INDUSTRIAL POLICY AND THE WORLD TRADE ORGANIZATION

The severe global financial crisis of 2008 could not be overcome without government interventions through industrial policy. This timely book analyzes industrial policy from the perspectives of trade law and economics under the WTO system. The author expertly examines both general tools of protecting and supporting domestic producers and specific topics like special economic zones, localization, greening measures, and creative economy. In addition to legal texts and jurisprudence, this book extensively utilizes other WTO materials to show what is actually discussed in WTO meetings and forums on relevant issues. Where applicable, the author advances practical recommendations for "right" or "optimal" industrial policy in certain contexts based on trade rules, case law, and some countries' real experiences. The author concludes this work with some thoughts on concrete actions to be taken at the WTO and national levels and in academic circles in order to better tackle industrial policy issues.

SHERZOD SHADIKHODJAEV is a Professor at the KDI School of Public Policy and Management. He obtained his LLB (with honors) from the University of World Economy and Diplomacy (Uzbekistan), and LLM and PhD in Law from Korea University. Previously, he worked for Korea Institute for International Economic Policy as a research fellow. He has done extensive academic and policy research in international economic law. His book *Retaliation in the WTO Dispute Settlement System* was published in 2009. His articles have been published in globally recognized journals, including *American Journal of International Law, Chinese Journal of International Law, Journal of International Economic Law, World Trade Review*, and *Journal of World Trade*.

CAMBRIDGE INTERNATIONAL TRADE AND ECONOMIC LAW

Series editors

Dr Lorand Bartels, *University of Cambridge*

Professor Thomas Cottier, *University of Berne*

Professor William Davey, *University of Illinois*

As the processes of regionalisation and globalisation have intensified, there have been accompanying increases in the regulations of international trade and economic law at the levels of international, regional and national laws.

The subject matter of this series is international economic law. Its core is the regulation of international trade, investment and cognate areas such as intellectual property and competition policy. The series publishes books on related regulatory areas, in particular human rights, labour, environment and culture, as well as sustainable development. These areas are vertically linked at the international, regional and national level, and the series extends to the implementation of these rules at these different levels. The series also includes works on governance, dealing with the structure and operation of related international organisations in the field of international economic law, and the way they interact with other subjects of international and national law.

Books in the series

INDUSTRIAL POLICY AND THE WORLD TRADE ORGANIZATION

Between Legal Constraints and Flexibilities

SHERZOD SHADIKHODJAEV

KDI School of Public Policy and Management

CAMBRIDGE
UNIVERSITY PRESS

University Printing House, Cambridge CB2 8BS, United Kingdom

One Liberty Plaza, 20th Floor, New York, NY 10006, USA

477 Williamstown Road, Port Melbourne, VIC 3207, Australia

314–321, 3rd Floor, Plot 3, Splendor Forum, Jasola District Centre, New Delhi – 110025, India

79 Anson Road, #06–04/06, Singapore 079906

Cambridge University Press is part of the University of Cambridge.

It furthers the University's mission by disseminating knowledge in the pursuit of education, learning, and research at the highest international levels of excellence.

www.cambridge.org
Information on this title: www.cambridge.org/9781107145085
DOI: 10.1017/9781316535172

© Sherzod Shadikhodjaev 2018

First published 2018

Printed and bound in Great Britain by Clays Ltd, Elcograf S.p.A.

A catalogue record for this publication is available from the British Library.

Library of Congress Cataloging-in-Publication Data
Names: Shadikhodjaev, Sherzod, author.
Title: Industrial policy and the World Trade Organization : between legal constraints and flexibilities / Sherzod Shadikhodjaev, KDI School of Public Policy and Management.
Description: Cambrdige [UK] ; New York, NY : Cambridge University Press, [2018] | Series: Cambridge international trade and economic law | Includes bibliographical references and index.
Identifiers: LCCN 2018009852 | ISBN 9781107145085 (hardback : alk. paper) | ISBN 9781316508459 (pbk. : alk. paper)
Subjects: LCSH: Foreign trade regulation. | World Trade Organization. | Industrial policy. | Economic development.
Classification: LCC K3943 .S525 2018 | DDC 382/.92–dc23
LC record available at https://lccn.loc.gov/2018009852

ISBN 978-1-107-14508-5 Hardback

To my Parents, Dinara, Asilakhon, Shodiyakhon, and Kadriyakhon

CONTENTS

FIGURES

TABLES

FOREWORD

In a couple of his publications, Paul Krugman has made the point that everyday life has not changed much since the 1970s. Indeed, it is the Industrial Revolution and its aftermath that shortened distances and made the world a bit more flat. We have yet to come to grips with the digital revolution (which some count as one, and some as two, distinct events). We have not seen much change in everyday life either. And yet change there is.

The digital revolution is a challenge for specific policies as it is for democracy itself. The questions it poses range from its impact on economic policy (What are the limits of automated production? What does it mean for employment policies? How does it affect the digital divide?) to pure moral if not moral/philosophical questions (What should our attitude toward artificial intelligence be? Can the object be "smarter" than the subject? Who controls the object?).

From domestic economic policy to trade is, of course, a short walk. Indeed, the liberalization of movement of factors of production has had as consequence the breakup of silos behind which national economic policies worked. The digital economy cuts across all issues discussed in both the multilateral system (the World Trade Organization or "WTO"), as well as (and even more so) free trade areas, where homogeneity of players and concerns helps advance faster and further the thinking about these issues. It also poses a formidable challenge to the institutional relevance of the multilateral regime. Its responsiveness to business concerns exacerbated by the emergence of digital economy is emerging as the key to its continuous policy-relevance. As time passes by, societal, development, and environmental concerns might weigh in as well.

Alas, so far, the signs do not lend to optimism. The WTO does not seem capable of absorbing challenges of more modest dimensions, as it grapples with its inability to provide the forum that will tame regulatory barriers at the multilateral level. Even if we accept that the current crisis is idiosyncratic, and due to extraordinary circumstances, the shaping of the multilateral agenda is a far cry from the challenges posed by the digital economy.

This book is a timely and wonderful contribution aiming to bridge the gap between the two. The author, a renowned expert in international trade, has managed to come up with a comprehensive and yet coherent inventory of the questions that the trading regime should be asking. As Voltaire used to say, what matters is to ask each time the right questions. If that much can be achieved, then the right answers will naturally arrive sooner or later.

This book does go one step beyond Voltaire's premise, and provides a roadmap that the WTO can only at its peril ignore. In my view, this volume is compulsory reading for the policy-maker and the researcher alike, and will illuminate the thinking of students of the multilateral trading regime as it is coming of age.

Petros C. Mavroidis
Edwin B. Parker Professor of Law at Columbia Law School,
New York City

ACKNOWLEDGMENTS

Inspiration for this book comes from my experience of teaching to graduate students and advising government officials. At Korea Development Institute (KDI) School of Public Policy and Management, I give lectures on "Industrial Policy and International Trade Regulation," among other things. This course has drawn a tremendous interest, as many students from different countries come from the public sector dealing with trade and industry. Moreover, I have occasionally advised government officials on trade law and policy issues. Through these interactions, the students and officials have shown a keen interest in the relationship between industrial policy and multilateral trade rules, the topic which I chose to address in this book.

This book would not have seen the light of day without the help of many people. First of all, I would like to thank my parents for having raised me to what I am and encouraging me in all stages of my life. I am thankful to my wife and my daughters for their constant love, support, and patience during this writing. I also appreciate the support of my brothers and parents-in-law.

In Korea, I am indebted to many people, including, but not limited to, dear professors, colleagues, students, and friends in Korea University, Korea Institute for International Economic Policy, and the KDI School. Two people are especially important to me. My mentor and academic supervisor Professor Nohyoung Park – the founding president of the Korean Society of International Economic Law – generously supported me during my Master's and doctoral studies at Korea University. It is he who introduced me to this intriguing world of international economic law, and I still have to learn many things from him, including his way of pioneering new fields. Professor Dukgeun Ahn from Seoul National University is one of the rare experts who has an impressive command of both the economics and law of international trade policy. It is actually he who once suggested that I write a book, so I came up with the idea of working on this project.

My special thanks go to Professor Petros C. Mavroidis – a world authority on international trade and economic law – for kindly agreeing to write a foreword for this book despite his busy schedule. I also thank Professor Julia Ya Qin – another great scholar – for her feedback and endorsement for this book.

I am much obliged to all professors and lecturers of the University of World Economy and Diplomacy in Uzbekistan, including Professors Akmal Saidov and Ravshan Khakimov, among others, whose valuable courses laid the foundations for my further studies and career.

Last but not least, I am grateful to the Series Editors of "Cambridge International Trade and Economic Law," Cambridge University Press, and its staff for enabling the publication of this book.

TABLE OF GATT/WTO CASES

(cont.)

Short Title	Full Title
	Aircraft – Recourse to Arbitration by Brazil under Article 22.6 of the DSU and Article 4.11 of the SCM Agreement, WT/DS46/ARB, 28 August 2000, DSR 2002:I, p. 19
Brazil – Retreaded Tyres	Appellate Body Report, *Brazil – Measures Affecting Imports of Retreaded Tyres*, WT/DS332/AB/R, adopted 17 December 2007, DSR 2007:IV, p. 1527
Brazil – Taxation	Panel Reports, *Brazil – Certain Measures Concerning Taxation and Charges*, WT/DS472/R, Add.1 and Corr.1/ WT/DS497/R, Add.1 and Corr.1, circulated to WTO Members 30 August 2017 [appealed by Brazil 28 September 2017]
Canada – Aircraft	Appellate Body Report, *Canada – Measures Affecting the Export of Civilian Aircraft*, WT/DS70/AB/R, adopted 20 August 1999, DSR 1999:III, p. 1377
Canada – Aircraft	Panel Report, *Canada – Measures Affecting the Export of Civilian Aircraft*, WT/DS70/R, adopted 20 August 1999, upheld by Appellate Body Report WT/DS70/AB/R, DSR 1999:IV, p. 1443
Canada – Autos	Appellate Body Report, *Canada – Certain Measures Affecting the Automotive Industry*, WT/DS139/AB/R, WT/DS142/AB/R, adopted 19 June 2000, DSR 2000: VI, p. 2985
Canada – Autos	Panel Report, *Canada – Certain Measures Affecting the Automotive Industry*, WT/DS139/R, WT/DS142/R, adopted 19 June 2000, as modified by Appellate Body Report WT/DS139/AB/R, WT/DS142/AB/R, DSR 2000:VII, p. 3043
Canada – FIRA	GATT Panel Report, *Canada – Administration of the Foreign Investment Review Act*, L/5504, adopted 7 February 1984, BISD 30S/140

(cont.)

(cont.)

(*cont.*)

(cont.)

Short Title	Full Title
EC – Approval and Marketing of Biotech Products	Panel Reports, *European Communities – Measures Affecting the Approval and Marketing of Biotech Products*, WT/DS291/R, Add.1 to Add.9 and Corr.1 / WT/DS292/R, Add.1 to Add.9 and Corr.1 / WT/DS293/R, Add.1 to Add.9 and Corr.1, adopted 21 November 2006, DSR 2006:III, p. 847
EC – Asbestos	Appellate Body Report, *European Communities – Measures Affecting Asbestos and Asbestos-Containing Products*, WT/DS135/AB/R, adopted 5 April 2001, DSR 2001:VII, p. 3243
EC – Bananas III	Appellate Body Report, *European Communities – Regime for the Importation, Sale and Distribution of Bananas*, WT/DS27/AB/R, adopted 25 September 1997, DSR 1997:II, p. 591
EC – Bed Linen	Panel Report, *European Communities – Anti-Dumping Duties on Imports of Cotton-Type Bed Linen from India*, WT/DS141/R, adopted 12 March 2001, as modified by Appellate Body Report WT/DS141/AB/R, DSR 2001:VI, p. 2077
EC – Chicken Cuts	Appellate Body Report, *European Communities – Customs Classification of Frozen Boneless Chicken Cuts*, WT/DS269/AB/R, WT/DS286/AB/R, adopted 27 September 2005, and Corr.1, DSR 2005:XIX, p. 9157
EC – Countervailing Measures on DRAM Chips	Panel Report, *European Communities – Countervailing Measures on Dynamic Random Access Memory Chips from Korea*, WT/DS299/R, adopted 3 August 2005, DSR 2005:XVIII, p. 8671
EC – Fasteners (China)	Appellate Body Report, *European Communities – Definitive Anti-Dumping Measures on Certain Iron or Steel*

(cont.)

(*cont.*)

Short Title	Full Title
EEC – Parts and Components	GATT Panel Report, *European Economic Community – Regulation on Imports of Parts and Components*, L/6657, adopted 16 May 1990, BISD 37S/132
EU – Biodiesel	Appellate Body Report, *European Union – Anti-Dumping Measures on Biodiesel from Argentina*, WT/DS473/AB/R and Add.1, adopted 26 October 2016
EU – PET (Pakistan)	Panel Report, *European Union – Countervailing Measures on Certain Polyethylene Terephthalate from Pakistan*, WT/DS486/R, Add.1 and Corr.1, circulated to WTO Members 6 July 2017 [appealed by the EU 30 August 2017]
India – Additional Import Duties	Appellate Body Report, *India – Additional and Extra-Additional Duties on Imports from the United States*, WT/DS360/AB/R, adopted 17 November 2008, DSR 2008: XX, p. 8223
India – Autos	Panel Report, *India – Measures Affecting the Automotive Sector*, WT/DS146/R, WT/DS175/R, and Corr.1, adopted 5 April 2002, DSR 2002:V, p. 1827
India – Quantitative Restrictions	Appellate Body Report, *India – Quantitative Restrictions on Imports of Agricultural, Textile and Industrial Products*, WT/DS90/AB/R, adopted 22 September 1999, DSR 1999:IV, p. 1763
India – Quantitative Restrictions	Panel Report, *India – Quantitative Restrictions on Imports of Agricultural, Textile and Industrial Products*, WT/DS90/R, adopted 22 September 1999, upheld by Appellate Body Report WT/DS90/AB/R, DSR 1999:V, p. 1799
India – Solar Cells	Appellate Body Report, *India – Certain Measures Relating to Solar Cells and Solar Modules*, WT/DS456/AB/R and Add.1, adopted 14 October 2016

(*cont.*)

Short Title	Full Title
India – Solar Cells	Panel Report, *India – Certain Measures Relating to Solar Cells and Solar Modules*, WT/DS456/R and Add.1, adopted 14 October 2016, as modified by Appellate Body Report WT/DS456/AB/R
Indonesia – Autos	Panel Report, *Indonesia – Certain Measures Affecting the Automobile Industry*, WT/DS54/R, WT/DS55/R, WT/DS59/R, WT/DS64/R, Corr.1 and Corr.2, adopted 23 July 1998, and Corr.3 and Corr.4, DSR 1998:VI, p. 2201
Indonesia – Import Licensing Regimes	Appellate Body Report, *Indonesia – Importation of Horticultural Products, Animals and Animal Products*, WT/DS477/AB/R, WT/DS478/AB/R, and Add.1, adopted 22 November 2017
Indonesia – Import Licensing Regimes	Panel Report, *Indonesia – Importation of Horticultural Products, Animals and Animal Products*, WT/DS477/R, WT/DS478/R, Add.1 and Corr.1, adopted 22 November 2017, as modified by Appellate Body Report WT/DS477/AB/R, WT/DS478/AB/R
Japan – Agricultural Products II	Appellate Body Report, *Japan – Measures Affecting Agricultural Products*, WT/DS76/AB/R, adopted 19 March 1999, DSR 1999:I, p. 277
Japan – Alcoholic Beverages II	Appellate Body Report, *Japan – Taxes on Alcoholic Beverages*, WT/DS8/AB/R, WT/DS10/AB/R, WT/DS11/AB/R, adopted 1 November 1996, DSR 1996:I, p. 97
Japan – Apples	Appellate Body Report, *Japan – Measures Affecting the Importation of Apples*, WT/DS245/AB/R, adopted 10 December 2003, DSR 2003:IX, p. 4391
Japan – DRAMs (Korea)	Appellate Body Report, *Japan – Countervailing Duties on Dynamic Random Access Memories from Korea*,

(*cont.*)

(cont.)

(cont.)

Short Title	Full Title
Turkey – Textiles	Appellate Body Report, *Turkey – Restrictions on Imports of Textile and Clothing Products*, WT/DS34/AB/R, adopted 19 November 1999, DSR 1999: VI, p. 2345
Turkey – Textiles	Panel Report, *Turkey – Restrictions on Imports of Textile and Clothing Products*, WT/DS34/R, adopted 19 November 1999, as modified by Appellate Body Report WT/DS34/AB/R, DSR 1999:VI, p. 2363
Ukraine – Passenger Cars	Panel Report, *Ukraine – Definitive Safeguard Measures on Certain Passenger Cars*, WT/DS468/R and Add.1, adopted 20 July 2015
US – Animals	Panel Report, *United States – Measures Affecting the Importation of Animals, Meat and Other Animal Products from Argentina*, WT/DS447/R and Add.1, adopted 31 August 2015
US – Anti-Dumping and Countervailing Duties (China)	Appellate Body Report, *United States – Definitive Anti-Dumping and Countervailing Duties on Certain Products from China*, WT/DS379/AB/R, adopted 25 March 2011, DSR 2011:V, p. 2869
US – Anti-Dumping and Countervailing Duties (China)	Panel Report, *United States – Definitive Anti-Dumping and Countervailing Duties on Certain Products from China*, WT/DS379/R, adopted 25 March 2011, as modified by Appellate Body Report WT/DS379/AB/R, DSR 2011:VI, p. 3143
US – Canadian Pork	GATT Panel Report, *United States – Countervailing Duties on Fresh, Chilled and Frozen Pork from Canada*, DS7/R, adopted 11 July 1991, BISD 38S/30
US – Clove Cigarettes	Appellate Body Report, *United States – Measures Affecting the Production and Sale of Clove Cigarettes*, WT/DS406/AB/R, adopted 24 April 2012, DSR 2012: XI, p. 5751

(*cont.*)

Short Title	Full Title
US – Clove Cigarettes	Panel Report, *United States – Measures Affecting the Production and Sale of Clove Cigarettes*, WT/DS406/R, adopted 24 April 2012, as modified by Appellate Body Report WT/DS406/AB/R, DSR 2012: XI, p. 5865
US – Continued Suspension	Appellate Body Report, *United States – Continued Suspension of Obligations in the EC – Hormones Dispute*, WT/DS320/AB/R, adopted 14 November 2008, DSR 2008:X, p. 3507
US – COOL	Appellate Body Reports, *United States – Certain Country of Origin Labelling (COOL) Requirements*, WT/DS384/AB/R / WT/DS386/AB/R, adopted 23 July 2012, DSR 2012:V, p. 2449
US – COOL	Panel Reports, *United States – Certain Country of Origin Labelling (COOL) Requirements*, WT/DS384/R / WT/DS386/R, adopted 23 July 2012, as modified by Appellate Body Reports WT/DS384/AB/R / WT/DS386/AB/R, DSR 2012:VI, p. 2745
US – COOL (*Article 21.5 – Canada and Mexico*)	Appellate Body Reports, *United States – Certain Country of Origin Labelling (COOL) Requirements – Recourse to Article 21.5 of the DSU by Canada and Mexico*, WT/DS384/AB/RW / WT/DS386/AB/RW, adopted 29 May 2015
US – Countervailing Duty Investigation on DRAMS	Appellate Body Report, *United States – Countervailing Duty Investigation on Dynamic Random Access Memory Semiconductors (DRAMS) from Korea*, WT/DS296/AB/R, adopted 20 July 2005, DSR 2005:XVI, p. 8131
US – Countervailing Measures on Certain EC Products	Appellate Body Report, *United States – Countervailing Measures Concerning Certain Products from the European*

(cont.)

(cont.)

(*cont.*)

(cont.)

EU CASE MATERIALS

ABBREVIATIONS

APEC	Asia-Pacific Economic Cooperation
BOP	balance of payment
BTA	border tax adjustment
CJEU	Court of Justice of the European Union
CPC	Central Product Classification
DOC	Department of Commerce (United States)
DSU	Dispute Settlement Understanding
DVD	digital video disc
EC	European Communities
EU	European Union
FDI	foreign direct investment
FTA	free trade agreement
GATS	General Agreement on Trade in Services
GATT	General Agreement on Tariffs and Trade
GDP	gross domestic product
GPA	Government Procurement Agreement
GSP	generalized system of preferences
HS	Harmonized System
ICT	information and communications technology
ILO	International Labor Organization
IPR	intellectual property right
ISO	International Standardization Organization
IT	information technology
LCR	local content requirement
LDC	least-developed country
MEA	multilateral environmental agreement
MERCOSUR	Southern Common Market
MFN	most-favored nation
NPR-PPMs	non-product-related processes and production methods
OECD	Organization for Economic Cooperation and Development
PPMs	processes and production methods
R&D	research and development

RTA	regional trade agreement
SCM	subsidies and countervailing measures
SME	small and medium enterprise
SPS	sanitary and phytosanitary
STC	specific trade concern
TBT	technical barriers to trade
TPP	Trans-Pacific Partnership
TPR	trade policy review
TPRB	Trade Policy Review Body
TPRM	Trade Policy Review Mechanism
TRIMs	trade-related investment measures
TRIPS	trade-related aspects of intellectual property rights
UAE	United Arab Emirates
UK	United Kingdom
UN	United Nations
UNCTAD	United Nations Conference on Trade and Development
UNDP	United Nations Development Program
UNESCO	United Nations Educational, Scientific, and Cultural Organization
US	United States
VAT	value-added tax
VCLT	Vienna Convention on the Law of Treaties
WCO	World Customs Organization
WIPO	World Intellectual Property Organization
WTO	World Trade Organization

~

Introduction

Treasure the moment, it will not last;
Only the fool lives in future or past.

Alisher Navoi (1441–1501)[1]

A series of "industrial revolutions" taking place from the eighteenth century onward has changed the production process tremendously. The first industrial revolution (about 1760–1840) mechanized manufacturing with water and steam power, marking a historic shift from a manual to machinery-based production. The second one (between the late nineteenth century and the early twentieth century) used electricity for mass production. The third or "digital" revolution (the 1960–1990s) automated production through the incorporation of electronics and information technology (IT). The current fourth industrial revolution builds on the digital revolution and creates a fusion of technologies – for example, artificial intelligence, the Internet of things, 3-D printing, nanotechnology, biotechnology, and so on – cutting across the physical, digital, and biological domains.[2]

Thanks to these significant developments, manufacturing now is much faster and less labor-intensive than it was centuries ago. The spectrum of end-products is significantly broader as well. Information and communications technology (ICT) and the Internet are transforming the present-day production, delivery, and consumption of goods and services in such a way that the lines between the tangible and the intangible, real and virtual worlds are getting blurred.

Industrialization without any government's involvement is hardly conceivable. In practice, many governments have played an undeniable

---

[1] *100 Pearls of Wisdom by Navoi* (Tashkent: Yangi Asr Avlodi, 2016), p. 65.
[2] Klaus Schwab, "The Fourth Industrial Revolution: What It Means and How to Respond," *Foreign Affairs*, 12 December 2015; Klaus Schwab, "The Fourth Industrial Revolution," World Economic Forum, 2016, pp. 6–7.

1

role in establishing, stimulating, and protecting domestic industries even when it was contrary to market principles.[3] Such a government's participation is captured by the concept of "industrial policy," which itself has never been defined in a commonly acceptable manner. Under a narrow understanding, this concept is closely associated with subsidies, but this book follows a definition that comprises a wider scope of public interventions directed at influencing industries through horizontal and selective policy tools.[4]

The global financial crisis and the Great Recession of 2008–2009 aroused a renewed interest in industrial policy. The crisis showed that market mechanisms were not necessarily efficient and that strong government interventions were even indispensable to save national economies from a devastating collapse. As a result, the importance of industrial policy is gaining wider recognition in academic and political circles.[5]

Today, many governments are in the process of modernizing their industrial policies with a view to coping with the crisis consequences, ongoing and new challenges caused by various internal and external factors, as well as technological advancements. Localization or industrial nationalism, digitization, innovation, and green growth are some key words that characterize current industrial policy-making in different parts of the world. It addresses both traditional and "new generation" issues often going far beyond national boundaries.

In 2017, the European Union (EU), for instance, announced a new Industrial Policy Strategy that highlights cybersecurity, free flow of nonpersonal data, renewable biological resources, intellectual property rights (IPRs), public procurement, sustainable finance, critical raw materials, mobility, and transport. The EU horizontal policies are

---

[3] See, e.g., Wilson Peres and Annalisa Primi, "Theory and Practice of Industrial Policy: Evidence from the Latin American Experience," CEPAL Desarrollo Productivo Serie No. 187, 2009; Ha-Joon Chang, *Kicking Away the Ladder: Development Strategy in Historical Perspective* (London: Anthem Press, 2003). For the literature review, see Wim Naudé, "Industrial Policy: Old and New Issues," UNU–WIDER Working Paper No. 2010/106, 2010, pp. 4–7.

[4] See Section 1.1.

[5] Joseph E. Stiglitz, Justin Yifu Lin, and Célestin Monga, "The Rejuvenation of Industrial Policy," Policy Research Working Paper No. WPS6628, World Bank, 2013, p. 2.

complemented by some sectoral measures affecting steel, space, defense, and automotive industries.[6]

Under the slogan "America First," the United States, in 2017, withdrew from the Trans-Pacific Partnership (TPP) and embarked on renegotiating some of its major trade agreements with the avowed objective to clinch deals that will "better" serve its industrial interests. Moreover, the US administration recently unveiled a plan to repeal the policy of curbing carbon emissions from power plants and to boost domestic production of fossil fuel energy in order to lessen the environmental burden on local manufacturers.[7]

In 2015, China launched an ambitious initiative called "Made in China 2025" to significantly upgrade Chinese industries and make them innovation-driven. It prioritizes basically ten sectors, including, inter alia, advanced IT, robotics, aerospace equipment, maritime equipment, and biopharmaceuticals, with the domestic content of core components and materials to be increased to 40 percent by 2020 and 70 percent by 2025.[8]

The "More Productive Brazil" project was introduced in 2016 to restructure the Brazilian industrial sector. It consists in the governmental cofinancing of consulting services that help local companies raise their productivity in compliance with the principles of lean manufacturing – methods of reducing waste, such as overproduction, waiting time, transportation, excess processing, inventory movements, and defects.[9]

The Indian government's new plans for a "future ready" industrial policy pursue the goal to strengthen global strategic linkages of domestic industries through brand-building and foreign direct investment (FDI),

---

[6] European Commission, "Investing in a Smart, Innovative and Sustainable Industry: A Renewed EU Industrial Policy Strategy," Communication from the Commission, 13 September 2017; European Commission, "State of the Union 2017 – Industrial Policy Strategy: Investing in a Smart, Innovative and Sustainable Industry," Press Release, 18 September 2017, http://europa.eu/rapid/press-release_IP-17-3185_en.htm.

[7] US White House, "An America First Energy Plan," www.whitehouse.gov/america-first-energy; US White House, "America First Foreign Policy," www.whitehouse.gov/america-first-foreign-policy; Lisa Friedman and Brad Plumer, "E.P.A. Announces Repeal of Major Obama-Era Carbon Emissions Rule," New York Times, 9 October 2017, www.nytimes.com/2017/10/09/climate/clean-power-plan.html.

[8] China's State Council, "Made in China 2025," http://english.gov.cn/2016special/madeinchina2025; Scott Kennedy, "Made in China 2025," Center for Strategic and International Studies, 2015, www.csis.org/analysis/made-china-2025.

[9] WTO, TPRB – TPR – Report by the Secretariat – Brazil, WT/TPR/S/358 (12 June 2017), para. 4.96.

to enhance industrial competitiveness, and adapt the innovative ecosystem to cutting-edge technologies and artificial intelligence.[10]

As for examples of some topic-specific practices, Australia, Canada, Russia, Turkey, Viet Nam, and some other countries restrict data outflows for the sake of information privacy and cybersecurity, which has serious implications for many IT companies and IT-reliant industries.[11] Global climate change and the deterioration of the environment have compelled most nations to adopt greening policies with actual or potential transboundary industrial impacts.[12] Creativity and innovation are what many politicians today consider as new engines for growth and make part of economic development strategies.[13]

Because industrial policies are designed and implemented with the internationalized nature of business linkages in mind, the domestic market is not the only focal point for national authorities. The authorities also pay attention to how to assist their producers in utilizing commercial opportunities abroad and expanding their presence in global value chains. All of these factors necessarily connect industrial policies to international trade.

When the General Agreement on Tariffs and Trade (GATT) was signed in 1947, the parties proudly declared the completion of "the most comprehensive, the most significant and the most far reaching negotiations ever undertaken in the history of world trade." At that time, twenty-three signatories shared approximately 70 percent of world trade.[14] The GATT's successor – the World Trade Organization (WTO) – now has 164 members accounting for about 98 percent of global trade.[15] The GATT/WTO multilateral trading system has effectively resisted the temptation of countries to resort to beggar-thy-neighbor actions even during the periods of severe

[10] India's Ministry of Commerce and Industry, "Formulation of a New Industrial Policy," 29 August 2017, http://pib.nic.in/newsite/PrintRelease.aspx?relid=170319; India's Ministry of Commerce and Industry, "Industrial Policy – 2017," Discussion Paper, 2017, http://dipp.nic.in/sites/default/files/Industrial_policy_2017_DP.pdf.

[11] See Section 5.5.   [12] See Chapter 6.   [13] See Chapter 7.

[14] European Office of the UN, "Adoption and Signature of the Final Act," Second Session of the Preparatory Committee of the UN Conference on Trade and Employment, Press Release No. 469, 27 October 1947.

[15] WTO, "Azevêdo: Global Trading System Has Constructive Role to Play to Help Drive Inclusivity," Speech, 30 October 2017, www.wto.org/english/news_e/spra_e/spra195_e.htm.

economic difficulties. This point is convincingly illustrated by WTO Director-General Roberto Azevêdo:

> [W]e all saw the value of the trading system during the financial crisis. In the 1930s, protectionist measures wiped out two-thirds of trade flows – with devastating consequences. In the crisis of 2008 we did not see the same escalation – precisely because governments knew they were bound by common rules. They held each other to the agreed standards. And these agreed standards are quite clear. We know when red lines are crossed – which we did not see in the 1930s. Our monitoring shows that trade restrictions imposed by the G20 economies since the 2008 crisis cover just 4.25 percent of world trade. This shows that the system is doing what it was created to do.[16]

Antiprotectionism is definitely an important but not the only part of the WTO domain that impacts on countries' sovereignty over their industrial policies.[17] Among many other relevant aspects, this system accepts qualifying unlawful industrial measures that are triggered by societal interests. Certain components of industrial policy are out of the WTO's reach.

The purpose of this book is to examine the extent to which industrial policy is regulated by the WTO regime with particular reference to legal constraints and flexibilities as applied to both general and topic-based industrial policies. The seven chapters are grouped into two parts.

Part I is dedicated to general tools of industrial policy. It explores the relationship between industrial policy and the world trading system and looks into governmental actions of protecting and supporting domestic industries. In particular, Chapter 1 begins with the economics and practice of industrial policy, followed by the discussion of the evolution of the GATT/WTO system, its major "controlling" functions, and implementation flexibilities vis-à-vis national industrial policies. Chapter 2 elaborates on most common protective measures, including border restrictions, taxes, product standards, and protection of services industries. Chapter 3 examines the stimulating side of industrial policy, namely, subsidies in manufacturing and services sectors and support measures involving upstream producers.

---

[16] *Ibid.*

[17] For one of the possible ways to define the WTO's regulatory domain on industrial policy, see, e.g., Bijit Bora, Peter J. Lloyd, and Mary Pangestu, "Industrial Policy and the WTO," UNCTAD Policy Issues in International Trade and Commodities Study Series No. 6, 2000, pp. 19–32.

Part II carries out a detailed study of some special topics of industrial policy. More specifically, Chapter 4 analyzes the issue of "zoning" of industrial policies, that is, when countries incentivize industrial activities within certain locations of their territory designated as, for example, special economic zones. Such free zones are regulated by multilateral customs rules and fall within the WTO jurisdiction. Chapter 5 concerns "localization" or import substitution measures that many governments used in the past and continue to rely on even these days. This chapter discusses some global trends, the economics and WTO-consistency of localization policies, with one section dealing with an emerging trend toward forced "localization" of electronic data. Chapter 6 is about the "greening" of industrial policies in the context of trade rules. It covers border carbon adjustments, renewable energy subsidies, environmental labeling programs, WTO environmental exceptions, and the problem of "trade–environment" harmonization at the international and domestic levels. Finally, Chapter 7 focuses on WTO issues associated with "creative economy" – an industrial policy of supporting economic development through a merger of culture, technology, and innovation.

PART I

General Tools of Industrial Policy

1

Industrial Policy under the Global Trade Regime

Industrial policy consists in a certain government intervention in the national economy, but there is no unified definition of what it is. Although the government has several industry-affecting tools at its disposal, officials, academics, and practitioners often differ on how to utilize them efficiently and properly. Trade and industrial policies considerably overlap in many aspects, which explains why trade economics and law are important for all stages of the industrial policy-making process. This chapter starts with the economics of industrial policy, highlighting some key theoretical findings, as well as practical issues derivable from the East Asian development experience. Then, we touch upon some important features of the multilateral trading system, briefly discussing its historical background, principal functions, and flexibilities in relation to national industrial policies. Overall, this chapter aims to provide an introductory analysis for more specific issues covered in the remainder of this book.

1.1 The Conceptual Framework for Industrial Policy

In spite of the widespread use, the term "industrial policy" has never been defined in a single way due to different perceptions changing over time. For example, an early definition by the Organization for Economic Cooperation and Development (OECD) stresses "promoting industrial growth and efficiency," and a working definition of the World Bank refers to "government efforts to alter industrial structure to promote productivity-based growth."[1] Diverse academic approaches to this

---

[1] OECD, "Objectives and Instruments of Industrial Policy: A Comparative Study," 1975, p. 7; World Bank, *The East Asian Miracle: Economic Growth and Public Policy* (New York: Oxford University Press, 1993), p. 304.

concept are common in accepting varying degrees of public intervention but are different in specifying the subject matter, purposes, and effects.[2]

On the basis of previous studies, Ken Warwick defines "industrial policy" in perhaps a most comprehensive way as "any type of intervention or government policy that attempts to improve the business environment or to alter the structure of economic activity toward sectors, technologies or tasks that are expected to offer better prospects for economic growth or societal welfare than would occur in the absence of such intervention." This description is quite inclusive for covering both horizontal and selective policies vis-à-vis industrial sectors and even certain technologies or tasks (design, logistics, and other stages of the value chain) and for pursuing wide-ranging goals on the economic, environmental, security, and other relevant fronts.[3] This book relies on this definition, as it provides an up-to-date conceptual foundation for our topic and substantially reflects a multitude of issues falling within the purview of today's global trade governance.

1.1.1 The Theory of Industrial Policy in a Nutshell

The theory of industrial policy goes back to the eighteenth century. Unlike Adam Smith, who had advocated a free market in which each agent would act in its own self-interest out of the government's reach, US Treasury Secretary Alexander Hamilton in his *Report on the Subject of Manufactures* (1791) advocated the use of bounties (subsidies) and the moderate tariff, as a source of revenue, for nurturing American producers in their "infancy" level.[4] Later, German economist Friedrich List in *The National System of Political Economy* (1841) elaborated on the government's role in protecting emerging industries from foreign competition. Drawing lessons from history, he suggested an economic development path to be followed in three consecutive stages, such as (i) the adoption of free trade with more advanced nations for the purpose of moving away from a state of "barbarism" and making progress in agriculture, (ii) the promotion of manufacturing by means of commercial restrictions, and (iii) a gradual reversion to free trade and competition at

---

[2] See Ken Warwick, "Beyond Industrial Policy: Emerging Issues and New Trends," OECD Science, Technology and Industry Policy Paper No. 2, 2013, p. 15.

[3] *Ibid.*, p. 16 (italics in the definition removed).

[4] For a critique, see Douglas A. Irwin, "The Aftermath of Hamilton's 'Report on Manufactures'," 64 *The Journal of Economic History* 800 (2004).

home and overseas.[5] Both Hamilton and List are widely recognized as intellectual pioneers of the infant industry argument. David Ricardo's *On the Principles of Political Economy and Taxation* (1817) presented the theory of comparative advantages, which explains how countries can gain from trade via industry specialization.

As Wim Naudé observes,[6] the intensive academic debate on industrial policies in modern times began after World War II, covering the periods of the reconstruction of Europe and Japan, the establishment of independent States in former colonies, and a series of financial crises of the regional and global scales. In the early postwar years, governments opted for selective interventions with an extensive use of import restrictions for infant industry protection. The then economic writings focused on such issues as coordination failures, economies of scale, and demand insufficiencies. By the 1980s, commentators justified government interventions only in limited areas of market failures and called for the loosening of import restrictions in accordance with the free market ideology. Such an antiinterventionist sentiment was influenced by the Washington Consensus prescriptions for economic liberalization and deregulation.[7] The 1997 Asian financial crisis spurred increasing skepticism about economic soundness of selective industrial policies. In contrast, the 2008 global financial crisis gave rise to scholarly defense of such policies, with some criticizing trade liberalization for inhibiting industrialization in Africa and other developing countries. Table 1.1 summarizes key findings of the economic literature since the 1940s.

1.1.1.1   Justifiability of Industrial Policy

Two extreme views on economic development treat industrial policy differently. Those who deny the need for an industrial policy insist that the market should be free so as to reach an efficient resource allocation.

---

[5] Friedrich List, *The National System of Political Economy* (originally published in 1841), translated by Sampson S. Lloyd (London: Longmans, Green and Co., 1909), p. 93.

[6] This paragraph is based on Naudé, Introduction, *supra* note 3, pp. 10–12.

[7] The "Washington Consensus" is a set of ten policy reforms for developing countries recommended by the US government and international financial organizations headquartered in Washington, DC. As summarized by John Williamson, the author of this concept, it includes "prudent macroeconomic policies, outward orientation, and free-market capitalism." See John Williamson, "What Washington Means by Policy Reform," in John Williamson (ed.), *Latin American Adjustment: How Much Has Happened?* (Washington, DC: Peterson Institute for International Economics, 1990), available at https://piie.com/commentary/speeches-papers/what-washington-means-policy-reform.

Table 1.1 *Evolution of Theory and Practice of Industrial Policy*

Phase	Key Idea	Representative Contributors
1940s to late 1960s	- Industrialization is necessary for development. - Market failures would prevent this from happening automatically. - Market failures are pervasive in developing countries. - Industrial policy is needed, particularly infant industry protection, state-ownership, and state coordination.	P. N. Rosenstein-Rodan, "Problems of Industrialisation of Eastern and South-Eastern Europe," 53 *Economic Journal* 202 (1943) Albert O. Hirschman, *The Strategy of Economic Development* (New Haven: Yale University Press, 1958) Gunnar Myrdal, *Economic Theory and Under-Developed Regions* (London: Duckworth, 1957)
1970s to 1990s	- Practical obstacles to industrial policy are considered significant. - Government failure is worse than market failure. Industrial policy is invitation to waste and rent-seeking. - Trade liberalization (exports), privatization and attracting FDI together with macroeconomic stability and minimum government interference are the basic requirements for growth and industrialization. - The era of the Washington consensus, especially after the debt crisis of the early 1980s and the ubiquity of structural adjustment programs.	Robert E. Baldwin, "The Case against Infant-Industry Tariff Protection," 77 *Journal of Political Economy* 295 (1969) Anne O. Krueger, "The Political Economy of the Rent-Seeking Society," 64 *American Economic Review* 291 (1974) Anne O. Krueger, "Government Failures in Development," 4(3) *Journal of Economic Perspectives* 9 (1990) Howard Pack, "Productivity and Industrial Development in Sub-Saharan Africa," 21 *World Development* 1 (1993) Howard Pack, "Industrial Policy: Growth Elixir or Poison?" *World Bank Research Observer* 47 (2000)
2000s to present	- Market and government failures are present.	Alice H. Amsden, *Asia's Next Giant: South Korea and Late*

Table 1.1 (*cont.*)

Phase	Key Idea	Representative Contributors
day	- The "how" rather than the "why" of industrial policy is important. - Institutional setting matters but design difficult. Need to understand political context. - Flexibility in the practice of industrial policy is important. - Differences exist with respect to the extent to which comparative advantage needs to be defied, not the principle. - Innovation and technological upgrading should be a central objective of industrial policy. - Promoting national innovation systems should be an important objective of industrial policy.	*Industrialization* (New York: Oxford University Press, 1989) Mario Cimoli, Giovanni Dosi, and Joseph E. Stiglitz, "The Political Economy of Capabilities Accumulation: The Past and Future of Policies for Industrial Development," in Mario Cimoli, Giovanni Dosi, and Joseph E. Stiglitz (eds.), *Industrial Policy and Development: The Political Economy of Capabilities Accumulation* (Oxford: Oxford University Press, 2009), pp. 1–16 Dani Rodrik, "Industrial Policy for the Twenty-First Century," Harvard University Faculty Research Working Paper No. RWP04–047, 2004 Ha-Joon Chang, *Kicking Away the Ladder: Development Strategy in Historical Perspective* (London: Anthem Press, 2003) Ha-Joon Chang, "Industrial Policy: Can We Go Beyond an Unproductive Confrontation?" Annual World Bank Conference on Development Economics, Seoul, 2009 Sanjaya Lall, "Selective Industrial and Trade Policies in Developing Countries: Theoretical and

Table 1.1 (*cont.*)

Phase	Key Idea	Representative Contributors
		Empirical Issues," QEH Working Paper No. 48 (2000)
		Justin Yifu Lin, "Learning from the Past to Reinvent the Future," in Justin Yifu Lin and Boris Pleskovic (eds.), *Lessons from East Asia and the Global Financial Crisis* (Washington, DC: World Bank, 2011), pp. 19–29
		Richard R. Nelson, *National Innovation Systems: A Comparative Analysis* (New York: Oxford University Press, 1993)
		James A. Robinson, "Industrial Policy and Development: A Political Economy Perspective," Annual World Bank Conference on Development Economics (Seoul, 2009)

Source: Wim Naudé, "Industrial Policy: Old and New Issues," UNU–WIDER Working Paper No. 2010/106, 2010, p. 10 (table 3), modified by the author.

In contrast, opponents stress the government's role in directing resources toward a particular course of growth. But in reality, virtually all successful industrial countries have followed mixed strategies under which the government has intervened in the marketplace at some point.[8]

In economics, public intervention is warranted when markets are distorted or incomplete. A market can be distorted by an externality – when the price of a good/service does not reflect the associated societal cost or benefit – or by an excessive market power attributable to, for

---

[8] Joseph E. Stiglitz, "Some Lessons from the East Asian Miracle," 11 *The World Bank Research Observer* 151 (1996), p. 155.

example, a monopoly. If a market does not exist for certain goods or services, it is incomplete. In either case, industrial policies may deliver a socially desirable outcome. Income redistribution can be another legitimate reason for governments to intervene.[9]

There is no consensus among economists on the optimal extent of government participation in the market. A laissez-faire approach says that, in a virtually unrestrained market, a government should be a passive player creating only favorable "framework conditions" for business like predictable and transparent governance and macroeconomic stability.[10] By contrast, a traditional approach supports more active interventions through sector-specific subsidies, nationalization, government-driven mergers, or preferential procurement practices, underlining possible intersectoral linkages and knowledge spillovers.[11] In this regard, one can distinguish functional (horizontal) and selective (vertical) industrial policies, with the former referring to economy-wide actions and the latter targeting specific sectors or regions.

In spite of its theoretical appeal, the pure laissez-faire policy lacks political popularity, as it "offers special interest benefits to nobody."[12] Not surprisingly, the literature justifies selective industrial policy sparingly, notably in the presence of market failures resulting from, inter alia, certain factors, as follows.[13]

First, this is the case of "coordination failures" when an individual agent does not invest in a particular project absent simultaneous investment in other related activities. For instance, a firm will not venture into production of clothes unless the government invests in transportation or financing facilities needed for the clothing industry.

Second, the government can respond to "information(al) externalities" arising from the lack of knowledge about potential business opportunities. A firm's innovative business plan is exposed to the risk of failure,

---

[9] See Howard Pack and Kamal Saggi, "Is There a Case for Industrial Policy? A Critical Survey," 21 *The World Bank Research Observer* 267 (2006), p. 268; Alan V. Deardorff, "The Economics of Government Market Intervention and Its International Dimension," in Marco Bronckers and Reinhard Quick (eds.), *New Directions in International Economic Law: Essays in Honour of John H. Jackson* (The Hague: Kluwer Law International, 2000), pp. 71–84.

[10] Warwick, *supra* note 2, p. 19.   [11] *Ibid.*

[12] Randall G. Holcombe, "South Korea's Economic Future: Industrial Policy, or Economic Democracy?," 88 *Journal of Economic Behavior & Organization* 3 (2013), p. 9.

[13] See, e.g., Pack and Saggi, *supra* note 9, pp. 272–9; Dani Rodrik, "Industrial Policy for the Twenty-First Century," Harvard University Faculty Research Working Paper No. RWP04–047, 2004, pp. 8–14.

but, if it succeeds, others will "copy" it and thereby cut that firm's profits from the project. This makes many firms reluctant to engage in new industrial activities. But the government can encourage discovery of novel business solutions by, inter alia, stimulating venture capital funding in specific sectors.

Third, it may be prudent for the government to invest in a particular infant industry that has the potential to generate manifold spillovers and linkage effects. Otherwise, individual agents will not invest on their own, as they cannot foresee new technologies and markets that can emerge once that industry becomes mature.

By contrast, critics point out a number of factors to disapprove of industrial targeting. In particular, selective State intervention distorts resource allocation and competition in the marketplace. This keeps many inefficient producers alive.

Furthermore, although optimal industrial targeting is warranted for imperfect markets in theory, making accurate policy prescriptions is extremely difficult in practice. Importantly, certain "government failures," such as the lack of information and capacity building, do not allow public practitioners to know exactly which industries or firms to support (i.e., "pick winners") and how. One study, for instance, lists fifteen areas (firm/industry-related knowledge spillovers, dynamic scale economies, comparative advantages, capital market failures, etc.) that government officials need to master in order to properly implement an industrial policy.[14]

In addition, it is not easy to evaluate precisely the costs and benefits (and the fact of success or failure) of industrial targeting even in retrospect.[15] Some "popular" criteria for selecting industries – such as high value-added per worker, usability of output across many sectors, future competitiveness, and defensive targeting in response to foreign industrial targeting – can, in fact, be destructive and counterproductive.[16]

Last but not least, industrial targeting provokes corruption and rent-seeking and results in preferences to politically connected entities.[17]

---

[14] Pack and Saggi, *supra* note 9, pp. 281–2.

[15] See Paul R. Krugman, "Targeted Industrial Policies: Theory and Evidence," Proceedings, Economic Policy Symposium, Jackson Hole, 1983, pp. 123–76.

[16] See *ibid.*, pp. 125–34.

[17] Dani Rodrik, "Normalizing Industrial Policy," Working Paper No. 3, Commission on Growth and Development, 2008, p. 8. For the literature review on this issue, see Naudé, Introduction, *supra* note 3, pp. 20–1.

In short, selective intervention necessitated by market failures may face practical constraints in the light of government failures. Therefore, some authors suggest moving away from price-distorting "hard" industrial policy to "soft" industrial policy, the concept that highlights cooperation between the government and industries. As Ann Harrison and Andrés Rodríguez-Clare explain, soft industrial policy seeks to develop "a process whereby government, industry and cluster-level private organizations can collaborate on interventions that can directly increase productivity":

> The idea is to shift the attention from interventions that distort prices to interventions that deal directly with the coordination problems that keep productivity low in existing or raising sectors. Thus, instead of tariffs, export subsidies, and tax breaks for foreign corporations, we think of programs and grants to, for example, help particular clusters by increasing the supply of skilled workers, encouraging technology adoption, and improving regulation and infrastructure. While "hard" [industrial policy] is easier to implement than "soft" [industrial policy] measures, tariffs and subsidies become entrenched and are more easily subject to manipulation by interest groups.[18]

Under soft industrial policy, governments could invite industry representatives to come forward with their well-grounded proposals for government support in various projects on infrastructure, education, innovation, research, and other fields. In countries with weak private sector organizations, the government should work to encourage different sectors to improve their level of organization. It is argued that, compared to "hard" measures such as trade protection or selective subsidies, soft industrial policy is less susceptible to corruption and rent-seeking, and it is more compatible with international trade and investment regimes.[19]

Finally, the infant industry argument for import protection deserves attention, as it is a "precursor of modern industrial policy."[20] The main idea is that the government should protect domestic industry in its early stage of formation from foreign competitors, because the latter have more experience in producing at lower costs. However, such protection should later be phased out as domestic producers will reduce costs throughout the learning-by-doing process to reach the production-efficiency

---

[18] Ann Harrison and Andrés Rodríguez-Clare, "Trade, Foreign Investment, and Industrial Policy for Developing Countries," in Dani Rodrik and Mark Rosenzweig (eds.), *Handbook of Development Economics* (North-Holland: Elsevier, 2010), vol. 5, p. 4112.
[19] *Ibid.*, p. 4113.   [20] Pack and Saggi, *supra* note 9, p. 269.

level of foreign rivals. A stronger version of the infant industry argument states that initial protection can even be of the global interest, because the true (but latent) comparative advantage may lie with the emerging domestic industry that will eventually be able to produce at a lowest world price thanks to the import protection.[21]

As with some justifications discussed earlier, economists regard the infant industry argument as a valid exception to the free trade philosophy in the presence of either market failure: (i) imperfect capital markets or (ii) problems of appropriability.[22] The first case refers to countries with a weak financial system that does not allow infant industries to secure sufficient funds for growth. The second case arises when pioneering companies are not compensated for generating social benefits (e.g., knowledge) in entering a new industry, while they incur startup costs of adapting technology to local circumstances, something that latecomers (free riders) would normally not bear.

1.1.1.2 Instruments of Industrial Policy

Because virtually all countries in the world, including economically advanced nations, have used – and will arguably continue to use – industrial policies even if disguised by other names like "investment promotion" or "export facilitation," a more pragmatic way today would be to focus on *how* (rather than *whether* or *why*) governments should pursue an industrial policy.[23] This hinges on what instruments governments may apply.

The scope of industrial policy tools ranges from trade measures, such as, for example, import restrictions and subsidies, to a broader array of actions aimed at the improvement of a business climate. In Table 1.2, Ken Warwick categorizes all available instruments by policy domains within the horizontal and selective action groups. The policy domains concern merchandise, labor, capital, land, technology, as well as some soft industrial policy measures ("systems/institutions") relating to interactions among markets, economic agents, and the government.

---

[21] *Ibid.*, pp. 268–9.

[22] Robert E. Baldwin, "The Case against Infant-Industry Tariff Protection," 77 *Journal of Political Economy* 295 (1969), p. 295; Paul R. Krugman, Maurice Obstfeld, and Marc J. Melitz, *International Economics: Theory and Policy*, 10th edn. (Boston: Pearson, 2015), pp. 277–8.

[23] Rodrik, *supra* note 17, p. 2; Wim Naudé, "New Challenges for Industrial Policy," UNU–WIDER Working Paper No. 2010/107, 2010, p. 1; Stiglitz, Lin, and Monga, Introduction, *supra* note 5, p. 9.

Table 1.2 *A Typology of Industrial Policy Instruments by Policy Domain*

Domain	Horizontal Policies	Selective Policies

Product markets	Competition and antitrust
	Indirect tax
	Product market regulation
	Exchange rate policy
		National champions
		Nationalization/
		  privatization
		Output subsidies/
		  State aids
		Export promotion
		Price regulation (e.g.,
		  pharma)
		Public procurement
		Trade policy
		Car scrappage

Labor and skills	Skills and education policies Training subsidies Wage subsidies Income and employment tax Management advisory services Labor market regulation	Targeted skills policies Apprenticeship policies Sector-specific advisory services

Capital markets	Loan guarantees
	Corporate tax/capital
	  allowances
	Macro/financial stability
	Financial market regulation
		Strategic investment fund
		Emergency loans
		State investment bank
		Inward investment
		  promotion

Land	Planning regulation Land use planning	Enterprise zones Place-based clusters policy Infrastructure

Technology	Research and development (R&D)
	  tax credit
	Science budget
	IPR regime
		Green technology
		Lead markets
		Public procurement for
		  innovation
		Patent box
		Selective technology
		  funding
		Centers of expertise

*Systems/
  Institutions*
	Entrepreneurship policy
	Scenario planning
	Distribution of information
	Overall competitiveness
	  strategy
		Indicative planning
		Foresight initiatives
		Identifying strategic sectors
		Sectoral competitiveness
		  strategy
		Clusters policy

Source: Ken Warwick, "Beyond Industrial Policy: Emerging Issues and New Trends,"
OECD Science, Technology and Industry Policy Paper No. 2, 2013, p. 27 (table 4).

Trade measures are usable across many domains of industrial policy. Whereas governments can, in principle, opt for any of the available trade instruments, the literature is not always conclusive on what is most suitable to particular cases. For instance, with respect to infant industry protection, Robert Baldwin argues that more direct and selective policy measures like subsidies handle special problems of infant industries better than a nondiscriminatory import tariff, as the latter distorts consumption and may decrease social welfare.[24] By contrast, Marc Melitz finds that a quota is preferable to a production subsidy or tariff, because politicians ideally wish to decrease and eventually terminate protection as learning by protected industries progresses and ends. Although subsidies or tariffs must be lowered over time to have this effect, this may not always be feasible in practice; in contrast, the fixed quota automatically reduces its level of protection as domestic costs fall.[25]

Horizontal policies utilize various instruments listed in Table 1.2 to affect the countrywide business climate. Selective industrial policies can take two forms. A defensive or reactive policy applies certain tools – such as, for example, bailout of banks during the 2008 financial crisis – in response to economic turbulences. A strategic industrial policy is about developing new sectors in a "frontier" or "catch-up" country based on existing or latent comparative advantages of that country.[26]

Industrial policy may have spatial dimensions when governments create and promote clusters – geographic concentrations of interlinked firms and associated institutions within the same sector, such as high-tech or textiles districts, – special economic zones, or any other type of industrial sites with/without clustering features. Concentration of production in a particular location can generate "agglomeration economies," notably benefits for inside firms through labor pooling, knowledge spillovers, and close proximity of specialized suppliers and buyers. Such benefits can result from either the clustering of similar activities ("localization economies") or the spatial concentration of diverse activities ("urbanization economies").[27]

---

[24] Baldwin, *supra* note 22, p. 304.
[25] Marc J. Melitz, "When and How Should Infant Industries be Protected?," 66 *Journal of International Economics* 177 (2005), p. 194.
[26] This paragraph is a summary of Warwick, *supra* note 2, pp. 28–30.
[27] Max Nathan and Henry Overman, "Agglomeration, Clusters, and Industrial Policy," 29 *Oxford Review of Economic Policy* 383 (2013), pp. 386–7.

Implementation of policy instruments is as important as the instruments themselves. In this respect, Dani Rodrik suggests three principles for optimization of an institutional framework. First, industrial policy must be "embedded" within society through various channels for strategic collaboration and coordination between public and private sectors. Advisory councils, sectoral round tables, and similar forums help the government "discover" key constraints to growth and find appropriate instruments to apply. The concept of soft industrial policy discussed earlier corresponds to the principle of embeddedness. Second, the policy must use both "carrots" and "sticks" in, respectively, promoting investment and discouraging bad projects by applying conditionality and sunset clauses, program reviews, monitoring, and periodic evaluations. Third, there must be accountability for success and failure in the conduct of industrial policy, with the persons in charge regularly reporting on the agenda implementation and the whole system operating in a transparent way.[28]

1.1.2   Industrial Policy in Practice: The Case of East Asia

No country has been capable of advancing to higher-income status without undergoing the process of industrialization.[29] The transformation from an agrarian to industrial economy starting in the eighteenth century was propelled by the first industrial revolution in Britain and subsequently in other parts of Europe, North America and eventually the entire world. But such transformation happened together with, and at least partially enabled by, industrial protectionism.[30] As Ha-Joon Chang concludes, virtually all "now-developed countries" actively used "interventionist industrial, trade and technology policies" in the past, so their today's preaching for free trade and laissez-faire industrial policy is, in fact, tantamount to "kicking away the ladder" with which they climbed to the top to become economically powerful.[31]

While the end of World War II gave new impetus to industrial development in many countries, the case of East Asia is phenomenal. Over the 1960–1990s, rapid industrialization in that region, including,

---

[28] Rodrik, *supra* note 17, pp. 25–30.
[29] Stiglitz, Lin, and Monga, Introduction, *supra* note 5, p. 10.
[30] See Chang, Introduction, *supra* note 3, pp. 19–51; Mehdi Shafaeddin, "How Did Developed Countries Industrialize? The History of Trade and Industrial Policy: The Cases of Great Britain and the USA," UNCTAD Discussion Paper No. 139, 1998.
[31] Chang, Introduction, *supra* note 3, pp. 125–41.

inter alia, Japan and "Four Tigers" – Hong Kong, South Korea (herein-after "Korea"), Singapore and Chinese Taipei – led to what the World Bank calls the "East Asian miracle." The East Asian nations attained unprecedentedly high-rate sustained growth throughout four decades, highly equal income distributions, and unusually rapid growth of exports.[32] Unlike the former Soviet Union and other planned economies that sought to correct market failures by *replacing* markets, the East Asian authorities intervened to *complement* markets where appropri-ate.[33] The role of FDI was vital in the economic growth of Hong Kong and Singapore, but comparatively minor in Korea and Chinese Taipei.[34] Except Hong Kong that generally adhered to the laissez-faire approach, the governments in the region in question made roughly three sets of industrial policy interventions: targeted (or sectoral) industrial promo-tion, directed credit, and export push.

With respect to the targeted industrial promotion, the governments in East Asia switched their attention chronologically from labor-intensive sectors (e.g., light industries) to capital-intensive ones (e.g., heavy and chemical industries) and then to high-technology and knowledge-based industries (e.g., ICT). Industrial targeting usually concerned export-oriented sectors and was subject to strict economic performance criteria, so many support schemes with unsatisfactory results were adjusted accordingly.[35] But there were, of course, some instances of nonexport factors that also shaped sectoral policies. For example, in 1982, Chinese Taipei announced "two-large, two-high and two-low" criteria for selecting "strategic industries," namely large linkage effect and large market potential, high technology intensity and high value-added, low energy consumption and low pollution.[36]

Moreover, the governments in East Asia repressed interest rates and directed "cheap" credits to different priority activities ranging from aiding specific firms or industries to promoting all exporters and small and medium enterprises (SMEs) and implementing social programs (e.g., provision of mass housing).[37] In comparison to many other developing

---

[32] World Bank, *supra* note 1, p. 8.   [33] Stiglitz, *supra* note 8, p. 156.

[34] Dwight H. Perkins, *East Asian Development: Foundations and Strategies* (Cambridge, MA: Harvard University Press, 2013), pp. 98–9.

[35] World Bank, *supra* note 1, p. 23.

[36] Francis T. Lui and Larry D. Qiu, "Taiwan: Thriving High-Technology Industries and SMEs," in Kwong Kai-Sun et al. (eds.), *Industrial Development in Singapore, Taiwan, and South Korea* (Singapore: World Scientific, 2001), p. 88.

[37] World Bank, *supra* note 1, pp. 280–4, 356–8.

countries, directed credits in this region were less subsidized and generally given to the private sector rather than public enterprises.[38] The allocation of resources was often based on contests.[39]

In Korea, the government supported large family-controlled business conglomerates to exploit scale economies in establishing new industries.[40] But excessive government-directed lending to the conglomerates in inefficient projects led to the accumulation of nonperforming loans that together with other factors eventually provoked the 1997–1998 financial crisis in the country.[41] Unlike Korea's case, SMEs have played a big role in industrialization of Chinese Taipei. SMEs there accounted for over 97 percent of the total number of enterprises in 1961–1988, constituting a major source of employment in the manufacturing sector.[42] There was little competition between State-owned enterprises and private SMEs, as the former were mainly upstream producers that supplied input materials to export-oriented downstream SMEs.[43]

The export-push strategy was probably the most successful part of the East Asian industrial policies.[44] All but Hong Kong started with import substitution, but later shifted to the export-promoting approach. The export push was implemented at the time when Europe and North America – important markets for East Asian goods – had quite liberal trade regimes in place. In contrast, industrialization in South America that began before World War II could not pursue an export-oriented development path due to unfavorable external conditions caused by the war and the Great Depression.[45] Export promotion in East Asia generated additional foreign exchange, expanded local companies' business opportunities and access to foreign technology with subsequent spillovers to the rest of economy.[46] The export-push strategy had four key components aimed at exporters:[47]

---

[38] *Ibid.*, pp. 280, 284–6.   [39] Stiglitz, *supra* note 8, p. 166.

[40] See Wonhyuk Lim, "The Chaebol and Industrial Policy in Korea," in Joseph E. Stiglitz and Justin Yifu Lin (eds.), *The Industrial Policy Revolution I: The Role of Government Beyond Ideology* (Basingstoke, UK: Palgrave Macmillan, 2013), pp. 359–60, 364.

[41] Jai S. Mah, "Industrial Policy and Economic Development: Korea's Experience," 41 *Journal of Economic Issues* 77 (2007), pp. 86–7. For an open access repository of diverse resources regarding Korea's development experience, see KDI School of Public Policy and Management, "K-Developedia," www.kdevelopedia.org.

[42] Lui and Qiu, *supra* note 36, p. 61.   [43] *Ibid.*, p. 63.

[44] World Bank, *supra* note 1, p. 358.   [45] Perkins, *supra* note 34, p. 54.

[46] World Bank, *supra* note 1, pp. 22–3; Stiglitz, *supra* note 8, p. 169.

[47] World Bank, *supra* note 1, pp. 143–5.

- access to imports at world prices via tariff exemptions or reductions, export-processing zones, bonded manufacturing warehouses, or duty drawbacks;
- access to export financing;
- government assistance for penetrating overseas markets, including fiscal incentives and administrative support;
- policy flexibility allowing timely changes to target priorities depending on circumstances.

The East Asian miracle is partly attributable to the existence of a system of active communication channels for public–private consultations and cooperation under which each participant from business circles could rely on a share of rents. In the 1960–1970s, the Korean president chaired monthly export promotion meetings attended by high-ranking government officials and business representatives where they discussed the progress on export performance relative to the government-set targets, overseas market conditions, problems and possible solutions in advancing exports.[48] The Japanese government operated both functional/thematic and sector-specific deliberation councils.[49] In Singapore, citizens participated in policy-making, serving as directors on public statutory boards or *ad hoc* government committees; chambers of commerce, trade associations, and professional societies were entitled to submit their views at the government's request.[50]

On the basis of this brief outline, what lessons can be drawn from the East Asian experience? Among the industrial policy interventions mentioned earlier, sectoral targeting per se made only a minor contribution to the economic miracle in the region, holding "little promise for other developing economies."[51] In contrast, it can be learned that outward-oriented export industrialization is more likely to succeed than the inward-looking development path.[52] Arguably, this would work

---

[48] Lim, *supra* note 40, pp. 356–7.   [49] World Bank, *supra* note 1, pp. 181–2.

[50] *Ibid.*, p. 184.

[51] *Ibid.*, pp. 325, 354; Marcus Noland and Howard Pack, *Industrial Policy in an Era of Globalization: Lessons from Asia* (Washington, DC: Institute for International Economics, 2003), p. 93 ("industrial policy" as perceived as selective industrial targeting, see p. 10 for definition.). For the opposite view, see Sanjaya Lall, "Industrial Policy in Developing Countries: What Can We Learn from East Asia?," in Patrizio Bianchi and Sandrine Labory (eds.), *International Handbook on Industrial Policy* (Cheltenham, the United Kingdom/Northampton, MA, the United States: Edward Elgar, 2006), p. 93.

[52] See World Bank, *supra* note 1, p. 23 (... "economies that are making the transition from highly protectionist import-substitution regimes to more balanced incentives would

especially for the countries that, like East Asia, enjoy easy access to major export markets via sea routes, as well as for economies whose domestic market is too small to rely on domestic consumption. For landlocked or other countries having logistical difficulties in reaching big (remote) markets, the export push could be effective if it is aimed at local producers of light but high-value-added goods or services industries that are less exposed to transportation constraints. Furthermore, the East Asian case suggests that incentives should be granted under stringent performance criteria and constantly monitored so as to allow timely modifications. Finally, well-functioning mechanisms of public–private interactions are indispensable to the efficient policy design and implementation. This is in line with soft industrial policy recommendations discussed above.

We acknowledge that the East Asian model cannot mechanically be applied in all parts of the world, given each nation's unique circumstances. Importantly, the economic miracle was happening at the time when the former GATT system, joined by most of the regional economies in question, was not as strict as the present WTO regime. While governments that wish to follow East Asia's approach of export industrialization must necessarily reconcile their measures with rigid WTO disciplines, its soft policy elements are less problematic in this respect for incorporating into the domestic system. In any event, smaller room for maneuver under the current trade rule book can be offset by better-than-GATT-offered export opportunities thanks to WTO-set lower barriers to wider trade geography.

1.2   The Multilateral Trading System and Industrial Policy

The multilateral trading system and industrial policy are intertwined in many ways. The industrialization of many countries after World War II has occurred under the GATT/WTO system. National industrial policies are often operationalized through trade instruments. For this reason, a number of countries run a single ministry for both trade and industry. Many academic writings in the trade and industry domains frequently discuss overlapping issues.

benefit from combining import liberalization with a strong commitment to exports and active export promotion, especially in those cases in which the pace of liberalization is moderate").

1.2.1 Evolution of the Multilateral Trading System

In 1947, twenty-three countries signed the GATT, the first multilateral trade agreement. The goal was to ensure postwar stability and prevent resurge of the beggar-thy-neighbor policies that major powers had practiced a nearly decade earlier. The then politicians had fresh memories of the Great Depression in the 1930s when the United States had imposed the protective Hawley–Smoot Tariff triggering retaliatory actions by Canada, Italy, Spain, Switzerland, and so on. Another worrisome fact was the rise of special trade arrangements by the United Kingdom, Germany, and Japan with their sphere-of-influence territories to the exclusion of other nations.[53] The new system was supposed to block protectionist and discriminatory policies of this kind in the future.

Industrialization issues have been in the spotlight since the very early years of the formation of the multilateral trade regime. Already during the drafting of the GATT, the US representative tabled five principles for shaping the contours of the future system, one of which was about ensuring that stabilization policies for industry and agriculture were consistent with trade policies.[54] The 1948 Havana Charter for an International Trade Organization aimed to "foster and assist industrial and general economic development, particularly of those countries which [were] still in the early stages of industrial development" and elaborated on this agenda in a discrete chapter on "Economic Development and Reconstruction."[55] But the failure of the Havana Charter left these parts aside, making the GATT a de facto international institution dealing with trade as a means of industrial development.

As in Table 1.3, five rounds of trade negotiations taking place between 1947 and 1961 concerned tariff reductions. These were market openings predominantly by developed countries, as the negotiations followed the "request-offer" (or "product-by-product") modality where most of the developing countries in the system were neither principal suppliers nor major importers of covered products.[56] In the 1950s, the Contracting

---

[53] See Douglas A. Irwin, Petros C. Mavroidis, and Alan O. Sykes, *The Genesis of the GATT* (New York: Cambridge University Press, 2008), pp. 5–7.

[54] UN Economic and Social Council – Preparatory Committee of the International Conference on Trade and Employment – Verbatim Report of the Second Plenary Meeting Held at Church House, Westminster, S.W.1, on 17 October 1946, E/PC/T/PV/2 (17 October 1946), p. 6.

[55] See Article 1 and Chapter II of the Havana Charter.

[56] Chad P. Bown, *Self-Enforcing Trade: Developing Countries and WTO Dispute Settlement* (Washington, DC: Brookings Institution, 2009), pp. 12–13.

Table 1.3 *GATT/WTO Negotiating Rounds*

Place/Name of Rounds	Number of Parties	Subjects and Modalities	Outcome
Geneva (1947)	23	Tariffs: product-by-product negotiations	15,000 tariff concessions
Annecy (1949)	13	Tariffs: product-by-product negotiations	5,000 tariff concessions; 9 accessions
Torquay (1951)	38	Tariffs: product-by-product negotiations	8,700 tariff concessions; 4 accessions
Geneva (1956)	26	Tariffs: product-by-product negotiations	Modest reductions
Dillon Round (1960–1961)	26	Tariffs: product-by-product negotiations	4,400 tariff concessions
Kennedy Round (1964–1967)	62	Tariffs: formula approach (linear cut) and product-by-product negotiations. Nontariff measures: antidumping	Average tariffs reduced by 35 percent; some 33,000 tariff lines bound; agreement on antidumping
Tokyo Round (1973–1979)	102	Tariffs: formula approach with exceptions. Nontariff measures: antidumping, customs valuation, subsidies and countervail, government procurement, import licensing, product standards, safeguards, special and differential treatment of developing countries	Average tariffs reduced by one-third to 6 percent for OECD manufactures imports; voluntary codes of conduct agreed for all nontariff issues except safeguards
Uruguay Round (1986–1994)	123	Tariffs: formula approach and product-by-product negotiations	Average tariffs reduced by one-third on average; agriculture and textiles and clothing subjected to

Table 1.3 (*cont.*)

Place/Name of Rounds	Number of Parties	Subjects and Modalities	Outcome
		Nontariff measures: all Tokyo issues plus services, intellectual property, preshipment inspection, rules of origin, trade-related investment measures (TRIMs), dispute settlement, transparency and surveillance of trade policies	rules; creation of the WTO; new agreements on services and trade-related aspects of intellectual property rights (TRIPS); majority of Tokyo Round codes extended to all WTO members
Doha Round (2001–)	164 in 2017	Tariffs and nontariff measures, including trade facilitation, rules, services, trade and environment, etc.	

Source: Based on WTO, "Six Decades of Multilateral Trade Cooperation: What Have We Learnt?," World Trade Report, 2007, p. 198 (table 4); WTO, "Understanding the WTO," 5th edn, 2015, p. 16 ("The GATT Trade Rounds").

Parties modified Article XVIII of the GATT (entitled "Governmental Assistance to Economic Development") to relax the rules on the use by developing countries of infant industry measures and balance-of-payment (BOP) restrictions and to essentially exempt these countries from the principle of full reciprocity.[57] In the early years, the GATT set out procedures of referring legal disputes to "working parties" – composed of both disputing and other interested parties – which was later replaced by "panels" as third-party adjudicators.[58]

---

[57] WTO, "Six Decades of Multilateral Trade Cooperation: What Have We Learnt?," World Trade Report, 2007, pp. 181–2.

[58] See Robert E. Hudec, *The GATT Legal System and World Trade Diplomacy*, 2nd edn (Salem, NH: Butterworth Legal Publishers, 1990), pp. 78–94.

From the Kennedy Round (1964–1967) onward, the GATT parties used a formula approach to cut tariffs across the board within product segments, having a greater impact on developing countries' exports.[59] Apart from tariff reductions, the Kennedy Round produced the Antidumping Agreement which detailed the existing provisions of Article VI of the GATT. During the 1960s, the interests of developing countries gained increasing attention from the world trading community. In 1965, the Contracting Parties added Part IV on "Trade and Development" to the GATT. The rise of the European Economic Community's preferential arrangements with former colonies in the 1960s provoked demands from nonparticipant developing countries for equal treatment. This issue was formally addressed first in the United Nations (UN) Conference on Trade and Development (UNCTAD) where in 1964 its Secretary-General floated the idea that developed countries should grant preferential market access to all developing countries. In 1968, the UNCTAD adopted the "generalized, non-reciprocal, non-discriminatory system of preferences" – the "Generalized System of Preferences" (GSP) – which granted selected products from developing countries reduced or eliminated tariff rates in preference-giving countries. According to Resolution 21(ii) of the UNCTAD (1968), this scheme pursued the objectives to increase export earnings of developing countries, promote their industrialization, and accelerate their economic growth.[60] In 1971, the GATT Contracting Parties approved a ten-year GSP waiver from Article I of the GATT on most-favored-nation (MFN) treatment.

The Tokyo Round (1973–1979) used a "Swiss formula" in tariff cuts to reduce the gap between high and low rates so as to reach greater harmonization of duties across tariff lines. The timing of this round coincided with the period when many countries were facing an economic downturn and BOP problems. This gave rise to the "new protectionism" with the extensive use of nontariff barriers amid multilateral tariff reductions. Therefore, negotiators focused on making trade fairer rather than freer, with nontariff issues coming into the spotlight.[61] As a result, the Tokyo Round produced a number of plurilateral agreements ("codes") on

---

[59] See J. M. Finger, "Effects of the Kennedy Round Tariff Concessions on the Exports of Developing Countries," 86 *The Economic Journal* 87 (1976).

[60] UNCTAD, "About GSP," http://unctad.org/en/Pages/DITC/GSP/About-GSP.aspx.

[61] See World Trade Report, 2007, *supra* note 57, pp. 185–6; Gerald M. Meier, "The Tokyo Round of Multilateral Trade Negotiations and the Developing Countries," 13 *Cornell International Law Journal* 239 (1980), pp. 241–2.

antidumping, subsidies, customs valuation, technical barriers, import licensing, government procurement and sectoral plurilaterals on civil aircraft, bovine meat, and dairy products. The 1979 Decision on Differential and More Favorable Treatment, Reciprocity and Fuller Participation of Developing Countries – known as the "Enabling Clause" – made the GSP waiver above permanent. A special "understanding" on dispute settlement provided details on notification, consultations, panel proceedings, surveillance, and technical assistance to developing countries and elaborated on the GATT "customary practice" in this field.

The Ministerial Declaration adopted at Punta del Este on 20 September 1986 launched the Uruguay Round with the most comprehensive and ambitious negotiation mandate in the GATT era. It took almost eight years for agreeing on a wide array of issues, including new areas like services and intellectual property. For the first time, agriculture has become the subject of tailor-made disciplines. At developing countries' request, it was decided to phase out existing quotas on textiles and clothing to eventually integrate this sector fully into the multilateral trading system. Before the end of the negotiations, a Trade Policy Review (TPR) Mechanism (TPRM) was introduced on a provisional basis as an "early harvest" to test. The Tokyo Round codes were improved and most of them "multilateralized" as part of a "single undertaking." Importantly, the Uruguay Round resulted in the creation of a full-fledged international organization – the WTO – although the original mandate had not even foreseen this. It was possible with Professor John Jackson's private initiative (1990) that was later taken over to the negotiations despite initial cool reactions by his home country, the United States, and other "majors" in the GATT system.[62]

Since its establishment in 1995, the WTO has continued the GATT work on strengthening the multilateral trading system. The first Ministerial Conference in Singapore (1996) gave birth to a new sectoral initiative on the MFN-based removal of duties on IT products, binding upon a subset of WTO members that constitutes the "critical mass" of respective world trade. The fourth Ministerial Conference held in Doha, Qatar, in 2001 launched a new round of multilateral negotiations on such areas as agriculture, nonagricultural market access, services, intellectual

---

[62] See Craig VanGrasstek, *The History and Future of the World Trade Organization* (Geneva: WTO, 2013), pp. 56–68.

property, trade and development, trade and environment, trade facilitation, WTO rules (antidumping, subsidies, and regional trade agreements (RTAs)), and dispute settlement. While not completed yet, the Doha Round reached some preliminary results in adopting the Transparency Mechanism for RTAs and the Agreement on Trade Facilitation.

1.2.2   The WTO's Role in Regulating National Industrial Policies

In this globalized world, the concept of "sovereignty" does no longer mean *absolute* autonomy of the State in pursuing its internal and external policies.[63] A nation adhering to complete self-reliance and isolationism is vulnerable to many challenges of regional and global scales, be it in economic, security, environmental, and other fields. Terrorism, climate change, refugees, and depleting natural resources are just few examples of acute problems that require joint government actions. Economic or financial crises in the last and current centuries had devastating cross-border effects. Such circumstances have obviously made the formally independent States interdependent, which naturally demands cooperation and coordination on the international plane, including the WTO.

The WTO-led multilateral trading system represents an international regime where national sovereignty over trade and industrial policies is circumscribed by many conditions and terms agreed upon by its stakeholders. All members must abide by WTO law regardless of what status it has under the respective domestic legal order. Article XVI:4 of the Marrakesh Agreement Establishing the WTO (hereinafter the "WTO Agreement") makes this point clear stating that "[e]ach Member shall ensure the conformity of its laws, regulations and administrative procedures with its obligations as provided in the annexed Agreements." Moreover, the adopted panel and appellate reports are legally binding on the disputing parties concerned, although the losing party has the discretion as to how to implement them.[64] As we will discuss in the next sections, the WTO system affects national industrial policies mainly through its rule-setting, judicial, and monitoring mechanisms.

---

[63] On this point, see, e.g., John H. Jackson, *Sovereignty, the WTO and Changing Fundamentals of International Law* (Cambridge: Cambridge University Press, 2006), pp. 57–78.

[64] See John H. Jackson, "International Law Status of WTO Dispute Settlement Reports: Obligation to Comply or Option to 'Buy Out'?," 98 *American Journal of International Law* 109 (2004).

1.2.2.1 Rule-Setting Function

Central, regional, and local governments should always consult the WTO rule book in all industrial policy stages. Agreements, ministerial decisions and declarations, as well as accession instruments together make up the WTO's statutory law. This is a member-driven organization, so its members are sole decision-makers endowed with a rule-making (or "legislative") power. Rules are developed through negotiations.

The WTO continues the GATT practice of taking decisions by consensus and has rarely used voting – a second-best option provided for under Articles IX and X of the WTO Agreement in the event of impasse in the consensus-building.[65] The consensus rule and the "single undertaking" principle of packaging WTO agreements strive to strengthen the sovereign equality of members and the integrity of the legal system. But in reality, this combination can well paralyze the decision-making process, as the number of members increases, the scope of subject matters expands, and many developing countries, especially the big ones, have more bargaining power today than they did in the past.[66]

In these circumstances, WTO members have explored several flexible ways of reaching agreement on new rules. As the case of the IT Agreement shows, the plurilateral approach to sectoral tariff liberalization with the "critical mass" and MFN elements has proved to be a worthwhile means of pushing the treaty-making forward. But systemic trade issues that need a WTO-wide response cannot be handled effectively enough in such a manner.

Another approach to reaching consensus consists in seeking less binding rules. The Trade Facilitation Agreement – the first post-Uruguay multilateral trade agreement – has been warmly applauded for the anticipated reduction of cross-border transaction costs. But in fact it contains many hortatory obligations on important issues, which downplays their enforceability. More specifically, around thirty-five technical measures on expedited customs procedures are written in nonmandatory "best efforts" language.[67]

---

[65] For instance, Ecuador's accession was approved by voting. See WTO, Accession of Ecuador – Decision of 16 August 1995, WT/ACC/ECU/5 (22 August 1995), n. 1.

[66] For the literature review and analysis on the WTO decision-making problems, see, e.g., Wenwei Guan, "Consensus Yet Not Consented: A Critique of the WTO Decision-Making by Consensus," 17 *Journal of International Economic Law* 77 (2014).

[67] OECD–WTO, "Aid for Trade at a Glance 2015: Reducing Trade Costs for Inclusive, Sustainable Growth," 2015, pp. 112–13.

Despite the existing practical constraints, it is unlikely that the WTO will be able to cancel the consensus rule, because amendment of the decision-making procedures requires *unanimous* support of its members.[68] Therefore, we believe that, in the current realities, members should rather switch from the failed consensus-building to voting – a permissible alternative to consensus.[69] Otherwise, the persistent stalemate in the WTO legislative process will make the whole system largely irresponsive to rapidly changing global challenges. This may compel the WTO "judiciary" to "creatively" interpret outdated provisions, which some may criticize as judicial overreaching.

The WTO legal texts are negotiated by trade officials, but it is extremely important for governments to consult with industries throughout the entire process of WTO rule-making. At the domestic level, the public–private interaction contributes to the formulation of the respective government's stance toward WTO initiatives and issues. However, not all countries have efficient channels of this kind in place. For instance, the Asia-Pacific Economic Cooperation (APEC) has been promoting the idea of "good regulatory practices" – affecting both trade and industries – for quite a long time, but only around half of its twenty-one member economies operate public consultation mechanisms as part of this agenda.[70]

In addition, WTO-level communications with the business community help governments obtain firsthand information on any problems faced by firms and explore new areas for possible regulatory reforms. As a striking example, "Trade Dialogues" with business representatives in the WTO have recently prioritized the pressing issues for future WTO legislative work, such as electronic commerce/digital trade, investment facilitation, support for SMEs and inclusive trade, trade finance, and

---

[68] See Article X:2 of the WTO Agreement referring to Article IX on decision making.

[69] It is also worth noting that the General Council agreed that the WTO decision-making procedure on waivers and accession requiring reaching consensus before voting proceeds "does not preclude a Member from requesting a vote at the time the decision is taken." WTO, Decision-Making Procedures under Articles IX and XII of the WTO Agreement – Statement by the Chairman – As Agreed by the General Council on 15 November 1995, WT/L/93 (24 November 1995).

[70] See Annex D of the 2011 APEC Leaders' Declaration, www.apec.org/Meeting-Papers/ Leaders-Declarations/2011/2011_aelm/2011_aelm_annexD.aspx; APEC, "Progress Report on 2011 Baseline Study on Good Regulatory Practices," APEC#213-CT-01.13, 2014, pp. 25–9.

global value chains.[71] Interestingly, over 50 percent of companies surveyed by the WTO Secretariat were keen to participate in networking events with WTO members and dedicated business forums at the WTO; 61 percent even wished to be allowed in WTO meetings.[72] These numbers point to the need for continuous interaction with business circles in the WTO.

1.2.2.2 Judicial Function

Virtually all disputes brought to the WTO address, directly or indirectly, certain aspects of industrial policy. Typically, the complainant's industries lose their market shares domestically or overseas because of the respondent's trade measures of industry promotion or protection. Pursuant to Article 3.2 of the Dispute Settlement Understanding (DSU), the WTO dispute settlement mechanism plays a central role in providing security and predictability to the WTO system and serves to preserve members' rights and obligations under the WTO agreements and to clarify the existing provisions of those agreements.

While the former GATT system dealt with around two hundred disputes over forty-seven years of its existence, the WTO already registered over five hundred disputes in some twenty-plus years only.[73] The increase in the caseload definitely stems from the growing number of members and expanded jurisdiction, but it may also indicate strong confidence in the WTO judicial procedures. However, this confidence may be damaged by procedural delays that happen quite frequently these days. The delays in the appellate procedures, for instance, are caused by the mismatch between the limited resources available to the Appellate Body and the increasing number of appeals.[74] The problem is

---

[71] WTO, "Businesses Share Ideas on Rules for Inclusive Trade," 28 September 2016, www.wto.org/english/news_e/news16_e/bus_28sep16_e.htm; WTO, "Business Leaders Call for WTO to Address Pressing Business Issues," 30 May 2016, www.wto.org/english/news_e/news16_e/bus_30may16_e.htm.

[72] WTO, "WTO Business Survey," www.wto.org/english/res_e/booksp_e/survey13_e.pdf.

[73] The GATT disputes here are those brought under Article XXIII of the GATT 1947. See GATT Analytical Index, *Guide to GATT Law and Practice*, updated 6th edn, 2 vols. (Geneva: WTO, 1995), vol. 2, pp. 771–87; WTO, "Chronological List of Disputes Cases," www.wto.org/english/tratop_e/dispu_e/dispu_status_e.htm.

[74] See Address by Ujal Singh Bhatia (Chairman of the Appellate Body), "The Problems of Plenty: Challenging Times for the WTO's Dispute Settlement System," 8 June 2017, www.wto.org/english/news_e/news17_e/ab_08jun17_e.pdf.

exacerbated by a recent setback in the selection of new Appellate Body members.[75] In this respect, the chairman of the Appellate Body rightly warned:

> When delays in WTO dispute resolution become the norm, they cast doubt on the value of the WTO's rules-oriented system itself. An erosion of trust in this system can lead to the re-emergence of power orientation in international trade policy. Delays compel WTO Members to look for other solutions, potentially elsewhere. And in this, it is the weaker countries that stand to lose the most.[76]

As the statistics for 1995–2015 show,[77] the frequency of the use of the WTO dispute settlement mechanism either as complainant or respondent directly correlates with the income status of participating members. During that period, the United States and the EU were the heaviest users, and some developing countries like Mexico, Brazil, India, China, and Chile were active as well. Most of the cases were concentrated in the goods sector. A comparatively large number of cases dealt with trade remedies, technical barriers to trade (TBT), licensing, sanitary and phytosanitary (SPS) measures, and investment-related trade measures.

The number of WTO complaints could have been much higher than it is now. But the government-to-government nature of disputes, the risk of procedural delays, largely prospective nature of remedies, and the potential for tit-for-tat actions by target members deter many dispute initiations. Moreover, many differences between or among members get resolved through WTO meeting discussions, as explained in the following section.

The way of handling industrial policy issues in one case will have important repercussions even outside that case. Indeed, the WTO jurisprudence creates "legitimate expectations" among WTO members. Thus, absent "cogent reasons," legal interpretations embodied in the adopted panel and Appellate Body reports must be followed in subsequent cases where relevant.[78] This makes *all* members keep a close eye on litigation developments, as many of them may well apply policies and measures akin to the challenged ones.

---

[75] See Bryce Baschuk, "U.S. Demands Exacerbate WTO Dispute Body Turmoil," Bloomberg BNA, *International Trade Daily*, 12 September 2017.

[76] Address by Ujal Singh Bhatia (Chairman of the Appellate Body), *supra* note 74.

[77] See Kara Leitner and Simon Lester, "WTO Dispute Settlement 1995–2015 – A Statistical Analysis," 19 *Journal of International Economic Law* 289 (2016), pp. 290–4.

[78] Appellate Body Report, *US – Stainless Steel (Mexico)*, paras. 158–60.

Article 5 of the DSU provides for good offices, conciliation, and mediation, but they remain largely inutile. In 2014, a new mediation procedure on SPS issues was adopted to encourage member-to-member consultations, with a facilitator involved. If such a topic-specific quasi-judicial mechanism turns out to be more successful than the Article 5 procedures, it will make sense to create a similar mechanism for other relevant trade areas as well.[79]

Because many WTO concepts are economic by nature, knowledge of the economics of trade (and industrial) policy would greatly help adjudicators reach economically sound findings within the permissible boundaries of treaty interpretation techniques as applied to specific provisions. However, only 16 percent of the serving WTO panelists (1995–2014) had an economics background predominantly from undergraduate studies.[80] As of 1 September 2017, only three[81] out of twenty-seven present and former members of the Appellate Body had academic degrees in economics. We believe that each panel and Appellate Body division should, to the maximum extent possible, include at least one member with an economics background, although ideally all panelists and Appellate Body members should have sufficient expertise in both law and economics of trade policy.

Last but not least, while economists engage in WTO affairs internally via domestic procedures of preparing government proposals and externally through participation in WTO meetings as member delegates,[82] they should also actively use the existing channels for outside experts[83] to have their say in the litigation process.

---

[79] Nohyoung Park and Myung-Hyun Chung, "Analysis of a New Mediation Procedure under the WTO SPS Agreement," 50 *Journal of World Trade* 93 (2016), p. 93.

[80] Louise Johannesson and Petros C. Mavroidis, "Black Cat, White Cat: The Identity of the WTO Judges," 49 *Journal of World Trade* 685 (2015), p. 688.

[81] They are Ujal Singh Bhatia (India, 2011–2019 (the term of office in the Appellate Body), M.A. in Economics and B.A. in Economics), Georges Michel Abi-Saab (Egypt, 2000–2008, MA in Economics), and Said El-Naggar (Egypt, 1995–2000, Master's and Doctoral degrees in Economics). See WTO, "Appellate Body Members," www.wto.org/english/tratop_e/dispu_e/ab_members_descrp_e.htm.

[82] See, e.g., Kym Anderson, "Setting the Trade Policy Agenda: What Roles for Economists?," World Bank Policy Research Working Paper No. 3560, 2005.

[83] See Gabrielle Z. Marceau and Jennifer K. Hawkins, "Experts in WTO Dispute Settlement," 3 *Journal of International Dispute Settlement* 493 (2012); Joost Pauwelyn, "The Use of Experts in WTO Dispute Settlement," 51 *International and Comparative Law Quarterly* 325 (2002).

1.2.2.3 Monitoring Function

The WTO also serves as a forum for multilateral surveillance over its members' trade and industrial policies. Although the existing mechanisms here lack an enforcing power – which is the sole jurisdiction of the WTO judiciary – they definitely increase transparency and accountability of domestic systems. By facilitating discussions among governments, these procedures greatly clarify many aspects of each member's internal regime and stimulate the feedback-giving process. This, in turn, may induce trade-friendlier policy adjustments and prevent formal disputes. But, of course, disputes can also arise in relation to the measures never discussed or monitored in the WTO before.

In general, multilateral oversight occurs in WTO meetings where each member can raise an issue with another member's policy in the related field. For instance, the Subsidies and Countervailing Measures (SCM) Committee examines subsidy notifications and members' reports on countervailing measures.[84] In 1995–2015, the TBT Committee and the SPS Committee discussed, respectively, 490 and 403 "specific trade concerns" (STCs) over proposed or adopted standard-related measures and their (potential) trade impacts.[85] The TBT-linked STCs mostly concerned the clarification about the measure at issue, followed by such issues as unnecessary barriers to trade, transparency, rationale or legitimacy, international standards, discrimination and others, with 68 percent of the STCs pertaining to notified measures.[86] The SPS-linked STCs were about animal health (39 percent), food safety (31 percent), plant health (25 percent), and other matters (5 percent), with about 44 percent of STCs being fully or partially resolved.[87]

Besides the topic-specific monitoring by the competent WTO bodies, two mechanisms below review national trade (and industrial) policies as a whole. One of them addresses their multilateral aspects, and the other focuses on regional aspects.

The TPRM looks at virtually all elements of national economic policies. The separate reports by the government and the WTO Secretariat

---

[84] Article 26 of the SCM Agreement.
[85] WTO, Committee on TBT – Twenty-First Annual Review of the Implementation and Operation of the TBT Agreement – Note by the Secretariat – Revision, G/TBT/38/Rev.1 (24 March 2016), Chart 14, para. 3.19; WTO, Committee on SPS Measures – STCs – Note by the Secretariat – Revision, G/SPS/GEN/204/Rev.16 (23 February 2016), para. 1.1.
[86] G/TBT/38/Rev.1, *supra* note 85, paras. 3.25, 3.28.
[87] G/SPS/GEN/204/Rev.16, *supra* note 85, paras. 1.2, 1.4.

on the member concerned provide information for discussion in the TPR Body (TPRB) meetings. The TPRM does not serve as a basis for dispute settlement proceedings, nor does it impose new policy commitments on the member under review.[88] Therefore, the panels in *Canada – Aircraft* and *Chile – Price Band System* explicitly refused to take account of the TPR reports regarding the respondent that the complainant had cited to support its own assertions.[89] But in fact as long as such reports are not explicitly quoted, the measures identified there may subsequently be challenged and adjudicated. This happened 53 percent of the time for Secretariat reports preceding the initiation of disputes.[90] Whether the disputes were actually triggered by the information in TPR reports – not cited in dispute materials – is difficult to prove, as complainants can learn about problematic measures from other sources as well. But the potential for such a trigger may discourage many members from disclosing substantive information in the TPRM process.

The Transparency Mechanism for RTAs adopted in 2006 is a miniaturized version of the TPRM that oversees members' regional trade policies as explained in the Secretariat's factual presentations on the notified agreements.[91] Like the TPRM, such transparency procedures are delinked from dispute settlement. The previous system of the multilateral surveillance of RTAs virtually failed to carry out its original mission to examine the lawfulness of the RTAs. As we observed elsewhere, the launch of the Transparency Mechanism in question marked a crucial shift in the WTO from legal "examination" of RTAs to their "consideration." This means that the new system no longer devotes any attention to the *WTO-consistency* of the RTAs, but rather represents a *transparency* review process. In our view, this pragmatic approach draws a clear-cut demarcation line between the WTO's monitoring and judicial bodies with respect to their jurisdiction over RTAs.[92]

---

[88] Section A of Annex 3 ("Trade Policy Review Mechanism") to the WTO Agreement.

[89] Panel Report, *Canada – Aircraft*, paras. 8.14, 9.274; Panel Report, *Chile – Price Band System*, n. 664 to para. 7.95.

[90] Arunabha Ghosh, "Information Gaps, Information Systems, and the WTO's Trade Policy Review Mechanism," GEG Working Paper No. 2008/40, University of Oxford, 2008, p. 21.

[91] See WTO, General Council – Transparency Mechanism for Regional Trade Agreements – Decision of 14 December 2006, WT/L/671 (18 December 2006).

[92] Sherzod Shadikhodjaev, "Checking RTA Compatibility with Global Trade Rules: WTO Litigation Practice and Implications from the Transparency Mechanism for RTAs," 45 *Journal of World Trade* 529 (2011), pp. 536–40.

1.2.3   Overview of WTO Flexibilities for Industrial Policy

This part provides a general outline of existing WTO flexibilities, leaving their detailed examination to other chapters. Technically, WTO law distinguishes between "derogation" and "exception." An exception justifies a measure that otherwise falls within, and violates, an applicable provision, while derogation excludes a measure from the scope of a legal provision altogether.[93]

To exemplify a legal derogation, Article XI:2 of the GATT says that the general ban on quantitative restrictions "shall not extend" to the specified nontariff import or export restrictions. In the same vein, Article III:8(a) of the GATT reads that the national treatment obligation "shall not apply" to government procurement. In contrast, the GATT does not "prevent" reasonable policy measures under Article XX exceptions or RTAs under an Article XXIV exception.

The WTO flexibility provisions apply either to specific provisions – for example, Article IV of the GATT on screen quotas as relevant to the GATT nondiscrimination rules – or horizontally, as discussed in the following section.

1.2.3.1   Horizontal Exceptions

The general and security exceptions apply across the board within a WTO agreement where they are inserted. As a most representative example, Article XX of the GATT lists general exceptions in paragraphs (a) to (j) for ten types of illegal but socially desirable trade measures.[94] These paragraphs use different terms – "necessary," "essential," "relating to," and so on – to express different degrees of "connection or relationship" between the illegal measure at issue and the covered policy interest.[95] To succeed, the party invoking Article XX must prove in two consecutive steps that the violating measure (i) seats under any of the exceptions in the related paragraph and (ii) satisfies the requirements of the opening clause (or "*chapeau*") of Article XX not to constitute "a means of arbitrary or unjustifiable discrimination" or "a disguised discrimination on international trade."[96] The first step appraises the

---

[93] Appellate Body Reports, *Canada – Renewable Energy/Canada – Feed-in Tariff Program*, para. 5.56; Appellate Body Reports, *China – Raw Materials*, para. 334.

[94] In Section 6.5.2, we argue that the GATT general exceptions do not apply to the non-GATT WTO instruments unless the latter explicitly suggest otherwise.

[95] Appellate Body Report, *US – Gasoline*, p. 17.

[96] *Ibid.*, p. 22; Appellate Body Report, *US – Shrimp*, paras. 119–20.

"general design" of a challenged measure under the applicable paragraph, whereas the second step checks the "manner" of application of that measure to ensure that the invoking member is not abusing or misusing the covered exceptions.[97]

As for the example of security exceptions, Article XXI of the GATT applies when members take measures relating to national security information, fissionable materials, and military goods; act in time of war or international emergencies; or comply with the UN peace and security obligations. But it is not clear yet whether and how these somewhat outdated security dimensions can address new challenges, such as, e.g., cybersecurity, energy security, and terrorism.[98]

With the proliferation of RTAs shown in Figure 1.1 and consequent repercussions for the multilateral trading system, the WTO exceptions for regional trade take on importance. RTAs in the goods sector are covered by Article XXIV of the GATT or the Enabling Clause (for South–South agreements), while those in the services sector are regulated by Article V of the General Agreement on Trade in Services (GATS). Articles XXIV and V are horizontal exceptions within the respective agreements, but the Enabling Clause is applicable to violations of Article I of the GATT only.[99] For the subject RTAs, they commonly impose an internal requirement to free (or liberalize) reciprocal trade and an external requirement not to raise barriers toward third-party trade, but they establish different parameters to comply with.

Three rulings on RTA issues are especially noteworthy. In *Turkey – Textiles*, the Appellate Body held that, for being justified under Article XXIV,

---

[97] Appellate Body Report, *US – Gasoline*, p. 22; Appellate Body Report, *US – Shrimp*, paras. 116, 156. See Lorand Bartels, "The Chapeau of the General Exceptions in the WTO GATT and GATS Agreements: A Reconstruction," 109 *American Journal of International Law* 95 (2015), p. 124 where the author criticizes this bifurcation approach denying the existence of any "analytic, structural, or even thematic difference" between the conditions in the *chapeau* and those in the paragraphs of Article XX, as all of those conditions work to "limit the right of a WTO member to adopt certain measures" for legitimate reasons under the general exceptions.

[98] See Ji Yeong Yoo and Dukgeun Ahn, "Security Exceptions in the WTO System: Bridge or Bottle-Neck for Trade and Security?," 19 *Journal of International Economic Law* 417 (2016); Shin-yi Peng, "Cybersecurity Threats and the WTO National Security Exceptions," 18 *Journal of International Economic Law* 449 (2015).

[99] Article XXIV:5 of the GATT reads that "the provisions of this Agreement shall not prevent" RTAs, and Article V of the GATS says "[t]his Agreement shall not prevent" services RTAs – both referring to the whole Agreement. In contrast, the Enabling Clause allows South–South RTAs "notwithstanding the provisions of Article I of the General Agreement."

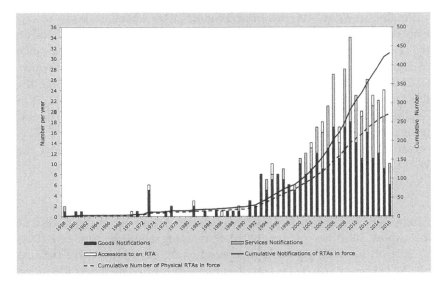

Figure 1.1   Evolution of RTAs in the World (1948–2016)
Source: WTO, "Recent Developments in Regional Trade Agreements (July–December 2016),"
INT/SUB/RTA/153, p. 2 (chart 1), www.wto.org/english/tratop_e/region_e/rtajuly-dec16_e.pdf.

an illegal measure relating to an RTA (i) must be introduced upon the
formation of a WTO-consistent RTA and (ii) must be necessary for the
formation of that RTA.[100] The first inquiry is especially difficult to handle,
as the overly vague language of Article XXIV has made the WTO adjudicators reluctant to interpret it for determining the WTO-consistency of
the RTA at issue.[101]

   Further, the Appellate Body in *Mexico – Taxes on Soft Drinks* affirmed
the WTO-admissibility of RTA-related issues reviewed in parallel procedures of a respective RTA. In particular, it concluded that WTO panels
could not decline to exercise jurisdiction over trade disputes properly
before them in favor of adjudicating bodies examining the same matter in
non-WTO forums, such as the North American Free Trade Agreement
(FTA) at issue.[102]

[100] Appellate Body Report, *Turkey – Textiles*, para. 58.
[101] They tried to avoid the issue of WTO-compatibility of the invoked RTAs in, inter alia,
Turkey – Textiles (DS34), *Argentina – Footwear (EC)* (DS121), *US – Line Pipe* (DS202),
and *Brazil – Retreaded Tyres* (DS332). See Shadikhodjaev, *supra* note 92, pp. 534–36.
[102] Appellate Body Report, *Mexico – Taxes on Soft Drinks*, paras. 45–54.

Finally, in *Peru – Agricultural Products*, the Appellate Body reconfirmed the *exclusive* role of the WTO rules on regional trade in checking the lawfulness of provisions of a member's RTA and denied the relevance of the provisions of the Vienna Convention on the Law of Treaties (VCLT) on *inter se* modifications within the WTO domain. Importantly, the Appellate Body sent a strong message against "WTO-minus" RTAs in holding that the Article XXIV requirement for an RTA to "facilitate" trade between its parties disables Article XXIV justification of RTA measures that "roll back on Members' rights and obligations under the WTO covered agreements."[103]

1.2.3.2 Member-Specific Flexibilities

Exemptions for historical preferences under Article I:2 of the GATT or for export subsidies of designated developing countries under Article 27.2(a) of the SCM Agreement represent rare examples where the text of a WTO treaty articulates certain carve-outs toward members identified by names. Most of the provided member-specific flexibilities can be found in the WTO's "secondary" law, as follows.

Article XII of the WTO Agreement reads that accession of an applicant "State" or "separate customs territory" is subject to "terms to be agreed between it and the WTO," which opens the door for negotiating specific commitments and tailor-made flexibilities. In addition to the scoping and timing of the market-opening commitments, the acceding government may negotiate grace periods for "grandfathering" some of its internal regulations when it needs more time for adapting to the WTO regime. Ecuador, for instance, managed to secure almost a four-year exemption for certain illegal investment-related measures in the automotive sector.[104]

Under Article XIII of the WTO Agreement (and formerly Article XXXV of the GATT), any existing and any acceding member may, for whatever reason, opt not to apply the WTO regime in bilateral trade. The United States used this mechanism most frequently by not extending MFN treatment vis-à-vis countries that, in its view, had low profiles on

---

[103] Appellate Body Report, *Peru – Agricultural Products*, paras. 5.111–5.113, 5.116. See Sherzod Shadikhodjaev, "The 'Regionalism vs Multilateralism' Issue in International Trade Law: Revisiting the *Peru–Agricultural Products* Case," 16 *Chinese Journal of International Law* 109 (2017).

[104] WTO, Report of the Working Party on the Accession of Ecuador, WT/L/77 (14 July 1995), paras. 75–6.

market economy or human rights. The nonapplication practice is, however, not widespread and, even in the case of invocation, tended to cease at a later point.[105]

According to Article IX (paragraphs 3 and 4) of the WTO Agreement, the Ministerial Conference can temporarily waive a requesting member from its WTO obligations in "exceptional circumstances," subject to the attached "terms and conditions." Waivers exceeding one year are to be reviewed until the full termination. In the former GATT system, waivers were granted in 115 cases targeting mostly the GATT scheduling and MFN provisions.[106] In the WTO, the number of waiver decisions exceeded two hundred,[107] with a few of them relating to the post-GATT agreements on agriculture, TRIMs, and TRIPS.[108] Most of the waivers were granted to individual members, but some were collective waivers concerning the Harmonized Commodity Description and Coding System (the "Harmonized System" or the "HS"), tariff preferences of developing countries for least-developed countries (LDCs), and certain TRIPS obligations of LDCs on pharmaceutical products.[109] Individual waivers typically address capacity problems of developing countries and allow developed countries to operate non-GSP preferential schemes, while collective waivers tend to deal with systemic (rather than incidental) difficulties.[110] In *EC – Bananas III*, the Appellate Body dismissed the respondent's argument that a waiver under Article I of the GATT had to be extended to Article XIII, another nondiscrimination clause. The Appellate Body stressed the "exceptional nature of waivers" and the need to interpret them "with great care," implying that waivers cannot apply beyond the provisions explicitly referred to in the waiver decisions concerned.[111]

1.2.3.3   Special and Differential (S&D) Treatment

Although roughly half of the GATT founding members were from the developing world, the original GATT text was written with arguably less

---

[105] See VanGrasstek, *supra* note 62, pp. 138–40, 143–6.

[106] GATT Analytical Index, *supra* note 73, pp. 892–905.

[107] Isabel Feichtner, *The Law and Politics of WTO Waivers: Stability and Flexibility in Public International Law* (New York: Cambridge University Press, 2011), p. 63.

[108] WTO, Council for TRIPS – Paragraph 6 of the Doha Declaration on the TRIPS Agreement and Public Health [...] – Note by the Secretariat, IP/C/W/387 (24 October 2002), para. 4.

[109] *Ibid.*, para. 5 and Annex 6.   [110] Feichtner, *supra* note 107, pp. 122, 157.

[111] Appellate Body Report, *EC – Bananas III*, paras. 184–7.

attention to their special needs and concerns. Over time, however, developing countries have been insisting on adopting more South-oriented flexibilities. As a result, 145 provisions under fifteen Uruguay Round agreements envisage S&D treatment of developing countries under the following categories: (i) provisions seeking to increase developing countries' trade opportunities; (ii) requirements to safeguard their interests; (iii) flexibility of commitments/action and use of policy instruments; (iv) transitional time-periods; (v) technical assistance; and (vi) LDC-specific provisions.[112] Over thirty Ministerial, General Council's, and other relevant decisions, mostly adopted after 1995, contain additional, albeit some repetitive, S&D provisions.[113]

The S&D regime has certain drawbacks. It mostly applies to developing countries as a group without further differentiation. Because its nature is already at odds with the fundamental principle of reciprocity that economic theory[114] considers as a key motivation for the multilateral trade cooperation, S&D treatment should be more customized to varying needs within that group, subject to objective criteria for differential application and graduation terms.[115]

Furthermore, many S&D provisions have failed to produce tangible results for developing countries because of the lack of implementation guidelines, vague formulations, and "soft law" obligations.[116] Therefore, the Doha Ministerial Declaration (2001) initiated review of the S&D rules with a view to rewriting them in stronger, more precise, effective, and operational language.[117] The Ministerial Conference in Bali (2013) established an S&D monitoring mechanism tasked to review all aspects of S&D implementation on the basis of inputs from members or WTO

---

[112] WTO, Committee on Trade and Development – S&D Treatment Provisions in WTO Agreements and Decisions – Note by the Secretariat, WT/COMTD/W/219 (22 September 2016), pp. 4–5.

[113] *Ibid.*, section 7.

[114] See, e.g., Kyle Bagwell and Robert W. Staiger, "An Economic Theory of GATT," 89 *American Economic Review* 215 (1999).

[115] For the literature review on this point, see Bernard Hoekman, "Operationalizing the Concept of Policy Space in the WTO: Beyond Special and Differential Treatment," 8 *Journal of International Economic Law* 405 (2005), pp. 412–13; Alexander Keck and Patrick Low, "Special and Differential Treatment in the WTO: Why, When and How?," WTO Staff Working Paper No. ERSD-2004-03, 2004, pp. 25–6.

[116] See Hoekman, *supra* note 115, p. 411, n. 14; Sonia E. Rolland, *Development at the World Trade Organization* (Oxford: Oxford University Press, 2012), pp. 109–38.

[117] WTO, Ministerial Conference – Fourth Session – Doha, 9–14 November 2001 – Ministerial Declaration – Adopted on 14 November 2001, WT/MIN(01)/DEC/1 (20 November 2001), para. 44.

bodies with the possibility to recommend negotiations on rule improvements.[118] To date, members have tabled over eighty proposals under the Doha mandate, but no submissions to the S&D monitoring mechanism.[119]

By contrast, an innovative S&D section of the newly adopted Trade Facilitation Agreement may well serve as a model for future legal texts to follow.[120] It is unique in giving developing countries the choice to self-designate the status of envisaged commitments and to link the implementation of some commitments to receipt of technical assistance and capacity building support from donor countries. This approach gives more room for member-specific flexibilities in complying with rules that – unlike flexibilities in market access commitments – have so far been largely regulated by universal or group-oriented provisions.[121]

1.3   Concluding Remarks

The economic literature justifies industrial policies, and in particular industrial targeting, under certain circumstances only. In essence, a public intervention is warranted where it creates new (or infant) industries that otherwise cannot emerge or where it addresses certain other market failures. But even within this delimited space, it is difficult to make economically reasonable and perfectly suitable policy prescriptions. When such prescriptions are nevertheless readily available, governments may still fall short of implementing them accurately due to the capacity building constraints.

As a practical matter, the story of the East Asian miracle provides some good lessons that may be followed by others, subject to the uniqueness of each country's conditions. This model of development highlights

---

[118] WTO, Ministerial Conference – Ninth Session – Bali, 3–6 December 2013 – Monitoring Mechanism on S&D Treatment – Ministerial Decision of 7 December 2013, WT/MIN (13)/45, WT/L/920 (11 December 2013).

[119] WTO, "Special and Differential Treatment: Grappling with 88 Proposals," www.wto.org/english/thewto_e/minist_e/min03_e/brief_e/brief21_e.htm; WT/COMTD/W/219, *supra* note 112, p. 4, para. 1.6.

[120] Antonia Eliason, "The Trade Facilitation Agreement: A New Hope for the World Trade Organization," 14 *World Trade Review* 643 (2015), p. 662.

[121] See Ben Czapnik, "The Unique Features of the Trade Facilitation Agreement: A Revolutionary New Approach to Multilateral Negotiations or the Exception Which Proves the Rule?," 18 *Journal of International Economic Law* 773 (2015).

the pros of an export-oriented, performance-based, and internally well-coordinated industrial policy.

In addition to economic considerations, the question as to "how" to design and carry out a proper industrial policy should necessarily be tackled from a legal perspective. This and the following chapters show that the WTO rule book considerably ties governments' hands in conducting their industrial policies as far as international trade is affected. Although this system does provide some flexibilities, they can be used mostly in exceptional cases only.

2

Protection of Domestic Industry

Protection of domestic producers from foreign competition and associated injury is an important component of any national industrial policy. Governments take many measures on the trade front to restrict market access to goods and services originating from other countries. This chapter discusses typical border restrictions (tariff, quantitative restrictions, and trade remedies), taxes, product standards, and service-affecting measures, showing some major legal constraints and flexibilities under respective WTO rules. Some of these measures, like trade remedies, are temporary and available only if and as long as certain prerequisites are met. Others, like customs duties or internal taxes, are virtually automatic in applying to imports whenever they enter the domestic market. Some product standards pursuing legitimate policy purposes may, in fact, be applied in a protectionist manner. Certain peculiarities of protecting services industries are attributable to the very nature of services and the relative novelty of trade regulation in this area.

2.1 Border Restrictions

2.1.1 Tariff

According to economic theory,[1] a tariff (or customs/import duty) reduces the local demand for the subject imported product by increasing its domestic price, which has different implications for national economies. For a "small" country unable to affect the world price of the product in question, this entails contraction of the national welfare. For a "big" country having considerable price influence in the world market,

---

[1] See Krugman, Obstfeld, and Melitz, Ch. 1, *supra* note 22, pp. 209–17; Kyle Bagwell and Robert W. Staiger, *The Economics of the World Trading System* (Cambridge, Massachusetts: MIT Press, 2002), pp. 13–36; WTO, "The WTO and Trade Economics: Theory and Policy," WTO E-Learning, 2012, pp. 13–17, https://ecampus.wto.org/admin/files/Course_492/CourseContents/TEC-E-Print.pdf.

the fall in the import demand lowers the world price to that country's favor. Despite this "terms-of-trade gain," the big country's tariff has an ambiguous impact on its welfare and may trigger retaliation by foreign countries that are forced to receive a lower price for their exports than if they would have earned without that tariff imposed. Such a trade war would make all countries worse off. Therefore, multilateral tariff reductions would deter such terms-of-trade manipulations and tit-for-tat restrictions and help governments resist internal antiliberalization pressures from import-competing sectors by mobilizing domestic exporters' lobbies for market openings abroad.

Tariff is a legitimate instrument "irrespective of the underlying objective," be it revenue generation or industry protection.[2] But it must comply with the MFN principle and tariff ceilings fixed in each member's schedule of concessions. Article II:1(a) of the GATT prohibits treatment less favorable to imports than that provided for in such schedule. Article II:1(b) safeguards tariff "bindings" by banning the application of "ordinary customs duties" in excess of the scheduled (or "bound") levels. While excess duties violating Article II:1(b) are automatically in breach of Article II:1(a) for treating imports less favorably per se,[3] nondiscriminatory below-binding "applied" (i.e., actually charged) duties are WTO-consistent.[4] Article II of the GATT does not prevent the use of a different *type* of tariff than that in the schedule (e.g., specific duty vs. *ad valorem* duty) as long as the bound amount is kept.[5]

In Table 2.1, the largest and the smallest binding (or scheduling) coverages are committed by many recently acceded members (100 percent) and Cameroon (13.3 percent) respectively vs. the WTO average of 79.9 percent. Bangladesh has the highest simple average bound tariff (169.3 percent), while Macao and Hong Kong have the lowest (0 percent each), but all three have low rates of the binding coverage. There is no difference ("water") between the bound and applied rates in, for example, the United States, but the gap is significant in, for example, some African countries.

Two typical patterns of schedule-related violations include (i) levying excess duties and (ii) customs reclassification leading to higher duties. As a fresh example for the first case, the panel in *Russia – Tariff Treatment* found that the applied duties of 10 percent and 15 percent at issue vs. the corresponding bound duties of 5 percent were inconsistent with Article II

---

[2] Appellate Body Report, *India – Additional Import Duties*, para. 159.
[3] Appellate Body Report, *Argentina – Textiles and Apparel*, para. 45.   [4] *Ibid.*, para. 46.
[5] *Ibid.*, paras. 54–5.

Table 2.1 *WTO Tariff Levels*

Member	Year of MFN Applied Tariff	Binding Coverage (in percent)	Simple Average	
			Bound	MFN Applied
1. Bangladesh	2015	15.5	169.3	13.9
2. Tanzania	2015	13.3	120.0	12.9
3. Nigeria	2015	19.1	118.3	12.1
4. Zambia	2015	16.8	106.0	13.6
5. The Gambia		13.7	102.8	
6. Kuwait	2015	99.9	97.8	4.7
7. Mauritius	2015	17.2	97.8	1.0
8. Mozambique	2014	13.6	97.4	10.1
9. Democratic Republic of the Congo	2015	100	96.1	10.9
10. Kenya	2015	14.8	95.1	12.9
11. Ghana		14.3	92.5	
12. Rwanda	2015	100	89.4	12.8
13. Zimbabwe	2015	22.2	88.0	16.8
14. Myanmar	2015	17.8	84.1	5.6
15. Togo	2015	13.9	80.0	12.2
16. Cameroon	2014	13.3	79.9	18.2
17. Chad	2015	13.4	79.9	17.9
18. Barbados		97.5	78.3	
19. Lesotho	2015	100	78.3	7.6
20. Solomon Islands	2015	100	78.3	9.6
21. Saint Kitts and Nevis	2015	97.5	76.0	9.1
22. Malawi	2015	31.9	74.7	12.6
23. Uganda	2015	15.7	73.1	12.8
24. Burundi	2015	22	67.1	12.8
25. Saint Vincent and the Grenadines	2015	99.7	62.9	10.0
26. Saint Lucia	2015	99.6	62.4	9.1
27. Pakistan	2015	98.7	60.0	12.3
28. Angola	2015	100	59.2	11.4
29. Antigua and Barbuda	2015	97.5	58.8	9.9
30. Dominica	2015	94.3	58.7	10.0
31. Belize	2015	97.6	58.2	10.9
32. Tunisia	2015	58	57.9	15.5
33. Grenada	2015	100	56.6	11.0

Table 2.1 (*cont.*)

Member	Year of MFN Applied Tariff	Binding Coverage (in percent)	Simple Average	
			Bound	MFN Applied
34. Guyana	2015	100	56.6	10.9
35. Trinidad and Tobago		100	55.8	
36. Jamaica	2015	100	49.6	8.5
37. Guinea-Bissau	2014	97.7	48.7	11.9
38. India	2015	74.4	48.5	13.4
39. Sierra Leone		100	47.4	
40. Niger	2015	96.7	44.7	12.2
41. Costa Rica	2014	100	43.1	5.6
42. Burkina Faso	2015	39.1	42.1	12.2
43. Colombia	2015	100	42.1	5.7
44. Djibouti	2014	100	41.3	20.9
45. Guatemala	2015	100	41.3	5.6
46. Morocco	2015	100	41.3	11.5
47. Nicaragua	2015	100	40.9	5.7
48. Fiji	2015	51.1	40.5	11.5
49. Bolivia	2015	100	40.0	11.6
50. Vanuatu	2015	100	39.7	7.4
51. Indonesia	2014	96.3	37.1	6.9
52. Egypt	2015	99.3	36.8	16.8
53. Maldives		96.8	36.8	
54. El Salvador	2015	100	36.7	6.0
55. Venezuela	2015	100	36.5	12.9
56. Mexico	2015	100	36.2	7.1
57. Central African Republic	2015	62	36.1	18.0
58. Bahrain	2015	72.8	34.8	4.7
59. Dominican Republic	2015	100	34.0	7.3
60. Paraguay	2015	100	33.5	9.8
61. Papua New Guinea	2014	100	32.1	4.7
62. Honduras	2015	100	31.9	5.7
63. Argentina	2015	100	31.8	13.6
64. Uruguay	2015	100	31.5	10.5
65. Brazil	2015	100	31.4	13.5
66. Sri Lanka	2015	38.3	30.4	9.3
67. Senegal	2015	100	30.0	12.2
68. Peru	2015	100	29.5	2.4
69. Turkey	2015	50.3	28.6	10.8

Table 2.1 (*cont.*)

Member	Year of MFN Applied Tariff	Binding Coverage (in percent)	Simple Average	
			Bound	MFN Applied
70. Mali	2015	39.9	28.5	12.2
71. Benin	2015	39.1	28.3	12.2
72. Thailand	2015	75	27.8	11.0
73. Madagascar	2015	30	27.3	11.7
74. Congo	2015	16.2	27.2	11.9
75. Liberia	2014	100	26.7	10.2
76. Nepal	2015	99.4	26.0	12.3
77. Philippines	2015	67	25.7	6.3
78. Brunei Darussalam	2014	95.3	25.4	1.2
79. Chile	2015	100	25.1	6.0
80. Iceland	2015	95	24.0	5.2
81. Panama	2015	100	22.9	6.8
82. Israel	2015	74.6	22.7	4.5
83. Malaysia	2014	84.3	22.3	6.1
84. Ecuador	2015	100	21.7	11.9
85. Gabon	2015	100	21.2	17.7
86. Samoa	2015	100	21.2	11.4
87. Yemen	2015	100	21.2	7.5
88. Cuba	2015	31.5	21.0	10.6
89. Norway	2015	100	20.2	6.6
90. Guinea		38.7	20.1	
91. Mauritania	2015	39.3	19.8	12.0
92. Cambodia	2014	100	19.1	11.2
93. Namibia	2015	96.1	19.0	7.6
94. South Africa	2015	96.1	19.0	7.6
95. Swaziland	2015	96.1	19.0	7.6
96. Botswana	2015	96.1	18.7	7.6
97. Haiti	2015	89	18.7	4.8
98. Lao People's Democratic Republic	2015	100	18.7	10.0
99. Suriname		26.8	18.0	
100. Tonga	2015	100	17.6	11.7
101. Mongolia	2015	100	17.5	5.0
102. Korea	2015	94.5	16.8	13.9
103. Jordan	2015	100	16.2	10.0
104. Cabo Verde	2015	100	15.8	10.0

Table 2.1 (*cont.*)

Member	Year of MFN Applied Tariff	Binding Coverage (in percent)	Simple Average	
			Bound	MFN Applied
105. Qatar	2015	100	15.6	4.7
106. United Arab Emirates (UAE)	2015	100	14.4	4.7
107. Oman	2015	100	13.8	5.5
108. Afghanistan		96.6	13.6	
109. Viet Nam	2015	100	11.5	9.5
110. Côte d'Ivoire	2015	33.3	11.1	12.2
111. Saudi Arabia	2015	100	11.1	5.1
112. New Zealand	2015	100	10.2	2.0
113. China	2015	100	10.0	9.9
114. Australia	2015	97	9.9	2.5
115. Singapore	2015	69.6	9.6	0.2
116. Seychelles	2015	100	9.5	2.9
117. Armenia	2015	100	8.5	6.1
118. Tajikistan	2015	100	8.1	7.6
119. Switzerland	2015	99.7	8.0	6.7
120. Russia	2015	100	7.6	7.8
121. Kyrgyz Republic	2015	99.9	7.5	7.4
122. Georgia	2015	100	7.3	1.5
123. The Former Yugoslav Republic of Macedonia	2015	100	7.2	6.8
124. Albania	2015	100	7.0	3.8
125. Moldova	2015	100	6.9	5.4
126. Canada	2015	99.7	6.8	4.2
127. Kazakhstan	2015	100	6.5	7.8
128. Chinese Taipei	2015	100	6.3	6.4
129. Ukraine	2015	100	5.8	4.5
130. Montenegro	2015	100	5.1	4.0
131. EU	2015	100	4.8	5.1
132. Japan	2015	99.7	4.4	4.0
133. United States	2015	100	3.5	3.5
134. Hong Kong	2015	45.9	0.0	0.0
135. Macao	2015	27.5	0.0	0.0
Average		*79.9*	*38.3*	*8.9 (126 members)*

Source: Based on WTO, "World Tariff Profiles," 2016, pp. 8–13 ("All Products").

of the GATT.[6] As for the second case, the European Communities (EC) in *EC – Chicken Cuts* reclassified frozen boneless chicken cuts impregnated with salt from HS heading 02.10 (salted chicken etc.) to HS heading 02.07 (frozen chicken etc.) that envisaged more burdensome bound duties. The EC argued that since the salting of the product at issue was not sufficient for its long-term preservation, it could not properly qualify as "salted" under heading 02.10. But the Appellate Body held that the term "salted" did not actually mean long-term preservation and that excess duties resulting from tariff reclassification contravened the scheduled concessions for heading 02.10.[7] In this era of the fourth industrial revolution when many multifunctional products are created with various technology converging features, the number of Article II disputes over the customs classification issue will likely increase.

Depending on industrial policy needs, applied tariffs may fluctuate over time. Imposing high duties does not make sense for goods that are not produced or are otherwise in short supply in the internal market. Low duties benefit domestic industries relying on intermediary imports. When, for instance, Korea temporarily reduced its tariff on crude oil from 3 percent to 1 percent in 2004, it did so to cope with world price hikes for this commodity.[8] In 2010, Canada decided to unilaterally eliminate applied MFN tariffs on 1,541 items (manufacturing inputs, machinery, and equipment) to increase competitiveness of local companies via cutting their import costs so as to "enhance their stock of capital equipment," "open the potential for new and different production technologies," and encourage innovation.[9]

But if need be, the bound levels for particular products may legally be raised following tariff rescheduling. Under Article XXVIII of the GATT, a member seeking to modify or withdraw a concession (i.e., an applicant member) must conduct negotiations with a member with whom that concession was initially negotiated and any other member with a "principal supplying interest," as well as consultations with other members having a "substantial interest" in that concession. The purpose is to "maintain a

---

[6] Panel Report, *Russia – Tariff Treatment*, paras. 7.57–7.62.
[7] Appellate Body Report, *EC – Chicken Cuts*, paras. 1–9, 347.
[8] WTO, "Trade Monitoring Database," referring to the Permanent Delegation of Korea to the WTO (March 2009), http://tmdb.wto.org.
[9] WTO, Committee on Market Access – Minutes of the Meeting Held on 29 April 2009, G/MA/M/51 (26 May 2010), para. 11.3; WTO, Committee on Market Access – Canadian Government Actions to Unilaterally Eliminate Certain Most-Favoured-Nation Applied Tariffs – Communication from Canada, G/MA/W/101 (19 April 2010).

[pre-rescheduling] general level of reciprocal and mutually advantageous concessions," which may require the applicant member's "compensatory adjustment" for other products. If this process fails, the applicant member is free to modify/withdraw the concession, but other participants are entitled to withdraw "substantially equivalent concessions."

Besides the Article XXVIII requirements, such tariff rescheduling must also respect other applicable WTO provisions. In *EC – Poultry*, Brazil argued that compensatory tariff-rate quotas resulting from Article XXVIII negotiations with the EC were exempt from the MFN principle. But the Appellate Body said that such perception would create "a serious loophole in the multilateral trading system" that would enable members (like Brazil here) to secure preferences on the pretext of "compensatory adjustment" under Article XXVIII.[10]

As for the practice, at least three hundred renegotiations under Article XXVIII were initiated in the GATT period, and over forty renegotiation requests have been made since 1995.[11] In 2012, Ukraine made an extremely ambitious request for modifying over 350 tariff concessions, explaining this with "very liberalized market access" commitments it had undertaken during the WTO accession as juxtaposed to no committed liberalization by other members under the stalled Doha Round. But many in the WTO objected, pointing to serious systemic implications of such a large-scale modification plan and virtual impossibility of negotiating an equivalent compensation.[12] Although Ukraine eventually withdrew its request,[13] this case provides a good practical lesson that each government should commit to market openings, considering actual and potential capacity of its industries and having possible renegotiation difficulties in mind.

Finally, Article XVIII of the GATT establishes less-demanding procedures for members with "low standards of living" and "in the early stages of development" in relation to protective or other import-affecting measures as part of their economic development policies. In line with the infant industry argument,[14] Article XVIII:A permits rescheduling of tariff concessions desirable "for the establishment of a particular industry." Unlike

---

[10] Appellate Body Report, *EC – Poultry*, paras. 100–1 citing the panel findings.
[11] WTO, Committee on Market Access – Situation of Schedules of WTO Members – Note by the Secretariat – Revision, G/MA/W/23/Rev.12 (11 April 2016), paras. 4.2, 4.5.
[12] WTO, Committee on Market Access – Minutes of the Meeting Held on 16 October 2012, G/MA/M/56 (8 January 2013), paras. 11.1–11.36.
[13] WTO, General Council – Minutes of the Meeting – Held in the Center William Rappard on 21 October 2014, WT/GC/M/153 (2 December 2014), paras. 7.1–7.3.
[14] See Section 1.1.1.1.

Article XXVIII, the provision in question is silent on the obligation to maintain the general level of concessions and negotiate with members having a "principal supplying interest." In case of failed negotiations, the Ministerial Conference may still allow unilateral tariff changes if it finds that the applicant member "has made every effort to reach an agreement," and that offered compensation is "adequate." But Article XVIII:A has been of very limited assistance to developing countries, as it was invoked only nine times in the 1950–1960s and the 1980s by Benelux (on behalf of Suriname), Greece, Indonesia, Korea, and Sri Lanka.[15]

2.1.2 Quantitative Restrictions

The WTO indicative list of notifiable quantitative restrictions includes trade-related prohibitions, quotas, nonautomatic licensing, State-trading restrictions, mixing regulations, minimum prices, and voluntary export restraints.[16] Article XI:1 of the GATT lays down a general ban on import or export "prohibitions or restrictions other than duties, taxes or other charges" whether implemented through "quotas, import or export licences or other measures." This derives from the GATT/WTO perception of tariffs as a more preferable form of border protection, as one can learn from a panel's observations:

> The prohibition against quantitative restrictions is a reflection that tariffs are GATT's border protection "of choice". Quantitative restrictions impose absolute limits on imports, while tariffs do not. In contrast to MFN tariffs which permit the most efficient competitor to supply imports, quantitative restrictions usually have a trade-distorting effect, their allocation can be problematic and their administration may not be transparent.[17]

Further, quantitative restrictions give rise to competition among interest groups to capture a quota "rent," sometimes even provoking illicit activities (e.g., bribery) by importers. Such rent-seeking makes quantitative restrictions costly, since it adds the value of the rents to the welfare loss of the tariff equivalents of those restrictions.[18] In the case of a monopoly, a quota has

---

[15] GATT Analytical Index, Ch. 1, *supra* note 73, vol. 1, p. 501; WT/COMTD/W/219, Ch. 1, *supra* note 112, p. 7.

[16] Annex 2 of the Decision on Notification Procedures for Quantitative Restrictions, adopted by the Council for Trade in Goods on 22 June 2012, G/L/59/Rev.1 (3 July 2012).

[17] Panel Report, *Turkey – Textiles*, para. 9.63.

[18] Anne O. Krueger, "The Political Economy of the Rent-Seeking Society," 64 *American Economic Review* 291 (1974).

greater import-restrictiveness than a tariff, as the domestic monopolist can charge consumers a monopoly price once the quota is filled.[19]

Article XI of the GATT is worded broadly to cover virtually any nonprice measure that restricts cross-border movement of goods. In addition to bans and quotas, the case-law examples of quantitative restrictions include, inter alia, minimum import/export price requirements, a discretionary licensing system, trade-balancing requirements, and restricted access to ports of entry.[20]

Import licenses are covered by Article XI:1, regardless whether they are automatic or nonautomatic.[21] They are also subject to the Agreement on Import Licensing Procedures. Article 1.3 thereof requires domestic rules in this area to be "neutral in application and administered in a fair and equitable manner." Automatic import licensing – approved "in all cases" and typically used for the collection of statistical information – must be employed in a way not causing an import-restrictive effect (Article 2 of the agreement in question). Nonautomatic import licensing – widely used for administering quotas (and tariff quotas) – must not have restrictive or distortive effects on imports "additional to those caused by the imposition of the [associated] restriction" (Article 3.2).

Article XI:2 of the GATT provides that the general ban does not apply to: export restrictions on foodstuffs and other essential products being in "critical shortages" (subparagraph (a)); trade restrictions pertaining to "the classification, grading or marketing of commodities in international trade" (subparagraph (b)); and certain import restrictions on agricultural and fisheries products imposed as part of governmental measures of limiting domestic production or removing temporary surpluses (subparagraph (c)).[22] The Appellate Body in *Indonesia – Import Licensing Regimes* found that the derogation under Article XI:2(c) was no longer available for agricultural products, as Article 4.2 of the Agreement on Agriculture prohibits quantitative import restrictions "which have been required to be converted into ordinary customs duties."[23]

Quantitative restrictions are also allowed in the case of safeguard measures, BOP restrictions, or general/security exception measures.

---

[19] Jagdish Bhagwati, "More on the Equivalence of Tariffs and Quotas," 58 *American Economic Review* 142 (1968).

[20] These measures were reviewed in *EEC – Minimum Import Prices* (GATT, 1978), *Japan – Semi-Conductors* (GATT, 1988), *India – Quantitative Restrictions* (DS90), *India – Autos* (DS146, 175), and *Colombia – Ports of Entry* (DS366).

[21] Panel Report, *Indonesia – Import Licensing Regimes*, paras. 7.55–7.57.

[22] For subparagraphs (a) and (b) of Article XI:2, see also Section 3.3.2.

[23] Appellate Body Report, *Indonesia – Import Licensing Regimes*, paras. 5.84–5.85.

Temporary BOP restrictions are permitted by Article XII of the GATT to "safeguard the external financial position" of an imposing member and by Article XVIII:B of the GATT to additionally "ensure a level of reserves adequate for the implementation of [a qualifying developing country's] programme of economic development." Since 1995, at least twenty members have applied BOP restrictions.[24] As the BOP preservation may well be used as a pretext for protectionism, the BOP Committee conducts consultations with the imposing member, including simplified procedures for developing countries, to review the restrictions.[25] But the WTO judiciary can examine this matter on its own.[26] In *India – Quantitative Restrictions*, India claimed that it applied import restrictions (like import licenses and "canalization" of imports through government agencies) on 2,714 tariff lines to protect its BOP situation under Article XVIII: B. But the panel found these measures unnecessary because of India's adequate monetary reserves. In particular, the panel referred to the information of the International Monetary Fund that India's reserves in 1997 – the year of the panel's establishment – were US$25.1 billion, while the then adequate level would have been US$16 billion.[27]

Even where quantitative restrictions are warranted, they must be administered in a nondiscriminatory way. Article XIII of the GATT prescribes the MFN application of import/export prohibitions or restrictions and an appropriate distribution of trade within import restrictions based on the supply patterns that would exist absent such restrictions. This also applies to tariff quotas (Article XIII:5) that are not considered as a genuine quantitative restriction.[28]

2.1.3   Trade Remedies

Depending on the results of investigations, governments may apply trade remedies to protect domestic producers from dumped, subsidized, or surging imports. Although not all initiations lead to actual impositions, the mere commencement of an investigation may have a chilling effect on foreign exporters. As Table 2.2 suggests, antidumping duties are used

---

[24] WTO Analytical Index, *Guide to WTO Law and Practice*, "General Agreement on Tariffs and Trade 1994," para. 780, www.wto.org/english/res_e/booksp_e/analytic_index_e/gatt1994_06_e.htm#article14.

[25] See the Understanding on the Balance-of-Payments Provisions of the GATT 1994.

[26] Appellate Body Report, *India – Quantitative Restrictions*, paras. 87–8, 94–5.

[27] Panel Report, *India – Quantitative Restrictions*, paras. 2.9–2.28, 5.174–5.184.

[28] GATT Panel Report, *EEC – Bananas II*, para. 138.

Table 2.2 Top Users and Top Targets in Trade Remedies (1995–2015)

TOP	Antidumping Duties		Countervailing Duties		Safeguards	
	Initiations	Measures	Initiations	Measures	Initiations	Measures
			Applying Members			
1	India (770)	India (572)	United States (179)	United States (95)	India (41)	India (19)
2	United States (569)	United States (359)	EU (76)	EU (36)	Indonesia (27)	Indonesia (17)
3	EU (480)	EU (309)	Canada (52)	Canada (26)	Turkey (21)	Turkey (15)
4	Brazil (392)	Argentina (239)	Australia (20)	Australia, Mexico (11 each)	Chile (19)	Jordan (9)
5	Argentina (322)	Brazil (228)	South Africa (13)	Brazil (7)	Jordan (17)	Chile, Philippines (8 each)
6	Australia (299)	China (181)	Brazil, Egypt (10 each)	China (6)	Egypt (13)	Egypt (7)
7	China, South Africa (229 each)	Turkey (170)	Peru (8)	Peru, South Africa (5 each)	Ukraine (12)	United States (6)
8	Canada (199)	South Africa (137)	China (7)	Argentina, New Zealand (4 each)	Philippines (11)	Czech Republic, Ecuador (5 each)
9	Turkey (196)	Australia, Canada (132 each)	Chile, Mexico, New Zealand (6 each)	Chile (2)	United States (10)	Argentina, Morocco, Poland, Ukraine (4 each)

10	Mexico (138)	Mexico (108)	Argentina (3)	Costa Rica, Japan, Turkey, Venezuela (1 each)	Czech Republic, Ecuador (9 each)	EU, Hungary, Russia, Thailand (3 each)
	Others (1,164)	Others (673)	Others (15)	Others (0)	Others (123)	Others (24)
	Total (4,987)	Total (3,240)	Total (411)	Total (216)	Total (312)	Total (151)
Target Members						As a principle, all exporting members should be affected on an MFN-basis.
1	China (1,123)	China (822)	China (99)	China (66)		
2	Korea (366)	Korea (225)	India (71)	India (36)		
3	Chinese Taipei (275)	Chinese Taipei (184)	Korea (27)	EU (12)		
4	United States (271)	United States (169)	Indonesia (20)	Italy, Korea (9 each)		
5	India (205)	Japan (139)	United States (15)	Brazil, Indonesia, United States (8 each)		
6	Thailand (200)	Thailand (138)	EU, Italy, Thailand (14 each)	France (6)		
7	Japan (195)	Indonesia (119)	Turkey (12)	Turkey (5)		
8	Indonesia (189)	India (116)	Chinese Taipei (10)	Argentina, Canada, South Africa, Chinese Taipei (4 each)		
9	Russia (143)	Russia (110)	Argentina, Brazil, Canada (9 each)	Malaysia, Thailand, Venezuela, Viet Nam (3 each)		

Table 2.2 (cont.)

TOP	Antidumping Duties		Countervailing Duties		Safeguards	
	Initiations	Measures	Initiations	Measures	Initiations	Measures
10	Brazil (129)	Brazil (90)	Malaysia (8)	Germany, Pakistan, Philippines (2 each)		
	Others (1,891)	Others (1,128)	Others (80)	Others (15)		
	Total (4,987)	Total (3,240)	Total (411)	Total (216)		
Target Sectors						
1	Base metals and articles (1,485 initiations)/(977 measures)		Base metals and articles (178)	Base metals and articles (101)	Base metals and articles (66)	Base metals and articles (31)
2	Products of the chemical and allied industries (1,000)/(690)		Resins, plastics, and rubber articles; rubber and articles (40)	Products of chemical and allied industries (20)	Products of chemical and allied industries (49)	Products of chemical and allied industries (30)
3	Resins, plastics, and articles; rubber and articles (659)/(416)		Products of chemical and allied industries (36)	Machinery and electrical equipment (16)	Articles of stone, plaster; ceramic products; glass (27)	Vegetable products / Prepared foodstuff; beverages, spirits, vinegar; tobacco / Articles of stone, plaster; ceramic products; glass (13 each)

4	Machinery and electrical equipment (416)/(271)	Prepared foodstuff; beverages, spirits, vinegar; tobacco (33)	Resins, plastics, and articles; rubber and articles (15)	Prepared foodstuff; beverages, spirits, vinegar; tobacco (25)	Live animals and products / Textiles and articles / Machinery and electrical equipment (9 each)
5	Textiles and articles (354)/ (256)	Machinery and electrical equipment (26)	Prepared foodstuff; beverages, spirits, vinegar; tobacco (14)	Vegetable products (21)	Paper, paperboard, and articles (5)
	Others (1,073)/(630)	Others (98)	Others (50)	Others (124)	Others (19)

Source: Compiled by the author on the basis of WTO statistics for trade remedies, available at www.wto.org.
Notes: Numbers in ( ) are the total number of initiations/measures by or vis-à-vis a respective member (country). Antidumping initiations and measures affected the same top-five sectors.

most frequently, followed by countervailing duties and safeguards. Antidumping and countervailing mechanisms are similar in being resorted to by both developed and developing countries as top users and in targeting primarily the nonagricultural sector. In contrast, safeguards are used mostly by developing countries and affect both industrial and agricultural goods as priority targets. The predominant use of safeguards by the developing world can be explained with the fact that, unlike the case of the other trade remedies, there is no need for burdensome fact-finding outside of the imposing country. As for major targets, all trade remedies affect base metals most often, and antidumping and countervailing duty investigations are initiated mainly vis-à-vis developing countries.

2.1.3.1 Antidumping Duties

Dumping refers to the selling of a product to a foreign market at a price lower than its home market price, that is, when, according to Article 2.1 of the Antidumping Agreement, "the export price of the product exported from one country to another is less than the comparable price, in the ordinary course of trade, for the like product when destined for consumption in the exporting country." As long as a firm's behavior meets this definition, the reason why it dumps is irrelevant, be it, for example, predatory dumping seeking to drive competitors out of the export market or cyclical dumping aimed to cope with over-capacity.[29] In order to impose an antidumping duty, the importing country must determine that dumped imports cause or threaten material injury to a domestic industry or materially retard the establishment of a domestic industry.

Like a tariff, an antidumping duty generates government revenues, protects local producers, and increases import costs for domestic consumers. A WTO report (2009) summarizes some economic studies on antidumping, as follows.[30] First, antidumping duties may cause trade diversion when imports from nondumping sources replace dumped imports, with no significant fall occurring in the overall level of imports. Second, prohibitive antidumping duties may push target foreign firms into shifting their production to the imposing country, which can even be of greater threat to domestic industries than dumping. Third, if foreign and domestic firms compete on quantity, the domestic firm will tend to

---

[29] Edwin Vermulst, *The WTO Anti-Dumping Agreement: A Commentary* (Oxford: Oxford University Press, 2005), p. 3.

[30] WTO, "Trade Policy Commitments and Contingency Measures," World Trade Report, 2009, pp. 68–73.

expand its local output to drive down prices so as to increase a foreign rival's dumping margin. Decreased prices in the importing country will benefit consumers there and thus increase national welfare. By contrast, if firms compete on price, an antidumping duty can result in a welfare loss, as it increases the price charged by both firms in the domestic market and thus harms local consumers. Fourth, domestic firms may use antidumping investigations as a mere threat to convince foreign firms to collude to fix prices or outputs with a view to obtaining better profits than what the actual antidumping duty could offer.

As for key legal requirements, the investigating authority must find a positive difference ("dumping margin") between the "normal value" (i.e., the home market price) and the "export price." For an injury determination, it must examine the volume of the dumped imports and their price effect on like products in the domestic market, as well as the consequent impact of these imports on the domestic producers concerned. The affirmative findings on dumping, injury, and a causal link between them entitle the government to levy antidumping duties in the amount not exceeding the dumping margin.

Two aspects of normal value calculations in the dumping determination have been used to indirectly counteract "industry-promoting" pricing policies either in nonmarket economies (NMEs) or NME-like circumstances.

First, the second *Ad* Note to Article VI:1 of the GATT allows discard of home market prices in countries where the State has "a complete or substantially complete monopoly" of trade and sets "all domestic prices." This provision is, on its face, applicable only to countries with these characteristics and not "lesser forms" of NMEs.[31] Investigators have typically substituted the prices in exporting NMEs for prices in a surrogate market economy country. Such an "analogue country" methodology inflates dumping margins, disfavoring NME-originating products. In this respect, Section 15(a)(ii) of China's Accession Protocol permits other members to use the analogue country methodology vis-à-vis Chinese producers that fail to prove "market economy conditions" in the relevant industry at home. Section 15(d) states further that this provision expires on 11 December 2016. But the United States and the EU continue to apply this methodology in the belief that the termination of the provision in question does not actually mean automatic granting of market

---

[31] Appellate Body Report, *EC – Fasteners (China)*, n. 460 to para. 285.

economy status to China. At the time of writing, China was challenging this practice in the WTO.[32] The outcome of this litigation will also have important repercussions for Viet Nam and Tajikistan whose accession instruments contain a similar NME clause.[33]

Second, Article 2.2 of the Antidumping Agreement allows constructing the normal value on the basis of the cost of production in the country of origin plus other relevant expenses and profits when the home market price of the investigated product is unreliable. Where prices of input materials (as part of the production cost) in an exporting *market economy* country are distorted by State interference, some importing authorities typically adjust them to market benchmarks, which inflates the corresponding dumping margin. In *EU – Biodiesel*, it was found that this practice contravened Article 2.2 by failing to consider *actual* costs in the country of origin.[34] But such invalidation of market-oriented cost adjustments is at odds with the permission of the analogue country methodology described earlier, as the general motive in both cases is the same, that is, distrust of State-distorted prices in the exporting market economy and NME. This asymmetry obviously highlights the need for amending WTO antidumping law.[35]

As for policy flexibilities, Article 15 of the Antidumping Agreement requires that developed countries give "special regard" to developing countries (first sentence) and that "[p]ossibilities of constructive remedies" be explored before applying antidumping duties vis-à-vis developing countries (second sentence). Despite the mandatory language, this clause represents de facto "soft law." Indeed, the first sentence contains "no specific or general obligation,"[36] and the second sentence merely contemplates the exploration of constructive remedies rather than the

---

[32] *United States – Measures Related to Price Comparison Methodologies* (DS515, consultation requested 12 December 2016), *EU – Price Comparison Methodologies* (DS516, consultation requested 12 December 2016).

[33] See WTO, Accession of the People's Republic of China – Decision of 10 November 2001, WT/L/432 (23 November 2001), section 15; WTO, Working Party on the Accession of Viet Nam – Accession of Viet Nam – Report of the Working Party on the Accession of Viet Nam, WT/ACC/VNM/48 (27 October 2006), para. 255; WTO, Working Party on the Accession of the Republic of Tajikistan – Report of the Working Party on the Accession of the Republic of Tajikistan, WT/ACC/TJK/30 (6 November 2012), para. 164.

[34] Appellate Body Report, *EU – Biodiesel*, paras. 5.11–5.14, 6.30. See also Section 3.3.2.

[35] See Sherzod Shadikhodjaev, "Input Cost Adjustments and WTO Anti-Dumping Law: A Closer Look at the EU Practice," *World Trade Review, forthcoming*. Published online 21 January 2018, DOI: 10.1017/S1474745617000568.

[36] Panel Report, *US – Steel Plate*, para. 7.110.

relinquishment of antidumping duties.[37] The Committee on Antidumping Practices recommends that developed countries elaborate on how they have complied with Article 15 in their semi-annual reports on antidumping actions.[38]

In our opinion, the current S&D treatment could become more meaningful with, for example, the introduction of "better-than-standard" conditions for an immediate termination of antidumping investigations vis-à-vis developing countries. This is an important issue, since developing countries are major targets of antidumping investigations as shown in Table 2.2. Under Article 5.8 of the Antidumping Agreement, the "standard" terms for *de minimis* dumping or negligible imports, which make the investigation stop, apply in relation to all exporting countries alike. But this sharply contrasts with countervailing duty cases, namely Article 27.10 of the SCM Agreement that sets certain thresholds, favorable to developing country exports, for *de minimis* subsidization and negligible imports.[39]

2.1.3.2 Countervailing Duties

Countervailing duties attack subsidized imports, but the economic literature is inconclusive on their desirability. On the one hand, these measures often decrease an importing country's welfare in a perfect market and may not combat foreign government-financed predatory pricing under imperfect competition.[40] By contrast, they may neutralize subsidies' harm in line with anti-beggar-thy-neighbor policies pursued by trade agreements and discourage subsidization if countervailing duties are imposed collectively.[41]

The investigating authority must establish the existence of a specific subsidy[42] and resulting material injury/threat thereof or material retardation of the establishment of the domestic industry concerned. Like in antidumping cases, the injury determination under Article 15 of the SCM Agreement focuses on the volume, price effect, and consequent impact of

---

[37] Panel Report, *EC – Bed Linen*, paras. 6.228–6.229.

[38] WTO, Committee on Antidumping Practices – Recommendation Regarding Annual Reviews of the Anti-Dumping Agreement – Adopted by the Committee on 27 November 2002, G/ADP/9 (29 November 2002).

[39] See Section 3.2.5.

[40] Alan O. Sykes, "Countervailing Duty Law: An Economic Perspective," 89 *Columbia Law Review* 199 (1989), pp. 214–15, 241–50.

[41] World Trade Report, 2009, *supra* note 30, p. 94.   [42] See Sections 3.2.1, 3.2.2, 3.2.3.

subsidized imports. Article 27 envisages S&D treatment for countervailing measures vis-à-vis developing countries.[43]

According to Article 19.3 of the SCM Agreement, a countervailing duty must apply "in the appropriate amounts." The Appellate Body in *US – Anti-Dumping and Countervailing Duties (China)* interpreted this as prohibiting "double remedies," that is, the offsetting of the same subsidization twice by the simultaneous imposition of countervailing duties and NME antidumping duties on the same product. In particular, the Appellate Body observed that an NME dumping margin could already cover some part of the subsidy so that a countervailing duty capturing the full amount of that subsidy could not be "appropriate."[44]

Article 19.4 of the SCM Agreement requires that the countervailing duty be not greater than the amount of the subsidy as expressed in "subsidization per unit of the subsidized and exported product." To calculate a per unit subsidization rate, the investigators may divide the total amount of the subsidy by the total sales value of the subsidized product, and in so doing they must properly match the elements in the numerator with those in the denominator.[45] For a multinational corporation, the amount of the subsidy tied to its domestic and overseas production in the numerator must be matched with the corresponding sales in home and foreign markets.[46]

In *US – Washing Machines*, the Korean government's tax credits were attributed only to Samsung's domestic production. The product at issue was produced by Samsung both at home and abroad. The Appellate Body faulted the US investigating authority for not assessing all relevant evidence. In particular, the US authority had mainly relied on official Korean sources that were silent on the government's intent to subsidize overseas production. But it had virtually ignored Samsung's argument that the R&D tax credits at issue were by nature linked to the company's activity benefiting its domestic *and* worldwide production alike.[47]

2.1.3.3 Safeguards

WTO-committed market openings make domestic industries vulnerable to foreign competition. Governments can use safeguard measures to

---

[43] See Section 3.2.5.
[44] Appellate Body Report, *US – Anti-Dumping and Countervailing Duties (China)*, para. 582.
[45] Appellate Body Report, *US – Softwood Lumber IV*, para. 153, n. 196 to para. 164.
[46] Appellate Body Report, *US – Washing Machines*, para. 5.297.
[47] *Ibid.*, paras. 5.288–5.289, 5.297–5.306.

temporarily shield local producers from a sudden influx of foreign goods so as to allow them some time for adjusting to new economic conditions. These are "extraordinary"[48] actions taken to cope with a particular economic emergency which itself is not caused by an unfair trade practice.

Economists argue that safeguards are necessary to restore competitiveness of protected industries facing hardship from trade liberalization, to serve as a second best policy for addressing inefficient unemployment caused by labor market failures, or to redistribute income toward workers displaced by import competition. Political economy justifies safeguards for being less-protectionist than the legislative protection, as they are subject to the strict administrative fact-finding process – a "safety valve" for interest groups' pressures. Further, while legalization of safeguards permits some "cheating" on trade obligations in the face of domestic lobbies, it also preserves multilateral cooperation and facilitates more trade concessions.[49]

Article 2.1 of the Agreement on Safeguards and Article XIX of the GATT, read together, provide that a safeguard measure is applicable to a product which, as a result of "unforeseen developments" and the effect of WTO obligations, including tariff concessions, is being imported in increased quantities causing (or threatening to cause) "serious injury" to domestic producers of "like or directly competitive products."

The "unforeseen developments" are developments that an importing member did not expect when it incurred a WTO obligation or granted a trade concession.[50] The importing authority must provide a "reasoned and adequate explanation" of how a development was unforeseen.[51] To trigger a safeguard, the increase in imports – absolute or relative to domestic production – must be sufficiently recent, sudden, sharp, and significant.[52] Article 4.1(a) of the Agreement on Safeguards defines "serious injury" as "a significant overall impairment in the position of a domestic industry." Such a stricter standard, as opposed to "material injury" in the antidumping and countervailing contexts, was set to make

[48] Appellate Body Report, *Argentina – Footwear (EC)*, para. 94.
[49] For a critique on these economic and political economy rationales for safeguards, see Alan O. Sykes, *The WTO Agreement on Safeguards: A Commentary* (New York: Oxford University Press, 2006), pp. 47–72.
[50] Appellate Body Report, *Korea – Dairy*, para. 86; Panel Report, *Argentina – Preserved Peaches*, paras. 7.25–7.28.
[51] Appellate Body Report, *US – Steel Safeguards*, para. 279.
[52] Appellate Body Report, *Argentina – Footwear (EC)*, para. 131.

it more difficult to restrict fair trade via safeguards. But this policy of constraining safeguards seems to be at odds with the broader scope of "like or directly competitive products" which actually increases the applicability of safeguards to an extended list of imports. Other distinctive features of the safeguard mechanism include the government's obligation to compensate to the affected countries, a shorter period of measures' application, usability of quantitative restrictions, safeguards' purpose to facilitate adjustment of domestic industries, and the MFN and progressive liberalization requirements for safeguards.

Under Article 12 of the Agreement on Safeguards, a member proposing to apply or extend a safeguard measure must notify the WTO with "all pertinent information" and conduct prior consultations with the exporting countries concerned to, inter alia, review that information. In *Ukraine – Passenger Cars*, Ukraine had not provided required information regarding the timetable for progressive liberalization before it held consultations with Japan. This was the basis for the panel to conclude that Ukraine acted inconsistently with Article 12.3 in failing to provide "adequate opportunity" for prior consultations.[53]

Article 9 of the Agreement on Safeguards (i) mandates an exclusion, from a safeguard measure, of those developing countries that individually account for less than 3 percent of the total imports concerned, provided that their collective import share does not exceed 9 percent; and (ii) allows developing countries to apply a safeguard measure for up to ten years instead of the normal eight-year maximum and to apply a new safeguard on the same product after a shorter-than-usual "waiting" period. The Appellate Body in *US – Line Pipe* clarified that the first rule did not require an importing country to provide a specific list of members that were included in, or excluded from, a safeguard measure, although such a list would be useful for transparency reasons.[54] But notification formats approved by the Committee on Safeguards in 2009 now instruct members to specify developing countries exempted from a safeguard measure under Article 9.[55]

---

[53] Panel Report, *Ukraine – Passenger Cars*, paras. 7.537–7.538.
[54] Appellate Body Report, *US – Line Pipe*, paras. 127–8.
[55] WTO, Committee on Safeguards – Formats for Certain Notifications under the Agreement on Safeguards – Note from the Secretariat, G/SG/1/Rev.1, G/SG/N/6/Rev.1, G/SG/89 (5 November 2009), p. 4.

2.2 Taxes

Internal taxes are a core component of each country's fiscal policy. WTO members are "sovereign in determining the structure and rates of their domestic tax regimes" and enjoy "some flexibility" in making adjustments thereto.[56] Liberalization of border restrictions makes governments tempted to manipulate their taxes in a manner that would disfavor imported goods in the domestic market. While there are no formal "bindings" for taxes, Article III of the GATT on national treatment deters this temptation, as high internal charges imposed on foreign products must equally apply to competing local counterparts.

Article III:2, the first and second sentences ban discriminatory "internal taxes or other internal charges of any kind" on foreign "like" products and "directly competitive or substitutable" products respectively.[57] A "like product" determination is typically based on physical characteristics of products, their end-uses, consumers' tastes and habits, and tariff classification of products.[58] The broader "directly competitive or substitutable" category may be specified through additional competitive-relationship criteria, such as, for example, cross-price elasticities or channels of distribution.[59] The first sentence of Article III:2 disallows even a marginal overtaxing on imports as compared to domestic products, but the second sentence permits *de minimis* tax differential which is defined on a case-by-case basis.[60]

Since national treatment does not apply to customs duties, governments may use this fact to defend their "tariff-like" discriminatory taxation. In *China – Auto Parts*, China imposed a 25 percent "charge" on imported auto parts qualified as "complete motor vehicles." This rate corresponded to the bound tariff for complete cars. According to China, the measure at issue sought to prevent circumvention of the 25 percent tariff when foreign cars were shipped in parts to pay only a 10 percent tariff for auto parts and subsequently reassembled in China. The Appellate Body found that this was actually a discriminatory "internal charge" within the meaning of Article III:2 rather than an "ordinary customs duty," because the obligation to pay it accrued internally – that is, after the auto parts had entered China – and constituted discrimination, as it

---

[56] Appellate Body Report, *US – Large Civil Aircraft (2nd complaint)*, para. 811.
[57] See also Section 5.4.1.
[58] Appellate Body Report, *Japan – Alcoholic Beverages II*, pp. 20–1.
[59] *Ibid.*, p. 25; Panel Report, *Korea – Alcoholic Beverages*, para. 10.61.
[60] Appellate Body Report, *Japan – Alcoholic Beverages II*, pp. 26–7.

did not apply to like domestic auto parts.[61] A proper distinction between a border and internal charge clearly preserves the importing country's right to apply customs duties to the full extent of bound rates, but it also precludes national treatment manipulations through measures akin to that in the case in question.[62]

WTO law permits members to adjust internal taxes at the border by charging imports and exempting exports as long as such adjustment concerns *indirect* (i.e., product-related) taxes and treats the products concerned alike.[63] Therefore, a recently proposed US destination-based cash flow tax that would allow companies in the United States, but not abroad, to deduct wage costs – not related to products as such – from the tax base could potentially provoke a WTO dispute.[64]

Finally, taxes on services industries are subject to the GATS. In *Argentina – Financial Services*, Argentina applied certain tax measures to services and service suppliers from those countries that did not exchange tax information with Argentina. Panama contended that this was discrimination against such "noncooperative" countries, but Argentina countered that its "defensive tax measures" served to prevent tax evasion in line with relevant international standards of fiscal transparency. The Appellate Body overturned the panel's finding of the GATS MFN and national treatment violations on the grounds of, inter alia, an erroneous likeness analysis. But it fell short of judging itself whether services/suppliers in noncooperative countries were "like" those in cooperative countries and Argentina.[65] This ruling is remarkable for examining trade restrictions used for combating offshore tax fraud.

2.3 Product Standards

The economic literature often refers to "standards" as a generic term for mandatory and voluntary TBT/SPS measures and provides rationales for some of them. First, since many products are valuable when consumed

---

[61] Appellate Body Report, *China – Auto Parts*, paras. 52, 113, 114–26, 162, 170–86.

[62] Sherzod Shadikhodjaev, "Customs Duty or Internal Charge? Revisiting the Delineation Issue within Treaty Interpretation in the *China – Auto Parts* Case," 7 *Asian Journal of WTO & International Health Law and Policy* 195 (2012), pp. 214–5.

[63] See Sections 4.3.3.1, 6.2.1.

[64] See Chad P. Bown, "Will the Proposed US Border Tax Provoke WTO Retaliation from Trading Partners?," Policy Brief No. PB17–11, Peterson Institute for International Economics, 2017.

[65] Appellate Body Report, *Argentina – Financial Services*, paras. 1.1–1.4, 6.49–6.80.

not in isolation but either together with other products (e.g., computers and DVD-writers) or simultaneously by many users (e.g., mobile phones), certain standards ensure compatibility across the variety of products and systems. Such compatibility standards increase welfare by allowing consumers to "mix and match" components from different producers or expanding the network of users.[66] Second, safety standards counter information asymmetry when producers, but no users, have information about a product being sold. Without proper information on quality goods, consumers tend to buy cheaper alternatives. Conversely, the adoption of safety standards (e.g., labeling requirements) can mitigate the undersupply of expensive high-quality goods.[67] Third, some standards help governments address environmental externalities.[68]

2.3.1 TBT Measures

The TBT Agreement deals with "technical regulations," "standards," and "conformity assessment procedures." Both technical regulations and standards lay down product characteristics and processes and production methods (PPMs), but compliance with technical regulations is mandatory. Conformity assessment refers to procedures (testing, verification, inspection, certification, etc.) determining whether requirements in technical regulations or standards are fulfilled. The TBT Agreement seeks to ensure a proper balance between pursued legitimate policies and trade liberalization.

Most of the case-law issues under the TBT Agreement have concerned technical regulations. With regard to technical regulations, Article 2.1 of the TBT Agreement seems to give more leeway than the corresponding GATT provisions for complying with the MFN and national treatment obligations. Indeed, the Appellate Body construed the required "treatment no less favourable" in Article 2.1 as *not prohibiting* a detrimental impact on imports that "stems exclusively from a legitimate regulatory distinction" as demonstrated by the design, architecture, revealing structure, operation, and application of a technical regulation.[69] The legal standard for nondiscrimination under Article 2.1 (including the relevance of a legitimate regulatory distinction to the

---

[66] WTO, "Exploring the Links between Trade, Standards and the WTO," World Trade Report, 2005, pp. 31–6.
[67] *Ibid.*, p. 42. [68] See Section 6.4.
[69] Appellate Body Report, *US – Clove Cigarettes*, paras. 175, 181–2.

detrimental impact on imports) "does not apply equally to ... Articles I:1 and III:4 of the GATT."[70]

An assessment under Article 2.2 of the TBT Agreement as to whether a technical regulation restricts trade more than necessary to achieve a legitimate objective involves a holistic weighing and balancing of:

> (i) the degree of contribution made by the measure to the legitimate objective at issue; (ii) the trade-restrictiveness of the measure; and (iii) the nature of the risks at issue as well as the gravity of the consequences that would arise from non-fulfilment of the objective pursued by the Member through the measure.[71]

The provisions on harmonization, equivalence, and mutual recognition aim to align divergent regulatory policies among members. Under the harmonization principle, members must use relevant international standards "as a basis" for their TBT measures, except where such standards are ineffective or inappropriate for the fulfillment of legitimate objectives (Articles 2.4, 5.4 and Annex 3.F). Technical regulations "in accordance with" international standards are presumed not to create an unnecessary obstacle to trade (Article 2.5).

In this context, an international standard is a standard approved by an international standardizing body,[72] an entity whose membership is "open on a non-discriminatory basis to relevant bodies of at least all WTO Members ... with respect to the participation at the policy development level and at every stage of standards development."[73] The lack of such membership openness was the basis for the Appellate Body in *US – Tuna II (Mexico)* to dismiss the qualification of the "dolphin-safe" definition and certification under the Agreement on the International Dolphin Conservation Program as a relevant international standard.[74] An international standard constitutes "a basis" for a technical regulation when the two are not mutually contradictory, and when the international standard

---

[70] Appellate Body Reports, *EC – Seal Products*, paras. 5.117, 5.130.

[71] Appellate Body Reports, *US – COOL*, para. 471; Appellate Body Reports, *US – COOL (Article 21.5 – Canada and Mexico)*, paras. 5.197–5.198.

[72] Appellate Body Report, *US – Tuna II (Mexico)*, para. 356

[73] Decision of the Committee on Principles for the Development of International Standards, Guides and Recommendations with Relation to Articles 2, 5 and Annex 3 of the [TBT] Agreement, contained in WTO, Committee on TBT – Decisions and Recommendations Adopted by the WTO Committee on TBT since 1 January 1995 – Note by the Secretariat – Revision, G/TBT/1/Rev.13 (8 March 2017).

[74] Appellate Body Report, *US – Tuna II (Mexico)*, paras. 396–401.

is used as "the principal constituent or fundamental principle for the purpose of enacting the technical regulation."[75]

It can be argued that the harmonization with international standards facilitates greater cross-country regulatory convergence and alignment than just an acceptance of a foreign TBT measure as equivalent to one's own or mutual recognition (Articles 2.7 and 6), as both of the latter do not generally require using *common* benchmarks.

Article 11 of the TBT Agreement obligates members to provide, upon request, advice and/or technical assistance to other members, especially developing countries, with respect to, inter alia, the establishment of national standardizing or conformity assessment bodies, the preparation of technical regulations and participation in international standardizing bodies. The key S&D elements of Article 12 include:

- the requirement to take account of "the special development, financial and trade needs" of developing countries;
- nonexpectation from developing countries to use international standards inappropriate to those needs;
- provision of technical assistance aimed at avoidance of unnecessary obstacles to the expansion and diversification of exports from developing countries;
- the TBT Committee's granting of time-limited exceptions if requested;
- the possibility of preparing international standards on products of special interest to developing countries;
- facilitation of active and representative participation in international bodies and systems.

In *US – COOL* and *US – Clove Cigarettes*, the panels turned down the allegations of Mexico and Indonesia respectively that the United States had failed to obey the Article 12.3 obligation to "take account of" their special needs.[76] This rejection was mainly due to the soft-law nature of that provision. Indeed, the term "take account of" was interpreted as entailing an obligation "to accord active and meaningful consideration to the special development, financial and trade needs of developing countr[ies]," but not an explicit requirement for members to document specifically in their rule-making process how actively they considered those needs.[77] Nevertheless, developing countries can still use the Trade

---

[75] Appellate Body Report, *EC – Sardines*, paras. 243–4, 248.
[76] Panel Reports, *US – COOL*, para. 7.799; Panel Report, *US – Clove Cigarettes*, para. 7.649.
[77] Panel Reports, *US – COOL*, paras. 7.786–7.787.

Facilitation Agreement as an S&D-inducing instrument, as they are entitled to link the implementation of the self-selected obligations there to receipt of donor countries' assistance in, for example, the TBT and SPS areas.

Last but not least, the adoption of "good regulatory practices" – best domestic procedures of developing high-quality and cost-effective regulations – can support the effective implementation of TBT obligations and minimize unnecessary trade barriers. Therefore, members in the TBT Committee have shared their experiences of incorporating good regulatory mechanisms in domestic procedures – like public consultations, transparency and regulatory impact assessments – and engaging in international regulatory cooperation.[78]

2.3.2 SPS Measures

SPS measures aim to protect animals or plants from pests or diseases; humans or animals from food-borne risks; humans from animal- or plant-carried diseases or pests; and the territory of a country from other damage caused by pests. Like the TBT Agreement, the SPS Agreement strives to strike a right balance between members' right to regulate and their trade commitments, and to align national standards based on the harmonization and equivalence principles.

Article 2 of the SPS Agreement obliges members to apply SPS measures only to the extent necessary to life/health protection, on the basis of scientific principles and sufficient scientific evidence (except Article 5.7 cases), without creating arbitrary or unjustifiable discrimination and a disguised restriction on international trade. The measures conforming to the SPS Agreement are presumed to comply with the relevant GATT provisions, including Article XX(b) on protection of human, animal, or plant life or health.

Article 5 requires that SPS measures be based on appropriate risk assessments, taking into account available scientific evidence, relevant PPMs, and other listed factors. While each member has the recognized autonomy in defining its own "appropriate level" of SPS protection, it

---

[78] See WTO, Committee on TBT – Seventh Triennial Review of the Operation and Implementation of the Agreement on TBT under Article 15.4, G/TBT/37 (3 December 2015), paras. 1.1–1.8, 2.1–2.3; WTO, Committee on TBT – Fifth Triennial Review of the Operation and Implementation of the Agreement on TBT under Article 15.4, G/TBT/26 (13 November 2009), paras. 5–16.

must consider the objective of minimizing adverse trade effects and avoid "arbitrary or unjustifiable distinctions" in such levels in different situations leading to discrimination or a disguised trade restriction.

An SPS measure's legality largely hinges upon its scientific justifiability. The scientific evidence must have a "rational relationship" to the SPS measure, sufficiently show the risk at issue, and be necessary for a risk assessment.[79] But in the absence of sufficient scientific evidence, Article 5.7 allows governments to adopt provisional SPS measures based on "available pertinent information" from, for example, international organizations or other members, provided that they will seek to obtain additional information for more objective risk assessments and review those measures accordingly "within a reasonable period of time." The triggering factor is the insufficiency of scientific evidence rather than mere scientific uncertainty or scientific controversy.[80] The "available pertinent information" in this context refers to an evidentiary basis that shows some possible risk but is not enough itself for a risk assessment.[81]

Article 6 requires "regionalization," that is, adaptation of measures to regional SPS characteristics. In particular, members must recognize the concepts of "pest- or disease-free areas" and "areas of low pest or disease prevalence." An exporting member claiming that some of its regions are such risk-free areas must provide an importing member with the necessary evidence and reasonable access for inspection and other relevant procedures. In *Russia – Pigs (EU)*, Russia was found to violate Article 6 by applying an EU-wide import ban on certain pig products, even though the EU authorities had objectively demonstrated to Russia that there were areas within the EU territory, outside of Estonia, Latvia, Lithuania, and Poland, which were free of African swine fever.[82]

The SPS Agreement provides for technical assistance (Article 9) and S&D treatment (Article 10). With respect to Article 10.1 requiring importing members to "take account of" developing countries' "special needs," the panel in *US – Animals* admitted that this provision imposed "a positive obligation that is subject to dispute settlement," but it ultimately rejected Argentina's S&D claim. The panel observed that not only

---

[79] Panel Report, *US – Poultry (China)*, para. 7.200; Appellate Body Report, *Japan – Agricultural Products II*, para. 84.
[80] Appellate Body Report, *Japan – Apples*, paras. 183–4; Appellate Body Report, *US – Continued Suspension*, para. 677.
[81] Appellate Body Report, *US – Continued Suspension*, para. 678.
[82] Panel Report, *Russia – Pigs (EU)*, para. 8.1; Appellate Body Report, *Russia – Pigs (EU)*, paras. 6.4–6.8.

an exporting developing country but also an importing country could identify the special needs under Article 10.1, but the latter did not bear "the burden" to "*necessarily* " do so.[83] The panel concluded:

> If a developing country Member can demonstrate that its special needs were expressly identified to or by the importing Member *and* can show a lack of documentation of the consideration that is likely enough to shift the burden on to the importing Member to show how it took account of those special needs. Conversely, if the importing Member was not made aware of the special needs of the developing country Member, we consider that it will be more difficult for the developing country Member to make its case.[84]

Considering developing country interests, Article 10 also calls for longer periods of compliance with qualifying new SPS measures, urges facilitation of active participation in relevant international organizations, and enables time-limited exceptions by the SPS Committee. But as it was rightly stated in the SPS Committee, the S&D provisions could be more effective if they were complemented with sufficient technical assistance to improve developing countries' ability to handle scientific issues and upgrade their laboratory facilities and technologies.[85]

2.4   Protection of Services Industries

Compared to the goods sector, economists widely accept more pervasive government interventions in services markets in the light of a greater likelihood of market failures (e.g., information asymmetry, imperfect competition due to monopolistic/oligopolistic supply of certain infrastructure- or network-based services, and externalities) and higher susceptibility of regulators to interest group pressures.[86]

This justifies considerable leeway that governments have under the GATS to protect their services industries. Specifically, they can define their market access and national treatment commitments only in relation to the scheduled sectors. WTO members have listed, on average, about

---

[83] Panel Report, *US – Animals*, para. 7.699 (emphasis in original).

[84] *Ibid.*, para. 7.700 (emphasis in original).

[85] WTO, Committee on SPS Measures – Summary of the Meeting Held on 21–22 June 2000 – Note by the Secretariat, G/SPS/R/19 (1 August 2000), para. 35; WTO, Committee on SPS Measures – SPS Agreement and Developing Countries – Statement by Egypt at the Meeting of 7–8 July 1999, G/SPS/GEN/128 (16 July 1999), para. 4.

[86] WTO, "Trade and Public Policies: A Closer Look at Non-Tariff Measures in the 21st Century," World Trade Report, 2012, pp. 74–7.

50 out of some 160 service subsectors in national schedules, with most often scheduled sectors being tourism, finance, business, telecommunications, and least frequently scheduled ones being education and health services.[87] Even the MFN obligation that applies horizontally irrespective of the sectoral coverage may be curbed by member-specific exemption lists.

Article XVI of the GATS allows members to restrict market access by any of the six types of limitations on: the number of service suppliers, the total value of service transactions or assets, the total number of service operations or the total quantity of service output, the total number of employees, types of legal entity or joint venture, and the participation of foreign capital. At the same time, not any conditioning of a market opening guarantees the anticipated level of protection. In *Mexico – Telecoms*, Mexico's schedule stated that market access for certain telecommunication services in mode 3 (commercial presence) was subject to permits which would not be granted "until the corresponding regulations are issued." Mexico refused to authorize the supply of corresponding services on the grounds that those regulations and permits were not issued yet. But the panel found that temporal limitations (e.g., the dates of the entry into force/implementation of commitments) as such did not constitute permissible market access limitations in the sense of Article XVI.[88]

Members may also qualify national treatment in their schedules, but, unlike the case of market access, they are not circumscribed by a fixed list of limitations. Article XVII of the GATS prohibits modification of "the conditions of competition" to the detriment of foreign services or suppliers. Footnote 10 to Article XVII stipulates that members are not required to compensate for "any inherent competitive disadvantages" resulting from "the foreign character" of the relevant service or supplier. The panel in *Canada – Autos*, however, cautioned that footnote 10 "does not provide cover for actions which might modify the conditions of competition against services and service suppliers which are already disadvantaged due to their foreign character."[89]

Governments may affect services industries through "domestic regulations" regarding qualifications, technical standards, licensing, and other

---

[87] WTO, "Trade in Services: The Most Dynamic Segment of International Trade," p. 5, www.wto.org/english/thewto_e/20y_e/services_brochure2015_e.pdf.

[88] Panel Report, *Mexico – Telecoms*, paras. 7.353–7.358.

[89] Panel Report, *Canada – Autos*, para. 10.300.

relevant matters that are neither discriminatory measures nor (quantitative) market access restrictions, subject to GATS Article VI obligations. The panel in *US – Gambling* suggested mutual exclusiveness between Articles VI, on the one hand, and XVI (and implicitly XVII), on the other.[90] For committed sectors, measures of general application (e.g., labor requirements, building regulations, etc.) must be administered "in a reasonable, objective and impartial manner." Where the supply of a scheduled service requires authorization, the government must decide on related applications "within a reasonable period of time." For commitments on professional services, there must be "adequate procedures" of verifying the competence of professionals from other members.

As in the merchandise trade rules, the GATS flexibility types include, inter alia, general and security exceptions, BOP restrictions, government procurement derogations, and schedule modifications. Article X of the GATS set a built-in agenda for negotiating new disciplines on emergency safeguards that would allow suspension of specific commitments for individual sectors incurring injury from excessive foreign supplies. But no legal text on this issue has been adopted so far.

The GATS contains thirteen S&D provisions aimed at increasing trade opportunities of developing countries, safeguarding their interests, ensuring flexibility of commitments, securing technical assistance, and LDCs.[91] To name a few, Article IV says that developing countries' participation in world trade must be facilitated by foreign specific commitments that strengthen their domestic services capacity, improve their access to distribution channels and information networks, and liberalize market access to their exports, giving special priority to LDCs. Under a WTO waiver operational until 31 December 2030, over twenty members notified their preferential market access to services and suppliers from LDCs.[92] Moreover, with respect to negotiations on progressive liberalization, Article XIX gives developing countries flexibility for opening fewer sectors, liberalizing fewer types of transactions, and extending market access "in line with their development situation."

---

[90] Panel Report, *US – Gambling*, paras. 6.305–6.313.
[91] WT/COMTD/W/219, Ch. 1, *supra* note 112, p. 68.
[92] See WTO, Preferential Treatment to Services and Service Suppliers of LDCs – Decision of 17 December 2011, WT/L/847 (19 December 2011); WTO, Ministerial Conference – Tenth Session – Nairobi, 15–18 December 2015 – Implementation of Preferential Treatment in Favour of Services and Service Supplier[...]al Decision of 19 December 2015, WT/MIN(15)/48, WT/L/982 (21 December 2015).

Finally, an additional policy space for governments can be found in certain sector-specific disciplines annexed to the GATS. For instance, paragraph 2(a) of the Annex on Financial Services makes an exception for "taking measures for prudential reasons, including for the protection of investors, depositors, policy holders or persons to whom a fiduciary duty is owed by a financial service supplier, or to ensure the integrity and stability of the financial system." Although this provision is entitled "Domestic Regulation," the Appellate Body in *Argentina – Financial Services* held that such prudential carve-out covered *all types* of measures in the financial sector contemplated by the Annex in question.[93]

2.5 Concluding Remarks

WTO members may employ a wide array of trade instruments to protect their industries. But this is subject to certain requirements and flexibilities which together serve to keep market restrictions at a reasonable level.

As final remarks to this chapter, it is noteworthy that some trends in world manufacturing and trade can impact on these instruments in various ways. In particular, with a growing international fragmentation of production, one can expect that the deeper countries are engaged in global value chains, the less "protectionist" they will be. This may happen because of the increasing shares of domestic content in target foreign final goods and of target foreign content in domestic final goods.[94] Furthermore, digitization in many fields leads to blurring distinctions within each segment of goods and services, as well as between goods and services so that associated trade restrictions may raise complex intersectional issues. Finally, the fourth industrial revolution may reshape certain trading patterns and related measures, as, for instance, the extensive use of new technologies like 3-D printers and artificial intelligence will, respectively, reduce reliance on imports of "printable" goods and replace humans in some service activities.

---

[93] Appellate Body Report, *Argentina – Financial Services*, paras. 6.251–6.272.
[94] See Emily J. Blanchard, Chad P. Bown, and Robert C. Johnson, "Global Supply Chains and Trade Policy," NBER Working Paper No. 21883, 2016.

3

Promotion of Domestic Industry

The promotion of domestic producers is another important component of any industrial policy. Governments intervene in their economies with various types of support measures – collectively known as "subsidies" – that may make the aid-receiving companies or industries better off in the marketplace, putting many foreign competitors at a disadvantage. Subsidies stimulate domestic output or exportation, but, when not provided horizontally, they distort resource allocation among market players. It is this selectiveness of subsidies that arouses considerable controversy in both the economics and law of international trade as to the soundness and validity of government support. This chapter commences with summarizing key findings in the economic literature on subsidies. Then we will turn to the WTO subsidy regime, discussing some important provisions of the SCM Agreement – a WTO treaty on industrial subsidies and antisubsidy measures – as well as specific subsidy issues pertaining to the services and upstream sectors.

3.1 The Economics of Government Subsidies

The economic literature does not define "subsidy" in a consistent way, but generally refers to a transfer of an economic value from the government to a private entity.[1] For economists, subsidies include direct governmental payments, government guarantees, tax credits, in-kind subsidies, implicit payments under government regulations affecting market prices/access, and other public favors.[2] Subsidies aim to reallocate resources to change an economic activity or behavior in a "more desirable" way than what would happen otherwise, which raises the issues of

---

[1] WTO, "Exploring the Links between Subsidies, Trade and the WTO," World Trade Report, 2006, p. xxiii.

[2] Gerd Schwartz and Benedict Clements, "Government Subsidies," 13 *Journal of Economic Surveys* 119 (1999), pp. 120–1.

efficiency and economic justifiability.[3] Compared to some other instruments, subsidies are more transparent when the amounts and recipients are known. But they make governments exposed to stronger lobbying – the fact that necessitates developing objective performance requirements as eligibility criteria.[4]

As for concrete policy objectives, subsidies are given, first, to promote industrial development. Economic theory accepts this in the presence of certain market failures and on the infant industry rationale.[5] Second, governments make R&D investments or pursue broader innovation policies for generating new knowledge and positive spillovers. But economists are inconclusive on whether R&D subsidies should be provided across the board or on a selective basis.[6] Third, subsidies may seek to obtain a national advantage in industries characterized by economies of scale. Where a foreign firm has a cost advantage because of its larger size, the government support (known as "strategic trade policy") can enable a domestic firm to expand and strategically win market share at the expense of a foreign competitor.[7] Fourth, subsidies can be part of national policies designed to redistribute income from the rich to the poor and across regions and to help declining industries adjust to economic difficulties. Being costly for society, such policies should target narrowly defined groups so as to avoid free-riding by undeserving recipients.[8] Finally, subsidization may also pursue some noneconomic objectives, such as, for example, the protection of the environment, cultural identity, and national security.[9]

Economists typically distinguish between production subsidies and export subsidies designed to stimulate domestic output and exports respectively. Jagdish Bhagwati and V. K. Ramaswami, and Harry Johnson argue that, in the presence of domestic market distortions, production subsidies are preferable to an import tariff which similarly raises domestic production but, unlike subsidies, creates the cost for consumers.[10]

---

[3] *Ibid.*, p. 126.   [4] World Trade Report, 2006, *supra* note 1, p. 107.
[5] See Section 1.1.1.1.   [6] World Trade Report, 2006, *supra* note 1, pp. 82–6.
[7] *Ibid.*, pp. 86–8.   [8] *Ibid.*, pp. 88–98.   [9] *Ibid.*, pp. 98–106.
[10] Jagdish Bhagwati and V. K. Ramaswami, "Domestic Distortions, Tariffs and the Theory of Optimum Subsidy," 71 *Journal of Political Economy* 44 (1963); Harry G. Johnson, "Optimal Trade Intervention in the Presence of Domestic Distortions," in R. E. Caves, H. G. Johnson, and P. B. Kenen (eds.), *Trade, Growth, and the Balance of Payments: Essays in Honor of Gottfried Haberler* (Chicago, IL: Rand McNally and Company, 1965), pp. 3–34. Many papers cited in this section are reproduced in Marc Bacchetta and Michele Ruta (eds.), *The WTO, Subsidies and Countervailing Measures* (Cheltenham, the United

However, the subsidy loses its merit if taxes needed to finance the subsidy are themselves distortionary. In this case, a tariff-and-subsidy combination or a tariff only would be the most optimal solution depending on the extent of tax and tariff distortions.[11]

As for export subsidies, James Brander and Barbara Spencer justify their use in markets with imperfect competition. Their model considers the case of one domestic and one foreign firm exporting an identical good to a third market. They show that, when these firms compete in quantities, an export subsidy can encourage the domestic firm to increase production, which will force the foreign rival to reduce its own output. This expands the domestic firm's market share and profits and ultimately boosts the subsidizing country's welfare if these profits surpass the total amount of the export subsidy.[12] Avinash Dixit extends this result to the cases where there are more than two competitors and finds the export subsidy to be optimal as long as the number of domestic firms is not too large.[13] But in a model where firms compete in prices rather than quantities, Jonathan Eaton and Gene Grossman argue that an export tax is better than an export subsidy.[14] Horst Raff and Young-Han Kim consider the pros and cons of export subsidies vs. export taxes in a situation where a domestic firm entering an overseas market initially faces informational barriers there, namely consumers' skepticism about unknown foreign brands. They suggest that an export subsidy is preferable when the informational barriers are large, but once consumers become informed about the new entrant's product, an export tax should be applied instead.[15]

With respect to actual effects of government support, Dani Rodrik provides an empirical analysis on export subsidies of different countries,

Kingdom/Northampton, MA, the United States: Edward Elgar, 2011) and summarized by Marc Bacchetta and Michele Ruta in Introduction to that book, pp. xv–xxviii.

[11] Daniel Brou, Edoardo Campanella, and Michele Ruta, "The Value of Domestic Subsidy Rules in Trade Agreements," WTO Staff Working Paper No. ERSD–2009–12, 2009, pp. 3–4.

[12] James A. Brander and Barbara J. Spencer, "Export Subsidies and International Market Share Rivalry," 18 *Journal of International Economics* 83 (1985).

[13] Avinash Dixit, "International Trade Policy for Oligopolistic Industries," 94 *Economic Journal* (supplement), 1984, pp. 1–16.

[14] Jonathan Eaton and Gene M. Grossman, "Optimal Trade and Industrial Policy under Oligopoly," 101 *The Quarterly Journal of Economics* 383 (1986).

[15] Horst Raff and Young-Han Kim, "Optimal Export Policy in the Presence of Informational Barriers to Entry and Imperfect Competition," 49 *Journal of International Economics* 99 (1999).

comparing success stories in Korea and Brazil, failures in Kenya and Bolivia, and mixed results in Turkey and India. He concludes that export promotion works best in the presence of both State autonomy (i.e., the government's independence from private interest groups' requests) and policy coherence (i.e., clearly defined, stable, and consistent set of policy priorities).[16] In the example of the commercial aircraft industry, Douglas Irwin and Nina Pavchik confirm subsidies' impact on world competition, inferring this from the effects – a 3.7 percent price hike for both Airbus and Boeing and a 5 percent increase in firms' marginal costs – that arose from the 1992 US–EU agreement on subsidy cuts for civil aircraft.[17] Mihir Desai and James Hines investigate stock price reactions to the initiation of a WTO dispute over US tax exemptions for foreign sales corporations and conclude that export subsidies do not only benefit foreign consumers of subsidized goods but also improve exporters' profitability.[18] By contrast, Hiroshi Ohashi attributes an unprecedented growth of the Japanese steel industry in the 1950s and 1960s to market mechanisms rather than export subsidies, because the estimated steel supply was inelastic to the subsidy level.[19]

Since subsidies distort trade by providing an artificial price advantage to target products, the GATT/WTO system has developed legal disciplines on the use of subsidies. Economists advance mainly two lines of arguments in support of having subsidy rules in place.

According to the standard theory of trade agreements, since negotiated tariff reductions can be eroded by subsequent domestic subsidies, the latter should be constrained by international regulation. But too strict rules may discourage subsidy-preferring members from tariff liberalization. Thus, subsidy disciplines should strike a right balance between the benefits and costs of government flexibility in using subsidies.[20]

---

[16] Dani Rodrik, "Taking Trade Policy Seriously: Export Subsidization as a Case Study in Policy Effectiveness," in Jim Levinsohn, Alan V. Deardorff, and Robert M. Stern (eds.), *New Directions in Trade Theory* (Ann Arbor, MI: University of Michigan Press, 1995), pp. 347–84.

[17] Douglas A. Irwin and Nina Pavchik, "Airbus versus Boeing Revisited: International Competition in the Aircraft Market," 64 *Journal of International Economics* 223 (2004).

[18] Mihir A. Desai and James R. Hines, "Market Reactions to Export Subsidies," 74 *Journal of International Economics* 459 (2008).

[19] Hiroshi Ohashi, "Learning by Doing, Export Subsidies, and Industry Growth: Japanese Steel in the 1950s and 1960s," 66 *Journal of International Economics* 297 (2005).

[20] See Brou, Campanella, and Ruta, *supra* note 11; Kyle Bagwell and Robert W. Staiger, "Will International Rules on Subsidies Disrupt the World Trading System?," 96 *American Economic Review* 877 (2006); Bagwell and Staiger, Ch. 1, *supra* note 114.

As a complement to this theory, the commitment theory adds that a subsidy-restricting agreement helps the government resist unjustified pressures from domestic interest groups that require protection following tariff reductions. Having signed such agreement, the government ties its hands and shields itself from the lobby's demand for inefficient over-subsidization.[21]

3.2   The WTO Subsidy Regime

As WTO jurisprudence suggests, not every government intervention that economists qualify as a trade-distorting subsidy would necessarily be captured by the SCM Agreement.[22] The agreement applies to a government action that represents (i) a "financial contribution" or "income or price support" conferring (ii) a "benefit" to (iii) a "specific" recipient.

Under the definition of "subsidy" in Article 1 of the SCM Agreement, the covered subsidizer is "a government or any public body" (collectively "government") or "a private body" acting in a government-like manner. Regarding the term "public body," the Appellate Body reversed a panel's finding that this is "any entity controlled by a government," and found instead that this term actually meant "an entity that possesses, exercises or is vested with governmental authority."[23] Under this interpretation, a public body must have essential governmental attributes, which requires verification of a de jure or de facto delegation of governmental authority.[24] This obviously makes it more difficult to challenge many support measures taken by State-owned enterprises and banks.

---

[21] See Daniel Brou and Michele Ruta, "A Commitment Theory of Subsidy Agreements," WTO Staff Working Paper No. ERSD–2012–15, 2012; Giovanni Maggi and Andres Rodriguez-Clare, "The Value of Trade Agreements in the Presence of Political Pressures," 106 *Journal of Political Economy* 574 (1998); Robert W. Staiger and Guido Tabellini, "Discretionary Trade Policy and Excessive Protection," 77 *American Economic Review* 823 (1987).

[22] Panel Report, US – *Export Restraints*, para. 8.63; Appellate Body Report, US – *Softwood Lumber IV*, n. 35 to para. 52.

[23] Appellate Body Report, US – *Anti-Dumping and Countervailing Duties (China)*, paras. 317, 322.

[24] *Ibid.*, para. 318.

3.2.1   Financial Contribution or Income/Price Support

The first definitional element of "subsidy" characterizes the form of a government intervention. A financial contribution involves a direct or indirect transfer of certain economic resources from a government or public body to recipients.[25] Article 1.1(a)(1) of the SCM Agreement, in subparagraphs (i) to (iv) listed here, provides an exhaustive list of financial contributions,[26] with the same measure being able to fall within more than one subparagraph:[27]

> (i)   a government practice involves a direct transfer of funds (e.g. grants, loans, and equity infusion), potential direct transfers of funds or liabilities (e.g. loan guarantees);
>
> (ii) government revenue that is otherwise due is foregone or not collected (e.g. fiscal incentives such as tax credits) [footnote omitted];
>
> (iii) a government provides goods or services other than general infrastructure, or purchases goods;
>
> (iv) a government makes payments to a funding mechanism, or entrusts or directs a private body to carry out one or more of the type of functions illustrated in (i) to (iii) above which would normally be vested in the government and the practice, in no real sense, differs from practices normally followed by governments[.]

Subparagraph (i) of Article 1.1(a)(1) covers a direct transfer of funds – "money, financial resources, and/or financial claims"[28] – in the form of "grants, loans, and equity infusion," as well as other relevant measures, including, inter alia, debt-to-equity swaps, interest reductions and deferrals, debt forgiveness, an extension of the loan maturity, and a share transfer.[29] Potential direct transfers (e.g., loan guarantees) imply the possibility of governmental transfer that is conditional upon future materialization of a triggering event (e.g., a recipient's failure to repay a loan). But that possibility is "due to uncertainty about whether the triggering event will occur, rather than uncertainty about whether the

---

[25] Panel Report, *US – Export Restraints*, para. 8.73.

[26] Appellate Body Report, *US – Large Civil Aircraft (2nd complaint)*, para. 613.

[27] Appellate Body Reports, *Canada – Renewable Energy / Canada – Feed-in Tariff Program*, para. 5.120.

[28] Appellate Body Report, *US – Large Civil Aircraft (2nd complaint)*, para. 614.

[29] Panel Report, *Korea – Commercial Vessels*, paras. 7.411–7.413, 7.420; Panel Report, *Japan – DRAMs (Korea)*, paras. 7.442–7.444; Appellate Body Report, *Japan – DRAMs (Korea)*, paras. 250–2; Panel Report, *EC and certain member States – Large Civil Aircraft*, paras. 7.1291, 7.1318.

transfer of funds will follow once the pre-defined event has transpired."[30] It is the mere existence of the governmental commitment to make a direct transfer – not the funds that may be transferred in the future – that qualifies as a potential direct transfer.[31]

Subparagraph (ii) applies to the foregoing of revenue otherwise due, that is, when the government deliberately raises less revenue than when it would have done in a different situation, something that must be established not in abstract, but against "some defined, normative benchmark" under a member's "tax rules."[32] In essence, this requires "a comparison between the tax treatment that applies to the alleged subsidy recipients and the tax treatment of comparable income of comparably situated taxpayers."[33] For this, the Appellate Body in *US – Large Civil Aircraft (2nd complaint)* developed a three-step analysis consisting of (i) identification of the tax treatment of the alleged recipient's income to see objective reasons for such treatment and taxation rule changes (if any), (ii) identification of a benchmark for comparison, notably the tax treatment vis-à-vis comparable taxpayers, and (iii) comparison of the reasons for the challenged tax treatment with the benchmark treatment.[34] This finding was made mainly in the context of income taxes, but government revenue also includes other taxes and customs duties. It remains to be seen if the Appellate Body's reference to the "reasons" in the first and third inquiries implies that legitimate objectives or reasons may "disqualify" some lower-than-otherwise-usual tax burden as a financial contribution.[35] Footnote 1 to Article 1.1(a)(1)(ii) carves out some policy space for export promotion in saying that nonexcess exemptions or remissions of duties and indirect taxes for exported goods are not considered as a subsidy.[36]

Subparagraph (iii) contemplates two alternative types of transactions. The first one, provision of goods or services, pertains to virtually any transferable item with a certain value – not necessarily commonly

---

[30] Panel Report, *US – Large Civil Aircraft (2nd complaint)*, para. 7.164.

[31] Panel Report, *EC and certain member States – Large Civil Aircraft*, paras. 7.302, 7.304, 7.1495.

[32] Appellate Body Report, *US – FSC*, para. 90.

[33] Appellate Body Report, *US – Large Civil Aircraft (2nd complaint)*, para. 812.

[34] *Ibid.*, paras. 812–14.

[35] *Cf.* Dominic Coppens, *WTO Disciplines on Subsidies and Countervailing Measures: Balancing Policy Space and Legal Constraints* (Cambridge: Cambridge University Press, 2014), p. 47.

[36] See Sections 4.3.3.1, 6.2.1.

perceived goods or services – *other than* general infrastructure. The "goods" here may include even nontradable items without an official HS number, such as, for example, trees before they are harvested.[37] The panel in *EC and certain member States – Large Civil Aircraft* construed "general infrastructure" as infrastructure "available to all or nearly all entities" and emphasized that no type of infrastructure was inherently "general" per se. This issue requires, the panel said, a case-by-case determination of relevant factors, such as access (or use) limitations, circumstances surrounding the creation of the infrastructure, the nature and type of the infrastructure, and others.[38] The second transaction covered by subparagraph (iii) is a government purchase of goods that, unlike the first transaction having the potential to artificially reduce a recipient's production cost, can generate artificial revenue for a selling entity.[39]

Subparagraph (iv) is set to prevent circumvention of the subsidy disciplines by the practices where governments make *indirect* financial contributions via a funding mechanism or private bodies acting as proxy.[40] In a private body's case, the government "entrusts" (i.e., gives a responsibility to) that body or "directs" (i.e., exercises a public authority over) it, which can involve "some form of threat or inducement."[41] But "mere policy pronouncements" or "mere acts of encouragement" do not, by themselves, amount to entrustment and direction.[42] In a series of allegations that the Korean government had entrusted or directed private creditors to save a domestic company from a financial trouble, WTO adjudicators found some factors relevant (but not necessarily decisive) to the entrustment/direction determination, such as commercial unreasonableness of "subsidization" by a private body, a government's exercise of its shareholder power over the private body, or its coercion in a related transaction.[43]

Finally, Article 1.1(a)(2) of the SCM Agreement refers to "any form of income or price support" within the meaning of Article XVI of the

---

[37] Appellate Body Report, *US – Softwood Lumber IV*, para. 67.

[38] Panel Report, *EC and certain member States – Large Civil Aircraft*, paras. 7.1036–7.1039.

[39] Appellate Body Report, *US – Softwood Lumber IV*, para. 53.

[40] Appellate Body Report, *US – Countervailing Duty Investigation on DRAMS*, paras. 108, 113.

[41] *Ibid.*, para. 116.   [42] *Ibid.*, para. 114.

[43] Appellate Body Report, *Japan – DRAMs (Korea)*, para. 138; Panel Report, *EC – Countervailing Measures on DRAM Chips*, para. 7.120; Appellate Body Report, *US – Countervailing Duty Investigation on DRAMS*, para. 156.

GATT. Although it broadens the scope of qualifying subsidies beyond financial contributions,[44] the panel in *China – GOES* cautioned against an unrestrained extension of the subject measures. The panel observed that since the previous jurisprudence had stressed the *nature* of government action rather than its effect as being pertinent to the finding of a financial contribution, Article 1.1(a)(2) should be interpreted narrowly so as not to capture government measures having only an indirect impact (or incidental side-effect) on the market. Accordingly, "price support" includes "direct government intervention in the market with the design to fix the price of a good at a particular level, for example, through purchase of surplus production when price is set above equilibrium."[45] Among recent cases, in *Canada – Renewable Energy / Canada-Feed-in Tariff Program*, a governmental scheme of purchasing "green" electricity at guaranteed prices was claimed to fall within Article 1.1(a)(2), but the panel exercised judicial economy.[46]

3.2.2   Benefit

In order to qualify as a subsidy, a financial contribution or income/price support must confer a "benefit," that is, something that makes a recipient ("a person, natural or legal, or a group of persons") better off in the market.[47] While the existence of a benefit is obvious for, for example, grants or tax exemptions, this may not be true for other industry-promoting measures. Article 14 of the SCM Agreement provides specific guidelines on benefit calculations for government-involved equity investments, loans, loan guarantees, provision of goods or services, and purchase of goods. Overall, Article 14 suggests that one should compare a transaction at issue with a relevant commercial (or market) practice to see if there is any difference in treatment favorable to the recipient.

Where the government has significant influence on the market, there is no appropriate *market* benchmark there. In *US – Softwood Lumber IV*, the US Department of Commerce (DOC) found the Canadian softwood lumber to be subsidized through supplies of underpriced standing timber. To calculate the amount of the subsidy, the DOC replaced

---

[44] Appellate Body Report, *US – Softwood Lumber IV*, para. 52.

[45] Panel Report, *China – GOES*, paras. 7.85–7.87.

[46] Panel Reports, *Canada – Renewable Energy / Canada – Feed-in Tariff Program*, para. 7.249.

[47] Appellate Body Report, *Canada – Aircraft*, paras. 154, 157–8.

State-distorted prices of timber in Canada with adjusted out-of-country prices. The Appellate Body approved of the use of out-of-country proxies for a subsidizing country's prices being distorted by the predominant role of the government.[48]

By contrast, a government's infant industry policy does not necessarily provide a benefit and hence a subsidy. Specifically, the Appellate Body in *Canada – Renewable Energy / Canada-Feed-in Tariff Program* differentiated creation of a *new* market from support of the *existing* market and held that "the creation of markets by a government does not *in and of itself* give rise to subsidies within the meaning of the SCM Agreement."[49] While securing some policy flexibility, this finding nevertheless raises a practical question as to how long an industry should be deemed to be in its infant stage so as to be "immune" from the WTO subsidy rules.[50]

When a State-owned company is fully privatized at arm's length and for a fair market price, there is a rebuttable presumption that a non-recurring subsidy – typically, a one-off subsidy (like an equity infusion) generating a long-lasting benefit for the recipient – given to that company before it was privatized ceases benefiting it after the privatization.[51] Thus, unless it is proved otherwise, the past subsidy here cannot be countervailed in the postprivatization period. The question as to whether such a rebuttable presumption extends to other forms of corporate ownership changes, notably partial privatizations or private-to-private sales, was an issue in *EC and certain member States – Large Civil Aircraft*. But the Appellate Body surprisingly failed to arrive at a single conclusion among its members.[52]

3.2.3 Specificity

The SCM Agreement regulates only "specific" subsidies that, unlike generally available subsidies, are believed to inefficiently allocate resources across an economy causing market distortions. Pursuant to

---

[48] Appellate Body Report, *US – Softwood Lumber IV*, paras. 77–8, 82–122; Appellate Body Report, *US – Anti-Dumping and Countervailing Duties (China)*, paras. 446, 483.

[49] Appellate Body Reports, *Canada – Renewable Energy / Canada – Feed-in Tariff Program*, para. 5.188 (emphasis in original).

[50] Sherzod Shadikhodjaev, "First WTO Judicial Review of Climate Change Subsidy Issues," 107 *American Journal of International Law* 864 (2013), p. 877.

[51] Appellate Body Report, *US – Countervailing Measures on Certain EC Products*, paras. 117–27.

[52] Appellate Body Report, *EC and certain member States – Large Civil Aircraft*, para. 726.

Article 2, subsidies are "specific" if they are bestowed, de jure or de facto, upon particular (groups of) enterprises or industries (collectively "certain enterprises") or geographical regions housing certain enterprises. Export and local content subsidies are deemed to be specific, but other subsidies require a separate specificity determination.

The term "certain enterprises" refers to a "known and particularized" enterprise/industry or a class thereof.[53] An "industry" (or a group of industries) generally covers producers of particular types of product, but the exact scope varies from case to case.[54] For instance, a subsidy's availability to certain agricultural crops and livestock as opposed to the entire agricultural sector was enough for a panel to characterize it as specific.[55] In *US – Softwood Lumber IV*, the panel considered a group of wood product industries as a whole as a specific recipient rather than the "wooden kitchen cabinet and bathroom vanity industry," the "wooden door and window industry," and the remaining twenty-one narrowly defined "industries" taken separately.[56]

Subsidies are not specific where they are subject to objective criteria or conditions regarding the automatic eligibility and the amount as clearly spelled out in official documents (Article 2.1(b)), or where generally applicable tax rates are set or changed by all levels of the government in charge (Article 2.2). Despite the objective criteria/conditions, a subsidy may still be found to be specific under other factors, including use by a limited number of, or predominant use by, certain enterprises; the allocation of disproportionally large amounts of subsidy to certain enterprises; and the manner of accepting or refusing subsidy requests (Article 2.1(c)).

3.2.4   Antisubsidy Measures

The SCM Agreement distinguishes prohibited subsidies (Part II of the agreement), actionable subsidies (Part III), and nonactionable (permissible) subsidies (Part IV). But Part IV has become inoperative since 2000 so that certain R&D subsidies, environmental subsidies, and regional development subsidies that were initially permitted under Part IV are currently either prohibited or actionable depending on the

---

[53] Appellate Body Report, *US – Anti-Dumping and Countervailing Duties (China)*, para. 373.
[54] *Ibid.*; Panel Report, *US – Upland Cotton*, para. 7.1142.
[55] Panel Report, *US – Upland Cotton*, paras. 7.1150–7.1152.
[56] Panel Report, *US – Softwood Lumber IV*, paras. 7.117 (and accompanying n. 180), 7.121.

subsidization terms. Subsidies contingent upon export performance (export subsidies) or the use of domestic over imported goods (local content or import substitution subsidies) are prohibited. All other specific subsidies are actionable.

An affected member can counteract a foreign subsidy by challenging it through the WTO dispute settlement mechanism (the multilateral track under Parts II and III) or by taking countervailing measures against subsidized imports (the national track under Part V). While both antisubsidy tracks can proceed in parallel, ultimately only one form of relief will be available (n. 35 to Article 10 of the SCM Agreement).

Under the multilateral track, a member complaining about an actionable subsidy must prove the existence of that subsidy and an associated "adverse effect" in the sense of Article 5 (i.e., injury to its domestic industry, nullification or impairment of its benefits, or serious prejudice to its interests). But no effect element is required for a prohibited subsidy.[57] The losing member-subsidizer must "take appropriate steps to remove the adverse effects or . . . withdraw the subsidy" in the case of actionable subsidies (Article 7.8) or must "withdraw the subsidy without delay" in the case of prohibited subsidies (Article 4.7).

Under the national track, an affected member can investigate relevant imports to check whether they are subsidized and injurious to the domestic industry. If confirmed so, it may impose a countervailing duty for up to five years on an extendable basis.

There are both the pros and cons of invoking either track. An import-competing industry may prefer the countervailing mechanism in anticipation of quick protection against subsidized imports. An importing government itself may feel more comfortable with launching a domestic investigation against foreign companies rather than lodging an official WTO complaint against a subsidizing government. Therefore, it is no wonder that the national track has been used far more frequently than the multilateral track as illustrated in Figure 3.1. In terms of the total numbers over 1995–2015, there were 69 WTO

---

[57] Prohibited subsidies are simply presumed to cause negative trade effects, irrespective of who exactly suffers those effects. Thus, the requirement not to grant a prohibited subsidy constitutes an *erga omnes* obligation "owed in its entirety to each and every [WTO] Member." Decision by the Arbitrators, *Brazil – Aircraft (Article 22.6 – Brazil)*, para. 3.48 (b); Decision by the Arbitrator, *US – FSC (Article 22.6 – US)*, para. 6.10. See also Sherzod Shadikhodjaev, *Retaliation in the WTO Dispute Settlement System* (Alphen aan den Rijn: Kluwer Law International, 2009), pp. 103–5.

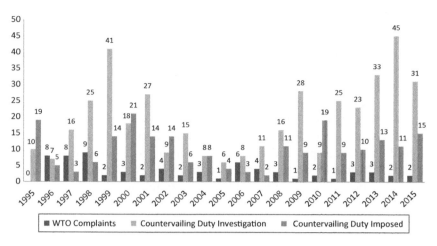

Figure 3.1   Antisubsidy Measures (1995–2015)

Source: Compiled by the author from data at WTO, "Disputes by Agreement: Subsidies and Countervailing Measures," www.wto.org/english/tratop_e/dispu_e/dispu_agreements_index_e.htm?id=A20#; WTO, "Statistics on Subsidies and Countervailing Measures," www.wto.org/english/tratop_e/scm_e/scm_e.htm.

Note: WTO complaints are consultation requests alleging violations by foreign subsidies of the SCM Agreement.

antisubsidy complaints vs. 411 countervailing duty investigations and 216 countervailing duties imposed.

By contrast, compared to countervailing duties,[58] multilateral remedies are more likely to lead to discontinuation of a subsidy program (at least in the case of a prohibited subsidy) and are available not only in the event of importation, but also when the subsidized product competes with the complaining member's product in the market of the subsidizing country or a third country. In the case of Part II remedies, the mere fact of the granting of a prohibited subsidy can be the sole basis for a WTO complaint by virtue of Articles 3.2 and 4.1 of the SCM Agreement.

---

[58] See Alan O. Sykes, "The Questionable Case for Subsidies Regulation: A Comparative Perspective," 2 *Journal of Legal Analysis* 473 (2010), p. 484 ("Unilateral countervailing duties . . . are unlikely to discourage the targeted subsidization practices systematically, as they are not coordinated multilaterally and generally apply to only a fraction of the production that benefits from subsidies.").

Initially, Article 13 of the Agreement on Agriculture (the "peace clause") temporarily insulated qualifying agricultural subsidies from SCM measures. That agreement distinguishes, in essence, permissible domestic subsidies, trade-distortive domestic subsidies, and export subsidies, with the latter two being subject to member-specific caps reflected in national schedules. Local content agricultural subsidies are prohibited by the SCM Agreement regardless of their legal status under the Agreement on Agriculture.[59] In the Ministerial Conference of 2015, developed countries committed themselves to eliminating scheduled export subsidies "immediately" except for some farm products, while developing countries pledged to do so by the end of 2018, with some longer timing given in specified cases.[60] Due to the expiry of the peace clause in 2003, agricultural support policies are currently prone to antisubsidy measures under the SCM Agreement.

3.2.5 S&D Treatment

Article 27 of the SCM Agreement on S&D treatment recognizes subsidies' "important role in economic development programs of developing country Members." The S&D provisions currently in force provide for, inter alia, (i) an exemption for export subsidies of certain developing countries and (ii) stricter requirements for applying the countervailing mechanism vis-à-vis developing countries.

Regarding the first category above, developing countries under Annex VII of the SCM Agreement – namely, LDCs and the listed developing countries with gross national product per capita below US$1,000 – remain exempt from the WTO's prohibition against export subsidies as long as export competitiveness of their subsidized product is below 3.25 percent in world trade of that product. In contrast, the original S&D exemption for local content subsidies expired and is no longer available. Since export and local content subsidies are equally banned, one may wonder why the S&D regime treats them asymmetrically. Indeed, just as local content subsidies can displace foreign inputs in a subsidizer's market, export subsidies can also displace foreign products abroad. The S&D asymmetry probably stems from what seems to be the WTO's

---

[59] Appellate Body Report, *US – Upland Cotton*, paras. 529–50.

[60] WTO, Ministerial Conference – Tenth Session – Nairobi, 15–18 December 2015 – Export Competition – Ministerial Decision of 19 December 2015, WT/MIN(15)/45, WT/L/980 (21 December 2015), paras. 6–11.

general preference for export promotion over import substitution. For example, while the requirement to use local content is circumscribed by, inter alia, Article III of the GATT, the requirement to export is not restricted by the GATT.[61] The economic literature is also more lenient toward export promotion.[62]

Under the second S&D category mentioned earlier, countervailing duty investigations against a developing country must be terminated if the *de minimis* subsidization rate does not exceed 2 percent or the volume of subsidized imports is negligible, that is, less than 4 percent of the overall imports of the like product unless below-four-percent imports from individual developing countries collectively exceed 9 percent of the overall imports concerned (Article 27.10). Such S&D thresholds make it more difficult to countervail developing country subsidies.

Article 27.13 exempts certain subsidies under privatization programs of developing countries from Part III of the SCM Agreement, provided that such programs and subsidies are appropriately notified, operate within a limited period, and eventually result in privatization of related enterprises.

Under Articles 27.14 and 27.15, the SCM Committee reviews, upon request, whether a developing country's "specific export subsidy practice" is consistent with its "development needs" or whether "a specific countervailing measure" against a developing country complies with the relevant S&D provisions. But so far, no such a request has been received.[63]

3.2.6   Subsidy Notifications

Article 25 of the SCM Agreement requires that every member notify its specific subsidies providing information on a subsidy's form, amount, policy objective/purpose, duration, and statistics on trade effects.

---

[61] The GATT panel in *Canada – FIRA* found that "that there is no provision in the General Agreement which forbids requirements to sell goods in foreign markets in preference to the domestic market." GATT Panel Report, *Canada – FIRA*, para. 5.18.

[62] World Trade Report, 2006, *supra* note 1, p. xxv ("A survey of the industrial policy literature indicates that from the point of view of implementation, export promotion has some advantages compared to import substitution."). Some commentators even question the very WTO wisdom of banning export subsidies, as such a prohibition actually limits the volume of trade in contrast to tariff liberalization. See Bagwell and Staiger, Ch. 2, *supra* note 1, p. 179.

[63] WT/COMTD/W/219, Ch. 1, *supra* note 112, pp. 59, 65.

Members must submit new and full notifications each third year, with 1995 being the year for the first notifications, and updating notifications in the intervening years.[64] Notifications do not prejudge the legal status of notified measures under the WTO system (Article 25.7).

It is particularly worrying that the portion of nonnotifying members relative to the overall number of members noticeably increased from 26 percent (in 1995) to 37 percent (2011), 42 percent (2013), and 65 percent (2015).[65] Such "chronic low compliance" with the notification requirement represents a serious transparency problem undermining the proper functioning of the multilateral subsidy regime.[66]

Nonnotification is attributable to the subsidizing government's capacity building constraints (e.g., the lack of professional staff or interagency coordination difficulties), fear of a potential legal dispute, and uncertainty about what to notify.[67] Yet, other members can still counternotify foreign subsidies (Article 25.10) or bring a complaint. For example, the United States counternotified Chinese and Indian subsidy programs in 2011 and challenged nonnotification in *China – Measures Concerning Wind Power Equipment*.[68]

In this connection, we suggest that, for greater transparency, the WTO Secretariat create a separate electronic database on member- and sector-specific subsidy programs based on (counter)notifications, WTO reports, dispute-related materials, and other available information. The accumulated data on subsidies in the fishery, energy, steel, and other relevant industries could be utilized for assessing subsidies' role in overcapacity, their environmental implications, and adequacy of the current WTO rules.[69]

---

[64] WTO, Committee on SCM – Questionnaire Format for Subsidy Notifications under Article 25 of the Agreement on Subsidies and Counte[...]cle XVI of GATT 1994 – Revision, G/SCM/6/Rev.1 (11 November 2003).

[65] WTO, Committee on SCM – Notification Requirements under the SCM Agreement – Background Note by the Secretariat – Revision, G/SCM/W/546/Rev.7 (31 March 2016), p. 4, para. 8.

[66] WTO, Committee on SCM – Minutes of the Regular Meeting Held on 25 October 2016, G/SCM/M/99 (16 January 2017), para. 72.

[67] Gregory Shaffer, Robert Wolfe, and Vinhcent Le, "Can Informal Law Discipline Subsidies?," 18 *Journal of International Economic Law* 711 (2015), p. 717.

[68] See WTO, Committee on SCM – Minutes of the Regular Meeting Held on 26 and 27 October 2011, G/SCM/M/79 (2 February 2012), paras. 101–9, 121; WTO, *China – Measures Concerning Wind Power Equipment* – Request for Consultations by the United States, WT/DS419/1, G/L/950, G/SCM/D86/1 (6 January 2011).

[69] The SCM Committee has already started discussion on the enhancement of transparency of fisheries subsidies and on the overcapacity issue. See, e.g., G/SCM/M/99, *supra* note 66, paras. 203–24, 225–50.

3.2.7   Subsidies in the Services Sector

Services industries benefit from government support as well. In terms of the number of subsidizing members, the WTO Secretariat's survey (2015) of TPR reports reveals a high concentration of service-related subsidies in five main areas: tourism and travel (81 members); transport including maritime (36), air (32), rail (17) and road (9); finance (44); telecommunication (33); software, ICT, data processing and telephone (30).[70] This database generally relies on the subsidy definition of the SCM Agreement,[71] as the GATS does not provide its own.

Article XV of the GATS set an agenda for negotiating multilateral disciplines on services subsidies that would address their "trade-distortive effects," the appropriateness of countervailing procedures, and development issues. Although the negotiations have not progressed, members do not have unfettered freedom to subsidize in this field. Article XV itself foresees the possibility of consultations between subsidizing and adversely affected members. Moreover, the GATS constrains discriminatory subsidies. Under Article II (MFN), a subsidy given to a foreign service and service supplier must "immediately and unconditionally" be extended to "like" services/suppliers of other members unless it falls within a member-specific exemption as exemplified in Table 3.1. Unlike the horizontally applicable MFN principle, national treatment of Article XVII applies only to the (sub)sectors listed in each member's schedule, subject to the inscribed conditions. Thus, the GATS scheduling guidelines stipulate that "any subsidy which is a discriminatory measure within the meaning of Article XVII would have to be either scheduled as a limitation on national treatment or brought into conformity with that Article."[72]

By contrast, the GATS disciplines do not apply to the subsidization of "services supplied in the exercise of governmental authority" (Article I:3). The MFN and national treatment provisions are inapplicable to government procurement of services (Article XIII). GATS-inconsistent

---

[70] WTO, Working Party on GATS Rules – Subsidies for Services Sectors – Information Contained in WTO TPRs – Background Note by the Secretariat – Revision, S/WPGR/W/25/Add.7/Rev.1 (13 January 2015), p. 12, para. 3.1.

[71] *Ibid.*, p. 11, para. 2.1.

[72] WTO, Trade in Services – Guidelines for the Scheduling of Specific Commitments under the GATS – Adopted by the Council for Trade in Services on 23 March 2001, S/L/92 (28 March 2001), para. 16.

Table 3.1 *Examples of GATS Article II (MFN) Exemptions for Service-Related Subsidies*

Member	(Sub)sector	Description of the Measure Indicating Its Inconsistency with Article II	Countries to Which the Measure Applies	Intended Duration	Conditions Creating the Need for the Exemption
Bulgaria	Medical and dental services	Public medical insurance, subsidization and compensation plans and programs, which cover the cost and expenses relating to medical and dental services provided to foreign citizens in the territory of the Republic of Bulgaria, are granted on the basis of reciprocity in the framework of bilateral agreements.	Countries with which such bilateral agreements are or will be concluded.	Indefinite	Obligations under international agreements
Russia	Audiovisual services	Measures based on coproduction agreements, which confer national treatment with respect to audiovisual works covered by these agreements, including in relation to subsidies for production and distribution.	Parties to the European Convention on Cinematographic Coproduction and countries with whom bilateral coproduction agreements are/may be concluded.	Indefinite	Development of cultural links and protection of cultural heritage

Table 3.1 (*cont.*)

Member	(Sub)sector	Description of the Measure Indicating Its Inconsistency with Article II	Countries to Which the Measure Applies	Intended Duration	Conditions Creating the Need for the Exemption
Tajikistan	Audiovisual services	Measures based on intergovernmental and plurilateral coproduction agreements, which confer national treatment with respect to audiovisual works covered by these agreements, including in relation to subsidies for production and distribution.	All countries with whom cultural cooperation may be desirable.	Indefinite	
Afghanistan	Audiovisual services		Parties to the European Convention on Cinematographic Coproduction and countries with whom bilateral or plurilateral coproduction agreements are/may be concluded.	Indefinite	

Source: Based on data from WTO, "I-TIP Services" (underlines added), http://i-tip.wto.org/services/.

subsidies are, in principle, defendable under general and security exceptions (Articles XIV and XIV *bis*).

In addition to the GATS, some product-linked subsidies involving services are subject to the SCM Agreement. In *Brazil – Aircraft (Article 21.5 – Canada II)*, Brazil's government made nonrefundable payments to lenders (financial service suppliers) that offered export credits to purchasers of Brazilian aircraft. The panel determined that a challenge under the SCM Agreement had to show that the benefit from these payments did not remain exclusively with the lender but passed through to aircraft producers.[73] In particular, the purchasers' access to the export credits on better-than-market conditions could act, the panel said, as *prima facie* evidence for conferral of a benefit on the producers as well, as "it lowers the cost of the product to their purchasers and thus makes their product more attractive relative to competing products."[74] This ruling may suggest the applicability of the SCM Agreement to services subsidies (e.g., a government's bailout of banks) that provide benefits to producers of goods (e.g., producers being bank clients).

Further, the *US – Large Civil Aircraft (2nd complaint)* case considered two R&D schemes each supported by the National Aeronautics and Space Administration and the Department of Defense respectively. These institutions representing the US government provided some funding and access to their research facilities, while Boeing contributed the work of its scientists and engineers and some financial resources. The agencies in question and Boeing shared the fruits of the research.[75] The panel observed that the omission of purchases of services in Article 1.1(a)(1) (iii) of the SCM Agreement (as opposed to the inclusion of purchases of goods there) would indicate members' "deliberate choice" to exclude purchases of services from the entire scope of financial contributions, including direct transfers of funds under Article 1.1(a)(1)(i). Thus, the panel declined to consider certain procurement contracts that qualified as purchases of services.[76] The Appellate Body concluded that the R&D arrangements at issue resembled joint ventures analogous to "equity infusion" under Article 1.1(a)(1)(i), but declared the panel's comment about exclusion of service purchases from the same provision "to be

---

[73] Panel Report, *Brazil – Aircraft (Article 21.5 – Canada II)*, para. 5.27, accompanying n. 41.
[74] *Ibid.*, n. 42 to para. 5.28.
[75] Appellate Body Report, *US – Large Civil Aircraft (2nd complaint)*, para. 611.
[76] *Ibid.*, paras. 550–2, 556–63.

moot and of no legal effect" because of its irrelevance to resolving this dispute.[77] It appears that despite noninclusion of governmental purchases of services in subparagraph (iii) of Article 1.1(a)(1), the remaining subparagraphs could still capture these transactions where relevant so that members could not easily circumvent the subsidy disciplines by distorting merchandise trade through "service contracts" with suppliers of goods.[78]

3.3   Industrial Policies in Upstream Sectors

Government policies in upstream (i.e., nonprocessing) sectors typically regulate the conservation, extraction, use, and sales of various minerals and fuels. Public international law recognizes a State's sovereignty over its natural resources.[79] The panel in *China – Raw Materials* held that this "principle of international law" allowed WTO members to use and exploit their natural resources in a manner that would promote their economic development in a sustainable way. But it also stressed that members "must exercise" such sovereignty "consistently with their WTO obligations" which derive from another component of the State sovereignty, namely a member's ability to enter into the WTO Agreement.[80]

3.3.1   *Pricing Measures*

A government's intervention in the upstream market may result in dual pricing, that is, low and high prices of raw materials destined for the domestic and overseas sales respectively. This can be achieved through direct measures like price controls or State monopolies, as well as indirect measures like export restrictions. Low input prices give a cost advantage to local downstream (i.e., processing) industries over foreign competitors. High export prices of inputs may "cross-subsidize" their underpriced domestic supplies.[81]

---

[77] *Ibid.*, paras. 620, 624–5.

[78] This concern was raised by the complainant and some third parties. See *ibid.*, para. 560.

[79] See UN General Assembly Resolution 1803 (XVII) on Permanent Sovereignty over Natural Resources, 14 December 1962.

[80] Panel Reports, *China – Raw Materials*, paras. 7.380–7.383.

[81] See WTO, Working Party on the Accession of the Russian Federation – Report of the Working Party on the Accession of the Russian Federation to the WTO, WT/ACC/RUS/70, WT/MIN(11)/2 (17 November 2011), para. 120; Julia Selivanova, "World Trade

A country's dual pricing policy has the beggar-thy-neighbor element when it increases that country's downstream exports and consequently lowers the corresponding world price. Economists argue that this can provoke (or result from) tariff escalation – a progressive increase in tariffs along processing chains seeking to restrict resource-intensive imports from the dual pricing country – and suggest that an agreement regulating both dual pricing and tariff escalation would be mutually beneficial for the exporting and importing countries concerned.[82]

The Uruguay Round negotiators wished to address dual pricing under the subsidy disciplines. A relevant draft text stated that, for the purpose of countervailing measures, a government's provision of a good would be considered as conferring a benefit if the government as a sole provider discriminated between the users of that good, except where the differential treatment was due to "normal commercial considerations."[83] This rule proposal might have banned upstream price differentiation between domestic and export markets, but it was eventually scrapped because of a fundamental concern about possible risks to the State sovereignty over natural resources.[84]

Even without such explicit wording in the SCM Agreement, dual pricing may, under certain circumstances, qualify as a "subsidy" in the form of, for example, the government provision of input goods at a less-than-adequate remuneration. But if the input, like natural gas or electricity, is used across many sectors of the subsidizing country, this fact would render the dual pricing scheme a nonspecific subsidy (at least on a de jure basis) outside of the SCM Agreement's reach. Neither would it be a genuine prohibited subsidy.[85]

Dual pricing could also be tested under Article XVII of the GATT on State trading enterprises – "[g]overnmental and non-governmental enterprises ... [with] exclusive or special rights or privileges, including

---

Organization Rules and Energy Pricing: Russia's Case," 38 *Journal of World Trade* 559 (2004), pp. 562, 597.

[82] WTO, "Trade in Natural Resources," World Trade Report, 2010, p. 188.

[83] This provision was supposed to be Article 14(e) of the SCM Agreement. See GATT, Uruguay Round – Group of Negotiations on Goods (GATT) – Negotiating Group on SCM – Draft Text on SCM, MTN.GNG/NG10/23 (7 November 1990).

[84] Selivanova, *supra* note 81, pp. 564–5.

[85] See *ibid.*, pp. 569–84; Sergey Ripinsky, "The System of Gas Dual Pricing in Russia: Compatibility with WTO Rules," 3 *World Trade Review* 463 (2004); Vitaliy Pogoretskyy, "Energy Dual Pricing in International Trade: Subsidies and Anti-dumping Perspectives," in Yulia Selivanova (ed.), *Regulation of Energy in International Trade Law: WTO, NAFTA and Energy Charter* (Alphen aan den Rijn: Kluwer Law International, 2011), pp. 199–214.

statutory or constitutional powers, in the exercise of which they influence through their purchases or sales the level or direction of imports or exports."[86] Pursuant to Article XVII:1(a), such entities must comply with "the general principles of non-discriminatory treatment prescribed in [the GATT] for governmental measures affecting imports or exports by private traders." Article XVII:1(b) adds that this obligation requires the purchases/sales by State trading enterprises to be in accordance with "commercial considerations." In *Canada – Wheat Exports and Grain Imports*, the Appellate Body clarified that the requirement under Article XVII:1(b) merely derived from the nondiscrimination obligation under Article XVII:1(a) rather than introduced a separate obligation triggering an additional inquiry into whether, in abstract, the enterprises were acting "commercially."[87] The panel in *Korea – Various Measures on Beef*, in a finding not reviewed by the Appellate Body, considered that nondiscrimination under Article XVII:1(a) included at least Articles I (MFN) and III (national treatment) of the GATT.[88] Thus, one may argue that dual pricing schemes involving State trading enterprises would violate national treatment by offering price advantages to domestic, but not foreign, producers. But a counterargument could be that Article XVII:1(a) actually covers only MFN, as it explicitly refers to nondiscrimination affecting "imports or exports" but not domestic sales. Following this proposition, dual pricing may be considered to be outside of the scope of Article XVII:1.[89]

Perhaps most direct WTO disciplines on pricing measures are contained in Article III:9 of the GATT which recognizes that "internal maximum price control measures" can have prejudicial effect on the interests of other members supplying imported products and thus stipulates that members with such measures "shall take account of the interests of exporting [members] with a view to avoiding to the fullest practicable extent such prejudicial effects." Yet, despite its mandatory language, this provision imposes rather a soft law obligation on the importing country.[90]

Some pricing policies were thoroughly scrutinized during accession negotiations. China pledged to "eliminate dual pricing practices as well as

---

[86] Understanding on the Interpretation of Article XVII of the GATT 1994.
[87] Appellate Body Report, *Canada – Wheat Exports and Grain Imports*, para. 145.
[88] Panel Report, *Korea – Various Measures on Beef*, para. 753.
[89] Pogoretskyy, *supra* note 85, pp. 197–8.
[90] See Selivanova, *supra* note 81, p. 594; Pogoretskyy, *supra* note 85, pp. 190–1.

differences in treatment accorded to goods produced for sale in China in comparison to those produced for export."[91] Saudi Arabia, Russia, and Tajikistan committed themselves to ensuring that their energy suppliers would operate under normal commercial conditions allowing full recovery of costs and reasonable profits.[92]

By contrast, several members retained the government's right to regulate prices of specific energy products and services, such as oil/natural gas and derivative products, electricity, gas transportation services, heat power transmission services, nuclear fuel cycle products, etc.[93] Russia, for instance, justified the price regulation of gas supplies to "households and other non-commercial users" (as opposed to "industrial users") with "domestic social policy" considerations, while Chinese Taipei explained its price control over petroleum, natural gas, and liquefied petroleum with the need to "maintain stability in energy prices."[94]

Finally, energy pricing policies of new WTO entrants have been subjected to enhanced transparency requirements. The members concerned normally included the list of price-regulated energy goods and services in their accession package and committed themselves to publishing any changes thereto in official domestic sources.[95] China's publication commitment also covers "price-setting mechanisms and policies."[96]

---

[91] WTO, Working Party on the Accession of China – Report of the Working Party on the Accession of China, WT/ACC/CHN/49 (1 October 2001), para. 18.

[92] See, e.g., WTO, Working Party on the Accession of Saudi Arabia – Report of the Working Party on the Accession of the Kingdom of Saudi Arabia to the WTO, WT/ACC/SAU/61 (1 November 2005), para. 33; WT/ACC/RUS/70, WT/MIN(11)/2, *supra* note 81, para. 132; WT/ACC/TJK/30, Ch. 2, *supra* note 33, para. 59.

[93] Juneyoung Lee et al., "Energy-Related Rules in Accession Protocols: Where are They?," in Uri Dadush and Chiedu Osakwe (eds.), *WTO Accessions and Trade Multilateralism: Case Studies and Lessons from the WTO at Twenty* (Cambridge: Cambridge University Press, 2015), pp. 719–20.

[94] WT/ACC/RUS/70, WT/MIN(11)/2, *supra* note 81, para. 132; WTO, Ministerial Conference – Fourth Session – Doha, 9–13 November 2001 – Report of the Working Party on the Accession of the Separate Customs Territory of Taiwan, Penghu, Kinmen and Matsu, WT/MIN(01)/4 (11 November 2001), para. 11.

[95] See, e.g., WT/ACC/RUS/70, WT/MIN(11)/2, *supra* note 81, para. 133; WTO, Working Party on the Accession of the Republic of Kazakhstan – Report of the Working Party on the Accession of the Republic of Kazakhstan, WT/ACC/KAZ/93 (23 June 2015), para. 170.

[96] WT/ACC/CHN/49, *supra* note 91, para. 60, Annex 4.

3.3.2   Export Restrictions

In general, export restrictions on goods can be defined in the way that the panel in *US – Export Restraints* described, namely:

> a border measure that takes the form of a government law or regulation which expressly limits the quantity of exports or places explicit conditions on the circumstances under which exports are permitted, or that takes the form of a government-imposed fee or tax on exports of the product calculated to limit the quantity of exports.[97]

The OECD inventory of restrictions on trade in raw materials (2014) records more than thirteen types of export-restraining measures – export licenses, export taxes, export bans/quotas, and so on – that are applied by sixty-five countries on minerals and metals, waste and scrap, wood and agricultural commodities.[98] Figure 3.2 shows a remarkable upward trend of using export restrictions worldwide during the last decade. In order to meet the soaring demand from boosting downstream industries at home, some emerging and developing economies have recently resorted to export restrictions on natural resources more extensively than ever. Since the production and international supply of minerals and other industrial raw materials are concentrated in a handful of countries, export restrictions inevitably limit global access to these resources and worsen the manufacturing capacity of import-dependent countries. In 2012, top-five resource-producing countries together accounted for over 90 percent of the world production of minerals and metals, such as antimony, lithium, platinum, tin, tungsten, and rare earth oxides.[99] The exhaustibility of these resources and the difficulty with their substitutability heighten concerns about export limitations.

Export restrictions aim to, inter alia, generate government revenues, conserve natural resources, promote downstream production, control foreign exchange, fight against illegal export activities, and protect health

---

[97] Panel Report, *US – Export Restraints*, para. 8.17.

[98] The data in this OECD inventory is summarized in Barbara Fliess, Christine Arriola, and Peter Liapis, "Recent Developments in the Use of Export Restrictions in Raw Materials Trade," in OECD, "Export Restrictions in Raw Materials Trade: Facts, Fallacies and Better Practices," 2014, pp. 17–61.

[99] *Ibid.*, p. 21.

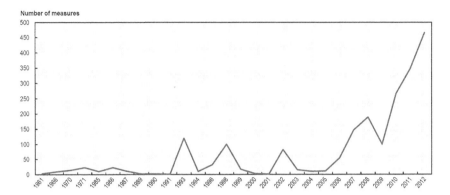

Figure 3.2 Global Trends in the Use of Export Restrictions on Industrial Raw Materials

Source: Barbara Fliess, Christine Arriola, and Peter Liapis, "Recent Developments in the Use of Export Restrictions in Raw Materials Trade," in OECD, "Export Restrictions in Raw Materials Trade: Facts, Fallacies and Better Practices," 2014, p. 23 (figure 1.2), citing "UN Comtrade."
Note: Measures are counted at the HS6 level of product classification. Restrictions that expired and then were reintroduced in the following year were counted as a new introduction of a measure.

and the environment.[100] Such measures may push up the world price of the subject commodity, while reducing its price at home creating indirect benefits to domestic processing industries. But they may discourage domestic producers of raw materials from further exploratory activities, investment, and technological improvements, eventually decreasing their productivity and overseas market shares.[101] Export restrictions may also boomerang against the imposing country itself:

> Experience shows that export controls can trigger similar actions in other supplier countries, driving up prices further, making price volatility worse, and creating a crisis of confidence that spreads from one resource to the next. Nobody benefits. Countries using export restrictions for some minerals are often heavily reliant on imports of other minerals, where

---

[100] See Barbara Fliess and Tarja Mård, "Taking Stock of Measures Restricting the Export of Raw Materials: Analysis of OECD Inventory Data," OECD Trade Policy Paper No. 140, 2012, pp. 17–18.
[101] K.C. Fung and Jane Korinek, "Economics of Export Restrictions as Applied to Industrial Raw Materials," OECD Trade Policy Paper No. 155, 2013, pp. 32–3.

they may face a restricted supply due to the use of similar trade instruments by other countries.[102]

Article XI:1 of the GATT explicitly bans quantitative export restrictions. The complainant in *Argentina – Hides and Leather* argued that the presence of domestic tanners' representatives in the Argentine customs inspection procedures for hides destined for export constituted a de facto export restriction. But the panel turned down this claim due to the lack of evidence, although it agreed that de facto export restrictions fell within Article XI:1.[103] In contrast, the *China – Raw Materials* ruling found the violation of Article XI:1 by the Chinese export quotas on bauxite, coke, fluorspar, silicon carbide, and zinc.[104]

While export duties as such are not prohibited by commonly applicable WTO disciplines, Julia Ya Qin distinguishes four groups of WTO members with different degrees of leeway in using export duties. In particular, 140-plus members have "nearly complete freedom" to restrict exports through duties, but the remaining members have certain accession obligations to bind export duties with the varying scope of goods, commitments, and WTO exceptions. Since export duties do have a restrictive trade effect, the process of scheduling them should eventually cover all WTO members similar to import duty bindings.[105] These measures can additionally be curbed at a regional trade level. Over sixty RTAs restrict export duties either through a standstill clause, which maintains the status quo for the existing duties and prohibits new ones, or through explicit bans modelled on the Article XI:1 prohibition against quantitative export restrictions.[106]

Like dual pricing, export duties can indirectly benefit the imposing country's downstream industries.[107] In *US – Export Restraints*, the DOC imposed countervailing duties on imports of downstream products

---

[102] OECD, "Export Restrictions in Raw Materials Trade: Facts, Fallacies and Better Practices," 2014, p. 12.

[103] Panel Report, *Argentina – Hides and Leather*, paras. 11.17, 11.22–11.55.

[104] Panel Reports, *China – Raw Materials*, para. 7.224.

[105] See Julia Ya Qin, "Reforming WTO Discipline on Export Duties: Sovereignty over Natural Resources, Economic Development and Environmental Protection," 46 *Journal of World Trade* 1147 (2012), pp. 1161–2, 1178–81, 1189.

[106] See Jane Korinek and Jessica Bartos, "Multilateralising Regionalism: Disciplines on Export Restrictions in Regional Trade Agreements," OECD Trade Policy Paper No. 139, 2012, pp. 24–30.

[107] World Trade Report, 2010, *supra* note 82, p. 188. See also, e.g., WT/ACC/RUS/70, WT/MIN(11)/2, *supra* note 81, para. 629.

which contained an input subjected to an export restraint. The United States argued that export restraints, including public charges on exports, amounted to government's entrustment of, or direction to, a private body to provide goods domestically, and hence a financial contribution. But the panel concluded that export restraints did not involve an "explicit and affirmative action of delegation or command" as implied by the concepts of entrustment or delegation, and that the mere effect of export restraints on the market did not differ from the effect of many other governmental (nonsubsidy) measures impacting on the marketplace.[108]

In a similar vein, the *EU – Biodiesel* ruling outlawed the use of the antidumping mechanism for offsetting cost advantages created by export restrictions. There, Argentina levied a higher tax on exports of soya beans and soybean oil (raw materials) than that on the exported biodiesel (the final product). The EU authorities investigating biodiesel imports determined that such taxation had effectively depressed the domestic prices of the raw materials to "an artificially low level" causing a downward pricing effect on biodiesel. Thus, in constructing the normal value of biodiesel due to such a "particular market situation," the EU authorities substituted the actual (low) input costs reflected in Argentine companies' records for adjusted (high) international reference prices. Such cost adjustment in the normal value inflated the dumping margin and the corresponding antidumping duty rate. The Appellate Body found the violation of Article 2.2 of the Antidumping Agreement under which the constructed normal value must include, inter alia, the production cost in the *country of origin*. It also invalidated the EU methodology under Article 2.2.1.1 of the Antidumping Agreement that requires that the costs be normally calculated on the basis of the investigated *exporter or producer's records* provided that those records, inter alia, "reasonably reflect" the relevant costs. Contrary to the EU view, the Appellate Body held that the phrase "reasonably reflect" implied the reasonableness (i.e., accuracy) of cost *records* rather than the costs as such.[109]

As for policy flexibilities, Articles XI:2(a) and XI:2(b) of the GATT exempt certain quantitative export restrictions from the Article XI:1 ban. Derogation under Article XI:2(a) is available to "[e]xport prohibitions or restrictions temporarily applied to prevent or relieve critical shortages of foodstuffs or other products essential to the exporting contracting party."

[108] Panel Report, *US – Export Restraints*, paras. 3.1, 8.20–8.22, 8.28–8.44.
[109] Appellate Body Report, *EU – Biodiesel*, paras. 5.2–5.10, 6.37, 6.56, 6.81–6.83. See also Shadikhodjaev, Ch. 2, *supra* note 35.

These are temporary measures addressing existing or imminent "critical" shortages, that is, those deficiencies of "foodstuffs or otherwise absolutely indispensable or necessary products" "that are crucial, that amount to a situation of decisive importance, or that reach a vitally important or decisive stage, or a turning point."[110]

Article XI:2(b) derogation extends to "[i]mport and export prohibitions or restrictions necessary to the application of standards or regulations for the classification, grading or marketing of commodities in international trade." In *Canada – Herring and Salmon*, Canada argued that its export prohibition on certain unprocessed fish was necessary for the marketing of high-quality processed fish abroad, but the GATT panel dismissed this claim. As the panel learned from the negotiating history, Article XI:2(b) was drafted to accommodate export restrictions aimed at "further[ing] the marketing of a commodity by spreading supplies of the restricted product over a longer period of time," but not "export restrictions on one commodity designed to promote [foreign] sales of another commodity."[111]

Moreover, the GATT general exceptions under Article XX may justify certain export restrictions, in particular those that are:

- "necessary to protect human, animal or plant life or health" (paragraph (b));
- imposed on gold or silver (paragraph (c));
- "relating to the conservation of exhaustible natural resources" and "made effective in conjunction with restrictions on domestic production or consumption" (paragraph (g));
- in pursuance of the obligations under a qualified "intergovernmental commodity agreement" (paragraph (h));
- imposed on "domestic materials necessary to ensure essential quantities of such materials to a domestic processing industry ... when the domestic price of such materials is held below the world price as part of a governmental stabilization plan" (paragraph (i));
- "essential to the acquisition or distribution of products in general or local short supply" (paragraph (j)).

Article XX was invoked in the WTO cases concerning Chinese export restrictions on certain natural resources widely used by the manufacturing industries. The panel in *China – Rare Earths* did recognize, under

---

[110] Appellate Body Reports, *China – Raw Materials*, paras. 324–7.
[111] GATT Panel Report, *Canada – Herring and Salmon*, para. 4.3.

Article XX(b), that the mining of rare earths, tungsten, and molybdenum was causing "grave harm" to the environment, life, and health inside the country. But China could not substantiate how its export duties on those products contributed to the protection from such damage and failed to explore other reasonably available alternatives, such as increased volume restrictions on the mining, higher resource taxes, or stricter pollution controls.[112] The defense faltered because of, inter alia, the very nature of the export duty to increase domestic demand for the restricted raw material to the detriment of the environment. According to an expert opinion of Gene Grossman cited by the panel, "a tax on exports of a good generates an increase in price in foreign markets, a fall in price in the home market, and an increase in domestic consumption" so that "the expansion of domestic sales that results from an export tax is an undesirable consequence for a policy designed to further environmental goals."[113]

Similarly, the panel in *China – Raw Materials* rejected China's defense under Article XX(g) for its export quotas and export duties on refractory-grade bauxite and fluorspar, the key inputs in the steel and aluminium production. The panel considered that a curb on extraction would better serve a conservation policy than export restrictions which could actually have a long-term adverse impact on the conservation due to the growing consumption by the downstream sector.[114] While the panel admitted that certain caps on domestic mining and production introduced during this litigation might help justify, in the future, the challenged measures under Article XX(g), for now, it said, China had failed to demonstrate that its export restrictions were made effective in conjunction with domestic production restrictions.[115]

3.3.3   Pass-Through of Upstream Subsidies[116]

Subsidies for upstream production may flow down to the downstream level when a subsidized input is used by a processed (finished) good. If the latter is exported, the importing government may countervail upstream subsidies, subject to the two-pronged pass-through principle. That is, where an input producer and a producer of the processed

---

[112] Panel Reports, *China – Rare Earths*, paras. 7.156, 7.171–7.187.   [113] *Ibid.*, para. 7.169.
[114] Panel Reports, *China – Raw Materials*, paras. 7.428, 7.430.   [115] *Ibid.*, para. 7.458.
[116] This section draws on Sherzod Shadikhodjaev, "How to Pass a Pass-Through Test: The Case of Input Subsidies," 15 *Journal of International Economic Law* 621 (2012).

product operate at arm's length, the investigating authority must establish (i) whether and (ii) to what extent the subsidy bestowed to the former has been passed through to the latter.[117]

WTO case law confirms the applicability of the national antisubsidy track to the pass-through of upstream subsidies under several provisions. In particular, Articles 10 (footnote 36) and 19.1 of the SCM Agreement and Article VI:3 of the GATT suggest that a countervailing duty can be imposed to offset "any subsidy bestowed directly or *indirectly* upon the manufacture, production or export of any merchandise," following "a final determination of the *existence* and *amount* of the subsidy" (emphasis added). Moreover, the prohibition on excess countervailing duties under Article 19.4 of the SCM Agreement would be meaningless for an upstream-subsidized finished product without a proper pass-through analysis.[118]

In addition, we believe that affected members can also invoke the multilateral track to challenge the pass-through of upstream subsidies. With respect to export subsidies, the pass-through issue may arise where an input producer obtains a subsidy from his government on condition that his input will be or has been used by downstream producers in making a product for export. As for local content subsidies, a subsidy for the production of some value-added inputs (e.g., leather), contingent upon the use of local raw materials (animal hides), may be claimed to pass through downstream (on the shoe-making industry).

As for actionable upstream subsidies under the multilateral track, the Appellate Body in US – Upland Cotton observed that while the countervailing pass-through analysis was "not critical" for the determination of a "significant price suppression" (i.e., a form of serious prejudice to a member's interests) under Article 6.3(c) of the SCM Agreement, it nevertheless acknowledged that a "subsidized product" mentioned in that provision had to be properly identified.[119] For the latter, it is necessary to clearly show that this product is indeed *subsidized*,[120] that is, that the input subsidy has flowed down to the processing industry, with no need to conduct a precise calculation of the benefit pass-

[117] Appellate Body Report, US – Softwood Lumber IV, paras. 141, 146.

[118] See ibid., paras. 140, 167(e); Panel Report, US – Softwood Lumber IV, para. 7.99; GATT Panel Report, US – Canadian Pork, para. 5.1.

[119] Appellate Body Report, US – Upland Cotton, para. 472.

[120] See Panel Report, US – Large Civil Aircraft (2nd complaint), paras. 7.282–7.286; Panel Report, EC and certain member States – Large Civil Aircraft, para. 7.197.

through.[121] Thus, for a serious prejudice claim, the pass-through principle is applicable only to the extent of the demonstration of the "whether" part, that is, the fact of the pass-through per se.

Although the panel in *US – Large Civil Aircraft (2nd complaint)* disagreed with the US argument that Article 1 of the SCM Agreement obligates the conduct of a pass-through analysis,[122] the "whether" element of such analysis is arguably derivable from Article 1.1(b) which reads "a benefit is thereby conferred." Indeed, this phrase does not preclude, on its face, *indirect* conferral of the benefit.

Since the concept of a "WTO-controlled" subsidy is comprised of a financial contribution (or income/price support), an associated benefit, and specificity, a pass-through determination must, in our view, cover all of these three components. The establishment of the financial contribution at the upstream level would already indicate its existence for the downstream producer.[123] But a determination of the benefit should be done twice, that is vis-à-vis both the direct and indirect recipients of the financial contribution.[124] So should be a specificity analysis.

A specificity determination for a subsidy's pass-through may disable counteractions against downstream products where upstream and downstream producers do not belong to the same sector as illustrated in two examples. As a first example, suppose country *A* provides a subsidy to all SMEs operating in all sectors. *A*'s big electronic companies purchase subsidized inputs of such SMEs, use them in the production of computers for export to country *B* where the computers are faced with *B*'s countervailing duties on the grounds of trade-distorting indirect subsidization. As a second example, suppose *A* subsidizes its steel industry whose products are widely used across all economic sectors, such as automobiles, shipbuilding, electronics, machinery, and so on. The products of one of such downstream industries are subject to *B*'s countervailing duties. In the first situation, the direct subsidy is not specific, as it does not target a specific enterprise or industry and is available to all enterprises falling within the category of SMEs, but it may be considered to be industry-specific at the downstream level benefiting the electronic sector.

---

[121] Appellate Body Report, *US – Upland Cotton*, para. 464; Panel Report, *US – Large Civil Aircraft (2nd complaint)*, para. 7.277.

[122] Panel Report, *US – Large Civil Aircraft (2nd complaint)*, para. 7.288.

[123] See also Panel Report, *US – Anti-Dumping and Countervailing Duties (China)*, para. 12.34.

[124] Appellate Body Report, *US – Softwood Lumber IV*, para. 143.

In the second situation, it is vice versa: the direct subsidy is industry-specific, while the indirect subsidy is not. But in either situation, counter-vailing duties are unlawful, as the subsidy in question is not specific at *both* upstream and downstream levels of production.

3.4   Concluding Remarks

The WTO sends a clear signal to its members not to subsidize in a trade-distortive manner. But the strict multilateral disciplines make it very difficult for governments to support local industries in a perfectly WTO-consistent way, as arguably most of the government support would be caught by the SCM Agreement in principle. As a practical matter, avoidance of localization, export promotion, and industrial targeting elements would minimize trade frictions in this field.

Another important point is that it is the subsidizing government itself that should evaluate the WTO-appropriateness and notifiability of its subsidy programs in the first place. For this purpose, it should operate a well-functioning self-screening mechanism based on a close collaboration of its trade officials, diplomats, lawyers, economists, academics/scholars, and businesses. In addition to reviews of internal measures, such mechanism should also cover regular monitoring and assessments of external factors, such as, for example, other members' reactions or feedback, foreign support policies, and antisubsidy actions. Since not all members have an effective screening system at home, the WTO should dedicate some of its meetings or workshops to an exchange of information and knowledge on such domestic procedures.

PART II

Special Topics of Industrial Policy

4

Free Zones and Industrial Development*

Special (or free) economic zones, free trade zones, export processing zones, enterprise zones, and other similar territorial schemes – commonly referred to in this chapter as "free zones" – have widely been utilized in many parts of the world. Examples include, inter alia, the Masan Free Trade Zone (Korea), the Shenzhen Special Economic Zone (China), the Bangalore Special Economic Zone (India), the Pomeranian Special Economic Zone (Poland), and the Navoi Free Economic Zone (Uzbekistan). Free zones are established to create a unique business environment within a designated site rather than on a nationwide basis with a view to achieving certain socioeconomic objectives. But governments pursuing such "zoning" or "localization" of industrial policies should take into account relevant multilateral customs and trade rules. After providing an overview of free zones, this chapter separately examines the relevant global customs and trade regimes to see if they can be applied in a mutually complementary manner as regards free zones. This is an important issue, as certain customs provisions admit the possibility of granting preferential duties or taxes to in-zone products, but these preferences may conflict with WTO law.

4.1 Free Zones as an Industrial Policy Tool

Notwithstanding a variety of types, most of the free zones are common in having a geographically delimited (usually fenced-in) area and single management and in providing incentives to qualifying companies. The prototypes of today's free zones – Gibraltar (1704), Singapore (1819), Hong Kong (1848), Hamburg (1888), and Copenhagen (1891) – were

---

* This chapter draws on, but substantially modifies and extends the author's article: Sherzod Shadikhodjaev, "International Regulation of Free Zones: An Analysis of Multilateral Customs and Trade Rules," 10 *World Trade Review* 189 (2011).

citywide zones located on international trade routes.[1] Modern free zones have globally proliferated since the establishment of the Shannon Free Zone in Ireland in 1959.[2] The number of free zones increased significantly from 79 in 25 countries in 1975 to around 3,500 zones in 130 countries in 2006.[3] Currently, most of the zones are concentrated in Asia and the Pacific, Latin America, Central and Eastern Europe, and Central Asia, with over 2,301 zones opened in 119 developing and transition economies.[4] The majority of in-zone companies are involved in labor-intensive and assembling activities in apparel, textiles, electrical, and electronic sectors, although their share in the world zone output gradually decreases.[5]

Free zones can be divided in six groups outlined in Table 4.1,[6] with the caveat that there may be differences in national systems as to the classification and definition of zones. "Free trade zones" are small, fenced-in, duty-free areas offering warehousing, storage, and distribution facilities for trade, transhipment, and reexport operations. "Export processing zones" are industrial sites working predominantly for exportation. While "traditional export processing zones" are open exclusively to export-oriented enterprises, "hybrid export processing zones" normally consist of a general zone open to all enterprises and a separate area reserved only for export-oriented enterprises. Unlike many Latin American countries, most Asian countries with such hybrid zones require those separate areas inside the zone to be fenced-in. "Free ports" typically occupy much larger areas and accommodate all types of activities, including tourism and retail sales, among other things, and allow people to reside. "Enterprise zones" are created mainly in developed countries like the United States, France, and the United Kingdom to revitalize underperforming urban or rural sites. Finally, "single-factory export processing zones" in, inter alia, Mauritius, Madagascar, Mexico, Costa Rica, the United States, and Sri Lanka support eligible individual enterprises regardless of their location.

---

[1] FIAS, "Special Economic Zones: Performance, Lessons Learned, and Implications for Zone Development," 2008, p. 9.

[2] Michael Engman, Osamu Onodera, and Enrico Pinali, "Export Processing Zones: Past and Future Role in Trade and Development," OECD Trade Policy Working Paper No. 53, 2007, p. 11.

[3] Jean-Pierre Singa Boyenge, "ILO Database on Export Processing Zones (Revised)," ILO Working Paper No. WP.251, 2007, p. 1.

[4] FIAS, *supra* note 1, p. 23.   [5] *Ibid.*, p. 25.

[6] This classification and definition of each category are based on FIAS, *supra* note 1, pp. 10–11.

Table 4.1 *Classification of Free Zones*

Type of Zone	Development Objective	Physical Configuration	Typical Location	Eligible Activities	Markets	Examples
Free Trade Zone (Commercial Free Zone)	Support trade	Size < 50 hectares	Ports of entry	Entrepôt and trade-related activities	Domestic, reexport	Colon Free Zone, Panama
Traditional Export Processing Zone	Export manufacturing	Size < 100 hectares; total area designated as an export processing zone	None	Manufacturing, other processing	Mostly export	Karachi Export Processing Zone, Pakistan
Hybrid Export Processing Zone	Export manufacturing	Size < 100 hectares; only part of the area designated as an export processing zone	None	Manufacturing, other processing	Export and domestic	Lat Krabang Industrial Estate, Thailand
Free Port	Integrated development	Size > 100 km^2	None	Multi-use	Domestic, internal and export	Aqaba Special Economic Zone, Jordan
Enterprise Zone, Empowerment, Urban Free Zones	Urban revitalization	Size < 50 hectares	Distressed urban or rural areas	Multi-use	Domestic	Empowerment Zone, Chicago
Single-Factory Export Processing Zone	Export manufacturing	Designation for individual enterprises	Countrywide	Manufacturing, other processing	Export	Mauritius, Mexico, Madagascar

Source: FIAS, "Special Economic Zones: Performance, Lessons Learned, and Implications for Zone Development," 2008, p. 10 (table 2), slightly modified by the author.

The role of free zones in economic development can be described in many ways.[7] First, they serve as "laboratories" for innovative regulatory approaches where the government first tests certain liberalization policies and then spreads successful policy elements across the entire country. For instance, the China (Shanghai) Pilot Free Trade Zone was launched in 2013 to experiment with a new FDI regulation method – eventually extendable to the rest of China – that permits, in principle, all foreign investment projects not covered by the pre-defined "negative" list of prohibitions and restrictions.[8] Second, many free zones promote and often diversify export manufacturing. For this purpose, countries may conduct liberal policies inside a zone, while keeping their protective barriers in outside areas. Third, free zones attract (foreign) investment with improved infrastructure, convenient access to overseas and local markets, a package of fiscal benefits, and a strengthened investment protection regime. Fourth, free zones create additional jobs in the zone and beyond. According to the International Labor Organization (ILO), the world level of employment in export processing zones in 2009 – sixty-six million jobs – was about 3.7 times higher than that in 1997.[9] Fifth, free zones may facilitate the transfer of technologies, know-how, and necessary skills from foreign enterprises operating in the zone to local enterprises and workers. Finally, free zones opened in a country's disadvantaged areas may contribute to more balanced regional development within that country.

Table 4.2 summarizes some key benefits and costs associated with free zones. A free zone can be said to be successful if benefits ultimately outweigh costs. With respect to economic performance, the Asian Development Bank's report (2015) states, for instance, that in 2007 free zones in China and Korea generated, respectively, 46 percent and 28 percent of FDI, 60 percent and 11 percent of exports, and over thirty million and thirteen thousand jobs. Malaysian zones in 2006 accounted for 72 percent of FDI, 83 percent of exports, and 5 percent of employment.[10] As for

---

[7] See Engman, Onodera, and Pinali, *supra* note 2, pp. 23–40.

[8] See Daqing Yao and John Whalley, "The China (Shanghai) Pilot Free Trade Zone: Background, Developments and Preliminary Assessment of Initial Impacts," 39 *The World Economy* 2 (2016); Zhongmei Wang, "Negative List in the SHPFTZ and Its Implications for China's Future FDI Legal System," 50 *Journal of World Trade* 117 (2016).

[9] ILO, "Good Practices in Labour Inspection in Export Processing Zones," 2012, p. 7.

[10] Asian Development Bank, "Asian Economic Integration Report 2015: How Can Special Economic Zones Catalyze Economic Development?," 2015, pp. 78–80.

Table 4.2 *Benefits and Costs of Free Zones for National Economies*

Benefits	Costs or Loss of Revenue

• Export growth
• FDI
• Foreign exchange
  earnings
• Employment
• Technology transfers
• Information exchange
  with companies
• Government revenue
	• Infrastructure investment
	• Administrative costs (setting up of separate
	  administrative arrangements)
	• Foregone tax revenue (tariffs, income tax, and
	  other taxes forgone)
	• Subsidies
	• Social and environmental costs (potential loss of
	  worker rights and protection afforded under
	  national laws and regulations and possible
	  degradation of the environment)

Source: Michael Engman, Osamu Onodera, and Enrico Pinali, "Export Processing Zones: Past and Future Role in Trade and Development," OECD Trade Policy Working Paper No. 53, 2007, p. 23 (table 3), citing "OECD Secretariat based on Madani (1999)."

examples of zone-level statistics, Wonsun Oh highlights impressive achievements of an export processing zone established in Korea's Masan city in the early 1970s. In particular, capital inflows into this zone increased from US$1.2 million in 1970 to US$88.9 million in 1975; the average investment per enterprise rose from US$238,700 in 1971 to US $1,871,100 in 1986. In 1970, there were only 4 firms there, but the number of firms sharply increased to 115 by 1973. In 1971–1991, exports from the Masan zone accounted for 2–4 percent of total Korean exports.[11]

Free zones raise a wide range of cross-border issues, such as trade, foreign investment, movement of capital and labor. Therefore, legal regulation of free zones extends to an international level. The remainder of this chapter examines multilateral rules on free zones, namely, the International Convention on the Simplification and Harmonization of Customs Procedures as amended (hereinafter the "Revised Kyoto Convention")[12] and WTO agreements.

---

[11] Wonsun Oh, "Export Processing Zones in the Republic of Korea: Economic Impact and Social Issues," ILO Working Paper No. 75, 1993, pp. 8–15.

[12] Done at Kyoto on 18 May 1973 and revised on 26 June 1999.

4.2   Free Zones under the Revised Kyoto Convention

The Revised Kyoto Convention concluded under the auspices of the World Customs Organization (WCO) deserves separate consideration, because it is, to our knowledge, the only multilateral treaty that contains specific provisions on free zones per se. This section starts with a brief introduction to this convention, followed by a review of relevant provisions.

4.2.1   Introduction to the Revised Kyoto Convention

The Revised Kyoto Convention represents a key international customs agreement governed by such important principles as, inter alia, transparency and predictability, standardization and simplification of customs documents, maximum use of IT, minimum necessary customs control, use of risk management and audit-based controls, and partnership with trade. This instrument entered into force on 3 February 2006 and had 110 contracting parties as of 15 May 2017.[13]

The convention consists of a Body, a General Annex, and Specific Annexes. The Body provides for definitions, the scope and structure of the convention, the administrative machinery, procedures of acceptance and amendment, dispute settlement, and so on. The General and Specific Annexes regulate customs administration issues. The General Annex is binding upon all parties, while Specific Annexes and chapters therein are optional.

Both the General and Specific Annexes set forth "standards" whose implementation is "recognized as necessary for the achievement of harmonization and simplification of Customs procedures and practices." Specific Annexes also contain "recommended practices" that are "recognized as constituting progress towards the harmonization and the simplification of Customs procedures and practices, the widest possible application of which is considered to be desirable." A party accepting a Specific Annex (or its chapter) is bound by all of its standards, but may make reservations to recommended practices. Each Annex is accompanied by nonbinding explanatory "guidelines."[14]

---

[13] WCO, "The Revised Kyoto Convention," www.wcoomd.org/en/topics/facilitation/instru ment-and-tools/conventions/pf_revised_kyoto_conv.aspx.

[14] See Articles 1, 4, and 12 of the Revised Kyoto Convention.

4.2.2 The Status of Free Zones

Chapter 2 of Specific Annex D of the Revised Kyoto Convention is dedicated to free zones. It defines "free zone" as "a part of the territory of a Contracting Party where any goods introduced are generally regarded, insofar as import duties and taxes are concerned, as being outside the Customs territory." This definition lets one distinguish two main characteristics of free zones: (i) free zones as an integral part of the national territory; and (ii) goods entering the zone as deemed, for the fiscal purposes, to be outside the customs territory, that is, "the territory in which the [party's] Customs law ... applies."[15] The word "generally" in the definition implies that some goods, such as, for example, machinery remaining permanently in the free zone, may not be considered outside the customs territory.[16] A number of countries (Korea,[17] India,[18] Panama,[19] etc.) go even further and exclude free zones per se (i.e., not just goods) from the scope of their customs territory.

Free zones possess three "extraterritorial" features. First, goods shipped from a free zone into the rest of the country's territory or vice versa are considered as if they were imported to or exported from the national customs territory respectively. Second, goods in free zones are normally subject to flexible customs control – measures applied by the customs authorities to ensure compliance with national customs law[20] – usually limited to general checks of goods only.[21] Third, goods entering free zones often enjoy exclusive tax and customs benefits not available in other parts of the country.

---

[15] Chapter 2, General Annex of the Revised Kyoto Convention.

[16] Guidelines on Section 2 ("Purpose and Scope"), Chapter 2, Specific Annex D of the Revised Kyoto Convention.

[17] Article 2.7 of the [Korean] Act on Designation and Management of Free Trade Zones (2004) defines the term "customs territory" as "a domestic area *other than a free trade zone*" (emphasis added).

[18] Paragraph 53 of the [Indian] Special Economic Zones Act (2005) states that "[a] Special Economic Zone shall, on and from the appointed day, be deemed to *be a territory outside the customs territory* of India for the purposes of undertaking the authorized operations" (emphasis added).

[19] WTO, TPRB – TPR – Report by the Secretariat – Panama – Revision, WT/TPR/S/186/Rev.1 (3 December 2007), p. 27.

[20] Chapter 2, General Annex of the Revised Kyoto Convention.

[21] Standard 4, Chapter 2, Specific Annex D of the Revised Kyoto Convention.

Whereas Chapter 2 of Specific Annex D constitutes the main basis for customs regulation of free zones, the relevant provisions of the General Annex are also applicable.[22] The latter include, inter alia, the rules on clearance and other customs formalities, duties, taxes, and customs control.[23] Chapter 2 in question lays down seventeen "standards" and four "recommended practices" grouped in the following categories.

4.2.2.1   Establishment and Control

National legislation must specify requirements for the establishment of free zones, admissible goods, and authorized operations, as well as customs control, including appropriate requirements for the suitability, construction, and layout of free zones. Customs authorities should be free to check the goods stored in the zone.[24]

4.2.2.2   Admission of Goods

Not only imported but also domestic goods must be authorized to be admitted to the free zone.[25] It is recommended that the rationales for restricting admission of imported goods be limited to public morality or order, public security, public hygiene or health, veterinary or phytosanitary considerations, and IPR protection.[26] Admissible goods entitled to duty/tax exemptions or refunds upon exportation must qualify for this immediately after they have been introduced into the zone.[27]

According to recommended practice 9, there should be no requirement for a goods declaration for goods introduced into the zone directly from abroad if the necessary information (e.g., commercial invoice) is already available in the documents accompanying the goods. But Korea, the United States, and Uganda made reservations, leaving their legislative requirement for import declarations for free zones unchanged,[28] perhaps in order to be able to track the goods that are processed in the zone and later admitted into the home market.

---

[22] Standard 1, Chapter 2, Specific Annex D of the Revised Kyoto Convention.
[23] Guidelines on Standard 1, Chapter 2, Specific Annex D of the Revised Kyoto Convention.
[24] Standards 2–4, Chapter 2, Specific Annex D of the Revised Kyoto Convention.
[25] Standard 5, Chapter 2, Specific Annex D of the Revised Kyoto Convention.
[26] Recommended practice 6, Chapter 2, Specific Annex D of the Revised Kyoto Convention.
[27] Standard 7, Chapter 2, Specific Annex D of the Revised Kyoto Convention.
[28] See Notifications to the WCO by Korea (PG0035E1, 31 March 2003), the United States (PG0117E, 19 January 2006), and Uganda (PG0029E1, 24 September 2002).

4.2.2.3   Security

Customs authorities usually require from declarants to provide a security that he/she discharges any obligations in regard to a customs procedure, such as the payment of duties and taxes. Recommended practice 10, however, states that no security (e.g., cash deposit or surety) should be required for the admission of goods to the zone.

4.2.2.4   Authorized Operations

Operations for preservation of goods (e.g., breaking bulk, grouping of packages, sorting, grading, and repacking) must be allowed. Rules on processing or manufacturing operations (if any) must be specified.[29]

4.2.2.5   Goods Consumed within Free Zones

National legislation must define requirements and circumstances in which goods to be consumed inside the zone may be admitted free of duties and taxes.[30] According to the guidelines, such free admission may apply to quite a broad range of goods, including, inter alia, catalysts and accelerators used in the industrial processing, goods consumed by people working inside the zone (office stores, fuel, food, and beverages), and construction materials.

4.2.2.6   Duration of Stay

Duration of the stay of goods in the zone must be defined only in exceptional circumstances.[31] The guidelines suggest that the "exceptional circumstances" may relate to time limits imposed on production or processing with due account of the nature of goods, their shelf life, or health and safety considerations.

4.2.2.7   Transfer of Ownership

The transfer of ownership of goods admitted to the zone must be allowed.[32] At the same time, the guidelines admit that retail sales within free zones may be prohibited, because such sales can be treated as a clearance for home use.

---

[29] Standards 11–12, Chapter 2, Specific Annex D of the Revised Kyoto Convention.
[30] Standard 13, Chapter 2, Specific Annex D of the Revised Kyoto Convention.
[31] Standard 14, Chapter 2, Specific Annex D of the Revised Kyoto Convention.
[32] Standard 15, Chapter 2, Specific Annex D of the Revised Kyoto Convention.

4.2.2.8   Removal of Goods

Goods admitted to or produced in the zone must be permitted to be removed to another free zone or placed under an applicable customs procedure. The only declaration required for goods on removal from a free zone must be the goods declaration normally required for the customs procedure to which those goods are assigned.[33] In the event of sending goods directly abroad, the customs should not require more information than already available on the documents accompanying the goods.[34]

4.2.2.9   Assessment of Duties and Taxes

National legislation must specify the point in time for the purpose of determining the value and quantity of goods that may be taken into home use on removal from the zone, as well as the rates of the customs duties and taxes applicable to them.[35] The guidelines indicate that, between the time when the goods were admitted into the zone and the time when they are placed on the domestic market, changes may occur in tariff/tax rates and the value or quantity of goods.

The required statutory provision on the timing for the determinations concerned – whether the time of entry into the zone or the time of delivery from the zone – is necessary to avoid uncertainties in customs and tax administration, which could otherwise lead to biased practices to the detriment of free zone enterprises. Moreover, the legislation must specify the rules for determining the amount of the customs duties and taxes chargeable on goods taken into home use after processing or manufacturing in the zone.[36]

4.2.2.10   Closure of Free Zones

In case of the zone's closure, producers must be given sufficient time to remove their goods to another free zone or to place them under a customs procedure concerned.[37] The guidelines say that such time is needed for arrangement for transport, for completing procedural formalities on obtaining permits, or paying duties and taxes if applicable.

---

[33] Standards 16–17, Chapter 2, Specific Annex D of the Revised Kyoto Convention.
[34] Recommended practice 18, Chapter 2, Specific Annex D of the Revised Kyoto Convention.
[35] Standard 19, Chapter 2, Specific Annex D of the Revised Kyoto Convention.
[36] Standard 20, Chapter 2, Specific Annex D of the Revised Kyoto Convention.
[37] Standard 21, Chapter 2, Specific Annex D of the Revised Kyoto Convention.

4.3   Free Zones under WTO Rules

Free zones are not mentioned in the text of multilateral trade agreements, but this does not mean their immunity from trade disciplines. Indeed, WTO law is legally binding[38] and applies, unless otherwise specified,[39] to the whole territory of each member, including free zones.[40] Moreover, many accession instruments explicitly recognize the WTO-applicability to free zones.[41] At least thirty-three acceded members undertook thirty-four specific commitments on free zones under which particular members (or a member):[42]

. confirm that free zones and special economic areas are fully subject to specific obligations in the Accession Protocols;
. clarify that normal customs formalities, tariffs, and taxes are applied when goods produced in, or imported into, the free zones under the special tax and tariff regimes of those zones enter the rest of the acceding governments' economy;
. accept the obligation to identify, list, and make precise those specific WTO agreements for which acceding governments would ensure enforcement and compliance of their WTO obligations in free zones and special economic areas;

---

[38] See Articles II:2 and XVI:4 of the WTO Agreement.
[39] Article XII:1 of the WTO Agreement provides for WTO accession by any State or eligible separate customs territory "on terms to be agreed between it and the WTO." Thus, if an applicant government wishes to exclude some part(s) of its territory from the WTO regulatory scope, it may negotiate such an exemption clause with WTO members. In addition, in the pre-WTO period some countries invoked Article XXVI:5 of the GATT to specify the territorial scope of acceptance of this agreement. Accession protocols of, for example, Japan, Portugal, and Spain contained special statements concerning territorial application of the GATT. In 1979, the United Kingdom accepted six of the Tokyo Round agreements on behalf of the territories for which it had international responsibility except for Antigua, Bermuda, Brunei, Cayman Islands, Montserrat, St. Kitts-Nevis, Sovereign Base Areas Cyprus, and the British Virgin Islands. For these and other relevant instances, see GATT Analytical Index, Ch. 1, *supra* note 73, pp. 917–23.
[40] The WTO applicability to free zones was recognized in a number of accession documents. See, e.g., WT/L/432, Ch. 2, *supra* note 33, Part I, para. 2(A)1; WTO, Working Party on the Accession of Ukraine – Report of the Working Party on the Accession of Ukraine to the WTO, WT/ACC/UKR/152 (25 January 2008), para. 84.
[41] See WTO, Technical Note on the Accession Process – Note by the Secretariat – Revision, WT/ACC/7/Rev.2 (1 November 2000), pp. 120–2.
[42] Chiedu Osakwe, "Contributions and Lessons from WTO Accessions: The Present and Future of the Rules-based Multilateral Trading System," in Uri Dadush and Chiedu Osakwe (eds.), *WTO Accessions and Trade Multilateralism: Case Studies and Lessons from the WTO at Twenty* (Cambridge: Cambridge University Press, 2015), pp. 270–1.

- accept the obligation to update and report to the WTO on the actual status of their relevant legislation on free zones and special economic areas to ensure compatibility of domestic laws with WTO principles and disciplines;
- accept the specific commitment to list and notify WTO-inconsistent requirements (such as export performance, trade balancing, or local content requirements) that shall be banned in the free zones and special economic areas of the acceding governments;
- accept the obligation for the nondiscrimination principle and its application to preferential arrangements provided to foreign-invested enterprises within the special economic areas;
- accept the obligation to notify the WTO with statistics on trade between the special economic areas and the other parts of the customs territory on a regular basis.

Due to the broad scope of trade law, we will focus only on those rules which have most frequently been discussed in connection with free zone policies as reflected in WTO documents. As a first reference in this regard, accession instruments of new members typically state:

> The representative of [X] stated that [X] would administer free zones or special economic areas established in its territory in compliance with WTO provisions, including those addressing subsidies, TRIMs and TRIPS, and that goods produced within the zones under tax and tariff provisions that exempt imports and imported inputs from tariffs and certain taxes would be subject to normal customs formalities when entering the rest of [X], including the application of tariffs and any taxes and charges.[43]

This passage lets us identify the issues, such as nondiscrimination covering "normal customs formalities," subsidies, TRIMs, and TRIPS. Additionally, there is a need to look into the question as to whether free zones are notifiable, as it was an issue in some WTO discussions. Our analysis below will consider these matters in separate sections, followed by the relevant WTO case-law part.

Most of the WTO discussions have concerned not free zones per se, but incentives offered therein. Commonly used incentives comprise:[44]

---

[43] Peter John Williams, *A Handbook on Accession to the WTO* (Cambridge: Cambridge University Press, 2008), p. 100.

[44] Engman, Onodera, and Pinali, *supra* note 2, p. 17.

- *Enhanced physical infrastructure*, such as enhanced access to transport and logistical networks, telecommunications networks and utility services, residential housing, and services institutions;
- *Streamlined administrative services*, such as "single window" or "one-stop" government services, fast track customs services, simplified licensing procedures, and so on;
- *Fiscal incentives*, such as:
  - Duty drawbacks or exemptions from import duties on raw material, intermediate inputs, and capital goods used in the production of goods and supply of services and various exemptions of customs fees and charges;
  - Exemptions from the payment of sales tax on exported products or services, as well as on all goods and services domestically purchased and used in the production;
  - Tax holidays, rebates, or reduced tax rates on corporate income or profits, often linked to the export performance of companies or to the share of exports in total production;
  - Indirect subsidies (e.g., special grants for education and training) and direct subsidies (e.g., the supply of water and electricity below market rates);
- *Relaxed legal and regulatory requirements* on, for example, foreign ownership, labor, environment, foreign exchange, and the lease or purchase of land;
- *Export promotion services*, including business advisory services, sales and marketing support, finance and export credit services.

4.3.1 Notification

As has been seen, accession documents may reflect members' notification commitments on free zones. As for common requirements, the Ministerial Decision on Notification Procedures (1994) annexed to the Final Act Embodying the Results of the Uruguay Round of Multilateral Trade Negotiations provides an indicative list of notifiable measures, including free zones. Section I of the Ministerial Decision states that the introduction or modification of national trade measures is subject to the notification requirements of the Understanding Regarding Notification, Consultation, Dispute Settlement and Surveillance adopted on 28 November 1979 (BISD 26S/210). The Understanding in question calls for an *ex ante* notification of measures wherever possible or, failing that, a prompt *ex post facto* notification. Such notification is required for the sake of transparency and is "without prejudice to views on the consistency of measures with or their relevance to rights and obligations under [WTO agreements]."[45]

In addition, various WTO agreements have their own notification clauses. For example, Article 25.2 of the SCM Agreement mandates notification of specific subsidies. Some members refused to notify free zone subsidies alleging their nonspecificity.[46] While the Ministerial Decision above qualifies free zones as a notifiable measure, it only "affirms" members' commitment to notification obligations under the multilateral/plurilateral trade agreements, whereas the annexed indicative list "does not alter existing notification requirements" in those agreements.[47]

Accordingly, the more specific notification provisions envisaged in the WTO agreements prevail over the corresponding provisions of the Ministerial Decision. It follows that free zone subsidies must be notified only if they meet the specificity standards of Article 2 of the SCM Agreement, albeit with one important caveat. The mere statement about nonspecificity will not always be sufficient to justify a subsidizing member's refusal to notify, as any other member may request explanation for such non-notification or counternotify an allegedly specific subsidy on its own.[48]

4.3.2 Nondiscrimination

Given that free zones typically offer *exclusive* incentives, the legal regime inside and outside of zones naturally differs, which may lead to allegations of discrimination. Therefore, one may raise the issues of "horizontal" and "parallel" application of the MFN and national treatment provisions in relation to free zones.

Suppose that a WTO member in Figure 4.1 provides a tariff and tax exemption to product X that enters its free zone from a foreign country, while imposing a tariff/tax of 10 percent on like product Y imported to the rest of its territory from a different country. Suppose also that the tax exemption applies to like domestic product Z if it is moved into the free zone. In this situation, a question may arise as to whether those benefits within the zone must be extended horizontally to the rest of the member's territory. In particular, can it be said that the principles of

---

[45] Section I of the Ministerial Decision on Notification Procedures.
[46] See Sections 3.2.6, 4.3.3.2.
[47] Section I and footnote 1 of the Ministerial Decision on Notification Procedures.
[48] Articles 25.8–25.10 of the SCM Agreement.

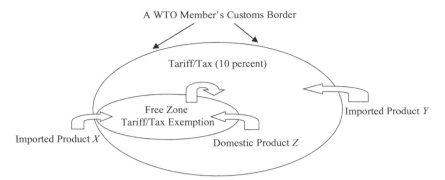

Figure 4.1   Diagram of Fiscal Benefits in Free Zone
Source: Drawn by the author.

MFN (*X* vs. *Y*) and national treatment (*Z* vs. *Y*) are breached here? One would be tempted to point to de facto discrimination if the given member's trade with many countries occurs beyond the zone, with the goods from those countries (or "outsiders") not enjoying zone benefits as a matter of practice. We believe that, given the absence of a clear-cut authoritative interpretation on this point, a commentator's answer to the question above will depend on the evidence he/she relies upon in each concrete case.

For those who answer in the affirmative and thus endorse the concept of "horizontal" application, main proof may be the fact that in our scenario WTO law does not, in principle, split the nondiscrimination rules over a member's territory. This is evident especially from the accession documents that confirm that WTO agreements and protocol commitments will be applied *uniformly* throughout the respective members' territories, including free zones, with domestic (enforcement) procedures and remedies being available in case of any nonuniform application.[49] The underlying purpose of the uniformity clause is arguably to ensure that WTO disciplines including MFN and national treatment are observed consistently by all levels of government and in all parts of the territory of members. The advocates of horizontal application might further claim that territorial fragmentation of such an important

---

[49] For an overview of individual commitments on the uniform application, see Williams, *supra* note 43, pp. 68–9.

pillar as nondiscrimination would endanger the rules-based multilateral trading system and provoke circumvention practices. They could also refer to the *Colombia – Textiles* case in which the panel determined, under the *chapeau* of Article XX of the GATT, that Colombia's exclusion of products entering its free zones from import restrictions applicable to the rest of its territory constituted "discrimination."[50]

In contrast, opponents could insist on the WTO-wide tacit acknowledgement of the *exclusive* nature of free zone preferences. Instead, they would rather support the "parallel" application of nondiscrimination by which the government concerned should accord equal treatment within and out of the zone, with no need for these "inside" and "outside" treatments to be the same. Thus, the concept of parallel application would have the internal and external components as discussed below.

With respect to the internal component, free zone incentives must equally benefit all enterprises meeting even-handed eligibility criteria. In many cases, foreign investors participate in free zones as a *locally incorporated* wholly owned enterprise or joint venture, which can minimize the risk of mistreatment of foreign investors to the favor of domestic counterparts. However, if access to a free zone or benefits therein is limited to investors from specific countries alone or otherwise subject to differential conditions based on the investor's nationality, "less favored" countries may question WTO-compatibility of these limitations. Interestingly, "in response to concerns raised by some members of the [accession] Working Party," China confirmed that "any preferential arrangements provided to foreign invested enterprises located within the special economic areas would be provided on a non-discriminatory basis."[51] While the records are silent on the substance of the "concerns," the Chinese commitment would certainly fall within the MFN rule.

As for the external component, if product X in Figure 4.1 is placed onto the domestic market either as such or as part of a final product, the duties, taxes, and other similar charges, from which it was initially exempted, must apply.[52] In other words, in-zone fiscal incentives must

---

[50] See Section 4.3.6.1.
[51] WTO, Ministerial Conference – Fourth Session – Doha, 9–13 November 2001 – Report of the Working Party on the Accession of China, WT/MIN(01)/3 (10 November 2001), para. 228.
[52] See, e.g., *ibid.*, para. 225; WTO, Working Party on the Accession of the Former Yugoslav Republic of Macedonia – Report of the Working Party on the Accession of the Former Yugoslav Republic of Macedonia, WT/ACC/807/27 (26 September 2002), para. 165; WT/ACC/VNM/48, Ch. 2, *supra* note 33, para. 339; WTO, Working Party on the Accession of

stop applying once the product concerned has been removed for home use. Such a parallel application of nondiscrimination is not only of interest to other WTO members, but also the host country itself. Indeed, should goods produced in free zones be taken into home use with no duties and taxes paid, they can harm the competing local companies. Thus, the external component is an important "insurance policy" protecting the interests of outsiders – both foreign and domestic businesses out of the zone.

At the same time, the mere existence of the normative requirement concerning the external (and internal) component would not always be sufficient. For example, the WTO Secretariat's TPR report on Kyrgyzstan (2007) reflects the fact, confirmed by the local authorities, that despite the existence of this requirement in Kyrgyz legislation, some of the free zones in that country have become "black holes" for tax evasion – "sale of imported fuel domestically, through [free economic zones], by a well-connected trading group without payment of excise tax."[53] In the pre-WTO period, similar practice in other countries alarmed some GATT contracting parties as well.[54] This clearly shows how proper enforcement of WTO obligations – in addition to their implementation – is important at a domestic level.

Whereas the arguments in support of horizontal application are not entirely groundless, it is, however, obvious that free zones would be deprived of their key merit of being an exclusive area if *all* incentives therein were extended to the rest of the WTO member's territory. Some of the incentives (e.g., border tax adjustments (BTAs) and duty drawbacks) could perfectly be applied across the country, but others would be restricted to free zones alone to make them more investment-attractive than the remaining home localities. Although many governments offer zone-specific preferences, they should not rule out a possibility that adversely affected WTO members – especially those whose companies operate out of the zone – may complain about nonhorizontal incentives.

Armenia – Report of the Working Party on the Accession of the Republic of Armenia, WT/ACC/ARM/23 (26 November 2002), para. 150.

[53] WTO, TPRB – TPR – Report by the Secretariat – Kyrgyz Republic – Revision, WT/TPR/S/170/Rev.1 (12 January 2007), pp. 68–9.

[54] For instance, in the course of Panama's accession to the GATT, the United States raised a question about "extensive unreported 'leakage' of products from the Colon Free Zone into the Panamanian customs territory without customs processing or taxation." GATT, Accession of Panama: Questions and Replies to the Memorandum on Foreign Trade Regime (L/7228), L/7426 (30 March 1994), p. 115.

To reduce the risk of discrimination-related challenges of outsiders, the host governments should at least guarantee parallel application of MFN and national treatment, providing all eligible companies with fair access to their zones and revoking fiscal incentives for products removed from their zones for the home market use.

4.3.3   SCM Agreement

4.3.3.1   "Subsidy"

The SCM Agreement lets one identify certain nonsubsidy measures that could be used in free zones without fear of antisubsidy actions. In particular, "general infrastructure" under Article 1.1(a)(1)(iii) does not constitute a financial contribution, hence a subsidy. The panel in *EC and certain member States – Large Civil Aircraft* noted various dictionary definitions of "infrastructure," such as, inter alia, "installations and services (power stations, sewers, roads, housing, etc.) regarded as the economic foundation of a country." It determined that "general infrastructure" is "available to all or nearly all entities," rather than "a single entity or limited group of entities." This issue requires a case-by-case assessment, so no infrastructure (including such well-known public goods as railroads or electricity distribution systems) is "inherently 'general' *per se*":[55]

> Take as an extreme example a 2 kilometer stretch of railway from a mine to a mineral processing plant, used for transporting raw ore for processing, on land owned by the mining company. It seems clear to us that the provision by a government of such a railway cannot properly be considered "general infrastructure" simply because it is a railway.[56]

Many free zones are deliberately established near (air)ports, railways, or highways so as to facilitate transportation of zone-related goods. A government's provision of these or other infrastructural facilities does not qualify as a subsidy if access thereto is not limited to free zones alone but is open to a sufficiently wide spectrum of users.

As the Appellate Body in *Canada – Renewable Energy / Canada – Feed-In Tariff Program* suggested that a government's support for an infant industry did not necessarily amount to a subsidy,[57] incubation

---

[55] Panel Report, *EC and certain member States – Large Civil Aircraft*, paras. 7.1036, 7.1039.
[56] *Ibid.*, n. 3870 to para. 7.1039.   [57] See Section 6.3.1.

of a country's new industries within free zones would likely escape the WTO's subsidy control.

Further, Article 14 of the SCM Agreement enumerates the cases where a financial contribution is deemed to confer a benefit. In essence, governmental loans, loan guarantees, and other specified measures that are offered on noncommercial terms are considered as conferring benefits. In contrast, any market-based support, including that in a free zone, does not provide a countervailable benefit.

In addition, free zones can also fully utilize BTAs and duty drawbacks that, pursuant to footnote 1 to Article 1 of the SCM Agreement, are not considered a subsidy:

> In accordance with the provisions of Article XVI of GATT 1994 (Note to Article XVI) and the provisions of Annexes I through III of this Agreement, the exemption of an exported product from duties or taxes borne by the like product when destined for domestic consumption, or the remission of such duties or taxes in amounts not in excess of those which have accrued, shall not be deemed to be a subsidy.

The "duties" in this passage are customs duties. The word "taxes" associated with products comprises only indirect taxes (e.g., excise tax, value-added tax (VAT), etc.) as opposed to direct taxes (e.g., taxes on wages and corporate income, etc.), which are not tied to products as such.[58] One GATT report referred to the opinion of most delegations to explain the differentiation between the two sets of taxes as follows:

> [I]ndirect taxes by their very nature bear on internal consumption and [are] consequently levied, according to the principle of destination, in the country of consumption, while direct taxes – even assuming that they [are] partly passed on into prices – [are] borne by entrepreneurs' profits or personal income.[59]

The aforementioned footnote 1 covers, in particular, imported or domestic inputs that are used in the production of a product for export. The eligible inputs are "inputs physically incorporated, energy, fuels and oil used in the production process and catalysts which are consumed in the course of their use to obtain the exported product."[60] Therefore,

---

[58] Appellate Body Report, *US – FSC*, para. 93.

[59] GATT, Report of the Working Party on Border Tax Adjustments, L/3464, adopted 2 December 1970, para. 21. But the Working Party also noted the lack of agreement on the extent of the pass-through of indirect/direct taxes to the product's price due to the "difficulty" and "a very complex nature" of this issue (para. 22).

[60] Footnote 61 to Annex II of the SCM Agreement.

tariff/tax preferences granted to *capital goods* (e.g., equipment), which are not listed as eligible inputs, can be considered as a subsidy within the meaning of the SCM Agreement.[61] Not surprisingly, under Article 27.4 of the SCM Agreement, Costa Rica asked for the extension of the transition period for export subsidies within its free zone and inward processing regimes, including, inter alia, exemption from any taxes or fees on imports of machinery and equipment used in the production of goods for export.[62] In the same vein, an EU countervailing duty investigation on polyethylene terephthalate from Iran, Pakistan, and the UAE determined that duty-free imports of capital goods to Iranian and UAE free zones did not fall within a permissible duty drawback scheme.[63]

To ensure that BTAs and drawback schemes do not circumvent the subsidy disciplines, Annexes II and III of the SCM Agreement authorize investigators to check whether an exporting country has an efficient system of verifying the use and amount of inputs. As an example from a national practice, the aforementioned EU investigation found some duty drawbacks in an Iranian petrochemical special economic zone to be a specific (export) subsidy due to certain operational "discrepancies and malfunctions," notably the absence of "a proper verification system to monitor the amount of duty-free imported raw materials consumed in the production of the resultant export product."[64] But the panel in *EU – PET (Pakistan)* held that the per se absence of such a system did not allow the importing country to countervail the entire, rather than excess, amount of duty (or tax) remissions.[65]

4.3.3.2   "Specificity"

In free zones that are open only to particular industries,[66] subsidies are industry-specific within the meaning of the SCM Agreement. But in

---

[61] See Raúl A. Torres, "Free Zones and the World Trade Organization Agreement on Subsidies and Countervailing Measures," 5 *Global Trade and Customs Journal* 217 (2007), p. 221.

[62] See WTO, Committee on SCM – Subsidies – Requests Pursuant to Article 27.4 of the SCM Agreement – Requests Pursuant to the Procedure in Document G/SCM/39 – Costa Rica, G/SCM/N/74/CRI (20 December 2001).

[63] Commission Regulation (EU) No. 473/2010 of 31 May 2010 Imposing a Provisional Countervailing Duty on Imports of Certain Polyethylene Terephthalate Originating in Iran, Pakistan, and the United Arab Emirates, OJ L 134/25 (1 June 2010), paras. 20, 29–37, 184, 194.

[64] *Ibid.*, paras. 29–37.   [65] Panel Report, *EU – PET (Pakistan)*, paras. 7.57–7.60.

[66] For example, Iran's Petrochemical Special Economic Zone, the UAE's Dubai Auto Free Zone, International Media Production Free Zone, and Dubai Flower Center Free Zone as

other zones, specificity of subsidies may not always be that obvious. In the past, Korea, for instance, believed that special treatment within its free trade zones was not a notifiable "subsidy specifically provided to an enterprise or industry or group of enterprises or industries."[67] Similarly, Panama refused to notify incentives in its export processing zones, because they were "not aimed at any product in particular or any specific industry."[68] The EC, however, disagreed with Panama and stated that even on the premise that there was no export performance requirement in the export processing zones, the subsidy was, in fact, available only to companies that were located in a certain region (zone).[69] We assume that Panama ultimately gave in and notified its subsidies concerned, because Panama's export processing zones were subsequently included in the list of programs that were granted transition period extensions under Article 27.4 of the SCM Agreement.[70] Korea also seems to have changed its mind, because it notified zone incentives later on.[71]

Many free zone subsidies would be regionally specific under Article 2.2 of the SCM Agreement in being "limited to certain enterprises located within a designated geographical region within the jurisdiction of the granting authority." Pursuant to the appellate interpretation in *US – Washing Machines*, the term "geographical region" here does not depend on the territorial size of the area covered by a subsidy. This means that, as with that case, a subsidy available to even 98 percent (i.e., almost all) of the territory under the granting authority's jurisdiction is considered regionally specific.[72]

As it follows from Article 2.2, if the central or regional/local governments confine subsidies to free zones only, while not extending them to the outside territories *under their respective jurisdictions*, these subsidies

---

investigated in Commission Regulation (EU) No. 473/2010 of 31 May 2010, *supra* note 63, paras. 22–3, 32, 190.

[67] WTO, TPRB – TPR – Report by the Secretariat – Republic of Korea – Revision, WT/TPR/S/204/Rev.1 (4 December 2008), p. 41, para. 22.

[68] WTO, Committee on SCM – Subsidies – Replies to Questions Posed by the EC Regarding the New and Full Notification of Panama – Revision, G/SCM/Q2/PAN/6/Rev.1 (13 April 1999), p. 2.

[69] WTO, Committee on SCM – Minutes of the Special Meeting Held on 4 May 1999, G/SCM/M/21 (21 September 1999), para. 39.

[70] See Section 4.3.3.3.

[71] WTO, Committee on SCM – Subsidies – New and Full Notification Pursuant to Article XVI:1 of the GATT 1994 and Article 25 of the A[...]Countervailing Measures – Korea, G/SCM/N/220/KOR (23 September 2011), section V.A.

[72] Appellate Body Report, *US – Washing Machines*, paras. 5.234, 5.236.

will have regional specificity. For example, a US countervailing duty investigation on coated free sheet paper from China found tax refunds for zone-located companies to be a regionally specific subsidy:

> [E]nterprises located in the Economic Development Zone of Hainan may enjoy several tax preferences ... Under "Preferential Policies Regarding Investment by Manufacturer," high-tech or labor intensive enterprises with investment over RMB 3 billion and more than 1000 local employees may be refunded 25 percent of the VAT paid on domestic sales (the percentage of the tax received by the local government) starting in the first year the company has production and sales. The VAT refund can continue for five years.
>
> One of [the target company]'s cross-owned companies was a qualifying manufacturing enterprise in the Economic Development Zone of Hainan and reported that it received the VAT refund in the [period of investigation]. This company added that because the capital and number of employees are registered with the local government, the tax refund is automatically granted.
>
> We determine that the domestic VAT refund confers a countervailable subsidy. The refund is a financial contribution in the form of revenue forgone by the local government and it provides a benefit to the recipient in the amount of the refunded taxes ... We further determine that the program is limited to enterprises located in a designated geographical region and, hence, is specific ...[73]

Should, however, a free zone be the sole territorial unit (e.g., a whole city as a free zone) within the jurisdiction of the granting authority (e.g., the city administration), the incentives enjoyed by all eligible companies in that zone would not be deemed geographically specific. In the aforementioned US investigation, the Chinese company under consideration claimed that the tax preference was not specific, as it was administered by the Yangpu *local* government in China and was available to "any high tech or labor-intensive industry in Yangpu" that had met certain requirements for investment and employment. But the petitioner rebutted the claim, saying that the tax benefit was part of the *central* government's program for free zones. The US authority sided with the petitioner.[74]

---

[73] US DOC, Decision Memorandum (17 October 2007), Final Determination in the Countervailing Duty Investigation of Coated Free Sheet from the People's Republic of China [C-570–907], 72 FR 60645, 25 October 2007. See part G "Domestic VAT Refunds for Companies Located in the Hainan Economic Development Zone."

[74] *Ibid.* See "Comment 16: Specificity of VAT Programs."

In countries, such as the United States and the Dominican Republic, where free zone status is granted to companies rather than territorial areas,[75] the regional specificity test may not work. But for such company-based designations of zones, enterprise or industry specificity could still be pertinent.

4.3.3.3   Prohibited Subsidies

Government support for export manufacturing or localization in free zones may conflict with Article 3 of the SCM Agreement that prohibits export subsidies and local content subsidies. Annex I of the SCM Agreement delegitimizes any export-related exemption, remission, or deferral of direct taxes or social welfare charges, as well as certain export-related deductions of the taxable base for direct taxes (paragraphs (e) and (f)). In contrast, nonexcess exemptions and remissions of import duties or indirect taxes are allowed for inputs used in making exported products. The SCM Agreement also permits, to a certain extent, substitution drawback systems under which domestic inputs are used as a substitute for imported inputs.[76]

In order to avoid possible attacks in the WTO, the most practical approach would be to exclude the export performance or local content conditions from subsidization. Before accession, Kazakhstan, for instance, removed the eligibility criteria of export orientation and import substitution from its legislation on free zones.[77] When Viet Nam entered the WTO, it promised that enterprises in its export processing zones would no longer be required to export their production, and "would only be entitled to incentives in the form, inter alia, of facilitation of procedures with respect to investment and rental of land and premises; and facilitation in the supply and training of labour and supply of water, power and other utilities."[78]

Developing countries listed in Annex VII of the SCM Agreement are exempt from the WTO prohibition on export subsidies, while other developing countries had an eight-year transition period (i.e., until 31 December 2002) extendable under Article 27.4. In accordance with the General Council's decision (2007), the SCM Committee continuously extended that transition period until the end of 2013, and the final two-

---

[75] Torres, *supra* note 61, p. 218. See also Section 4.1.
[76] See Annexes I(i) and III of the SCM Agreement.
[77] WT/ACC/KAZ/93, Ch. 3, *supra* note 95, paras. 920–1.
[78] WT/ACC/VNM/48, Ch. 2, *supra* note 33, para. 285.

year phase-out period expired on 31 December 2015.[79] The beneficiaries of the last extension were nineteen members, of which eleven requested extensions for free zone programs.[80] As for local content subsidies, the related transition periods under the SCM Agreement have already expired. But acceding countries may still negotiate tailor-made transition periods for prohibited subsidies.

4.3.4   TRIMs Agreement

WTO disciplines prohibit TRIMs – localization requirements, trade balancing requirements, foreign exchange limitations, and export restrictions – that violate Articles III and XI of the GATT on national treatment and the general ban against quantitative restrictions.[81] Because many free zones are created mainly with a view to attracting investment, they may contribute to easing at least some restrictive TRIMs. For instance, a government conducting a tight foreign exchange policy can decide to remove its currency restrictions for free zone companies. By contrast, it may wish to apply localization measures in free zones, which is incompatible with, inter alia, the TRIMs Agreement. Thus, during the accession talks, the Former Yugoslav Republic of Macedonia pledged not to provide local content incentives to enterprises working in its special economic zones.[82]

The TRIMs Agreement set out extendable S&D transition periods for notified illegal TRIMs: seven years for LDCs and five for developing countries.[83] The transition periods under the subsidy and TRIMs disciplines for, respectively, local content subsidies and local content TRIMs do not coincide, even though they target essentially the same localization policy. In particular, a requirement on local content "compliance with which is necessary to obtain an advantage"[84] can be granted an extended grace period under the TRIMs Agreement, subject to certain conditions. But if the same measure qualifies as a local content subsidy, it is not

---

[79] WTO, General Council – Article 27.4 of the SCM Agreement – Decision of 27 July 2007, WT/L/691 (31 July 2007). See also WT/COMTD/W/219, Ch. 1, *supra* note 112, pp. 63–4.

[80] Nineteen members are Antigua and Barbuda, Barbados, Belize, Costa Rica, Dominica, Dominican Republic, El Salvador, Fiji, Grenada, Guatemala, Jamaica, Jordan, Mauritius, Panama, Papua New Guinea, St. Lucia, St. Kitts and Nevis, St. Vincent and the Grenadines, and Uruguay. See G/SCM/W/546/Rev.7, Ch. 3, *supra* note 65, Annex I.

[81] Article 2.1 of the TRIMs Agreement.   [82] WT/ACC/807/27, *supra* note 52, para. 154.

[83] Articles 5.1, 5.2, and 5.3 of the TRIMs Agreement. See also Section 5.4.2.

[84] Paragraph 1 (*chapeau*) of the Annex of the TRIMs Agreement.

tolerated under the SCM Agreement any longer. It should, however, be recalled that S&D treatment for TRIMs creates a temporary exemption from GATT Articles III and XI only, but not from the subsidy rules.[85]

The S&D provisions of the TRIMs Agreement do not seem to have widely been invoked in the context of free zones, as only few countries notified their unlawful free zone TRIMs to which transition periods were applicable.[86] This may suggest that many WTO members have been reluctant either to use prohibited TRIMs in free zones or to notify them to the WTO.

4.3.5   TRIPS Agreement

The TRIPS Agreement provides for the protection of IPRs with regard to international trade, elaborating on basic principles, IPR standards, domestic enforcement, WTO dispute settlement, and special transitional arrangements. To our knowledge, no serious TRIPS claims have, so far, been raised in connection with free zones, although newly acceded members have usually made a generic TRIPS commitment as mentioned earlier.

Because free zones are part of a national territory, they are not exempt from the TRIPS rules. Therefore, the local authorities must, inter alia, block any attempt to use their free zones as areas for transshipping counterfeit or pirated goods to the domestic or foreign market.

4.3.6   WTO Litigation Practice

The following subsections discuss WTO disputes that have dealt with two sets of measures affecting free zones: special (or favorable) treatment of goods produced in or imported to domestic zones and restrictions on imports from foreign zones.

---

[85] See also Section 5.3.2.

[86] We could find only two instances of such notifications. See WTO, Committee on TRIMs – Notification under Article 5.1 of the Agreement on TRIMs – Dominican Republic, G/TRIMS/N/1/DOM/1 (10 May 1995); WTO, Committee on TRIMs – Notification under Article 5.1 of the Agreement on TRIMs – Thailand, G/TRIMS/N/1/THA/1 (28 April 1995). For the list of TRIMs notifications, see WTO, Report (2008) of the Committee on TRIMs, G/L/860 (29 October 2008), Annex 1.

4.3.6.1   Special Treatment of Goods in Domestic Free Zones

In a consultation request in *Brazil – Taxation*, the EU complained about discriminatory tax advantages given to goods produced in Brazilian free trade zones – "Zona Franca de Manaus" (the Manaus Free Trade Zone) and "Áreas de Livre Comércio." Brazil allegedly provided certain tax exemptions only to the goods manufactured in such zones and sold to the rest of Brazil, but not to imported goods, including those stored in those zones, marketed in other parts of Brazil's territory. In the EU's view, this was a violation of Article III:2 of the GATT, "since the same tax benefits [did] not apply to the importation and sale of imported goods in Brazil, whether or not they transit[ted] through a Free Trade Zone." The EU also claimed that certain "operations involving goods produced in [those zones] [were] subject to a lower tax burden than the tax burden applicable in the case of other goods, including all imported goods sold in Brazil."[87]

But in the panel proceedings, the EU specifically challenged free zone treatment in relation to the mandatory minimum level of R&D investments under the so-called Informatics program on tax incentives in the IT sector. For accreditation under that program, companies had to invest annually in R&D activities in Brazil a certain percentage of their domestic sales. But the value of their purchases of, inter alia, products manufactured in the Manaus Free Trade Zone was deducted from such sales. Thus, the higher a company's purchases were of those (and other incentivized domestic) products, the less it had to invest in R&D. The panel concluded that the Informatics program was inconsistent with Article III:4 of the GATT for promoting purchases of local products to the detriment of the imported like products.[88] At the time of writing, the panel report was under appeal.

In another dispute, *Colombia – Textiles*, the panel found that the compound tariff on textiles, apparel, and footwear exceeding the binding level violated Article II of the GATT. Colombia countered, however, that its compound tariff fought against "illicit trade" – money laundering via importation at "artificially low prices." But it failed to prove, under Articles XX(a) and XX(d) of the GATT, that this

---

[87] WTO, *Brazil – Certain Measures Concerning Taxation and Charges* – Request for Consultations by the EU, WT/DS472/1, G/L/1061, G/SCM/D100/1, G/TRIMS/D/39 (8 January 2014), pp. 4–5.

[88] Panel Reports, *Brazil – Taxation*, paras. 7.231–7.243.

measure was "necessary" to protect public morals and to secure compliance with its criminal law.[89]

As for the compliance with the *chapeau* of Article XX, the panel noted that the compound tariff did not apply to goods entering Colombia's Special Customs Regime Zones unless those goods were introduced into the rest of its customs territory. Colombia explained that the zones in question represented "border zones with very low levels of development, or in a situation of isolation or economic integration with another state, which need to be managed differently from the rest of the national customs territory."[90] But in the analysis not reviewed by the Appellate Body, the panel concluded that such an inconsistent application of the compound tariff throughout its territory failed to meet the *chapeau* requirements, constituting "a means of arbitrary or unjustifiable discrimination" and "a disguised restriction on international trade":[91]

> The above-mentioned exclusion [of the Special Customs Regime Zones] establishes a difference in treatment between products entering the Special Customs Regime Zones and products entering the rest of the Colombian customs territory. Therefore, there is discrimination in the application of the measure.
>
> Colombia tries to justify this discrimination by pointing out that imports into these zones are for local consumption, because they are border zones with a population living in conditions of extreme poverty, and that the goods would not be marketed in the rest of the national territory. However, Colombia has not shown that imports of textiles, apparel and footwear that enter these zones, and are consumed inside the zone, cannot be used for money laundering, nor that they pose a lower risk of being used for money laundering. Even if there is a different risk, Colombia has not explained what other measures it is taking in these zones to reduce the incentives for imports to be used for money laundering.
>
> Taking into account the arguments and the evidence available, the Panel does not consider that Colombia has shown that the discrimination resulting from the application of the compound tariff, with respect to the exemption of goods entering Special Customs Regime Zones, bears any relation to the pursuit of the declared objective of combating money laundering. As a matter of fact, Colombia has not shown that imports into Special Customs Regime Zones cannot be used for money laundering

---

[89] Panel Report, *Colombia – Textiles*, paras. 7.189, 7.471, 7.536–7.537; Appellate Body Report, *Colombia – Textiles*, paras. 5.117, 5.147–5.150.

[90] Panel Report, *Colombia – Textiles*, para. 7.576.

[91] *Ibid.*, paras. 7.577–7.580 (footnotes omitted). See also Appellate Body Report, *Colombia – Textiles*, para. 5.153.

in accordance with the methodologies that Colombia has described. Consequently, in view of the stated objective of the measure, Colombia has not demonstrated that the discrimination in the application of the compound tariff, with respect to the exemption of goods entering Special Customs Regime Zones, is justified.

Both of these cases are common in pertaining to the nondiscrimination issue discussed earlier. The EU consultation request in the first case concerns parallel nondiscrimination, as Brazil's out-of-zone treatment of zone-produced goods was allegedly better than that of foreign goods. The second case underscores the relevance of the concept of horizontal nondiscrimination, albeit in the context of the *chapeau* of Article XX.

4.3.6.2   Restrictions on Imports from Foreign Free Zones

In *Colombia – Ports of Entry*, textiles, apparel, and footwear from Panama and Panama's Colon Free Zone (CFZ) were allowed to enter Colombia only at two ports – Bogota airport and Barranquilla seaport – despite the existence of eleven ports for textile and apparel imports out of twenty-six ports of entry for international trade. This case was handled at the panel level without proceeding to the appellate stage.

The panel determined that limited access to the Colombian ports constituted a prohibited quantitative restriction on imports in the sense of Article XI:1 of the GATT.[92] However, Colombia argued, under Article XX(d) of the GATT, that its measure was necessary to counteract under-invoicing, customs fraud, smuggling, money laundering, and drug trafficking.[93] In particular, Colombia pointed to weak enforcement mechanisms in the CFZ:

> The CFZ is the world's second largest free zone after Hong Kong, and serves as an originating or transshipment point for some goods purchased with narcotics proceeds (mainly dollars obtained in the United States) through the Colombian Black Market Peso Exchange ... The CFZ has limited resources to conduct supervisory programs and monitor for illegal activities, with a legal staff of approximately five people who, among other things, oversee efforts to detect money laundering, trans-shipment, goods smuggling, counterfeit products and intellectual property rights violations.[94]

Recognizing that combating illicit activities at issue was indeed of particular importance to Colombia, the panel, nevertheless, faulted

---

[92] Panel Report, *Colombia – Ports of Entry*, paras. 7.209–7.275.
[93] *Ibid.*, paras. 7.483–7.492.   [94] *Ibid.*, n. 892 to para. 7.554.

Colombia for the lack of evidence showing how the ports-of-entry restriction contributed to its goals without causing a significant negative impact on legitimate trade. On this basis, the panel concluded that Colombia did not establish that the measure at issue was necessary to ensure compliance with national customs laws and regulations.[95]

This case has certain implications on both sides of trade involving free zones. For importing WTO members, it shows that even restrictions imposed on goods from other members' free zones are subject to WTO rules. Although no one in this case contested the existence of Colombia's right to take protective measures in relation to imports from the CFZ, the way this right was exercised gave rise to the dispute. The size of a foreign zone and trade involved certainly impacts on government's decision whether or not to restrict related imports. As the largest free zone in the Americas and the second largest free zone in the world,[96] the CFZ may indeed have posed some threat to producers in Colombia, which is the biggest export destination of CFZ goods.[97] In addition, over 80 percent of Panamanian imports to Colombia arrived from the CFZ[98] – another important fact that explains why CFZ goods were of particular concern to Colombia. As for the coverage of subject goods, money laundering, smuggling, and other similar practices associated with the CFZ may have occurred in relation to a wider range of products, but the Colombian government chose to target textiles, apparel, and footwear goods which constitute an "important national industry in Colombia."[99]

For countries that export from free zones, the panel's decision suggests that benefits available under the WTO umbrella are as applicable to their free zones as to the rest of their territories, irrespective of the legal status of the zones under national legislation. The fact that free zones, including the CFZ, are not regarded as part of Panama's customs territory[100] did not prevent the panel from ruling against Colombia's restrictions on the CFZ exports.[101] It follows that if a free zone under a member's jurisdiction is not explicitly excluded from the WTO's regulatory domain, this

[95] *Ibid.*, paras. 7.482–7.620.
[96] *Ibid.*, n. 892 to para. 7.554; Wikipedia, "Colón Free Trade Zone," http://en.wikipedia.org/wiki/Col%C3%B3n_Free_Trade_Zone.
[97] Wikipedia, *supra* note 96.
[98] Panel Report, *Colombia – Ports of Entry*, n. 978 to para. 7.592.   [99] *Ibid.*, para. 2.14.
[100] WT/TPR/S/186/Rev.1, *supra* note 19, p. 27.
[101] While "extraterritoriality" of the CFZ was not the issue before the panel, we doubt that even if Colombia had raised this issue, the panel would have ruled otherwise.

enables this zone to fully enjoy WTO benefits, including, inter alia, MFN-based market access concessions enforceable through the DSU procedures.

Conversely, exactly the same fact allows the importing country to invoke exception clauses, such as, for example, Articles XX and XXI of the GATT, in relation to foreign free zones. In this regard, the panel under Article XX(d) acknowledged the importance to Colombia of the battle against CFZ-related illicit activities:

> The Panel recalls its earlier conclusions that the fight against under-invoicing and smuggling is an important interest in consideration of the particular conditions faced by Colombia. The Panel is satisfied that problems with under-invoicing and contraband occur *in connection with the CFZ, which falls within Panama's jurisdiction.*[102] (emphasis added)

The full applicability of WTO benefits to free zones, as inferred from this case, stands, however, in contrast to limitations maintained by certain RTAs on intrabloc trade in free zone goods. Most "restrictive" RTAs do not extent preferential treatment to goods enjoying duty draw-backs in an exporting country's customs territory/free zones or specifically to goods imported from free zones.[103] This stems from the fact that, as with Panama, free zones can be deemed to be outside of a customs territory to which an RTA may explicitly confine regional trade preferences. The restrictions on free zones are aimed at, inter alia, preventing free riding on RTA preferences by non-RTA countries whose products (raw materials, inputs, etc.) already benefit from duty-free access to RTA signatories' free zones. Whereas RTAs are by definition bilateral or regional arrangements with a very limited membership, the WTO is a nearly universal organization where MFN benefits are enjoyed by the largest part of the global trading community. This explains why the free-riding effect tied to free zones has been of more concern to RTAs than to the WTO.

---

[102] Panel Report, *Colombia – Ports of Entry*, para. 7.612.

[103] For an overview of the treatment of free zones under RTAs, see, e.g., Jaime Granados, "Export Processing Zones and Other Special Regimes in the Context of Multilateral and Regional Trade Negotiations," Occasional Paper No. 20, Inter-American Development Bank, 2003, pp. 5–10; Engman, Onodera, and Pinali, *supra* note 2, pp. 50–1. See also Sherzod Shadikhodjaev, "Duty Drawback and Regional Trade Agreements: Foes or Friends?," 16 *Journal of International Economic Law* 587 (2013).

4.4   Customs and Trade Rules: Some Questions of Concurrent Application

In the preceding parts, we separately examined multilateral customs and trade disciplines concerning free zones. The Revised Kyoto Convention of the WCO and trade agreements of the WTO are independent legal regimes dealing with the specific subject matters. Nevertheless, they are interconnected in at least two ways. First, the Revised Kyoto Convention may be consulted for the purposes of WTO affairs including, inter alia, interpretation of certain customs terminology. For instance, in *China – Auto Parts*, the WCO Secretariat advised the panel on clarification of some issues regarding the HS and relating to the Revised Kyoto Convention.[104] Second, as of 15 May 2017, 102 out of 110 contracting parties to the Revised Kyoto Convention were members of the WTO,[105] and these numbers will increase with the passage of time. Such overlapping membership requires that the countries concerned honor their obligations under both legal systems.

Given such a linkage between two regimes, a question arises as to whether they may be applied concurrently with no discrepancies in their implementation. With respect to free zones, we do not see any visible conflict between them. On the contrary, the Revised Kyoto Convention complements global trade rules by setting forth some specific customs standards and procedures for free zones that are not detailed in current WTO law.

Even the "extraterritorial" features of free zones under the Revised Kyoto Convention do not seem to be in an apparent conflict with WTO agreements. We recall that the term "free zone" is defined in the text of the convention as "*a part of the territory* of a Contracting Party" where imported goods are "*generally* regarded, *insofar as import duties and taxes are concerned*, as being *outside the Customs territory* " (emphasis added). The italicized words indicate full jurisdiction of countries over their free zones and, together with other provisions,[106] admit the possibility of using customs or tax preferences for the goods in the zone.

---

[104] See WTO, *China – Measures Affecting Imports of Automobile Parts* – Reports of the Panel – Annexes B, C, D and E – Addendum, WT/DS339/R/Add.2, WT/DS340/R/Add.2, WT/DS342/R/Add.2 (18 July 2008), Annexes C-3 and C-4.

[105] The lists of WTO members and signatories to the Revised Kyoto Convention are available at www.wto.org and www.wcoomd.org, respectively.

[106] For example, as considered in Section 4.2.2.5, standard 13 provides that "[n]ational legislation shall enumerate the cases in which goods to be consumed inside the free zone may be admitted free of duties and taxes and shall lay down the requirements which must be met."

However, the mere fact that the Revised Kyoto Convention recognizes such possibility should not be read as suggesting absolute freedom of WTO members in this field. As the convention is silent on how the governments should grant incentives, countries with overlapping membership must do so in a WTO-compliant fashion. To conclude, nothing in the multilateral customs and trade rules prevents the governments from applying them in a mutually complementary manner in relation to free zones.

4.5   Concluding Remarks

The optional application of provisions of the Revised Kyoto Convention on free zones coupled with the possibility of making reservations to recommended practices provides quite a flexible regulatory framework for operation of such zones. Although the convention is binding on its contracting parties to the extent of accepted obligations, nonparty countries may still use the convention as a source of reference for designing or improving their legislation on free zones.

In contrast to the Revised Kyoto Convention, WTO agreements extend beyond the customs issues and are more rigid and comprehensive in regulating free zones, with virtually no room left for reservations.[107] The fact that none of the WTO agreements specifically deals with free zones per se simply means that they treat free zones as part of a member's territorial jurisdiction and hence remain fully applicable there.

Thus, the WTO dispute settlement procedures have been invoked to raise some free-zone-related issues. The WTO's accession, monitoring, and discussion mechanisms have been utilized more actively to keep free zones under multilateral control. Last but not least, WTO-based domestic trade procedures like countervailing duty investigations provide another route to address foreign free zone measures.

---

[107] See Article XVI:5 of the WTO Agreement.

5

Local Content Requirements and Industrialization

In spite of stringent GATT/WTO restrictions, local content requirements (LCRs) have remained, and will likely continue to be, in wide use. It is not surprising. LCRs are politically attractive, as they can have immediate import-substitutive and job-creative effects even at no, or at insignificant, cost to the government. They tend to flourish in time of economic recessions when internal pressures for protectionism are particularly high. In this chapter, we first explain some global trends concerning localization policies and briefly discuss the economics of LCRs. Then we examine the relevant WTO provisions on national treatment, subsidies, and government procurement, covering both merchandise and services trade. With the advancement of digital technologies and the spread of public sentiments on information security and privacy in cyberspace, several countries these days have recourse to the so-called data localization measures that are considered at the end of this analysis.

5.1   LCRs and World Practice

National authorities use LCRs with a view to creating jobs at home, promoting local firms, nurturing infant industries, or diversifying the economy as a whole. Typical examples include requirements for purchasing domestic inputs (goods and/or services) in the production chain, subsidies conditional on the use of local content, obligations of service suppliers to use local infrastructure, and price preferences to domestic bidders in public procurement. In addition, forced localization of data storage and processing is becoming a "trendy" LCR in the digital age.

According to a WTO–UNCTAD joint study (2002), LCRs and other trade-restrictive investment measures in the past applied to the automotive sector most extensively. In particular, Canada established a local content scheme in the 1920s providing tariff reductions on auto parts to manufacturers using at least 50 percent of inputs from the Canadian sources, with that threshold being increased to 60 percent in 1936.

Australia introduced its foreign investment policy in the mid-1930s aimed at production of motor vehicles with substantial local content. During the 1950–1960s, Argentina, Brazil, and Chile prescribed localization rates varying from 60 percent to 95 percent for commercial vehicles, passenger cars, trucks, and other finished vehicles. In the 1970–1980s, a common regional import substitution policy of the Andean Pact countries allocated production of specific cars across the region and operated LCRs. In the same time frame, Indonesia maintained lists of parts and components to be sourced domestically. In the mid-1990s, China adopted an industrial policy obligating carmakers to increase domestic content from 40 percent in the first year of production to 80 percent by the third year. In addition, the automotive LCR "club" included, at different times, the United Kingdom, Ireland, New Zealand, Korea, India, Malaysia, Thailand, Mexico, South Africa, and so on.[1]

LCRs are politically appealing because of their effect of creating immediate employment in targeted sectors and channelling in-country business opportunities to domestic firms. During economic difficulties, governments may resort to LCRs even more frequently than ever. Susan Stone, James Messent, and Dorothee Flaig identified 146 localization measures implemented by about 40 economies between 2008 and 1 April 2014 as a response to the financial crisis of 2008. This study finds that big economies – those with a large gross domestic product (GDP) and population – used most of the surveyed LCRs, apparently in the belief that their market was attractive enough for inducing firms to change their production methods toward boosting a local industry. Whereas input measures were adopted mainly by low-income countries generally for the industrial development reasons, most of the data localization measures were concentrated within the high-income group probably because of the greater role of the services sector there. The LCR-imposing countries in the database in question collectively accounted for nearly 52 percent of world exports, which rebuts a common perception that localization policies are typical of closed economies.[2]

Localization policies have restrictive impacts on international trade. According to Gary Clyde Hufbauer et al., LCRs affected nearly US$928

---

[1] This paragraph summarizes WTO, Council for Trade in Goods – TRIMs and Other Performance Requirements – Joint Study by the WTO and UNCTAD Secretariats – Part II – Addendum, G/C/W/307/Add.1 (8 February 2002), paras. 5–25.

[2] Susan Stone, James Messent, and Dorothee Flaig, "Emerging Policy Issues: Localisation Barriers to Trade," OECD Trade Policy Paper No. 180, 2015, pp. 14–16.

billion of global trade in goods and services in 2010, or almost 5 percent of the US$18.5 trillion of total global trade. They estimate that LCRs may have reduced world trade by as much as US$93 billion a year.[3]

Despite the widespread proliferation of LCRs, relevant WTO bodies can scrutinize them, as a rule, only on request, which is why some of the existing LCRs may well be off the WTO's radar. Taking discussions in the Committee on TRIMs as an illustrative example, we explain some dynamics on how LCRs are dealt with in WTO meetings.

Between 1995 and 2015, the Committee on TRIMs discussed thirty-four local content measures of sixteen WTO members, breaking down as follows: six measures (by Indonesia), four (by Brazil, China, and India each), three (by Russia), two (by Korea, Nigeria, and the United States each), and one (by Argentina, Colombia, Colombia/Ecuador/Venezuela, Malaysia, Turkey, Ukraine, and Uruguay each). Only seven (or 21 percent) of these measures were challenged in the WTO dispute settlement procedures.[4]

Figure 5.1 shows the trend of addressing LCRs in the Committee on TRIMs since 1995. Some passivism in the first several years may partly be attributed to members' entitlement to the transition periods for illegal TRIMs, including LCRs. The period of 2010–2015 witnessed high frequency of LCRs appearing on the agenda, with many of them being discussed in several meetings over multiple years. This is perhaps due to protectionism provoked by the 2008 global financial crisis and its consequences.

As is evident from Figure 5.2, the localization measures targeted various sectors, led by energy, automobiles, combination of various sectors, and ICT/telecom. It is remarkable that renewables were affected by six (or 67 percent) of nine energy-related LCRs.

As for "justification" of the LCRs covered by the agenda of the Committee on TRIMs, some members stated that the measures were necessary to improve international competitiveness and technological capacity of domestic (input) industries or to support SMEs.[5] Four measures were said to be part of government procurement in the sense of

---

[3] Gary Clyde Hufbauer et al., *Local Content Requirements: A Global Problem* (Washington, DC: Peterson Institute for International Economics, 2013), pp. 37–8.

[4] See Annex 5.1 of this chapter.

[5] WTO, Committee on TRIMs – Minutes of the Meeting Held on 30 September and 1 November 1996, G/TRIMS/M/5 (27 November 1996), para. 24; WTO, Committee on TRIMs – Minutes of the Special Meeting Held on 1 October 2012 – Note by the Secretariat, G/TRIMS/M/33 (22 November 2012), para. 22; WTO, Committee on

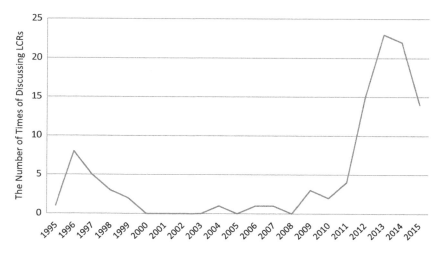

Figure 5.1   Frequency of Discussing LCRs in the Committee on TRIMs (1995–2015)
Source: Drawn by the author on the basis of information in Annex 5.1 of this chapter.
Note: When a particular LCR was discussed in, for example, two meetings in the same year, the number of discussing times for that LCR was two (i.e., discussed twice) in that year

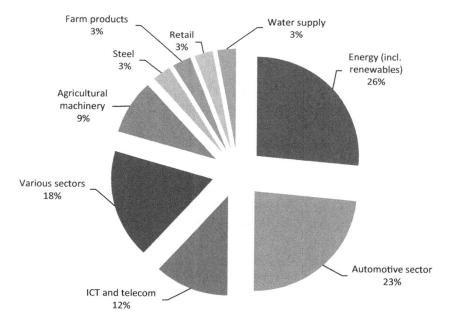

Figure 5.2   LCR-Affected Sectors in Discussions of the Committee on TRIMs (1995–2015)
Source: Drawn by the author on the basis of information in Annex 5.1 of this chapter.
Note: "Various sectors" refers to several sectors affected by a single LCR.

Article III:8(a) of the GATT.[6] One member linked its LCRs for wind power equipment to the UN climate change regime.[7]

5.2   Review of the Economic Literature

The work (1981) of Gene Grossman is generally considered as the first fundamental economic research in the field of local content policies. This analysis uses a partial equilibrium model to assess LCRs' impacts on the resource reallocation in perfectly competitive markets, assuming that a domestic downstream producer can purchase inputs of both domestic and foreign origin, but domestic inputs are more expensive due to low technological capability. The author concludes that LCRs may not succeed in achieving policy-makers' goal to increase the domestic value added in a multi-staged industry. Although LCRs increase the output of the domestic upstream producers, they decrease the demand and production at the downstream level, as higher prices of domestic inputs pass through to the prices of the related final goods. Which of these effects prevails depends on the sensitivity of the input production to changes in the output price, and of the final good production to changes in the input's price.[8]

With respect to oligopolistic markets, Kala Krishna and Motoshige Itoh find that the effects of LCR schemes depend on the form of protection, the degree of substitution between inputs, and on whether an input's demand increases or falls when the other input's price rises. They conclude that LCRs lower or raise profits of domestic producers of intermediate goods if the inputs are, respectively, a complement or substitute for the foreign goods.[9]

Carl Davidson, Steven Matusz, and Mordechai Kreinin consider the case where a local firm competes with a subsidiary of a foreign investor in

---

TRIMs – Minutes of the Meeting Held on 8 October 2014, G/TRIMS/M/37 (21 November 2014), para. 56.

[6] WTO, Committee on TRIMs – Minutes of the Meeting Held on 16 April 2015, G/TRIMS/M/38 (27 July 2015), para. 55; G/TRIMS/M/33, *supra* note 5, para. 41; WTO, Committee on TRIMs – Minutes of the Meeting Held on 4 October 2013, G/TRIMS/M/35 (20 December 2013), para. 36; WTO, Committee on TRIMs – Minutes of the Meeting Held on 4 October 2013, G/TRIMS/M/35 (20 December 2013), para. 98.

[7] G/TRIMS/M/35, *supra* note 6, para. 107.

[8] Gene M. Grossman, "The Theory of Domestic Content Protection and Content Preference," 96 *Quarterly Journal of Economics* 583 (1981).

[9] Kala Krishna and Motoshige Itoh, "Content Protection and Oligopolistic Interactions," 55 *Review of Economic Studies* 107 (1988).

a duopolistic market of final goods. The authors argue that foreign investment performance standards, including LCRs, cut the investing country's welfare because of the transfer of monopoly rents from a foreign to domestic firm, and that they reduce the host country's welfare due to a decline in consumer surplus that outweighs the increase in the monopoly rent. Although the minimum content standard may positively impact on employment in the host country to some point, marginal increases in the content requirement can, in fact, reduce employment because of decline in FDI.[10] Martin Richardson adds that certain LCRs can increase foreign profits at the cost of domestic producers in the case of a duopoly where a domestic producer of final goods can use only local inputs. In particular, the price hikes for local inputs, resulting from LCR-caused rising demand, increase the price of domestic final goods. This consequently reduces demand, and the domestic production contracts. The foreign producer, unlike domestic competitors, can still rely on cheaper foreign inputs and make higher profits.[11]

Susan Stone, James Messent, and Dorothee Flaig conclude that LCR-imposing countries experience an increasing concentration of domestic activity in a few targeted sectors and a fall in exports in non-LCR-affected sectors, which undermines potential growth and innovation on a broader scale.[12]

On the other hand, some analyses point to certain positive aspects of localization measures for home economies. Theodore Moran takes the view that LCRs could compensate for market distortions and increase the imposing country's economic welfare when foreign subsidiaries producing final goods exercise monopolistic power to drive down domestic input prices causing reduction of domestic output.[13] Considering the case of inputs as imperfect substitutes in the industry with monopolistic characteristics, Michael Mussa argues that LCRs avoid "the excess consumption distortion loss generated by a tariff on imported inputs or a subsidy on domestic inputs." Therefore, such content protection measures constitute a second best policy for increasing the ratio of domestic

---

[10] Carl Davidson, Steven J. Matusz, and Mordechai E. Kreinin, "Analysis of Performance Standards for Direct Foreign Investments," 18 *Canadian Journal of Economics* 876 (1985).

[11] Martin Richardson, "The Effects of a Content Requirement on a Foreign Duopsonist," 31 *Journal of International Economics* 143 (1991).

[12] Stone, Messent, and Flaig, *supra* note 2, p. 2.

[13] Theodore H. Moran, "The Impact of TRIMs on Trade and Development," 1 *Transnational Corporations* 55 (1992).

input to imported input.[14] In addition, Kazutaka Takechi and Kazuharu Kiyono recognize that while local content protection has no price effect in a small country, LCRs can make large countries better off when they lower the price of foreign intermediate goods.[15]

Some recent studies suggest that the presence of certain factors – like learning-by-doing effects, technological transfer, economies of scale, and technological spillovers – could bring benefits that would mitigate some negative effects of LCRs. But there is no clear evidence that shows that these benefits override the negative effects.[16] Moreover, sector-specific analyses on, for example, renewable energy, automotive, and hydrocarbon industries generally conclude that, while LCR policies may achieve certain short-term objectives, they undermine industrial competitiveness in the long run.[17]

To sum up, there is no unanimous agreement about the cumulative effect of localization policies. While LCRs can indeed generate some gains to the domestic input industry, it is not certain whether those gains can outweigh the LCR-associated losses to domestic final good producers and consumers. Yet, the economic literature generally tends to maintain a negative attitude toward LCRs.

Gary Clyde Hufbauer et al., as well as Susan Stone, James Messent, and Dorothee Flaig suggest various alternatives to better promote domestic industries and employment – the key policy rationales for LCRs. First of all, governments should undertake fiscal, administrative, and other necessary reforms to improve a business climate at home. This may be inferred from the fact that around 60–70 percent of LCRs imposed during 2008–2014 were implemented by countries with comparatively low rankings in terms of ease of doing business.[18] Next, the improvement of logistics cuts trade costs, makes local companies more competitive abroad, and creates in-country jobs. Further, an increase in infrastructural investment effectively responds to unemployment and boosts

---

[14] Michael Mussa, "The Economics of Content Protection," NBER Working Paper No. 1457, 1984.

[15] Kazutaka Takechi and Kazuharu Kiyono, "Local Content Protection: Specific-Factor Model for Intermediate Goods Production and Market Segmentation," 15 *Japan and the World Economy* 69 (2003).

[16] For a brief overview of the literature on factors mitigating the LCR harm, see Stone, Messent, and Flaig, *supra* note 2, pp. 19–20.

[17] Stone, Messent, and Flaig, *supra* note 2, p. 12; See also country- and industry-specific case studies in Hufbauer et al., *supra* note 3, pp. 41–150.

[18] Stone, Messent, and Flaig, *supra* note 2, p. 17.

domestic production. As for trade-specific measures, tariffs or subsidies are preferable to LCRs because of more visible costs and simple and transparent administration.[19]

5.3   The Scope of the WTO-Applicability to LCRs

Public measures mandating, by law or in practice, compliance with trade-affecting LCRs fall within the scope of WTO law. But governments may also impose LCRs by asking firms to "voluntarily" use local content. This section considers the extent to which the WTO rule book covers such private undertakings. Because LCRs can be subjected to several WTO provisions at once, we also discuss the issue of overlapping application.

5.3.1   Private Actions on LCRs

LCRs can be operationalized through certain arrangements between the government and manufacturers. In the process of negotiations with the government, producers (investors) can agree to commit themselves to using local content in order to gain governmental approval for their activities or enjoy certain (non)fiscal benefits.

In *Canada – FIRA*, the Canadian legislation provided for the *possibility* of written "undertakings" by foreign investors to purchase local products. Submission of such purchase undertakings was not mandatory, but it could secure the authorities' positive decision on a proposed investment project. The acceptance of such undertakings created compulsory legal conditions for investors.[20] Similarly, a "Memorandum of Understanding" containing indigenization terms in *India – Autos* entitled manufacturers to import restricted auto parts. Once signed, such memoranda became binding and enforceable.[21] In *Canada – Autos*, Canadian motor vehicle producers wishing to enjoy import duty exemptions signed "Letters of Undertaking" with the commitment to increase domestic value added in motor vehicles. The commitments were requested and monitored by the government, and the companies accepted responsibility vis-à-vis the government.[22]

---

[19] *Ibid.*, pp. 61–9; Hufbauer et al., *supra* note 3, pp. 17–34.
[20] GATT Panel Report, *Canada – FIRA*, paras. 2.4–2.12.
[21] Panel Report, *India – Autos*, paras. 7.188–7.190.
[22] Panel Report, *Canada – Autos*, paras. 2.4–2.5, 10.122.

The WTO-lawfulness of such arrangements was tested under the national treatment provisions. As emphasized in case law, the private undertakings should not interfere with the rights of other countries deriving from Article III of the GATT and exercised on behalf of their exporters.[23] While legislation or government instruments obligating the use of products from local sources fall under the category of "laws" or "regulations" in Article III:4 of the GATT, private actions above may constitute internal "requirements" covered by that provision only if they are closely attributed to the State conduct. Irrespective of the way of materialization, legally enforceable private arrangements or undertakings accepted by firms to obtain an advantage from the government represent such "requirements."[24] But legal enforceability or a linkage between the private action and an advantage conferred by the government is not the only criterion for making the private action a "requirement" under Article III:4. Rather, one needs to consider "a broad variety of forms of government action that can be effective in influencing the conduct of private parties."[25]

5.3.2   Cumulative Application of WTO Provisions to LCRs

Depending on the circumstances, the same LCR can be subjected to multiple WTO rules. In the case of LCRs for goods, the relevant GATT, TRIMs, and SCM provisions can come into play. As explained here, they apply cumulatively despite some overlap.

The national treatment provisions of the GATT and the TRIMs Agreement remain applicable as full-fledged or stand-alone rules to covered LCRs. The Appellate Body in *EC – Bananas III* suggested that a panel would normally be expected to examine the more specific agreement before the more general one where two agreements apply simultaneously.[26] But the panels have differently sequenced the claims raised under both sets of rules in question. The *Indonesia – Autos* panel started with the TRIMs provisions in the belief that they were more specific than the GATT's national treatment, but exercised judicial economy on the latter.[27] However, the panels in *Canada – Autos* and *India –*

---

[23] GATT Panel Report, *Canada – FIRA*, para. 5.6.
[24] *Ibid.*, para. 5.4; GATT Panel Report, *EEC – Parts and Components*, para. 5.21.
[25] Panel Report, *Canada – Autos*, paras. 10.106–10.107.
[26] Appellate Body Report, *EC – Bananas III*, para. 204.
[27] Panel Report, *Indonesia – Autos*, paras. 14.63, 14.93.

Autos questioned such an order of analysis and chose to consider Article III issues first.[28] Although the finding under either agreement would, in principle, obviate the need to proceed with a similar claim under the other agreement, the panel in *India – Solar Cells* decided to turn to Article III even after it had found the violation of the corresponding TRIMs provisions.[29]

Further, the GATT and the SCM Agreement can overlap in the case of local content subsidies, but they still apply on their own.[30] The panel in *Indonesia – Autos* disagreed with an argument that the SCM Agreement overrides Article III of the GATT in relation to such subsidies. Invoking the public international law concept of a presumption against conflict and previous jurisprudence, the panel explained why these two agreements were not mutually exclusive:

> Article III continues to prohibit discrimination between domestic and imported products in respect of internal taxes and other domestic regulations, including local content requirements. It does not "proscribe" nor does it "prohibit" the provision of any subsidy *per se*. By contrast, the SCM Agreement prohibits subsidies which are conditional on export performance and on meeting local content requirements, provides remedies with respect to certain subsidies where they cause adverse effects to the interests of another Member and exempts certain subsidies from actionability under the SCM Agreement. In short, Article III prohibits discrimination between domestic and imported products while the SCM Agreement regulates the provision of subsidies to enterprises.[31]

Similarly, the TRIMs Agreement and the SCM Agreement target different aspects of LCRs. According to a panel's findings, the SCM Agreement bans *subsidies* contingent on LCRs rather than LCRs as such, while the TRIMs Agreement prohibits *LCRs* as such, not the granting of associated advantages, including subsidies. Thus, inconsistency with Article 3.1(b) of the SCM Agreement can be remedied with removal of the subsidy, with the LCR possibly being intact, whereas a TRIMs violation can be remedied with removal of the LCR with no need for discontinuation of the related subsidy.[32] It follows that both the subsidy and TRIMs regimes apply to LCRs, without one overriding the other.

---

[28] Panel Report, *Canada – Autos*, paras. 10.63–10.64, 10.91; Panel Report, *India – Autos*, paras. 7.157, 7.161.
[29] Panel Report, *India – Solar Cells*, paras. 7.78–7.79.
[30] Panel Report, *Indonesia – Autos*, paras. 14.39–14.40.   [31] *Ibid.*, para. 14.33.
[32] *Ibid.*, paras. 14.50–14.51.

When it comes to LCRs challenged under Article III of the GATT and the TRIMs Agreement, on the one hand, and under Article 3.1(b) of the SCM Agreement, on the other, there is no "obligatory sequence of analysis." It is in the panel's "margin of discretion" to decide whether to commence its analysis with the former or the latter.[33] Nevertheless, panels cannot exercise judicial economy on the SCM claims after making findings on LCRs under the GATT and the TRIMs Agreement. Otherwise, complainants could be deprived of their rights under the SCM Agreement to enjoy faster-than-usual litigation and special remedies against prohibited subsidies, such as adjudicators' recommendation to withdraw the subsidy without delay and antisubsidy countermeasures.[34]

5.4   Legality of LCRs under WTO Rules

5.4.1   GATT

Article III of the GATT on national treatment forbids governments to discriminate against foreign goods through taxes and regulatory measures. It is designed to prevent protectionism inside the market and protect tariff concessions.[35] Paragraph 1 of Article III states that internal measures "should not be applied to imported or domestic products so as to afford protection to domestic production." This "general principle" informs the rest of Article III, constituting part of the context of the other paragraphs therein.[36]

Paragraph 2 of Article III prohibits tax discrimination. It consists of two sentences to be read together with *Ad* Article III:2, with the first sentence banning *excess* taxes on "like" imported products and the second outlawing *dissimilar* taxes on "directly competitive or substitutable" imported products:

> The products of the territory of any contracting party imported into the territory of any other contracting party shall not be subject, directly or indirectly, to internal taxes or other internal charges of any kind in excess of those applied, directly or indirectly, to like domestic products. Moreover, no contracting party shall otherwise apply internal taxes or other internal charges to imported or domestic products in a manner contrary to the principles set forth in paragraph 1.* [asterisk in original]

---

[33] Appellate Body Reports, *Canada – Renewable Energy / Canada – Feed-in Tariff Program*, paras. 5.5, 5.8.

[34] *Ibid.*, para. 5.7.   [35] Appellate Body Report, *Japan – Alcoholic Beverages II*, pp. 16–17.

[36] *Ibid.*, pp. 17–18.

Article III:2 applies to indirect taxes, but direct taxes are still covered by paragraphs 4 and 5 of Article III on regulatory measures.[37] The word "indirectly" in the earlier passage prevents, inter alia, discriminatory content-targeting taxes like taxes directly levied on finished goods containing foreign inputs or taxes on services (e.g., distribution services) related to finished goods using foreign inputs.[38] By the same token, Article III:2 bans tax preferences to final products or services that use input products from local sources.

Article III:4 prohibits discriminatory regulatory measures other than indirect taxes, whereas Article III:5 explicitly proscribes any quantitative regulation that mandates utilization of local products in a "specified amount or proportion":

> 4. The products of the territory of any contracting party imported into the territory of any other contracting party shall be accorded treatment no less favourable than that accorded to like products of national origin in respect of all laws, regulations and requirements affecting their internal sale, offering for sale, purchase, transportation, distribution or use . . .
>
> 5. No contracting party shall establish or maintain any internal quantitative regulation relating to the mixture, processing or use of products in specified amounts or proportions which requires, directly or indirectly, that any specified amount or proportion of any product which is the subject of the regulation must be supplied from domestic sources. Moreover, no contracting party shall otherwise apply internal quantitative regulations in a manner contrary to the principles set forth in paragraph 1.* [asterisk in original]

The provisions of Article III certainly ban LCRs setting a required *minimum* for the consumption of local goods. But they also cover LCRs with *maximum* limits for foreign goods. In *US – FSC (Article 21.5 – EC)*, the US legislation conditioned the granting of a direct tax exemption to the 50 percent ceiling for the use of imported inputs. The Appellate Body held that such a limitation on the foreign content was in breach of Article III:4, as it constituted a "considerable impetus" for manufacturers to use domestic inputs instead of imported ones.[39]

As for flexibilities, members are entitled to use LCRs as part of government procurement or screen quotas.[40] In addition, Article III:8

---

[37] See also Section 6.2.1.

[38] Panel Report, *Mexico – Taxes on Soft Drinks*, paras. 8.44, 8.49.

[39] Appellate Body Report, *US – FSC (Article 21.5 – EC)*, paras. 212, 220–2.

[40] See Sections 5.4.4, 7.4.1.

(b) of the GATT accepts certain production subsidies given to domestic (but not foreign) producers:

> [Article III] shall not prevent the payment of subsidies exclusively to domestic producers, including payments to domestic producers derived from the proceeds of internal taxes or charges applied consistently with the provisions of this Article and subsidies effected through governmental purchases of domestic products.

Article III:8(b) covers only the payment of subsidies involving the expenditure of revenue by a government (as opposed to, e.g., tax exemptions/reductions).[41] This provision excuses *discriminatory* channelling of covered subsidies to domestic producers, but does not exempt those subsidies from the SCM Agreement.

The general and security exceptions or other common flexibilities are also available to LCR-related GATT violations. In *India – Solar Cells*, India invoked Articles XX(j) and XX(d) of the GATT to justify its LCRs for solar cells and solar modules imposed on renewable electricity generators. While the Appellate Body did not question the applicability of these provisions to the LCRs per se, it rejected the legal defense as tied to the factual circumstances of that case. With respect to Article XX(j) pertaining to measures "essential to the acquisition or distribution of products in general or local short supply," the Appellate Body said that such a "short supply" could exist only where there was a shortage of products from *all* available sources, including imports, and downplayed the presented rationale for the LCRs as being necessary for addressing low domestic capacity to manufacture solar cells and modules. As for Article XX(d) that excuses illegal trade measures securing compliance with GATT-consistent laws or regulations, the Appellate Body found that the instruments cited by India were not proper "laws or regulations" under that provision.[42]

Finally, governments may utilize rules of origin of RTAs as an indirect way of localizing or "regionalizing" multistage production in a WTO-permitted manner. Rules of origin make only qualifying originating goods – typically, goods produced with substantial domestic or regional content – eligible for preferential treatment. However, one should bear in

---

[41] Appellate Body Report, *Canada – Periodicals*, p. 34.
[42] Appellate Body Report, *India – Solar Cells*, paras. 5.51–5.52, 5.67–5.77, 5.133–5.135, 5.138–5.148. See also Sherzod Shadikhodjaev, "India – Certain Measures Relating to Solar Cells and Solar Modules," 111 *American Journal of International Law* 139 (2017), pp. 140–7.

mind that RTAs with too restrictive rules of origin may violate Article XXIV of the GATT or the Enabling Clause for raising high trade barriers toward third countries.

5.4.2 TRIMs Agreement

As the GATT panel in *Canada – FIRA* noted, the GATT "does not prevent [a member] from exercising its sovereign right to regulate foreign direct investments." It is only trade-related elements of investment measures that can be subjected to the GATT disciplines.[43] Reflecting this logic, Article 2.1 of the TRIMs Agreement prohibits TRIMs that conflict with Articles III or XI of the GATT. Investment measures prescribing LCRs are automatically deemed to be trade-related, as they "always favour the use of domestic products over imported products, and therefore affect trade."[44]

Besides certain new procedural provisions, the TRIMs Agreement adds some value to the existing rules by providing an illustrative list of illegal TRIMs, which reduces a complainant's burden of proving the WTO-applicability to the listed measures. More specifically, the Annex of the agreement exemplifies LCRs as unlawful TRIMs, as follows:

1. TRIMs that are inconsistent with the obligation of national treatment provided for in paragraph 4 of Article III of GATT 1994 include those which are mandatory or enforceable under domestic law or under administrative rulings, or compliance with which is necessary to obtain an advantage, and which require:
   (a) the purchase or use by an enterprise of products of domestic origin or from any domestic source, whether specified in terms of particular products, in terms of volume or value of products, or in terms of a proportion of volume or value of its local production; or
   (b) that an enterprise's purchases or use of imported products be limited to an amount related to the volume or value of local products that it exports.

While subparagraph (a) above captures commonly perceived LCRs, subparagraph (b) also confirms the applicability of Article III:4 to the LCRs that promote localization indirectly by balancing between the

---

[43] GATT Panel Report, *Canada – FIRA*, para. 5.1.
[44] Panel Report, *Indonesia – Autos*, para. 14.82.

domestic use of foreign products and the exportation of domestic products. Paragraph 2(a) of the Annex of the TRIMs Agreement considers similar balancing between importation and exportation as being contrary to the ban on quantitative restrictions under Article XI:1 of the GATT.

As indicated in *Indonesia – Autos*, LCRs violating Article 2.1 of the TRIMs Agreement "may be justified" under Articles 3 or 5 of the TRIMs Agreement.[45] Article 3 accepts all exceptions under the GATT. Article 5 grants transition periods of two, five, and seven years to developed, developing, and LDC members respectively for notified WTO-inconsistent TRIMs. Under Article 5.3 of the TRIMs Agreement, the Council for Trade in Goods may extend the transition period of a developing country or LDC "with particular [implementation] difficulties," taking into account "the individual development, financial and trade needs" of the respective member. In 2001, the Council for Trade in Goods prolonged those periods of seven developing countries to specific dates.[46] With respect to LDCs, the Hong Kong Ministerial Declaration (2005) established new extendable transition periods of seven years for existing measures and five years for future measures, subject to the condition that the covered measures must be phased out by 2020.[47]

Whereas these periods apply to the existing members concerned, the acceding countries may negotiate some flexibility for their localization policies during accession talks. China, Ecuador, and Russia were granted transition periods for maintaining TRIMs in the automotive sector after the accession.[48] For example, Russia is committed to removing preferential tariffs or tariff exemptions under certain automobile investment programs by 1 July 2018, while keeping the localization cap of 25 percent for auto parts and components during the transition period.[49]

---

[45] *Ibid.*, para. 14.92.

[46] See WTO Analytical Index, *Guide to WTO Law and Practice*, "Agreement on Trade-Related Investment Measures," para. 34, www.wto.org/english/res_e/booksp_e/analytic_index_e/trims_01_e.htm#article5A.

[47] WTO, Ministerial Conference – Sixth Session – Hong Kong, 13–18 December 2005 – Doha Work Programme – Ministerial Declaration – Adopted on 18 December 2005, WT/MIN(05)/DEC (22 December 2005), Annex F, p. F–2.

[48] Chiedu Osakwe and Juneyoung Lee, "The Future of Multilateral Investment Rules in the WTO: Contributions from WTO Accession Outcomes," in Uri Dadush and Chiedu Osakwe (eds.), *WTO Accessions and Trade Multilateralism: Case Studies and Lessons from the WTO at Twenty* (Cambridge: Cambridge University Press, 2015), pp. 823–5.

[49] WT/ACC/RUS/70, WT/MIN(11)/2, Ch. 3, *supra* note 81, para. 1090.

5.4.3   SCM Agreement

Article 3 of the SCM Agreement prohibits members from giving local content (or import substitution) subsidies:

> 3.1 Except as provided in the Agreement on Agriculture, the following subsidies, within the meaning of Article 1, shall be prohibited:
>
>   ...
>
>   (b) subsidies contingent, whether solely or as one of several other conditions, upon the use of domestic over imported goods.
>
> 3.2 A Member shall neither grant nor maintain subsidies referred to in paragraph 1.

The meaning of "goods" in subparagraph (b) can indirectly be ascertained from the appellate interpretation of the same word used in the legal definition of "subsidy." In *US – Large Civil Aircraft (2nd complaint)*, the Appellate Body construed the term "goods" in Article 1.1(a)(1)(iii) of the SCM Agreement as referring to "tangible items" as contrasted against "services" "which are intangible."[50] In *US – Softwood Lumber IV*, the Appellate Body stretched the scope of "goods" to even nontradable and non-HS-classifiable items, but again had "tangible items" in mind.[51] But in *Canada – Renewable Energy / Feed-In Tariff Program*, the Appellate Body seems to have departed from this emphasis on tangibility by implicitly agreeing with the description of electricity – which is definitely intangible – as a "good" purchased by the government.[52] Accordingly, the granting of a subsidy conditional upon the use of, for example, local electricity or digital products should fall under the Article 3.1(b) prohibition.

Surprisingly, subparagraph (b) of Article 3.1 does not mention contingency "in law or in fact" as juxtaposed to subparagraph (a) thereof that bans "subsidies contingent, in law or in fact, ... upon export performance." But the Appellate Body did *not* consider this omission as the drafters' intention to outlaw only de jure local content subsidies. Rather, it drew a parallel with Article III:4 of the GATT, Articles II and XVII of the GATS prohibiting both de jure and de facto discriminations to conclude that Article 3.1(b) actually extends to de

---

[50] Appellate Body Report, *US – Large Civil Aircraft (2nd complaint)*, n. 1295 to para. 619.

[51] Appellate Body Report, *US – Softwood Lumber IV*, paras. 58–9, 67.

[52] Shadikhodjaev, Ch. 3, *supra* note 50, p. 871.

facto (along with de jure) local content subsidies so as to prevent "easy" circumvention of SCM obligations.[53]

In *Canada – Autos*, the government granted import duty exemptions to the manufacturers that complied with the Canadian Value Added (CVA) and production-to-sales ratio requirements. The CVA represented the aggregate of several local content components, including the cost of domestic parts and materials, direct labor costs, manufacturing overheads, general and administrative expenses, depreciation in respect of machinery and permanent plant equipment, and a capital cost allowance for land and buildings.[54] Thus, for receiving tariff benefits, the eligible automakers could, in principle, use local workforce rather than domestic goods to satisfy the CVA requirements. This gave the grounds for the panel to conclude that the tariff exemption was not a de jure local content subsidy. But the Appellate Body criticized the panel for basing its reasoning on the mere existence of multiple possibilities for compliance with the CVA requirements without looking into the specified *level* at which the CVA requirements would actually operate:

> It seems to us that whether or not a particular manufacturer is able to satisfy its specific CVA requirements without using any Canadian parts and materials in its production depends very much on the *level* of the applicable CVA requirements. For example, if the level of the CVA requirements is very high, we can see that the use of domestic goods may well be a necessity and thus be, in practice, required as a *condition* for eligibility for the import duty exemption. By contrast, if the level of the CVA requirements is very low, it would be much easier to satisfy those requirements *without* actually using domestic goods; for example, where the CVA requirements are set at 40 percent, it might be possible to satisfy that level simply with the aggregate of other elements of Canadian value added, in particular, labour costs. The multiplicity of *possibilities* for compliance with the CVA requirements, when these requirements are set at low levels, may, depending on the specific level applicable to a particular manufacturer, make the use of domestic goods only one *possible* means (means which might not, in fact, be utilized) of satisfying the CVA requirements.[55]

The practical lesson from this finding is that governments should keep localization rates at a low level, on the one hand, and permit multiple

---

[53] Appellate Body Report, *Canada – Autos*, paras. 140–3.
[54] Panel Report, *Canada – Autos*, para. 10.204.
[55] Appellate Body Report, *Canada – Autos*, para. 130 (emphasis in original). See also para. 131.

price/cost elements – including those not related to goods – to meet that level, on the other. This would help the localizing country resist de jure challenges under Article 3.1(b) of the SCM Agreement. To avoid de facto allegations in the same factual and legal contexts, governments should not, inter alia, grant disproportionately large amounts of subsidy to those producers that use domestic *goods* to comply with the localization levels or make such producers predominant users of subsidy as opposed to producers relying on nongood factors (labor cost, etc.).

Another implicit "flexibility" derivable from a combination of the WTO rules is in that members interested in localization will be on a safer footing if they subsidize their input-supplying industries *directly* rather than through subsidies given to input-using industries. The economic effect could be roughly the same.[56] Such direct subsidies would make domestic inputs cheap and hence attractive to input users at home (and probably abroad). As for the legal nature, direct subsidization of input manufacturing is far less hindered by WTO strictures, as it is *not banned* as such. Depending on the subsidy terms and factual circumstances, it could qualify as an actionable subsidy under the SCM Agreement, which may be countered only in the presence of associated adverse effects, and as a production subsidy defendable under Article III:8(b) of the GATT.

Article 27.3 of the SCM Agreement exempted developing countries and LDCs from the Article 3.1(b) prohibition for five and eight years, respectively. But currently this S&D treatment is no longer available. At the same time, as we stated earlier, some developing countries can avail themselves of the renewed transition periods for illegal TRIMs, including LCRs. Because the SCM Agreement and the TRIMs Agreement impose *cumulative* obligations,[57] the eligible members should delink their LCRs from subsidies to enjoy S&D treatment under the TRIMs Agreement without violating the SCM Agreement.

5.4.4   Government Procurement

Certain LCRs in government procurement projects are tolerated under Article III:8(a) of the GATT which reads:

---

[56] Alan O. Sykes, "The Economics of WTO Rules on Subsidies and Countervailing Measures," John M. Olin Law & Economics Working Paper No. 186, University of Chicago Law School, 2003, p. 19.

[57] Panel Report, *Indonesia – Autos*, para. 14.52.

The provisions of [Article III of the GATT] shall not apply to laws, regulations or requirements governing the procurement by governmental agencies of products purchased for governmental purposes and not with a view to commercial resale or with a view to use in the production of goods for commercial sale.

As a legal derogation, Article III:8(a) excludes covered measures from the scope of the national treatment obligations under Article III of the GATT and Article 2 of the TRIMs Agreement.[58] The word "procurement" in the passage above refers to the process of obtaining products by a governmental agency, whereas the word "purchased" describes a way of how procurement can materialize.[59]

In order to fall within Article III:8(a), public purchases must simultaneously meet both conditions of being (i) "for governmental purposes" and (ii) "not with a view to commercial resale ..."[60] The "products purchased for governmental purposes" comprise products "purchased for the use of government, consumed by government, or provided by government to recipients in the discharge of its public functions."[61] Government purchases for "commercial resale" – excluded from the scope of Article III:8(a) – are arm's length transactions, which is determined by the nature of the relationship between a seller and buyer.[62]

The derogation above applies when the imported product being discriminated against is in a "competitive relationship" with – that is, "like"/ "directly competitive or substitutable" in relation to – the domestic product purchased.[63] Thus, legal defense based on Article III:8(a) was rejected in renewable energy disputes, because the LCR at issue discriminated against foreign electricity-generating *equipment*, while the government was actually purchasing renewable *electricity* linked to that LCR.[64]

In considering the policy space under Article III:8(a), one also needs to check if an LCR-imposing member is a party to the Government Procurement Agreement (GPA) which was revised in 2012. This plurilateral treaty applies only to the GPA signatories with respect to "any measure regarding covered procurement." Article II:2 of the revised GPA limits this agreement's scope to the public procurement by specified procuring entities – governmental and other entities involved in

---

[58] Appellate Body Reports, *Canada – Renewable Energy / Canada – Feed-In Tariff Program*, paras. 5.20–5.33, 5.56.
[59] *Ibid.*, para. 5.59.   [60] *Ibid.*, para. 5.69.   [61] *Ibid.*, paras. 5.68, 5.74.
[62] *Ibid.*, para. 5.71.   [63] *Ibid.*, para. 5.79.
[64] *Ibid.*, para. 5.79; Appellate Body Report, *India – Solar Cells*, paras. 5.25, 5.40–5.41.

"covered procurement" – of scheduled goods and services that exceeds certain numeric thresholds:

> For the purposes of this Agreement, covered procurement means procurement for governmental purposes:
>
> a. of goods, services, or any combination thereof:
>   i. as specified in each Party's annexes to Appendix I; and
>   ii. not procured with a view to commercial sale or resale, or for use in the production or supply of goods or services for commercial sale or resale;
> b. by any contractual means, including: purchase; lease; and rental or hire purchase, with or without an option to buy;
> c. for which the value, as estimated in accordance with paragraphs 6 through 8, equals or exceeds the relevant threshold specified in a Party's annexes to Appendix I, at the time of publication of a notice in accordance with Article VII;
> d. by a procuring entity; and
> e. that is not otherwise excluded from coverage in paragraph 3 or a Party's annexes to Appendix I.

With respect to covered procurement, Article IV of the revised GPA provides for nondiscrimination (MFN and national treatment) of goods, services, and suppliers and bans "offsets" – actions encouraging local development or improving the BOP accounts, such as, for example, the use of domestic content. Thus, if a particular WTO member is a GPA party, it cannot take a localization measure involving covered procurement vis-à-vis other GPA parties. By contrast, its LCRs fall outside the purview of the GPA if they apply to below-threshold procurements, nonscheduled goods/services, or transactions by nonlisted public agencies.

In 2014 and 2015, the Committee on Government Procurement discussed new legislative initiatives of the United States regarding public procurements by federal, State, and municipal governments in certain transportation, construction, and other infrastructural projects.[65] In particular, the US administration sought to secure an expanded budget for those projects over the next several years and to increase the "Buy

---

[65] See WTO, Committee on Government Procurement – Minutes of the Formal Meeting of 11 February 2015, GPA/M/59 (4 May 2015), paras. 2.1–2.16; WTO, Committee on Government Procurement – Minutes of the Formal Meeting of 29 October 2014, GPA/M/57 (22 December 2014), paras. 2.1–2.26; WTO, Committee on Government Procurement – Minutes of the Formal Meeting of 25 June 2014, GPA/M/56 (4 September 2014), paras. 2.1–2.18.

America" localization ratio for qualifying inputs from current 60 percent to 100 percent. The "Buy America" provisions have normally not applied to the goods and services from the parties to the GPA and the US FTAs in relation to covered procurement. But Canada, the EU, Switzerland, and other members argued that the legislative proposals concerning, inter alia, the GROW America Act, Made in the U.S.A. Act, and the Invest in American Jobs Act would, if enacted, contravene Article XXII:6 of the revised GPA. Article XXII:6 states that "[e]ach Party shall seek to avoid introducing or continuing discriminatory measures that distort open procurement."[66] In Canada's view, this provision would apply to the parties' procurement measures, "regardless of whether such measures applied to procurement not covered by the GPA."[67] Similarly, Norway asserted that the US bills "sent a negative signal also for non-covered procurement contrary to … Article XXII:6."[68] But the United States disagreed:

> The United States took its international obligations seriously and insured that all covered procurement was conducted in a manner consistent with its obligations. It strongly supported efforts to combat localization. While the United States maintained certain Buy America requirements, these were applied consistently with its international obligations, and were designed and implemented transparently.
>
> …
>
> [A]ll Parties to the Agreement excluded certain segments of their procurement from coverage under the Agreement. These exclusions had long been understood to provide the required flexibility that Parties needed to simultaneously open up other sectors of their procurement. The United States saw no disconnect between combatting localization broadly and allowing GPA countries to exclude certain procurements from coverage under the Agreement.[69]

As a modified version of Article XXIV:7(c) of the Uruguay Round GPA (1994), Article XXII:6 of the revised GPA addresses the gap in the government procurement regime where certain market-opening concessions in parties' GPA schedules are conditional on reciprocity – that is, made available only vis-à-vis the parties with equivalent concessions – and are thus discriminatory in not applying on a strict MFN-basis.[70]

---

[66] GPA/M/59, *supra* note 65, paras. 2.2, 2.9, 2.13.   [67] *Ibid.*, para. 2.2.
[68] GPA/M/57, *supra* note 65, para. 2.23.   [69] *Ibid.*, paras. 2.25–2.26.
[70] Robert D. Anderson and Sue Arrowsmith, "The WTO Regime on Government Procurement: Past, Present and Future," in Sue Arrowsmith and Robert D. Anderson (eds.), *The WTO Regime on Government Procurement: Challenge and Reform* (Cambridge:

In other words, this provision seems to counter such MFN conditionality as applied to *covered* procurement. Therefore, it is not likely that the Article XXII:6 obligation extends to noncovered procurement as some members argued.

5.4.5   GATS

The GATS disciplines are applicable to LCRs in the services sector. Article XVII:1 provides for national treatment vis-à-vis foreign services and service suppliers in listed (sub)sectors, subject to the terms written in members' schedules:

> In the sectors inscribed in its Schedule, and subject to any conditions and qualifications set out therein, each Member shall accord to services and service suppliers of any other Member, in respect of all measures affecting the supply of services, treatment no less favourable than that it accords to its own like services and service suppliers.

The GATS forbids both de jure and de facto discrimination. Pursuant to paragraphs 2 and 3 of Article XVII, the appropriate yardstick of less-favorableness is not whether the treatment is "[f]ormally identical" or "formally different," but whether the treatment "modifies the conditions of competition" to the detriment of foreign services or service suppliers.

Table 5.1 illustrates some instances of service-related LCRs by selected members without prejudice to their lawfulness.

In *Canada – Autos*, producers of motor vehicles could meet certain LCRs partly through the purchase of locally supplied services. For this, they could bear the following costs incurred in Canada: the cost of maintenance and repair work on buildings, machinery, and equipment used for production purposes; the cost of engineering services, experimental work, and product development work; and administrative and general expenses.[71] With respect to national treatment allegations under Article XVII of the GATS, the panel noted that Canada had made specific commitments in all affected services. It found further that none of the scheduled Canadian limitations on national treatment could capture the

---

Cambridge University Press, 2011), p. 20; Robert D. Anderson and Kodjo Osei-Lah, "The Coverage Negotiations under the Agreement on Government Procurement: Context, Mandate, Process and Prospects," in Sue Arrowsmith and Robert D. Anderson (eds.), *The WTO Regime on Government Procurement: Challenge and Reform* (Cambridge: Cambridge University Press, 2011), pp. 156–61.

[71] Panel Report, *Canada – Autos*, para. 10.291.

Table 5.1 *Illustrative List of LCRs in the Services Sector*

Imposing Country	Sector Description	Localization Measure	Source
Brazil	Telecommunications	"In June 2012, ANATEL auctioned radio spectrum in the 450 Mhz and 2.5 Ghz bands for commercial mobile services. The notice required that winning bidders commit to purchase goods, products, equipment, and systems for telecommunications and data networks with national technology, and ensure that, after five years, 50% of the equipment, telecommunications systems, and networks be produced locally (regardless of the origin of capital), and 20% be produced with technology developed in the country."	WT/TPR/S/283/Rev.1, 26 July 2013 (p. 160, para. 4.198)
Congo	Energy	"Oil companies must give priority to local personnel when recruiting and to Congolese suppliers for services."	WT/TPR/S/169, 23 August 2006 (p. 58, para. 41)
Ecuador	Mining	"The quota of manual workers of Ecuadorian nationality in mining operations was reduced from 95% to at least 80% . . ."	WT/TPR/S/254, 10 October 2011 (p. 90, para. 32)
Senegal	Tourism	"The [National Tourism Charter adopted in April 2003] also stresses the protection of tourists and cultural or natural heritage, and requires local labour to be preferred in conditions of equal skill."	WT/TPR/S/223/SEN/Rev.1, 7 October 2009 (p. 226, para. 228)
South Africa	Banking	"[A] foreign bank establishing a branch may be required to employ a minimum number of local residents to obtain a banking licence, and may be obliged to have a minimum capital base."	WT/TPR/S/114, Annex 4 (South Africa), 24 March 2003 (p. A4–233, para. 24)

Source: Compiled by the author from information in the WTO Secretariat's TPR reports.

LCRs properly, as they were neither LCR-specific limitations nor the entry "unbound" – the *only* limitations that would have covered LCRs.[72] While the LCRs in this particular case worked against foreign services supplied through modes 1 (cross-border supply) and 2 (consumption abroad), these measures did not discriminate between domestic and foreign services/suppliers operating within Canada under modes 3 (commercial presence) and 4 (movement of natural persons). Nevertheless, the panel concluded that the LCRs, in fact, incentivized the target manufacturers to purchase services in modes 3 and 4, which are supplied within Canada, to the detriment of "like" foreign services supplied through modes 1 and 2, that is, from and in the territory of other members.[73]

As we can learn from the *Canada – Autos* case, LCRs in the scheduled sectors will, in principle, be contrary to the GATS provisions on national treatment unless the imposing member included explicit LCR-permitting or alternatively generic "unbound" records in the relevant parts of its schedule. We believe that such records should mean *services* to be an input, not the goods. Indeed, it does not make sense to inscribe LCRs obligating service suppliers to use certain local goods, as such LCRs arguably would not be tolerated under WTO rules on goods. The following examples show LCR-specific entries recorded in GATS schedules as limitations on national treatment:

- "The foreign service supplier must prove commitment to recruit and develop more local human resources."[74]
- "Preferential use of local services to the extent they are available under conditions of quality, price and delivery equivalent to those of like services of foreign origin."[75]
- "With regard to personnel, materials, equipment, facilities and services required in the petroleum operations, priority shall be given to the employment of national subcontractors, provided that they are competitive in delivery, time, price and quality."[76]
- "Travel Agencies should employ at least one Israel-licensed Travel Expert."[77]

[72] *Ibid.*, para. 10.296.   [73] *Ibid.*, paras. 10.305–10.307.
[74] S/L/92, Ch. 3, *supra* note 72, p. 18.
[75] WTO, Côte d'Ivoire – Schedule of Specific Commitments, GATS/SC/23 (15 April 1994).
[76] S/L/92, Ch. 3, *supra* note 72, p. 18.
[77] WTO, Israel – Schedule of Specific Commitments, GATS/SC/44 (15 April 1994).

- "Thirty per cent of screen time must be devoted to Mexican films. For each copy screened in Mexico, a copy must be processed in a Mexican laboratory."[78]
- "Not less than 80% of all employed personnel engaged in realization of a production sharing agreement should be citizens of the Russian Federation."[79]
- "[For subsurface operations] Kazakhstan may require investors, in procuring services, to procure up to 50% of such services from juridical persons of Kazakhstan."[80]

In nonscheduled sectors, governments are free to utilize their service localization policies. In addition, the national treatment disciplines do not apply to government procurement of services defined by Article XIII:1 of the GATS as "the procurement by governmental agencies of services purchased for governmental purposes and not with a view to commercial resale or with a view to use in the supply of services for commercial sale." Although multilateral negotiations on government procurement foreseen by Article XIII:2 of the GATS have not produced additional rules yet, one still needs to check if a particular public procurement of services is covered by the GPA. Finally, illegal LCRs may be defended under the general or security exceptions where appropriate.

5.5   Data Localization Requirements as an Emerging Issue

The widespread use of the Internet and digital technologies may necessitate public actions on the domestic plane to strengthen information security and safeguard customers' privacy. This section discusses government restrictions on electronic data flows as part of data protection policies and the status of such measures under international trade rules.

5.5.1   Overview of Data Localization Measures

National practices on data protection are largely inconsistent. For example, the US model prescribes the free movement of data unless there is a good reason to block the transfer of data abroad. Thus, the

---

[78] WTO, Mexico – Schedule of Specific Commitments, GATS/SC/56 (15 April 1994).

[79] WTO, Trade in Services – Russian Federation – Schedule of Specific Commitments, GATS/SC/149 (5 November 2012).

[80] WTO, Trade in Services – The Republic of Kazakhstan – Schedule of Specific Commitments, GATS/SC/154 (15 February 2016).

United States generally allows data outflows, subject to restrictions in certain sensitive sectors, such as health care and financial services. By contrast, the EU model prevents personal information from leaving the home country, except where there is a legal basis for the contrary. Accordingly, the EU bans personal data transmissions to a third country unless the latter is determined to have an adequate EU-like level of protection.[81]

In pursuing the policy of restricting the movement of data beyond national boundaries, governments can employ certain data localization measures. First, local data storage (or data residency) requirements mandate storage and/or processing of data within the imposing country. Second, local data center requirements demand that firms, wishing to provide certain digital services in a particular country, establish a data center in that country. Either or both of such LCRs are imposed by several developed and developing countries, including Australia, France, Canada, Greece, Brazil, China, India, Russia, Turkey, Viet Nam, and so on.[82]

Such LCRs in the digital environment have been especially pervasive since the revelations by Edward Snowden, a former contractor for the Central Intelligence Agency, in 2013 and afterward about the US National Security Agency's expansive secret gathering of private data from US-based Internet companies. These localization measures apparently intend to insulate in-country digitized information from undesirable third-country checks.

Moreover, a US court decision in 2016 rejecting the US government's request for compelling Microsoft to disclose customers' emails stored on servers abroad shows some loopholes in domestic law enforcement procedures. This may additionally incentivize more countries to adopt data localization policies to avoid such problems at home.[83]

Google, Microsoft, Amazon Web Services, and many other IT companies operate data centers – which are both capital- and electricity-intensive – in

---

[81] See Lawrence A. Kogan, "Coherent International Trade Policies Hasten, Not Retard, Cloud Computing," 7 *Global Trade and Customs Journal* 379 (2012), pp. 382–5; Renee Berry and Matthew Reisman, "Policy Challenges of Cross-Border Cloud Computing," 4 (2) *Journal of International Commerce and Economics* 1 (2012), pp. 10–13.

[82] See Stephen J. Ezell, Robert D. Atkinson, and Michelle A. Wein, "Localization Barriers to Trade: Threat to the Global Innovation Economy," Information Technology and Innovation Foundation, 2013, pp. 16–19.

[83] Shin-yi Peng and Han-wei Liu, "The Legality of Data Residency Requirements: How Can the Trans-Pacific Partnership Help?," 51 *Journal of World Trade* 183 (2017), pp. 199–200.

different parts of the world to serve multiple countries. The selection of a suitable site for data centers depends on several factors, such as cost-efficiency, access to the existing and potential markets, political risks, and technical feasibility.[84] The forced data localization works against this business practice and creates extremely high compliance costs for the firms.[85]

The data localization requirements negatively affect cloud services – typically, online data storage and backup solutions, database processing, Web-based emails, photo hosting, social networks, and mobile applications – because "the geographical independence is a central aspect of cloud computing as a supplier model,"[86] as data can be collected, stored, processed, and used in multiple places.

Data privacy laws in some European countries allow local bank customers to refuse to have their information processed by service providers in third countries, which represents an option "that is extremely difficult to address in business planning."[87] The prohibition of the overseas storage or processing of citizens' health records disables medical outsourcing abroad.

Such LCRs are generally motivated by privacy or cybersecurity considerations, as imposing governments believe that these measures make data more secure within their territory. But LCRs may also be used as a disguised industrial development strategy with the aim to attract foreign IT companies' investment or promote a domestic Internet industry.[88]

5.5.2   Legal Status under Trade Rules

In the context of services regulation, data localization measures can be characterized as trade barriers to cloud computing, as well as other services (finance, health care, etc.) having cross-border data transfer elements. While the UN Statistics Division currently singles out "cloud computing, Web hosting, application hosting" as a separate service category under Central Product Classification (CPC) Ver. 2.1 for the

---

[84] Shamel Azmeh and Christopher Foster, "The TPP and the Digital Trade Agenda: Digital Industrial Policy and Silicon Valley's Influence on New Trade Agreements," Working Paper No. 16–175, London School of Economics and Political Science, 2016, pp. 25–6.

[85] US International Trade Commission, "Digital Trade in the U.S. and Global Economics, Part 2," 2014, p. 84.

[86] National Board of Trade (Sweden), "How Borderless is the Cloud? An Introduction to Cloud Computing and International Trade," 2012, p. 14.

[87] US International Trade Commission, *supra* note 85, p. 91.   [88] *Ibid.*

statistical purposes only,[89] no explicit reference to cloud services can be found in the older CPC version relied upon by the current GATS scheduling guidelines.[90] But this does not mean that cloud computing should qualify as a totally new service not covered by members' commitments. In particular, as we will see in Section 7.2.2, there appears to be a general acceptance of, albeit no current consensus on, the concept of "technological neutrality" that, in essence, keeps scheduled commitments largely unaffected by technological transformations in the supply of services. Following this logic, there seems to be sufficient room in the current WTO classification system for accommodating cloud activities in the existing sectors. Cloud computing would likely fall within the spectrum of "computer and related services" that comprise "data processing services" (CPC 843) and/or "data base services" (CPC 844).[91] Otherwise, certain telecommunication services, such as, for example, "on-line information and/or data processing (incl. transaction processing)" under CPC 843** [asterisks in original] could include certain cloud activities.[92]

WTO case law on the GATS does not shed enough light on the status of trade measures with the privacy protection intent in general[93] and data localization elements in particular. One can argue that, by restricting business opportunities, the LCRs in question limit access to an imposing country's market with respect to, inter alia, the number of foreign cloud providers (Article XVI:2(a) of the GATS), the number of service operations in banking, health care, and so on, or the quantity of service output (Article XVI:2(c) of the GATS). These limitations would impact on mode 1 where providers abroad cannot use "export-restricted" data to satisfy the needs of the consumers in the restricting member and/or on mode 3 where commercial presence of IT companies in the host country is conditioned on the local data center requirement. Therefore, data

---

[89] See WTO, Committee on Specific Commitments – Report of the Meeting Held on 14 October 2015 – Note by the Secretariat, S/CSC/M/74 (27 November 2015), paras. 2.2–2.6.

[90] See S/L/92, Ch. 3, *supra* note 72, Attachment 8 containing the "Services Sectoral Classification List," MTN.GNS/W/120 (10 July 1991).

[91] See MTN.GNS/W/120, *supra* note 90.

[92] There is no consensus among WTO members as to whether it is computer and related services or telecommunication services that better accommodate cloud computing. See, e.g., WTO, Council for Trade in Services – Report of the Meeting Held on 18 March 2015 – Note by the Secretariat, S/C/M/122 (1 May 2015), paras. 4.11–4.48.

[93] Rolf H. Weber, "Regulatory Autonomy and Privacy Standards under the GATS," 7 *Asian Journal of WTO & International Health Law and Policy* 25 (2012), p. 33.

localization measures can be questioned under Article XVI of the GATS on market access, absent any relevant terms in a host country's schedule.

In addition, there is some potential, in appropriate circumstances, for challenging these measures under Article VI of the GATS on domestic regulation. But this is an alternative track, as the *US – Gambling* panel opined that Articles VI and XVI are mutually exclusive.[94] In our particular case, the legal validity of data localization in the scheduled sectors can be checked, inter alia, under Article VI:5. The latter, in conjunction with Article VI:4, requires that members' licensing/qualification requirements and technical standards be "based on objective and transparent criteria" and be "not more burdensome than necessary to ensure the quality of the service," and that the licensing procedures should not act as "a restriction on the supply of the service."

Data localization requirements found to violate the GATS may be justified under the general exceptions as being "necessary to secure compliance" with GATS-consistent laws or regulations relating to "the protection of the privacy of individuals in relation to the processing and dissemination of personal data and the protection of confidentiality of individual records and accounts" or as relating to "safety" (Articles XIV (c)(ii) and XIV(c)(iii), respectively). Alternatively, the measures in question can be said to be "necessary . . . to maintain public order" (Article XIV(a)). In *US – Gambling*, the panel held – and the Appellate Body did not deny – that the content of "public order" depends on "prevailing social, cultural, ethical and religious values," and that it is for members to define "public order" for themselves "according to their own systems and scales of values."[95]

Whether data localization is indeed "necessary" in the sense of the general exceptions seems to be a tricky question especially in the case of outright bans on data outflows. Industry representatives argue that in-country data are even more susceptible to the loss in the event of a security breach than data that are encrypted and stored in out-of-country clouds.[96] The United States – a strong supporter of the free cross-border movement of information – contends that data security can, in fact, be enhanced "through external storage, where economies of scale in specialized security practiced by best-in-class data processors may surpass what

[94] Panel Report, *US – Gambling*, para. 6.305.
[95] *Ibid.*, para 6.461; Appellate Body Report, *US – Gambling*, para. 296.
[96] US International Trade Commission, *supra* note 85, p. 84.

is available in storage facilities within one particular jurisdiction."[97] Even the EU, which has traditionally been very sensitive about data protection, suggests trade-friendlier alternatives to the strict ban on transmissions, such as permission of data transfers on the basis of adequacy-of-protection determinations for foreign countries, binding corporate rules, or contractual clauses.[98]

Unlike WTO agreements, some recent RTAs introduced specific rules constraining data localization requirements. To our knowledge, the Korea–US FTA is the first trade agreement that recognizes the principle of the free cross-border transmission of digitized information and urges the parties, albeit in a hortatory way, not to raise "unnecessary barriers" (Article 15.8):

> Recognizing the importance of the free flow of information in facilitating trade, and acknowledging the importance of protecting personal information, the Parties shall endeavor to refrain from imposing or maintaining unnecessary barriers to electronic information flows across borders.

The TPP Agreement[99] adopts a more comprehensive approach to this issue. Article 14.8 recognizes the importance of the policy for personal information protection, obliges the parties to maintain related domestic legal frameworks, and encourages them to develop mechanisms that would promote compatibility between different regimes of data protection. Compared to the Korea–US FTA, this agreement is more "aggressive" in (i) requiring its parties to adopt a free-flow-friendly environment for data (Article 14.11.2) and (ii) banning forced localization of computing facilities (Article 14.13.2). Both clauses, nevertheless, accept reasonable government actions taken to attain "a legitimate public policy objective":

> Article 14.11: Cross-Border Transfer of Information by Electronic Means
>
> 1. The Parties recognise that each Party may have its own regulatory requirements concerning the transfer of information by electronic means.
> 2. Each Party shall allow the cross-border transfer of information by electronic means, including personal information, when this activity is for the conduct of the business of a covered person.

---

[97] WTO, Council for Trade in Services – Communication by the US – Work Programme on Electronic Commerce, S/C/W/359 (17 December 2014), para. 4.4.

[98] S/C/M/122, *supra* note 92, para. 4.29.

[99] At the time of writing, the fate of the TPP Agreement following the US withdrawal was not clear.

3. Nothing in this Article shall prevent a Party from adopting or maintaining measures inconsistent with paragraph 2 to achieve a legitimate public policy objective, provided that the measure:
    (a) is not applied in a manner which would constitute a means of arbitrary or unjustifiable discrimination or a disguised restriction on trade; and
    (b) does not impose restrictions on transfers of information greater than are required to achieve the objective.

[Article 14.12 . . .]

Article 14.13: Location of Computing Facilities

1. The Parties recognise that each Party may have its own regulatory requirements regarding the use of computing facilities, including requirements that seek to ensure the security and confidentiality of communications.
2. No Party shall require a covered person to use or locate computing facilities in that Party's territory as a condition for conducting business in that territory.
3. Nothing in this Article shall prevent a Party from adopting or maintaining measures inconsistent with paragraph 2 to achieve a legitimate public policy objective, provided that the measure:
    (a) is not applied in a manner which would constitute a means of arbitrary or unjustifiable discrimination or a disguised restriction on trade; and
    (b) does not impose restrictions on the use or location of computing facilities greater than are required to achieve the objective.

5.6   Concluding Remarks

Many LCRs intend to stimulate domestic input manufacturing and consumption, but they actually limit producers' option of using cost-efficient and quality inputs to be competitive in the marketplace. In line with the mainstream economic findings, WTO law maintains generally a negative attitude toward localization measures. The past GATT/WTO jurisprudence delegitimized even government-directed "voluntary" commitments to utilizing local content. This prevents circumvention of trade disciplines by disguised public LCRs.

Critics may accuse the WTO regime of working against genuine efforts of countries to boost domestic industries with business opportunities kept within the borders. But without such multilateral strictures, those industries themselves will be vulnerable to LCRs abroad.

In any event, the current WTO rule book does not completely block localization. More specifically, trade regulation of government procurement and services leaves enough space for operating relevant LCR programs legally. Properly designed rules of origin under RTAs can contribute to localizing some parts of the supply chain. Subsidies may not be considered prohibited local content subsidies if the associated localization rate is sufficiently low and can be met by multiple cost components, including service costs. Finally, subsidies given to input suppliers directly are more tolerated in the WTO than local content subsidies granted to input users.

Annex 5.1 *LCRs Discussed in the WTO Committee on TRIMs (1995–2015)*

Applying Member	Agenda Item	Measure Description	Target Sector	WTO Source	WTO Dispute
Argentina	Notifications under Article 5.1 of the TRIMs Agreement	Decree No 33/1996 increased the level of local content from 60 to at least 67.5 percent in car industry and expanded the coverage of LCRs to include auto parts manufacturers.	Automotive	G/TRIMS/M/8 (20 July 1998); G/TRIMS/M/7 (6 November 1997); G/TRIMS/M/5 (27 November 1996); G/TRIMS/M/4 (2 May 1996)	None
Brazil	Brazil – Tax Preferences Linked to Local Content Conditions in Several Sectors	Since the end of 2011, Brazil has operated various tax programs conditional on LCRs for automobiles, telecommunication network equipment, semiconductors, certain digital goods, fertilizers, etc.	Various	G/TRIMS/M/37 (21 November 2014); G/TRIMS/M/36 (5 September 2014); G/TRIMS/M/35 (20 December 2013); G/TRIMS/M/34 (19 June 2013)	DS472, 497
Brazil	Brazil – Tax Preferences to Domestically Manufactured Automotive Vehicles	The 2013–2017 "INOVAR AUTO" automotive regime provides tax benefits for compliance with LCRs on	Automotive	G/TRIMS/M/33 (22 November 2012)	DS472, 497

Annex 5.1 (*cont.*)

Applying Member	Agenda Item	Measure Description	Target Sector	WTO Source	WTO Dispute
		domestic or MERCOSUR inputs.			
Brazil	Brazil – Certain Local Content Provisions in the Telecommunications Sector	A series of measures (2012–2014) on radio frequency spectrum obligated winning bidders to purchase products, equipment, and systems for telecommunications and data networks with national technology or use 70 percent of local content in the infrastructure deployment.	ICT and telecom	G/TRIMS/M/36 (5 September 2014); G/TRIMS/M/35 (20 December 2013); G/TRIMS/M/34 (19 June 2013); G/TRIMS/M/33 (22 November 2012); G/TRIMS/M/32 (14 June 2012)	None
Brazil	Notifications under Article 5.1 of the TRIMs Agreement	In 1995 and 1996, the government introduced provisional tax and tariff benefits to automobile manufacturers meeting certain targets for local content and export performance.	Automotive	G/TRIMS/M/6 (12 May 1997); G/TRIMS/M/4 (2 May 1996); G/TRIMS/M/3 (13 December 1995)	DS51, 52, 65, 81

Country	Measure	Description	Sector	Reference	
China	China – Local Content Requirements for Purchases of Technology by the Banking Sector	On 26 December 2014, the China Banking Regulatory Commission issued guidelines that prescribe certain indigenous innovation requirements. For instance, banking ICT equipment must contain indigenous Chinese intellectual property.	ICT and telecom	G/TRIMS/M/38 (27 July 2015)	None
China	China – Certain Investment Measures Pertaining to the Steel Sector	Under the 2005 Development Policies for the Iron and Steel Industry for the Eleventh Five Year Period, foreign steel companies were not allowed to invest in greenfield sites and assume more than 50 percent of equity stake in steel investments in China.	Steel	G/TRIMS/M/34 (19 June 2013); G/TRIMS/M/33 (22 November 2012)	None
China	Transitional Review Mechanism Pursuant to Paragraph 18 of the Protocol of Accession of the People's Republic of China to the WTO	Clean Development Mechanism projects on renewable energy appeared to be subject to certain LCRs. The National Development and Reform	Energy (renewables, petrochemicals)	G/TRIMS/M/26 (9 November 2007); G/TRIMS/M/25 (27 October 2006)	None

Annex 5.1 (*cont.*)

Applying Member	Agenda Item	Measure Description	Target Sector	WTO Source	WTO Dispute
		Commission drafted a legislation aimed at increasing the localization rate of large-scale petrochemical projects by 2010.			
China	Transitional Review Mechanism Pursuant to Paragraph 18 of the Protocol of Accession of the People's Republic of China to the WTO	China's Automobile Industry Development Policy (2004) and Administrative Measures for the Imports of Automobile Components Fulfilling the Characteristics of a Whole Vehicle could lead to the localization of automobile production.	Automotive	G/TRIMS/M/19 (5 November 2004)	DS339, 340, 342
Colombia	Notifications under Article 5.1 of the TRIMs Agreement	Under the agricultural absorption policy, the granting of import licenses for farm products depended on the quantity of local content absorbed.	Farm products	G/TRIMS/M/6 (12 May 1997); G/TRIMS/M/4 (2 May 1996)	None

Colombia, Ecuador, and Venezuela	Notifications under Article 5.1 of the TRIMs Agreement	A proposed amendment to the Andean common automotive regime foresaw an increased localization level.	Automotive	G/TRIMS/M/8 (20 July 1998)	None
India	India – Local Content Requirement in Solar Power Generation Projects	In December 2014 and February 2015, the Union Cabinet approved two solar power schemes with LCRs for photovoltaic cells and modules.	Energy (renewables)	G/TRIMS/M/39 (2 February 2016); G/TRIMS/M/38 (27 July 2015)	None
India	India – Certain Preferences to Domestically Manufactured Electronic Goods and Telecommunications Products	In February 2012, the Department of Electronics and Information Technology issued a policy notice requiring at least 30 percent of all government procurement of electronic products to be manufactured domestically. In October 2012, the Department of Telecommunications issued a notification on the requirements for preferences to domestically manufactured telecom products in government procurement.	Various	G/TRIMS/M/38 (27 July 2015); G/TRIMS/M/37 (21 November 2014); G/TRIMS/M/35 (20 December 2013); G/TRIMS/M/34 (19 June 2013); G/TRIMS/M/33 (22 November 2012); G/TRIMS/M/32 (14 June 2012)	None

Annex 5.1 (*cont.*)

Applying Member	Agenda Item	Measure Description	Target Sector	WTO Source	WTO Dispute
India	India – Mandatory Local Content Requirements in Project Guidelines for Phase I (Batch 1 and Batch 2) of the Jawaharlal Nehru National Solar Mission	In July 2010, the Ministry of New and Renewable Energy issued guidelines for the selection of projects under Phase I of the Jawaharlal Nehru National Solar Mission. For photovoltaic projects based on crystalline silicon technology, the guidelines required that all project developers use modules manufactured in India; for such projects selected in FY2011–2012, developers had to use both modules and cells manufactured in India. For projects based on solar thermal technology, the guidelines required 30 percent of local content in all plants and installations.	Energy (renewables)	G/TRIMS/M/33 (22 November 2012); G/TRIMS/M/32 (14 June 2012); G/TRIMS/M/31 (10 November 2011)	DS456

Country	Case	Description	Sector	G/TRIMS references	DS
India	Export and Import Policy, April 1997–March 2002	Public Notice No. 60 (1997) conditioned the import of wholly and partially knocked down kits on the requirement to achieve 50–70 percent localization.	Automotive	G/TRIMS/M/10 (15 April 1999); G/TRIMS/M/9 (13 January 1999); G/TRIMS/M/8 (20 July 1998)	DS146, 175
Indonesia	Indonesia – Local Content Requirements for 4G LTE Mobile Devices	In January 2015, the Ministry of Communication and Information Technology issued two draft regulations related to mandatory LCRs for the 4G LTE spectrum – including LTE smart phones – sold on the Indonesian market.	ICT and telecom	G/TRIMS/M/39 (2 February 2016); G/TRIMS/M/38 (27 July 2015)	None
Indonesia	Indonesia – Certain Measures Addressing Local Content in Investment in the Telecommunications Sector	Ministerial Decree No. 7/2009 requires that 30 percent of Broadband Wireless Access devices using the 2.3 GHz and the 3.3 GHz and 40 percent of base stations be domestically manufactured; that electric and telecommunication equipment be manufactured with at least	ICT and telecom	G/TRIMS/M/39 (2 February 2016); G/TRIMS/M/38 (27 July 2015); G/TRIMS/M/37 (21 November 2014); G/TRIMS/M/36 (5 September 2014); G/TRIMS/M/35 (20 December 2013);	None

Annex 5.1 (cont.)

Applying Member	Agenda Item	Measure Description	Target Sector	WTO Source	WTO Dispute
		50 percent of domestically procured components in five years.		G/TRIMS/M/34 (19 June 2013); G/TRIMS/M/33 (22 November 2012); G/TRIMS/M/32 (14 June 2012); G/TRIMS/M/31 (10 November 2011); G/TRIMS/M/30 (1 November 2010); G/TRIMS/M/29 (30 November 2009); G/TRIMS/M/28 (18 June 2009)	
Indonesia	Indonesia – Certain Local Content Provisions in the Energy Sector (Mining, Oil, and Gas)	The 2009 Mining Law and its implementing regulations state that operators must "prioritize" the utilization of local manpower and domestic goods and services in the mining, oil, and gas sectors.	Energy (mining, oil and gas)	G/TRIMS/M/39 (2 February 2016); G/TRIMS/M/38 (27 July 2015); G/TRIMS/M/37 (21 November 2014); G/TRIMS/M/36 (5 September 2014);	None

Country	Measure	Description	Sector	References	
				G/TRIMS/M/35 (20 December 2013); G/TRIMS/M/34 (19 June 2013); G/TRIMS/M/33 (22 November 2012); G/TRIMS/M/32 (14 June 2012); G/TRIMS/M/31 (10 November 2011); G/TRIMS/M/30 (1 November 2010); G/TRIMS/M/29 (30 November 2009)	None
Indonesia	Indonesia – Newly Adopted Industry Law and Trade Law	The Trade Law (2014) and the Industry Law (2014) contain LCRs for domestic products.	Various	G/TRIMS/M/39 (2 February 2016); G/TRIMS/M/38 (27 July 2015); G/TRIMS/M/37 (21 November 2014); G/TRIMS/M/36 (5 September 2014)	None
Indonesia	Indonesia – Minimum Local Product Requirement for Modern Retail Sector	The 2012 and 2013 regulations require modern shops and franchise establishments to	Retail	G/TRIMS/M/39 (2 February 2016); G/TRIMS/M/38 (27 July 2015);	

Annex 5.1 (*cont.*)

Applying Member	Agenda Item	Measure Description	Target Sector	WTO Source	WTO Dispute
		sell/use 80 percent of domestic products/services.		G/TRIMS/M/37 (21 November 2014); G/TRIMS/M/36 (5 September 2014)	
Indonesia	Notifications under Article 5.1 of the TRIMs Agreement	The 1996 National Car Program instituted fiscal incentives conditional on LCRs.	Automotive	G/TRIMS/M/6 (12 May 1997); G/TRIMS/M/5 (27 November 1996); G/TRIMS/M/4 (2 May 1996)	DS54, 55, 59, 64
Korea	Republic of Korea – Assistance Measures for Agricultural Machinery	The Ministry of Agriculture, Food, and Rural Affairs plans to introduce new criteria for evaluating certain agricultural machinery that can be purchased by farmers with a government loan, such as the machinery's performance scores in job creation in Korea,	Agricultural machinery	G/TRIMS/M/39 (2 February 2016)	None

Country	Measure	Description	Sector	Document	
Korea	Notifications under Article 5.1 of the TRIMs Agreement	contribution to exports from Korea, numbers of parts suppliers in Korea, and R&D in Korea. The government appears to have applied LCRs for certain types of tractors of less than fifty horsepower.	Agricultural machinery	G/TRIMS/M/5 (27 November 1996)	None
Malaysia	Notifications under Article 5.1 of the TRIMs Agreement	The government applied LCRs to certain investment incentives in manufacturing projects and local material content policy on motor vehicles.	Various	G/TRIMS/M/5 (27 November 1996)	None
Nigeria	Nigeria – Certain Measures Taken in the "Act to Provide for the Development of Nigerian Content in the Nigeria Oil and Gas Industry" of April 2010	The Nigerian Act (2010) contains LCRs for oil and gas projects.	Energy (oil and gas)	G/TRIMS/M/39 (2 February 2016); G/TRIMS/M/38 (27 July 2015); G/TRIMS/M/37 (21 November 2014); G/TRIMS/M/36 (5 September 2014); G/TRIMS/M/35 (20 December 2013); G/TRIMS/M/34 (19 June 2013);	None

Annex 5.1 (*cont.*)

Applying Member	Agenda Item	Measure Description	Target Sector	WTO Source	WTO Dispute
				G/TRIMS/M/33 (22 November 2012); G/TRIMS/M/32 (14 June 2012); G/TRIMS/M/31 (10 November 2011)	
Nigeria	Notifications under Article 5.1 of the TRIMs Agreement	The Industrial Policy of Nigeria granted incentives for the use of local raw materials.	Various	G/TRIMS/M/6 (12 May 1997)	None
Russia	Russian Federation – Local Content Requirements for Purchases by State-owned Enterprises	In 2014–2015, Russia adopted LCRs in the procurement of medical devices, textiles, machinery, vehicles, and software and appears to have extended them to purchases by State-owned enterprises.	Various	G/TRIMS/M/39 (2 February 2016); G/TRIMS/M/38 (27 July 2015)	None
Russia	Russian Federation – Local Content Requirements for Agricultural Equipment	In 2012–2013, Russia applied LCRs for agricultural equipment.	Agricultural machinery	G/TRIMS/M/39 (2 February 2016); G/TRIMS/M/38 (27 July 2015); G/TRIMS/M/37 (21 November 2014);	None

Russia	Russian Federation – Support Measures for the Automotive Sector; Russia – Certain Measures Relating to Industrial Assembly; Russia – Local Content Conditions in the "Auto Investment Program"	The Auto Investment Program and recent regulations (of, e.g., 2014, 2015) foresee subsidies and LCRs for industrial assembly, production, or purchase of automobiles.	Automotive	G/TRIMS/M/36 (5 September 2014); G/TRIMS/M/35 (20 December 2013); G/TRIMS/M/34 (19 June 2013)	None
Turkey	Turkey – Local Content Requirements in the Electricity Generation	Amendments to the Renewable Energy Law (2005) appear to grant larger subsidies to electricity generators using local content.	Energy (renewables)	G/TRIMS/M/39 (2 February 2016); G/TRIMS/M/38 (27 July 2015); G/TRIMS/M/37 (21 November 2014); G/TRIMS/M/36 (5 September 2014); G/TRIMS/M/34 (19 June 2013) G/TRIMS/M/38 (27 July 2015)	None
Ukraine	Ukraine – Certain Local Content Provisions in the Law "On Amendments to the Law	Under the 2012 amendments to the Law on Electricity Production, raw materials, fixed assets, works and	Energy	G/TRIMS/M/35 (20 December 2013); G/TRIMS/M/34 (19 June 2013);	None

Annex 5.1 (*cont.*)

Applying Member	Agenda Item	Measure Description	Target Sector	WTO Source	WTO Dispute
	of Ukraine 'On Electric Power Industry'"	services, and so on used in the development of energy power plants must be at least 50 percent locally sourced.		G/TRIMS/M/33 (22 November 2012)	
Uruguay	Uruguay – Local Content Requirements for Wind Power Equipment	Decree 403/009 (2009) imposes LCRs for construction of wind farms.	Energy (renewables)	G/TRIMS/M/36 (5 September 2014); G/TRIMS/M/35 (20 December 2013)	None
United States	United States – Certain Local Content Requirements in Some of the Renewable Energy Programs	Some State-level renewable energy programs appear to contain LCRs.	Energy (renewables)	G/TRIMS/M/39 (2 February 2016); G/TRIMS/M/38 (27 July 2015); G/TRIMS/M/37 (21 November 2014); G/TRIMS/M/36 (5 September 2014); G/TRIMS/M/35 (20 December 2013); G/TRIMS/M/34 (19 June 2013)	None

| United States | United States – Domestic Content Requirement in Procurement by Water Utilities in the United States | Procurement by water utilities in South Carolina, Pennsylvania, West Virginia, and some New England States is linked to LCRs with regard to the supply of ductile iron pipes and fittings for use in water projects. | Water supply | G/TRIMS/M/36 (5 September 2014); G/TRIMS/M/35 (20 December 2013); G/TRIMS/M/34 (19 June 2013) | None |

Source: Compiled by the author on the basis of the relevant WTO sources.

Notes:

* The database was completed on 18 March 2016.

** Total: thirty-four measures. The measure's description is generally based on the background information provided by a member taking issue on that measure and requesting committee-level discussion.

6

The Greening of Industrial Policy

Industrialization can have negative effects on the environment, causing global warming, air and water pollution, depletion of natural resources, extinction of species, and destruction of ecosystems. Many environmental problems typically cross national boundaries, sometimes reaching the global scale. This necessitates adequate counteractions on the domestic and international planes. Governments employ various measures at the central and regional/local levels to mitigate or adapt to environmental degradation. Quite often such actions impact on international trade and hence fall within the WTO legal order. Therefore, the greening of industrial policies occurs at the intersection of trade and environmental issues. Due to spatial constraints, this chapter focuses on border carbon adjustments, renewable energy subsidies, ecolabeling schemes, environmental exceptions of Article XX of the GATT, and the "trade–environment" harmonization problem.

6.1 Environmental Dimensions of Industrial Policy and Trade

The environmental situation on our planet has seriously deteriorated since the recent past. Just to consider the case of air pollution as an example, around half of the anthropogenic carbon dioxide (CO_2) emissions since 1750 have occurred in the last forty years.[1] Whereas OECD countries – commonly known as most advanced economies – were responsible for nearly 77 percent of total greenhouse gas (GHG) emissions in the past, about two-thirds of new emissions are attributable to non-OECD (developing) countries.[2] With worldwide climate mitigation efforts, substantial cuts in GHG emissions over the next few decades can

---

[1] Intergovernmental Panel on Climate Change, "Climate Change 2014: Synthesis Report," 2015, pp. 4, 45.
[2] WTO and UNEP, "Trade and Climate Change," Joint Report, 2009, p. viii.

greatly reduce risks of climate change in the second half of the twenty-first century and beyond.[3]

According to economic theory, activities of one agent can affect others in causing environmental costs (negative externality) or providing societal benefits (positive externality). Since the market price of that agent's product fails to reflect the true value of such external costs or benefits, its product will be overproduced in the case of a negative externality or underproduced in the case of a positive externality. In other words, such a market failure leads to the overproduction of environment-damaging goods and the underproduction of ecofriendly goods. Therefore, the government intervenes to "internalize" external costs and benefits into the price-setting by, respectively, imposing an additional burden (e.g., tax) on polluters and incentivizing greening activities.[4]

The panel in *China – Raw Materials* noted that, although a higher level of wealth can stimulate public demand for a cleaner environment, environmental improvement is unlikely to occur unless the government responds with environmental protection policies.[5] The panel made this remark with respect to the "environmental Kuznets curve" hypothesis that presumes that environmental degradation increases in the early stages of economic growth, but, beyond a certain level of income per capita, this trend reverses so that economic growth at high income levels leads to environmental improvement.[6]

The world trade has grown tremendously by at least thirty-two times compared to its level in 1950[7] thanks to, inter alia, global reductions of tariff and nontariff barriers. Trade liberalization affects the environment, and particularly the climate, in different ways. With a "scale effect," the expansion of economic activity spurred by market openings worsens the environment when the consumption of energy in production and transportation and consequent GHG emissions increase. By contrast, open trade reduces emission intensity of output through a "technique effect" by lowering the cost of environmental goods and services. Thus, the contribution of trade to promoting the transfer of environmentally sound

---

[3] Intergovernmental Panel on Climate Change, *supra* note 1, pp. 17–18.
[4] This paragraph is based on the summarized explanation of the economics in World Trade Report, 2010, Ch. 3, *supra* note 82, pp. 49–50.
[5] Panel Reports, *China – Raw Materials*, paras. 7.551–7.552.
[6] See David I. Stern, "The Rise and Fall of the Environmental Kuznets Curve," 32 *World Development* 1419 (2004).
[7] WTO and UNEP, *supra* note 2, p. 48.

technologies has gained international recognition.[8] Finally, a "composition effect" takes place when trade changes the structure of a country's production and thereby increases or decreases emissions depending on whether carbon-intensive industries expand or contract.[9]

International initiatives on sustainable development and environmental issues advanced in the last few decades have catalyzed implementation of green economy policies in both developed and developing countries. Governments have used a mix of policy instruments for internalizing externalities, enhancing institutional and regulatory capabilities, boosting green investment across key sectors, and strengthening information-related and social policies.[10] The State leaders in the UN Conference on Sustainable Development (2012) acknowledged the role of green economy in achieving sustainable development, but affirmed that related national policies should comply with international law and should not constitute "a means of arbitrary or unjustifiable discrimination or a disguised restriction on international trade."[11]

The preamble of the WTO Agreement stresses the importance of the optimal use of the world's resources in accordance with sustainable development goals and the need for protection and preservation of the environment. But as the Appellate Body observed, the recognized autonomy of WTO members to define their own environmental policies is circumscribed by their multilateral trade obligations.[12]

6.2 Border Carbon Adjustments

As of 31 August 2015, thirty-nine national and twenty-three subnational jurisdictions put a price on carbon through taxes and cap-and-trade (or emission trading) systems. These carbon pricing mechanisms have remarkably expanded by 90 percent since 2012 and cover about 12 percent of the annual global GHG emissions.[13] But nonuniversal

---

[8] See UN General Assembly Resolution, "The Future We Want," A/RES/66/288 (27 July 2012), para. 271.

[9] For a review of the economic literature on these three effects, see WTO and UNEP, *supra* note 2, pp. 49–52.

[10] See UN Division for Sustainable Development, "A Guidebook to the Green Economy – Issue 3: Exploring Green Economy Policies and International Experience with National Strategies," 2012, pp. 7–9, 14.

[11] UN General Assembly Resolution, *supra* note 8, paras. 56, 58.

[12] Appellate Body Report, *US – Gasoline*, p. 30.

[13] World Bank and Ecofys, "State and Trends of Carbon Pricing," Joint Report, 2015, p. 20.

application of such measures is a cause for concern. They impose extra costs on domestic firms, making them less competitive than firms from countries that do not operate similar schemes. This, in turn, can trigger "carbon leakage" when affected firms move to countries with weaker climate policies (i.e., "carbon heavens"). In order to level the playing field, governments applying carbon pricing measures may decide to make border adjustments thereto.

6.2.1 The Case of Carbon Taxes

Carbon taxes generally refer to taxes on the carbon content of fossil fuels, that is, CO_2 emitted during their combustion. A carbon tax was initially introduced in Finland in 1990, followed later by three other Nordic countries, Slovenia, Italy, Estonia, Switzerland, and others. Canada adopted a carbon tax at a regional level. Furthermore, energy taxes – special charges based on the energy content of energy sources – act as "implicit carbon taxes" for their de facto impact on CO_2 emissions associated with fossil fuels.[14]

Whether the carbon tax is indeed a "tax" in the WTO terminology is crucial for defining the scope of applicable law.[15] Since a carbon charge applies to domestic carbon-intensive products, this fact alone would arguably suffice to characterize it as a "tax" rather than a customs duty that by definition applies to imported products only.[16] Thus, our analysis below is based on the premise that carbon charges are internal taxes.

Carbon taxes become a WTO issue if they affect foreign products through BTA (or border tax adjustment). As it follows from a GATT working party report (1970), BTA is the practice of charging imports with, and exempting exports from, internal taxes, namely:

> any fiscal measures which put into effect, in whole or in part, the destination principle (i.e. which enable exported products to be relieved of some or all of the tax charged in the exporting country in respect of

[14] For an overview of carbon tax systems, see WTO and UNEP, *supra* note 2, pp. 90–1 and accompanying footnotes.

[15] On this issue, see, e.g., Joost Pauwelyn, "U.S. Federal Climate Policy and Competitiveness Concerns: The Limits and Options of International Trade Law," Working Paper No. NI WP 07–02, Nicholas Institute for Environmental Policy Solutions at Duke University, 2007, pp. 17–21.

[16] WTO, Committee on Trade and Environment – Taxes and Charges for Environmental Purposes – Border Tax Adjustment – Note by the Secretariat, WT/CTE/W/47 (2 May 1997), para. 55.

> similar domestic products sold to consumers on the home market and
> which enable imported products sold to consumers to be charged with
> some or all of the tax charged in the importing country in respect of
> similar domestic products).[17]

Unlike the origin principle under which goods are taxed in the country
of production, the destination principle prescribes the collection of taxes
at the final point of consumption. The BTA system intends to level the
playing field between taxed domestic and untaxed foreign products and
to prevent double taxation on the same product in different markets.
Only indirect taxes are eligible for BTA.[18]

Pursuant to footnote 58 to Annex I(e) of the SCM Agreement, direct
taxes are "taxes on wages, profits, interests, rents, royalties, and all other
forms of income, and taxes on the ownership of real property"; indirect
taxes include "sales, excise, turnover, value added, franchise, stamp,
transfer, inventory and equipment taxes, border taxes and *all taxes other
than direct taxes and import charges*" (emphasis added). The SCM
Agreement elaborates Article XVI of the GATT so this chategorization
of taxes may well be relevant to the GATT provisions. From the italicized
words it may be inferred that carbon taxes qualify as indirect taxes,
because they are not mentioned among direct taxes and do not fall within
"import charges" – a fiscal measure that footnote 58 distinguishes from
domestic *taxes*.[19]

BTAs on the import side are subject to Articles II and III of the GATT.
Article II:2(a) permits members to impose "at any time on the importation of any product":

> a charge equivalent to an internal tax imposed consistently with the provi-
> sions of paragraph 2 of Article III* [asterisk in original] in respect of the like
> domestic product or in respect of an article from which the imported
> product has been manufactured or produced in whole or in part.[20]

Article III:2 – mentioned in Article II:2(a) – requires that internal taxes
or charges applied, "directly or indirectly," on domestic products be not
more burdensome for competing imported products. The drafters of the

---

[17] L/3464, Ch. 4, *supra* note 59, para. 4.   [18] See Section 4.3.3.1.
[19] See also Christine Kaufmann and Rolf H. Weber, "Carbon-Related Border Tax Adjustment: Mitigating Climate Change or Restricting International Trade?," 10 *World Trade
Review* 497 (2011), p. 520.
[20] This provision is complemented by *Ad* Article III, which says that an internal tax or
charge collected at the point of importation and applicable to both the imported and like
domestic product is to be regarded as a tax measure within the meaning of Article III.

GATT explained the term "equivalent" in Article II:2(a) as meaning that "if a [charge] is imposed on perfume because it contains alcohol, the [charge] to be imposed must take into consideration the value of the alcohol [i.e., the content] and not the value of the perfume."[21] The drafters also introduced the word "indirectly" to Article III:2 to embrace taxes on production of goods.[22] In short, the GATT negotiation records suggest that both provisions apply even to taxes on the *processing* of a product.

But the scope of the processing covered by BTAs is not clear. In particular, the aforementioned 1970 working party report could not conclude whether border adjustment was allowed for "tax occultes" (e.g., taxes on advertising, energy, machinery, or transport) that target certain items and services used in the transportation and production of goods.[23] Taxes targeting CO_2 emissions during the production process arguably belong to such tax occultes. In *US – Superfund*, the GATT panel examined a US tax on certain chemicals and imported substances manufactured with the use of those chemicals. The complainant submitted that such tax was not eligible for the BTA, as it was designed to counter polluting activities within the United States, and the "Polluter-Pays Principle" would require the US authorities to tax only domestic products – the sole cause of pollution in the United States.[24] But the panel found that policy purposes of taxation were not relevant to the tax's eligibility for BTA.[25] The panel acknowledged the lawfulness of the BTA on imported final products with the chemical inputs being a taxable base and thus leaned some support to the idea that tax occultes are adjustable at the border.[26]

But the *US – Superfund* panel did not specify whether BTA is available exclusively to the inputs that are *physically present* in the final product. WTO provisions on export-related BTAs seem to bring some clarity to this issue, providing a legal context for interpretation of the reference in Article II:2(a) to "an article from which the imported product has been

---

[21] EPCT/TAC/PV/26, p. 21, quoted in GATT Analytical Index, Ch. 1, *supra* note 73, vol. 1, p. 86.

[22] EPCT/C.II/W.5, p. 5 and EPCT/A/PV/9, p. 19 quoted in GATT Analytical Index, Ch. 1, *supra* note 73, vol. 1, p. 141.

[23] L/3464, Ch. 4, *supra* note 59, para. 15.

[24] GATT Panel Report, *US – Superfund*, para. 5.2.3.   [25] *Ibid.*, para. 5.2.4.

[26] *Ibid.*, paras. 5.2.7–5.2.8.

manufactured or produced in whole or in part."[27] In particular, footnote 1 to Article 1.1(a)(1)(ii) of the SCM Agreement accepts border adjustment (i.e., the exemption or remission) of indirect taxes on exports "in amounts not in excess of those which have accrued." Furthermore, Annex I(h) of the SCM Agreement allows the nonexcess exemption or remission of "prior-stage cumulative indirect taxes" on inputs consumed in the production of exported products. As stated in footnote 61 to Annex II of the SCM Agreement, the inputs here refer to "inputs physically incorporated, energy, fuels and oil used in the production process and catalysts which are consumed in the course of their use to obtain the exported product." With the reference to "energy, fuels and oil," the SCM Agreement permits BTAs for these nondetectable inputs of exports. This contrasts with the corresponding provision of the Tokyo Round Subsidies Code that confined BTAs only to inputs "physically incorporated" in the exported product.[28] Therefore, the explicit permission of export-side BTAs for a finished product's invisible components in question (energy, etc.) should logically support permissibility of such BTAs on the import side.

To conclude, WTO law seems to be tolerant of appropriately designed border carbon tax adjustments as long as carbon is deemed to fall within the scope of consumed "energy, fuels and oil" or perhaps "catalysts." While BTA-based carbon taxes help in fighting climate change, they are undesirable if they act as a cover for protectionist policies in selected sectors.[29] As for the practical use, they may not be easily introduced everywhere. Indeed, the idea of imposing a carbon *tax*, hence an extra financial burden, is itself not appealing to domestic stakeholders; and measuring and verifying the carbon footprint of products is technically difficult.[30]

---

[27] Robert Howse and Antonia L. Eliason, "Domestic and International Strategies to Address Climate Change: An Overview of the WTO Legal Issues," in Thomas Cottier, Olga Nartova, and Sadeq Z. Bigdeli (eds.), *International Trade Regulation and the Mitigation of Climate Change* (New York: Cambridge University Press, 2009), p. 66.

[28] See paragraphs (h) and (i) of the Annex of the Agreement on Interpretation and Application of Articles VI, XVI and XXIII of the GATT (Tokyo Round). See also WT/CTE/W/47, *supra* note 16, para. 74.

[29] See Henrik Horn and Petros C. Mavroidis, "To B(TA) or Not to B(TA)? On the Legality and Desirability of Border Tax Adjustments from a Trade Perspective," 34 *The World Economy* 1911 (2011), pp. 1932–6.

[30] Gary Clyde Hufbauer, Steve Charnovitz, and Jisun Kim, *Global Warming and the World Trading System* (Washington, DC: Peterson Institute for International Economics, 2009), pp. 68–9.

6.2.2   The Case of Emission Allowances

Under the cap-and-trade system, the government distributes emission permits ("allowances") among pollutants within a predetermined cap on total emissions in the designated territory. The cap is lowered over time to reduce the amount of gaseous discharges into the atmosphere. Producers that exceed the level of permitted emissions can buy allowances from those who pollute less. The price paid for allowances – in essence, the carbon price – is set, ideally, by market forces through trading or auctioning. The cap-and-trade scheme is currently implemented or planned in the EU members, Norway, Iceland, Liechtenstein, New Zealand, Kazakhstan, and Korea; and at a regional/local level in Alberta, Beijing, California, Chongqing, Connecticut, Delaware, Guangdong, Hubei, Kyoto, New York, Quebec, Tokyo, and so on.[31]

The first international scheme was launched in the EU. According to the European Commission, it covers around 45 percent of overall EU GHG emissions and applies to more than eleven thousand power stations and industrial plants located in the region, as well as aviation activities. Companies there must surrender allowances for every tonne of CO_2 (or the equivalent amount of certain other GHGs) that they emitted in the previous year. They receive some allowances for free, but for the remaining emissions they need to buy extra allowances or use any surplus allowances they have saved from previous years. Failure to comply with the permit levels entails heavy fines.[32]

With respect to the border adjustment issue, a key question is whether the obligation to purchase allowances constitutes an internal tax or charge in the sense of Article III:2 of the GATT. In the case of a positive answer, imposition of this obligation on foreign carbon-emitting products would be warranted under Article II:2(a) of the GATT with respect to carbon as a potentially acceptable part of "an article" used in manufacturing the products in question.

The OECD defines taxes as compulsory payments to the government which are "unrequited." This means that benefits provided by the government to taxpayers are not necessarily in proportion to their payments.[33] Following this definition, the obligation to hold an emission

---

[31] World Bank and Ecofys, *supra* note 13, p. 22.
[32] European Commission, "The EU Emissions Trading System (EU ETS)," 2016, https://ec.europa.eu/clima/sites/clima/files/factsheet_ets_en.pdf.
[33] OECD, "Tax: Tax Revenue," https://data.oecd.org/tax/tax-revenue.htm.

permit could be considered a tax, as it serves community interests, and affected companies do not receive anything identifiable in return.[34] But the same definition can also work against this view, as companies, in fact, obtain a (marketable) permission to emit CO_2 within the level directly proportional to the amount paid.[35]

The judgment (2011) of the Court of Justice of the EU (CJEU) in *Air Transport Association of America and Others* supports the "nontax" view. There, American airline companies challenged EU Directive 2008/101/ EC before a UK court for the inclusion of aviation activities in the EU emission trading scheme and asked for a preliminary ruling from the CJEU. Under the EU system at issue, from 2012 onward all domestic and foreign airlines were supposed to hold allowances for CO_2 emitted during all flights entering and leaving EU airspace, including the part performed over third countries and the high seas. The EU plan envisaged allocation of 85 percent of allowances free of charge and the remaining 15 percent for sale. The number of allowances for aircraft operators was calculated on the basis of their fuel consumption for the covered flights in the preceding year and an emission factor.[36] The claimants alleged that, inter alia, the EU scheme violated the obligation under the EU–US Open Skies Agreement to exempt the fuel load from any fiscal charges. But the CJEU found that the scheme was not "a tax, duty, fee or charge" in the sense of that obligation for the following reasons: there was no direct nexus between the quantity of fuel consumed by an aircraft and the actual cost of obtaining allowances; the scheme did not intend to generate public revenues; and the price of allowances was set by the market rather than predetermined by the government.[37] Should the CJEU's finding hold true for the WTO treatment of taxes, one may argue that emission permits do

---

[34] See Pauwelyn, *supra* note 15, p. 21; R. Ismer and K. Neuhoff, "Border Tax Adjustments: A Feasible Way to Address Nonparticipation in Emission Trading," CMI Working Paper No. 36, 2004, p. 11.

[35] Tracey Epps and Andrew Green, *Reconciling Trade and Climate: How the WTO Can Help Address Climate Change* (Cheltenham, the United Kingdom/Northampton, MA, the United States: Edward Elgar, 2010), p. 138.

[36] See Directive 2008/101/EC of the European Parliament and of the Council of 19 November 2008 Amending Directive 2003/87/EC so as to Include Aviation Activities in the Scheme for Greenhouse Gas Emission Allowance Trading within the Community, OJ L 8, 13.1.2009, pp. 3–21.

[37] Judgment of the Court (Grand Chamber), *Air Transport Association of America and Others v Secretary of State for Energy and Climate Change*, Case C-366/10, 21 December 2011, paras. 142–3.

not constitute an internal tax/charge under Article III:2 of the GATT,[38] and are thus not eligible for BTAs permitted by Article II:2(a) of the GATT.

The cap-and-trade regime can nevertheless fall within the scope of Article III:4 of the GATT as "laws, regulations and requirements affecting [the] internal sale, offering for sale, purchase, transportation, distribution or use [of products]." *Ad* Article III of the GATT accepts adjustability of such regulatory measures on the import side, subject to the national treatment obligation:

> [A]ny law, regulation or requirement of the kind referred to in paragraph 1 which applies to an imported product and to the like domestic product and is ... enforced in the case of the imported product at the time or point of importation, is nevertheless to be regarded as ... a law, regulation or requirement of the kind referred to in paragraph 1, and is accordingly subject to the provisions of Article III.

Pursuant to WTO jurisprudence, Article III:4 is violated if (i) the imported and domestic products at issue are "like products"; (ii) the challenged measure is a "law, regulation, or requirement"; and (iii) the imported products are accorded "less favourable" treatment than that accorded to like domestic products.[39] The cap-and-trade legislation satisfies the second condition, but may not meet the remaining ones.

Under the first condition, a key question is whether different carbon intensity per se – resulting from the production process – makes physically identical or similar domestic and imported products "unlike" so as to warrant more burdensome requirements on "carbon-rich" imported products than on "carbon-poor" domestic counterparts. WTO case law on Article III:4 does not directly elucidate this issue in comparable situations. Specifically, the panel in *EC – Approval and Marketing of Biotech Products* practiced judicial economy as to whether genetically modified and non-genetically-modified products were "like."[40] In *US – Tuna II (Article 21.5 – Mexico)*, the panel simply accepted the parties' agreement that tuna products at issue were "like," without commenting further on

---

[38] See Lorand Bartels, "The WTO Legality of the Application of the EU's Emission Trading System to Aviation," 23 *European Journal of International Law* 429 (2012), pp. 439–40. For the opposing view, see Joshua Meltzer, "Climate Change and Trade – The EU Aviation Directive and the WTO," 15 *Journal of International Economic Law* 111 (2012), pp. 130–1.

[39] Appellate Body Report, *Korea – Various Measures on Beef*, para. 113.

[40] Panel Reports, *EC – Approval and Marketing of Biotech Products*, para. 7.3422.

whether the difference in fishing methods affected the likeness of those products.[41] Similarly, the panel in *EC − Seal Products* merely relied on the absence of the parties' doubt about the likeness of seal products regardless of seal hunting.[42]

But in the past, the unadopted GATT panel report in *US − Tuna (Mexico)* was more straightforward in saying that a difference in PPMs − not detectable in the product − was not relevant to the likeness determination, as national treatment covered only measures affecting products as such.[43] Following this logic, CO_2 emissions that do not affect the product as such should, in principle, fall outside of the Article III likeness consideration. By contrast, if, for example, a carbon footprint label enables consumers to distinguish between facially like products and this affects their purchasing decisions, the carbon intensity would make the products "unlike" in the context of consumers' tastes and habits − one of the accepted "like product" criteria. There also seems to be some possibility to consider the products at issue as "unlike" from the perspective of suppliers if the latter cannot easily shift from the production of one product to the other because of different PPMs.[44] Indeed, the Appellate Body's recognition of a product's supply-side substitutability in defining a proper market in different legal contexts may offer a potentially new "like product" criterion for Article III issues.[45] But unlikeness of the products cannot be proved only by consumer tastes/habits or the supply-side factor, each taken separately, because, as the Appellate Body emphasized, the "like product" standard requires a *cumulative* analysis of *all* relevant criteria.[46] Thus, in the light of the jurisprudence so far, Article III hardly accepts product distinctions based on non-product-

---

[41] Panel Report, *US − Tuna II (Mexico)* (*Article 21.5 − Mexico*), paras. 7.496, 7.71. But in the original dispute, the panel stipulated that its likeness analysis under Article 2.1 of the TBT Agreement involved a comparison of tuna products from different sources rather than dolphin-safe vs. not dolphin-safe tuna. See Panel Report, *US − Tuna II (Mexico)*, para. 7.250.

[42] Panel Reports, *EC − Seal Products*, paras. 7.607, 7.138−7.139.

[43] GATT Panel Report, *US − Tuna (Mexico)*, paras. 5.11, 5.15.

[44] For supply-side substitutability as a possible likeness standard, see Won-mog Choi, *"Like Products" in International Trade Law: Towards a Consistent GATT/WTO Jurisprudence* (New York: Oxford University Press, 2003), pp. 34−49, 66−71.

[45] Shadikhodjaev, Ch. 3, *supra* note 50, p. 875; Shadikhodjaev, Ch. 5, *supra* note 42, p. 145.

[46] Appellate Body Report, *EC − Asbestos*, para. 109.

related PPMs (NPR-PPMs) – those that do not leave any physically detectable traces on the product.[47]

As for the third element of the Article III:4 test above, different treatment of imported products is not necessarily "less favourable."[48] Treatment is "less favourable" only when a measure modifies the conditions of competition in the same market to the detriment of the imported like products.[49] Such import-biased modification takes place where, for instance, free allocation of emission permits is not (equally) available to foreign goods as compared to domestic counterparts. Another example can be derived from the Lieberman–Warner Bill (2007) that intended (but eventually failed) to introduce a cap-and-trade system in the United States. Under the bill in question, the number of allowances for domestic companies was proportional to their *own* emissions in relation to a *particular good*, but that for importers was based on the *average* of emissions by the exporting country's all companies producing *multiple goods within a particular category*.[50] One can well argue that such a proposed scheme was designed not even-handedly with an underlying purpose to protect domestic industries. Obviously, the cap-and-trade system applied in these or similar ways is likely to be found to treat imported goods less favorably in contravention of Article III:4. But this would also open the door for a legal defense under the WTO (general) exceptions.

6.3   Renewable Energy Subsidies

As environmentally friendly and virtually nonexhaustible resources, renewables typically include hydropower, solar energy, wind power, geothermal power, bioenergy, and ocean power. They are used in the

---

[47] Erich Vranes, *Trade and the Environment: Fundamental Issues in International Law, WTO Law, and Legal Theory* (New York: Oxford University Press, 2009), p. 324. By contrast, some commentators defend source-neutral PPMs as being consistent with Article III. See Robert Howse and Donald Regan, "The Product/Process Distinction – An Illusory Basis for Disciplining 'Unilateralism' in Trade Policy," 11 *European Journal of International Law* 249 (2000); Steve Charnovitz, "The Law of Environmental 'PPMs' in the WTO: Debunking the Myth of Illegality," 27 *Yale Journal of International Law* 59 (2002).

[48] Appellate Body Report, *Korea – Various Measures on Beef*, para. 135.

[49] Appellate Body Report, *Dominican Republic – Import and Sale of Cigarettes*, para. 93.

[50] Paul-Erik Veel, "Carbon Tariffs and the WTO: An Evaluation of Feasible Policies," 12 *Journal of International Economic Law* 749 (2009), p. 769.

electricity, heating/cooling, and transport sectors.[51] In 2015, 173 countries had renewable energy targets, and 146 countries had renewable energy support policies in place at the national or provincial level.[52]

Apart from general fiscal stimuli, specific support programs in this sphere comprise feed-in tariff (FIT) and premiums, quota obligations, public tenders or auctions, and net metering.[53] Under the FIT system, generators sell green electricity on a contractual long-term basis at a fixed price that covers both production costs and profits. Unlike FITs, feed-in premiums are paid on top of the electricity market price and fluctuate over time. Quota schemes oblige utilities, electricity suppliers, consumers, or other actors to purchase a predetermined minimum share of green electricity or else pay a fine for noncompliance. The quota obligations are usually accompanied with tradable specific certificates or credits that prove the renewable electricity utilization. Public tenders or auctions assure winning generators of stable purchases of renewable electricity within a defined period at a price set through the bidding process. Finally, net metering allows households or small businesses that have generating facilities – like solar photovoltaic installations or small-scale wind turbines – to send back nonused green electricity produced from those facilities into the grid and obtain a credit from their electricity meter running backward which they can use against the electricity taken from the grid at other times. In 2015, the feed-in policies were most popular and implemented in 110 countries, followed by a quota system (100 countries), tendering (64), and net metering (52).[54]

6.3.1   Government Support as a "Subsidy"

Trade frictions over renewable energy subsidies have unfolded since recently. At the domestic level, the United States, the EU, and other economies importing green-power-generating equipment and components (e.g., solar panels) or renewable energy sources (e.g., biofuels) have used the countervailing duty mechanism to offset subsidized prices.[55]

---

[51] International Energy Agency, "Renewables," www.iea.org/topics/renewables.
[52] REN21, "Renewables 2016: Global Status Report," 2016, p. 20.
[53] See Heymi Bahar, Jagoda Egeland, and Ronald Steenblik, "Domestic Incentive Measures for Renewable Energy with Possible Trade Implications," OECD Trade and Environment Working Paper No. 2013/01, 2013.
[54] REN21, *supra* note 52, pp. 19–20.
[55] See Sherzod Shadikhodjaev, "Renewable Energy and Government Support: Time to 'Green' the SCM Agreement?," 14 *World Trade Review* 479 (2015), pp. 488–92.

At the multilateral level, seven WTO complaints have challenged government support for renewables in the EU, Canada, China, India, and the United States.[56]

The *Canada – Renewable Energy / Canada – Feed-In Tariff Program* case[57] examined a FIT program of Canadian province Ontario that entitled generators of solar- or wind-based electricity to a guaranteed price per kWh of electricity under twenty-year or forty-year contracts if they met the "Minimum Required Domestic Content Level" for installation of related equipment.[58] The Appellate Body characterized FIT-based electricity purchases by the Ontario Power Authority as a financial contribution in the form of the government purchase of goods within the meaning of Article 1.1(a)(1)(iii) of the SCM Agreement.[59] As for the benefit determination, the Appellate Body examined whether FIT prices were more advantageous than non-FIT electricity prices in the marketplace and made two remarkable points in this respect.

First, the definition of an appropriate market – where government-supported prices should be compared with nonsupported relevant prices – necessitates consideration of both demand-side (consumer-based) and supply-side (producer-based) factors to check if renewable electricity and conventional electricity are sufficiently substitutable to be deemed to be in the same market. Notwithstanding the demand-side factors that preclude consumers from distinguishing electricity based on its source of generation, the Appellate Body stressed the supply-side factors to conclude that the price comparison should be conducted not within the entire blended electricity market, but exclusively within wind- and solar-energy-generated electricity markets.[60] Under this market

---

[56] These are *US – Renewable Energy* (DS510, consultation requested 9 September 2016), *European Union – Certain Measures on the Importation and Marketing of Biodiesel and Measures Supporting the Biodiesel Industry* (DS459, 15 May 2013), *India – Solar Cells* (DS456, 6 February 2013), *European Union and Certain Member States – Certain Measures Affecting the Renewable Energy Generation Sector* (DS452, 5 November 2012), *Canada – Feed-In Tariff Program* (DS426, 11 August 2011), *China – Measures Concerning Wind Power Equipment* (DS419, 22 December 2010), and *Canada – Renewable Energy* (DS412, 13 September 2010).

[57] The following discussion on *Canada – Renewable Energy / Canada – Feed-In Tariff Program* is largely drawn on this author's extensive analysis of these disputes. See Shadikhodjaev, Ch. 3, *supra* note 50.

[58] Panel Reports, *Canada – Renewable Energy / Canada – Feed-In Tariff Program*, paras. 7.64–7.68.

[59] Appellate Body Reports, *Canada – Renewable Energy / Canada – Feed-In Tariff Program*, para. 5.128.

[60] *Ibid.*, para. 5.178.

definition, one cannot compare renewable electricity prices paid by the government with conventional electricity prices – which are typically lower than the former – to find an advantage (i.e., "more than adequate remuneration") to renewable electricity generators.

Second, the government's support for creation of a *new* market, such as the market of renewable electricity, does not "in and of itself" qualify as a benefit, and hence a subsidy:

> [A] distinction should be drawn between, on the one hand, government interventions that create markets that would otherwise not exist and, on the other hand, other types of government interventions in support of certain players in markets that already exist, or to correct market distortions therein. Where a government creates a market, it cannot be said that the government intervention distorts the market, as there would not be a market if the government had not created it. While the creation of markets by a government does not *in and of itself* give rise to subsidies within the meaning of the SCM Agreement, government interventions in existing markets may amount to subsidies when they take the form of a financial contribution, or income or price support, and confer a benefit to specific enterprises or industries.[61]

This passage reflects economic justification of public interventions where markets are incomplete.[62] More specifically, it allows some room for the development of infant industries, not necessarily confined to renewable energy. Any government involved in the establishment of a new industrial sector can, in principle, rely on this finding to avoid antisubsidy measures. But the appellate decision is silent on how to determine whether that sector indeed represents a new market in its early stages of formation. One can assume that the longer a government's support lasts for an "infant" industry, the lesser its chance is that it will escape the SCM Agreement's constraints.

Despite some commentators' criticism of the benefit analysis,[63] the appellate findings should be commended from, at least, the

---

[61] *Ibid.*, para. 5.188 (emphasis in original).   [62] See Section 1.1.1.1.

[63] See, e.g., Aaron Cosbey and Petros C. Mavroidis, "A Turquoise Mess: Green Subsidies, Blue Industrial Policy and Renewable Energy: The Case for Redrafting the Subsidies Agreement of the WTO," 17 *Journal of International Economic Law* 11 (2014); Rajib Pal, "Has the Appellate Body's Decision in *Canada – Renewable Energy/Canada – Feed-in Tariff Program* Opened the Door for Production Subsidies?," 17 *Journal of International Economic Law* 125 (2014); Luca Rubini, "'The Good, the Bad, and the Ugly.' Lessons on Methodology in Legal Analysis from the Recent WTO Litigation on Renewable Energy Subsidies," 48 *Journal of World Trade* 895 (2014); Rolf H. Weber and Rika Koch,

environmental point of view.[64] While WTO members have been reluctant to "green" the current subsidy rule book, the Appellate Body interpreted the SCM Agreement in a manner that carves out some policy space for promotion of clean energy. Indeed, the two points considered above make it more difficult for a challenger to prove that a green stimulus scheme is a WTO-disciplined "subsidy" particularly where *only* government intervention can make high-cost and economically inefficient green projects implementable. This probably explains why the United States omitted the SCM Agreement in its panel request in *India – Solar Cells*, although it did invoke that agreement in the consultation request when the appellate ruling in *Canada – Renewable Energy / Canada – Feed-In Tariff Program* was not issued yet.[65]

Certainly, the legislative way of "greening" the existing subsidy rules is better than the interpretative way in accommodating clean energy support policies. The SCM Agreement could be amended to incorporate a due restraint clause that would prevent WTO members from taking antisubsidy measures in the renewable energy sector. To minimize possible trade distortions, due restraint should apply to narrowly defined renewable energy products, subject to (i) specified competitiveness criteria that would determine a member's eligibility for, and graduation from, the due restraint shelter and (ii) member-specific ceilings for subsidy amounts to be cut over time.[66]

Until the SCM Agreement is rewritten accordingly, members can still rely on the policy space carved out by the Appellate Body above. But for practical reasons, they should refrain from imposing local content and export performance conditions to be on a safer footing. In this case, even if a particular green measure meets the subsidy definition of the SCM Agreement, the challenger must additionally establish specificity and adverse effects to substantiate the existence of an injurious actionable subsidy.

"International Trade Law Challenges by Subsidies for Renewable Energy," 49 *Journal of World Trade* 757 (2015).

[64] Shadikhodjaev, Ch. 3, *supra* note 50, p. 877; Shadikhodjaev, *supra* note 55, p. 487.

[65] See Panel Report, *India – Solar Cells*, n. 1 to para. 1.1.

[66] For this and other greening proposals, see Shadikhodjaev, *supra* note 55, pp. 493–505.

6.3.2   Territorial Limitations of Support Programs[67]

Article 34 of the Treaty on the Functioning of the EU prohibits "[q]uantitative restrictions on imports and all measures having equivalent effect" between EU member States. Some decisions of the CJEU related to such ban are notable for considering the impact of public support schemes on the cross-border movement of electricity produced from renewable sources of energy.

In *PreussenElectra*, the CJEU found that the German law requiring electricity suppliers to purchase green electricity produced within their area of supply was able to prevent the use of that type of electricity from non-German sources,[68] notably renewable electricity produced in Sweden at a lower cost.[69] But the CJEU concluded that that law was not inconsistent with the EU ban on import restrictions given the contribution of the contested measure to the implementation of the EU policy for protection of the environment and the health and life of humans, animals, and plants.[70]

In two recent cases, the CJEU again approved of a public support's territorial limitations. In *Ålands Vindkraft*, the Swedish authorities refused to award a green certificate – a special document that can be sold to local suppliers and users who have a quota obligation for renewable electricity – to a wind farm in Finland on the grounds that only electricity-generating facilities within Sweden were eligible for obtaining green certificates.[71] In *Essent Belgium*, a Belgian supplier surrendered to its government both green certificates for domestically produced electricity and guarantees of origin obtained in Denmark, Sweden, the Netherlands, and Norway to fulfill its quota obligation, but those guarantees were not accepted.[72] Guarantees of origin are documents – mutually

---

[67] This section draws on Sherzod Shadikhodjaev, "Promotion of 'Green' Electricity and International Dispute Settlement: Trade and Investment Issues," 49 *International Lawyer* 343 (2016), pp. 352–61.

[68] Judgment of the Court, *PreussenElektra AG v Schhleswag AG*, Case C-379/98, 13 March 2001, para. 71.

[69] Opinion of Advocate General Jacobs in Case C-379/98, *PreussenElektra AG v Schhleswag AG*, 26 October 2000, para. 200.

[70] See Judgment of the Court, *PreussenElektra AG v Schhleswag AG*, *supra* note 68, paras. 72–81.

[71] Opinion of Advocate General Bot in Case C-573/12, *Ålands Vindkraft AB v Energimyndigheten*, 28 January 2014, paras. 24–6.

[72] Judgment of the Court (Fourth Chamber), *Essent Belgium NV v Vlaamse Reguleringsinstantie voor de Elektriciteits - en Gasmarkt*, Joined Cases C-204/12 to C-208/12, 11 September 2014, paras. 1–42.

recognizable among EU members – that prove the green nature of electricity and facilitate trade in renewable electricity.[73]

In *Ålands Vindkraft* and *Essent Belgium*, the Advocate General opined that the territorial restrictions of public support at issue violated the EU principle of the free movement of goods and contradicted the goal of the EU renewable energy policy to "promote cross-border exchanges of green electricity."[74] But the CJEU disagreed. While acknowledging the import-impeding effect on foreign green electricity, the CJEU found the territorial restrictions justified, as the current EU law had not yet harmonized the related national support schemes across the region.[75] Moreover, it observed that the environmental objective of reducing carbon emissions could be pursued primarily at the production stage, because the green nature of electricity could easily be verified when electricity was produced rather than consumed.[76] In *Essent Belgium*, the CJEU simply assumed that the guarantees of origin were "goods," and held that the restriction of the free movement of such goods could be justified on the similar grounds.[77]

Since the CJEU judgments were based on the *current* EU law that does not require extension of renewable energy schemes to out-of-country generation, a possible formation of a single European market of renewable electricity in the future will likely render the "localized" support schemes unjustifiable any longer. The fact that Norway and Sweden have managed to merge their green certificate support schemes suggests that regional integration of this kind is an achievable goal.[78]

With the global trend of growing support and production of green electricity, the factual situations of EU cases may well be subjected to the

---

[73] *Ibid.*, para. 79.
[74] Opinion of Advocate General Bot in Case C-573/12, *supra* note 71, paras. 79–121; Opinion of Advocate General Bot in Joined Cases C-204/12 to C-208/12, *Essent Belgium NV v Vlaamse Reguleringsinstantie voor de Elektriciteits - en Gasmarkt*, 8 May 2013, paras. 70–116.
[75] Judgment of the Court (Grand Chamber), *Ålands vindkraft AB v Energimyndigheten*, Case C-573/12, 1 July 2014, paras. 49–54, 94; Judgment of the Court (Fourth Chamber), *Essent Belgium NV v Vlaamse Reguleringsinstantie voor de Elektriciteits - en Gasmarkt*, *supra* note 72, paras. 88–116.
[76] Judgment of the Court (Grand Chamber), *Ålands vindkraft AB v Energimyndigheten*, *supra* note 75, paras. 94–6.
[77] Judgment of the Court (Fourth Chamber), *Essent Belgium NV v Vlaamse Reguleringsinstantie voor de Elektriciteits - en Gasmarkt*, *supra* note 72, paras. 73–81.
[78] Judgment of the Court (Grand Chamber), *Ålands vindkraft AB v Energimyndigheten*, *supra* note 75, paras. 22, 101.

WTO's legal scrutiny someday. For instance, if WTO member *A*'s renewable energy programs do not apply to green imports from member *B*, the latter could, in principle, challenge *A*'s incentives as a prohibited import restriction under Article XI of the GATT or as a discriminatory measure under Article III of the GATT. Articles XI and III apply to import restrictions at the border and within the border respectively. The threshold criterion in distinguishing internal measures from border measures is whether the factor triggering those measures takes place inside the border.[79] As public favors in our case are triggered by the *internal* production and use of green electricity, Article III is more relevant than Article XI. But even when an Article III violation is confirmed, the measure in question may be defended under other GATT provisions, including, where appropriate, Article III:8(a) on government procurement, Article III:8(b) on production subsidies, or Article XX on general exceptions. The WTO exceptions for RTAs can come into play if green support schemes are "regionalized" within a trading bloc and closed to outside countries.

Finally, renewable energy programs have created new types of commercial items, such as green certificates and guarantees of origin that are marketable as such.[80] But the legal nature of these items – that is, whether they are goods or not – remains unclear. The CJEU avoided this tricky issue through the assumption technique. Under the WTO system, there is no across-the-board definition of "goods." At least the SCM Agreement appears to be applicable to green certificates and guarantees of origin as part of subsidies, since the Appellate Body construed the term "goods" in the subsidy definition broadly enough as comprising even items that are not tradable as such and not subject to tariff classification.[81]

6.4   Environmental Labels

Agenda 21 of the UN Conference on Environment and Development (Earth Summit, 1992) recommended that governments encourage

---

[79] See Appellate Body Reports, *China – Auto Parts*, paras. 161–3; Shadikhodjaev, Ch. 2, *supra* note 62, pp. 198–202.

[80] At the *Essent Belgium* hearing, it was acknowledged that "a guarantee of origin may, like a green certificate, be sold separately from electricity." See Opinion of Advocate General Bot in Joined Cases C-204/12 to C-208/12, *supra* note 74, para. 112.

[81] Appellate Body Report, *US – Softwood Lumber IV*, para. 67.

environmental labeling to assist consumers to make environmentally sound purchasing decisions.[82] Environmental labeling is "the use of labels in order to inform consumers that a labeled product is more environmentally friendly relative to other products in the same category."[83] The International Standardization Organization (ISO) distinguishes three categories of environmental labeling under the ISO 14020 series of standards: a multiattribute label developed by a third party, a single-attribute label developed by the producer, and an ecolabel whose awarding is based on a full life-cycle assessment.[84] Whereas the ISO treats ecolabels distinctly from the other environmental labeling types, many sources seem to use these terms interchangeably, so we will also follow this common usage pattern for the sake of convenience.

In general, environmental labeling programs can be voluntary or mandatory, governmental or private, verifiable by a third party or self-declarable by producers. As of April 2016, there were 463 ecolabels in 199 economies and 25 industrial sectors.[85] These include, inter alia, The Blue Angel (Germany), Nordic Swan (Nordic countries), Korea Eco-Label, Eco Mark (Japan), Green Choice Philippines, and Qualidade Ambiental (Brazil). Ecolabeling traditionally focuses on energy efficiency, sustainability of the resource production, and recycling capacity, but may also extend to other environment-related policies, such as, for example, animal welfare.[86] Carbon footprint labels, for instance, display the total

---

[82] UN Conference on Environment and Development, "Agenda 21," 1992, para. 4.21.

[83] UNEP, "Criterial in Environmental Labelling: A Comparative Analysis of Environmental Criteria in Selected Labelling Schemes," Environment and Trade, No. 13, cited in WTO, Committee on Trade and Environment – Market Access Impact of Eco-Labelling Requirements – Note by the Secretariat, WT/CTE/W/79 (9 March 1998), para. 4.

[84] International Institute for Sustainable Development, "The ISO 14020 Series," www.iisd.org/business/markets/eco_label_iso14020.aspx. See also WTO, Committee on Trade and Environment – Internationally Agreed Definitions of Environmental Labelling within the International Organization for Standardization[...]rk – Communication from the ISO, WT/CTE/W/114 (31 May 1999); Richard Bonsi, A.L. Hammet, and Bob Smith, "Eco-labels and International Trade: Problems and Solutions," 42 *Journal of World Trade* 407 (2008), pp. 409–11.

[85] Ecolabel Index (the global directory of ecolabels), www.ecolabelindex.com. The glossary of this source (www.ecolabelindex.com/glossary/#E) defines "ecolabels" as "a sign or logo that is intended to indicate an environmentally preferable product, service or company, based on defined standards or criteria."

[86] Ilona Cheyne, "Proportionality, Proximity and Environmental Labelling in WTO Law," 12 *Journal of International Economic Law* 927 (2009), p. 929.

amount of GHG (grams of CO_2 equivalent per unit) emitted during the entire life cycle of a product or service.[87]

Ecolabels can contribute to the development of environmentally conscious markets by raising consumers' awareness of environmental matters, while inducing manufacturers to green the production process.[88] The rate of consumers' recognition of ecolabels in different countries varies, amounting to, for example, 65 percent for US Energy Star or 94 percent for Australian energy efficiency labels.[89]

Eligibility criteria for ecolabeling are deliberately set in such a way that only a small portion (about 5–30 percent) of products in the covered category can meet them. Such a strict approach seeks to balance between the number of ecolabeled products and the stringency of the criteria to produce optimum environmental effects.[90] But this may also give rise to trade restrictions contrary to WTO rules and principles. Many public and private schemes tend to be voluntary, but they can, in fact, create de facto market access requirements.[91]

6.4.1   Applicability of WTO Rules to Environmental Labeling

Environmental labeling can be scrutinized under many WTO provisions depending on the features of a related program and particular issues involved. The GATT provisions on nondiscrimination (Articles I and III), general elimination of quantitative restrictions (Article XI), and general exceptions concerning environmental matters (Article XX) can certainly come into play. Moreover, ecolabeling may contribute to the

---

[87] WTO, Committee on Trade and Environment – Summary Report of the Information Session on Product Carbon Footprint and Labelling Schemes – 17 February 2010 – Note by the Secretariat – Addendum, WT/CTE/M/49/Add.1 (28 May 2010).

[88] OECD, "Effects of Eco-Labelling Schemes: Compilation of Recent Studies," Joint Working Party on Trade and Environment, COM/ENV/TD(2004)34/FINAL, 2005, pp. 5, 7.

[89] WTO, Committee on Trade and Environment – Report of the Meeting Held on 2 May 2007 – Note by the Secretariat, WT/CTE/M/44 (13 June 2007), para. 79; WTO, Committee on Trade and Environment – Report of the Meeting Held on 3 November 2008 – Note by the Secretariat, WT/CTE/M/46 (12 January 2009), para. 41.

[90] OECD, *supra* note 88, p. 20.

[91] WTO, Committee on Trade and Environment – Report of the Meeting Held on 16 October 2013 – Note by the Secretariat, WT/CTE/M/56 (31 January 2014), para. 1.59; WTO, Committee on Trade and Environment – Report of the Meeting Held on 6 July 2011 – Note by the Secretariat, WT/CTE/M/52 (6 September 2011), para. 19.

greening of government procurement[92] as part of "technical specifications to promote the conservation of natural resources or protect the environment" that procuring entities may adopt for purchasing of goods or services pursuant to Article X:6 of the revised GPA. Annex A(1) of the SPS Agreement refers to "labelling requirements directly related to food safety." But the scope of this agreement is actually broader than this and covers any labeling requirements that are imposed to protect human, animal, or plant life or health from diseases and other risks and damage specified in Annex A(1).[93]

The TBT Agreement is particularly specific to environmental labeling.[94] The preamble recognizes members' autonomy in protecting the environment at the appropriate level, subject to the rules established in the agreement. Ecolabeling schemes can qualify as mandatory technical regulations or nonmandatory standards. The WTO definitions of both "technical regulation" and "standard" include labeling *requirements* – "provisions that set out criteria or conditions to be fulfilled in order to use a particular label."[95] In *US – Tuna II (Mexico)*, the Appellate Body held that the per se fact that those criteria or conditions are binding is not dispositive of the proper characterization of a TBT measure, as not only technical regulations but also standards may include compulsory, binding, or enforceable elements. To determine whether labeling requirements are part of a technical regulation or standard, one would need to consider all characteristics of the measure and the circumstances of the case at issue, and in particular "whether the measure consists of a law or a regulation enacted by a WTO Member, whether it prescribes or prohibits particular conduct, whether it sets out specific requirements that constitute the sole means of addressing a particular matter, and the nature of the matter addressed by the measure."[96]

Most contention about trade effects of environmental labeling has centered on life-cycle assessments of ecolabels that typically look at a product's environmental impacts from initial stages of its production to

---

[92] See WTO, Committee on Trade and Environment – Report of the Meeting Held on 22 June 2015 – Note by the Secretariat, WT/CTE/M/59 (3 September 2015), para. 2.5; WTO, Committee on Trade and Environment – Report of the Meeting Held on 29 September 2010 – Note by the Secretariat, WT/CTE/M/50 (2 November 2010), paras. 65–6.

[93] Panel Reports, *EC – Approval and Marketing of Biotech Products*, paras. 7.390–7.391.

[94] Labeling measures under the TBT Agreement were addressed in *US – Tuna II (Mexico)* (DS381), *US – Cool* (DS384, 386), *EC – Seal Products* (DS400, 401), and *EC – Sardines* (DS231).

[95] Appellate Body Report, *US – Tuna II (Mexico)*, para. 186.   [96] *Ibid.*, paras. 187–8.

its final disposal.[97] This raises an issue of validity of NPR-PPMs concerning, for example, air or water pollution in the course of production.

Given what we considered earlier, Article III of the GATT is quite unlikely to allow ecolabeling programs to discriminate against foreign products solely on the basis of different NPR-PPMs.[98] Even voluntary NPR-PPMs schemes administered by the government or by private bodies with governmental involvement can fall under the GATT anti-discrimination provisions or give rise to nonviolation complaints under Article XXIII:1(b) of the GATT.[99] But Article XX exceptions still remain available to such schemes if they are found to be breaking the GATT.[100]

As for the TBT Agreement, the first sentence of Annex 1.1 defines "technical regulation" as a binding document that lays down "product characteristics or their related [PPMs]"; and the first sentence of Annex 1.2 defines "standard" as a nonbinding document on "characteristics for products or related [PPMs]." In *EC – Seal Products*, the Appellate Body disagreed with the panel that the identity of the hunter, the type or the purpose of hunt constituted seal products' characteristics, but it was unable to complete a legal analysis on whether the EU Seal Regime laid down PPMs.[101] Nevertheless, the Appellate Body interpreted the phrase "their related [PPMs]" in the first sentence of Annex 1.1 as covering only the PPMs that are closely connected to the characteristics of a product:

> A plain reading of Annex 1.1 thus suggests that a "related" PPM is one that is "connected" or "has a relation" to the characteristics of a product. The word "their", which immediately precedes the words "related processes and production methods", refers back to "product characteristics". Thus, in the context of the first sentence of Annex 1.1, we understand the reference to "or their related processes and production methods" to indicate that the subject matter of a technical regulation may consist of a process or production method that is *related* to product characteristics. In order to determine whether a measure lays down related PPMs, a panel thus will have to examine whether the processes and production methods

---

[97] See WTO, Committee on Trade and Environment – Report to the 5th Session of the Ministerial Conference in Cancún – Paragraphs 32 and 33 of the Doha Ministerial Declaration, WT/CTE/8 (11 July 2013), paras. 34, 36; WTO, Committee on Trade and Environment – Report of the Meeting Held on 27–28 June 2001 – Note by the Secretariat, WT/CTE/M/27 (8 August 2001), paras. 87–99.

[98] See Section 6.2.2.

[99] See Seung Wha Chang, "GATTing a Green Trade Barrier: Eco-Labelling and the WTO Agreement on Technical Barriers to Trade," 31 *Journal of World Trade* 137 (1997).

[100] See also Section 6.5.1.

[101] See Appellate Body Reports, *EC – Seal Products*, paras. 5.1–5.70.

prescribed by the measure have a sufficient nexus to the characteristics of a product in order to be considered related to those characteristics.[102]

While the TBT Agreement undoubtedly applies to product-related PPMs, the status of NPR-PPMs is not clear. For example, the first sentence of Annex 1.1 speaks of "their related" PPMs – that is, PPMs related to product characteristics – while the first sentence of Annex 1.2 mentions only "related" PPMs without "their." According to one view, the legal definitions at issue and the negotiating history[103] suggest that only product-related PPMs are subject to the disciplines of the TBT Agreement.[104] The Appellate Body held that "the line between PPMs that fall, and those that do not fall, within the scope of the TBT Agreement raises important systemic issues."[105] Accordingly, one can say that what falls within the purview of the TBT Agreement is product-related PPMs, and what does not is NPR-PPMs.

Yet, this understanding can be questioned under the second sentence of each Annex 1.1 and Annex 1.2, which states that a technical regulation/standard "may also include or deal exclusively with . . . labelling requirements as they apply to a product, process or production method." The second sentence in question omits the words "their related"/"related" for a PPM, which textually delinks the latter from a product. The Appellate Body found that the words "also include" and "deal exclusively with" indicate that the second sentence covers elements that "are additional to, and may be distinct from," those in the first sentence.[106] Therefore, it appears that this interpretation implicitly leaves some room for NPR-PPMs under the second sentence at least. In this context, it is noteworthy that the panel in *US – Tuna II (Mexico)* concluded that the US dolphin-safe labeling requirements fell within the scope of the second sentence of Annex 1.1 simply on the grounds that they "apply to a product," namely tuna products, in accordance with the language of that

---

[102] *Ibid.*, para. 5.12 (emphasis in original).

[103] The words "their" and "related" were inserted in the definitions in question at the request of Mexico which wished to make it clear that only product-related PPMs would be covered by the TBT Agreement. See WTO, Committee on Trade and Environment – Committee on TBT – Negotiating History of the Coverage of the Agreement on TBT [. . .]stics – Note by the Secretariat, WT/CTE/W/10, G/TBT/W/11 (29 August 1995), paras. 146–7.

[104] For a review on this issue, see, e.g., Christiane R. Conrad, *Processes and Production Methods (PPMs) in WTO Law: Interfacing Trade and Social Goals* (Cambridge: Cambridge University Press, 2011), pp. 376–81.

[105] Appellate Body Reports, *EC – Seal Products*, para. 5.69.   [106] *Ibid.*, para. 5.14.

sentence.[107] This finding was not appealed, but it shows how NPR-PPMs, like fishing methods here that do not leave any traces on the tuna as a subject product, can be examined under the TBT Agreement on a de facto basis, that is, without an explicit acknowledgement of the existence of NPR-PPMs as such.

6.4.2   WTO Discussions on Environmental Labeling

According to the WTO Secretariat's most recent statistics we could find, members made TBT notifications for environmental labeling measures in relation to genetically modified organisms, emissions reductions, energy efficiency, toxic substances, waste management, organic products, and natural resources. Between 2000 and 2011, the number of such notifications reached 425 in total and showed a steady upward trend over the reviewed period. In 1995–2011, the TBT Committee addressed 31 STCs on environmental labeling (out of 117 related to labeling) regarding unnecessary barriers to trade, transparency, informational lack, discrimination, legitimacy and rationale, international standards, S&D treatment, and others.[108]

With respect to the NPR-PPMs issue, the TBT Committee has pragmatically dealt with labeling requirements irrespective of the label content. First, the TBT Committee stated in its decision that members' obligation under Article 2.9 of the TBT Agreement "to notify all mandatory labelling requirements . . . is not dependent upon the kind of information which is provided on the label, whether it is in the nature of a technical specification or not."[109] In the same vein, the TBT Committee agreed that, "without prejudice to the views of Members concerning the coverage and application of the [TBT] Agreement," the obligation to publish notices of draft standards on "voluntary labelling requirements" under paragraph L of the Code of Good Practice exists regardless of "the kind of information provided on the label."[110] Second, as of 1 January 2016,

---

[107] Panel Report, *US – Tuna II (Mexico)*, para. 7.78.

[108] WTO, "Detailed Presentation of Environmental Requirements and Market Access, including Labelling for Environmental Purposes," WTO E-Learning, 2013, pp. 26–7, https://ecampus.wto.org/admin/files/Course_385/Module_2423/ModuleDocuments/TE_Req-L2-R2-E.pdf.

[109] WTO, Committee on TBT – Decisions and Recommendations adopted by the WTO Committee on TBT since 1 January 1995 – Note by the Secretariat – Revision, G/TBT/1/Rev.12 (21 January 2015), p. 22 (section 4.3.1.4).

[110] *Ibid.*, p. 29 (section 4.3.2.3).

NPR-PPMs were targeted in 43 out of 489 STCs considered by the TBT Committee since the WTO establishment.[111] In particular, members questioned labeling of a variety of items, ranging from genetically modified products and transgenic foods (measures by the EU, Japan, Brazil, New Zealand, Chile, and Peru) to dolphin-safe tuna (the United States), halal food (the UAE, Saudi Arabia, Bahrain, Kuwait, and Indonesia), organic products (the EU and Chinese Taipei), and seal products (the EU and some EU members). Such a flexible approach of the TBT Committee may eventually result in treaty amendments that would accept NPR-PPMs explicitly.[112]

The TBT Committee is not the sole WTO forum on environmental labeling programs. The Doha Ministerial Declaration (2001) in paragraph 32 instructed the Committee on Trade and Environment to identify any need for clarification of existing WTO rules on "labelling requirements for environmental purposes." While some members believe that this Committee's discussions could produce some inputs for further debate in other relevant WTO bodies, others argue that the TBT Committee is better suited for this task.[113]

The Committee on Trade and Environment discussed environmental labeling programs of a handful of members, including China, Chinese Taipei, Canada, Singapore, Chile, Australia, New Zealand, and the United States.[114] For example, Singapore presented six ecolabeling schemes (Mandatory Energy Labelling, Fuel Economy Labelling, Green Label, Energy Smart Building Label, Green Mark, and Green Building Product Certification), four of which are administered by the government and two are managed by nongovernmental organizations. These

---

[111] WTO, "Technical Barriers to Trade Information Management System," http://tbtims .wto.org. The key word is "non-product related processes and procedural methods" in the entry "Issues" for "Specific Trade Concerns (STCs)."

[112] Conrad, *supra* note 104, p. 381.

[113] See WTO, Committee on Trade and Environment – Report of the Meeting Held on 20 April 2004 – Note by the Secretariat, WT/CTE/M/36 (19 May 2004), paras. 14–28; WTO, Committee on Trade and Environment – Report of the Meeting Held on 20 April 2004 – Note by the Secretariat, WT/CTE/M/34 (29 July 2003), paras. 54–95.

[114] See WT/CTE/M/59, *supra* note 92, paras. 2.1–2.5; WTO, Committee on Trade and Environment – Report of the Meeting Held on 14 November 2011 – Note by the Secretariat, WT/CTE/M/53 (27 January 2012), para. 40; WTO, Committee on Trade and Environment – Report of the Meeting Held on 9 November 2010 – Note by the Secretariat, WT/CTE/M/51 (31 May 2011), paras. 22–35; WT/CTE/M/50, *supra* note 92, paras. 64–9; WT/CTE/M/46, *supra* note 89, para. 41; WT/CTE/M/44, *supra* note 89, paras. 60–83.

programs aim to raise environmental awareness among consumers and enhance energy efficiency and energy security. Some of them certify "green" buildings together with "conventional" goods.[115] As another example, the United States has run a voluntary energy efficiency program called "Energy Star" since 1992, applying it initially to computer monitors but later also to home appliances, office equipment, and commercial food services. The US authorities have worked to internationalize Energy Star through bilateral arrangements with foreign counterparts.[116]

While the role of environmental labeling schemes in informing consumers is widely recognized, many members are still concerned about possible negative ramifications for trade,[117] including, inter alia, reduced market access opportunities for exporters especially from developing countries[118] or carbon footprint labels' disfavors to imports from distant countries.[119] Some urge international harmonization of ecolabeling requirements with greater participation of developing countries in the drafting process and transparent domestic standard-setting with engagement of all related stakeholders.[120]

Many members take the view that WTO rules, including the TBT Agreement, are already adequate to address environmental labeling and related STCs with "the appropriate balance of rights and obligations for both mandatory and voluntary labelling programmes." Thus, they consider further clarification unnecessary.[121] But as we saw earlier, the applicability of the TBT Agreement to NPR-PPMs is not clear enough so that rule amendments on this issue would, in fact, be useful.

6.5   Environmental Exceptions under GATT Article XX

GATT-inconsistent environmental measures can be defended under Article XX of the GATT if they are "necessary to protect human, animal or plant life or health" (paragraph (b)); or "relating to the conservation of exhaustible natural resources" as applied "in conjunction with restrictions on domestic production or consumption" (paragraph (g)). The invoking

---

[115] See WT/CTE/M/51, *supra* note 114, paras. 22–35.
[116] See WT/CTE/M/44, *supra* note 89, paras. 60–83.
[117] WT/CTE/8, *supra* note 97, para. 30.
[118] *Ibid.*, para. 31; WTO, Committee on Trade and Environment – Report of the Meeting Held on 30 June 2014 – Note by the Secretariat, WT/CTE/M/57 (30 September 2014), paras. 1.47–1.55; WT/CTE/M/53, *supra* note 114, para. 41.
[119] WT/CTE/M/50, *supra* note 92, para. 73.
[120] WT/CTE/M/52, *supra* note 91, para. 20.   [121] WT/CTE/8, *supra* note 97, para. 37.

member has to prove the relevance of a respective paragraph to a contested measure and compliance with the *chapeau* requirements.

6.5.1   Litigation Practice over the "Trade and Environment" Issue

The "trade and environment" disputes involving the aforementioned provisions of Article XX concerned government actions aimed at reduction of air pollution caused by gasoline consumption, elimination of health risks posed by asbestos, protection of sea turtles and dolphins from life-threatening fishing methods, reduction of environmental harm from growing volumes of waste tires, conservation of certain natural resources (rare earth, etc.), and minimization of extraction-related health- or environment-hazard effects.[122]

The first step in an Article XX(b) analysis – the necessity test – consists in (i) "weighing and balancing" of the importance of the protected interests and values at stake, the challenged measure's contribution to the achievement of the policy objective, and its impact on trade, as well as (ii) comparison of the measure with less-trade-restrictive alternatives that are "reasonably available" to the imposing member.[123] In the context of the second component, an alternative measure which is impossible to implement cannot be said to be reasonably available, but it will not cease to be reasonably available simply because of "administrative difficulties" of implementation.[124] Besides being implementable, the alternative measure must be consistent or otherwise less inconsistent with the GATT than the challenged measure to achieve the policy objective at issue.[125] As for the practice, the Appellate Body in *EC – Asbestos* found that the proposed alternative, that is, "controlled use" of – instead of the EC ban on – asbestos products, lacked scientific evidence that would prove the efficacy of that alternative in halting the spread of asbestos-related health risks.[126] Similarly, the Appellate Body concluded in *Brazil – Retreaded Tyres* that enhanced waste management and disposal measures were remedial in nature and could not be real substitutes for the contested Brazilian import ban on retreaded tires, which was a preventive measure

---

[122] The related cases are *US – Gasoline* (DS2), *EC – Asbestos* (DS135), *US – Shrimp* (DS58), *US – Tuna II (Mexico)* (DS381), *Brazil – Retreaded Tyres* (DS332), *China – Raw Materials* (DS394, 395, 398), and *China – Rare Earths* (DS431, 432, 433).
[123] Appellate Body Report, *Brazil – Retreaded Tyres*, paras. 178, 182.
[124] Appellate Body Report, *EC – Asbestos*, para. 169.   [125] *Ibid.*, paras. 170–1.
[126] *Ibid.*, paras. 172–4.

and thus "apt to produce a material contribution to the achievement of its objective" to reduce the accumulation of hazardous waste tires.[127]

As regards Article XX(g), the term "exhaustible natural resources" has been interpreted broadly enough to reflect today's realities. It covers not only mineral or nonliving resources, but also living animals and plants susceptible of extinction, as well as clean air, which can deplete because of the atmospheric pollution.[128] It is the challenged measure itself rather than its WTO-inconsistent aspect that must be "relating to" the conservation policy.[129] This necessitates "a close and genuine relationship of ends and means" between that measure and the applying member's conservation objective.[130] Article XX(g) additionally imposes "a requirement of even-handedness" by demanding the applying member to limit domestic production or consumption. The domestic production/consumption must be subject to real restrictions rather than possible limitations sometime in the future.[131] An Article XX(g) analysis basically looks into the challenged measures' structure and design in connection with the features of the relevant market, such as the exhaustible natural resource at issue, the structure, and the product and geographical scope of the market, as well as the role of foreign and local market participants.[132]

With respect to the practice under Article XX(g), the United States in *US – Gasoline* adopted a measure regulating the composition and emission effects of gasoline in order to reduce air pollution in the country. The Appellate Body found that the US standards on "clean" gasoline were "primarily aimed at" the goal of conservation of clean air in the United States and were consistent with the even-handedness requirement, as they affected both imported and domestic products.[133] In *US – Shrimp*, the United States prohibited imports of shrimp from countries that the US authorities did not certify as using turtle-safe harvesting methods. The Appellate Body concluded that such an import ban – found to violate Article XI of the GATT – constituted a measure relating to the conservation of an exhaustible natural resource (here, sea

---

[127] Appellate Body Report, *Brazil – Retreaded Tyres*, paras. 151, 210–11.

[128] Appellate Body Report, *US – Shrimp*, paras. 128–31; Panel Report, *US – Gasoline*, para. 6.37.

[129] Appellate Body Report, *US – Gasoline*, p. 16.

[130] Appellate Body Report, *US – Shrimp*, para. 136; Appellate Body Reports, *China – Raw Materials*, para. 355.

[131] Appellate Body Reports, *China – Rare Earths*, paras. 5.92– 5.93.

[132] *Ibid.*, paras. 5.96–5.97.   [133] Appellate Body Report, *US – Gasoline*, pp. 19, 21.

turtles) and implemented in conjunction with the restrictions on domestic harvesting of shrimp.[134]

Two points made in US – Shrimp have far-reaching implications for environmental policies. First, the Appellate Body noted that sea turtles migrate to or traverse waters under the US jurisdiction and determined on that basis that there was a sufficient nexus between migratory marine populations in question and the United States.[135] Importantly, it found that conditioning market access on whether exporting members comply with a policy unilaterally prescribed by an importing member did not render such a measure a priori incapable of enjoying Article XX defense.[136] Second, the Appellate Body accepted the applicability of Article XX to the US restrictions which actually were triggered by the difference in NPR-PPMs. Therefore, this appellate ruling left some room under the general exceptions for accommodating properly designed unilateral policy prescriptions and NPR-PPMs affecting the global or transboundary environment.

Once the challenged measure is provisionally justified under the relevant Article XX paragraph, the next step is to verify its validity under the chapeau requirements for it not to constitute "a means of arbitrary or unjustifiable discrimination" or "a disguised restriction on international trade." The Appellate Body in US – Gasoline found the inconsistency with the chapeau on the grounds that the United States failed to cooperate with the complaining members with a view to mitigating administrative problems that had triggered the introduction of discriminatory gasoline standards and counting the costs for foreign refiners that would result from the imposition of such standards.[137] The import ban in US – Shrimp did not meet the chapeau conditions for two reasons: the United States required other governments to establish the same harvesting regulation without taking into account different circumstances that could exist in different countries; and the procedures of certifying countries with turtle-safe shrimping were not transparent and predictable.[138] In Brazil – Retreaded Tyres, Brazil exempted the Southern Common Market (MERCOSUR) countries from its import ban on retreaded tires in order to comply with a MERCOSUR tribunal's ruling that had condemned Brazil for increasing trade barriers within that economic bloc. But the Appellate Body found that ruling to be an unacceptable excuse for

---

[134] Appellate Body Report, US – Shrimp, paras. 142–5.   [135] Ibid., para. 133.
[136] Ibid., para. 121.   [137] Appellate Body Report, US – Gasoline, pp. 28–9.
[138] Appellate Body Report, US – Shrimp, paras. 161–5, 180–1.

the discriminatory application of the ban, as it had nothing to do with the measure's policy objective to reduce exposure to the risks arising from the accumulation of waste tires. Therefore, it was held that the MERCOSUR exemption resulted in "arbitrary and unjustifiable discrimination" against non-MERCOSUR countries in the sense of the Article XX *chapeau*.[139] To conclude, the appellate findings under the *chapeau* suggest that environmental policies involving trade should be implemented in a consistent way, with enough attention being paid to the interests and difficulties of affected foreign countries.

6.5.2   Time for Harmonization of WTO Exceptions?

Whether the general exceptions under Article XX of the GATT can justify violations of WTO agreements other than the GATT is a controversial question. In the environmental context, this issue can arise with respect to, inter alia, renewable energy subsidies under the SCM Agreement or ecolabels under the TBT Agreement. Table 6.1 distinguishes three categories of the WTO legal texts approaching the general exceptions differently. The first category foresees the applicability of Article XX in relation to all or some of the covered obligations. The provisions in China's Accession Protocol examined in WTO dispute settlement show that Article XX can be treated differently even within the same accession document. The second category does not leave any room for the application of Article XX as a whole or some of its parts because of several factors, such as, e.g., the omission of Article XX as juxtaposed to the inclusion of Article XXI on security exceptions, the presence of *lex specialis* on general exceptions, or the absorption of Article XX flexibilities into the respective text. The third category is silent on the applicability issue because of the absence of any textual indication.

As we reviewed elsewhere,[140] the WTO jurisprudence has accepted the invocability of Article XX in a non-GATT context only in the presence of a specific textual basis. It follows that whereas ecolabels not complying with the TBT Agreement can enjoy certain Article XX-like flexibilities in the TBT Agreement itself, renewable energy subsidies violating the SCM Agreement are not eligible for the GATT general exceptions. But depriving green subsidies of Article XX defense, as well as different availability of the general and security exceptions within the same system are

---

[139] Appellate Body Report, *Brazil – Retreaded Tyres*, paras. 226–8.
[140] See Shadikhodjaev, *supra* note 55, pp. 499–505.

Table 6.1 *Applicability of GATT Article XX within the WTO Legal Regime*

Applies		Does Not Apply		Not Clear	
Legal Text	Why?	Legal Text	Why?	Legal Text	Why?
TRIMs	Acceptance of all GATT exceptions	SPS (vis-à-vis Art. XX(b))	Elaboration of Art. XX (b) through the SPS text	Customs Valuation	No indication in the text
Preshipment (vis-à-vis some transparency obligations)	Recognition of Art. XX emergency situations	Import Licensing	Reference to Art. XXI (security) but not Art. XX	Safeguards	No indication in the text
IT Agreement (vis-à-vis binding commitments)	Incorporation of binding commitments in GATT schedules	TBT	Incorporation of Art. XX flexibilities in the TBT text itself	Rules of Origin	No indication in the text
China's Accession Protocol, para. 5.1	Insertion of the "without prejudice" condition vis-à-vis China's right to regulate trade under the WTO Agreement	Agriculture (vis-à-vis binding commitments on subsidies)	Subjection of the binding commitments to the provisions of this agreement alone	Antidumping	The Appellate Body's *arguendo* assumption (but not final confirmation) of Art. XX applicability to specific actions against dumping under Art. 18.1; No indication in the rest of the text

Table 6.1 (*cont.*)

Applies		Does Not Apply		Not Clear	
Legal Text	Why?	Legal Text	Why?	Legal Text	Why?
		GATS	Inclusion of *lex specialis* on general exceptions	SCM	Art. XX availability under footnote 56 to Art. 32.1 not clear; No indication in the rest of the text
		TRIPS	Cumulative application of TRIPS and GATT obligations; Inclusion of the single clause on a security exception (but none on general exceptions) in the TRIPS text		
		Civil Aircraft (vis-à-vis binding commitments)	Textual indication preventing Art. XX application		
		China's Accession Protocol, para. 11.3	Inferred (implicit) exclusion of Art. XX from applicable justifications		

Source: Sherzod Shadikhodjaev, "Renewable Energy and Government Support: Time to 'Green' the SCM Agreement?," 14 *World Trade Review* 479 (2015), p. 504 (table 4).

something that is difficult to accept. Thus, we suggest that members adopt a new instrument (agreement, ministerial decision, declaration, etc.) that would reiterate or even update the text of GATT Articles XX and XXI and stipulate that these provisions would apply in the WTO across the board "without prejudice" to the comparable exceptions and flexibilities. This would make the use of the general and security exceptions – that are equally important in principle – more consistent, thereby rectifying the puzzling situation where some WTO agreements explicitly mention Article XXI but omit Article XX. The words "without prejudice" could arguably prevent or at least minimize any overlap with existing exceptions and flexibilities. Importantly, the proposed blanket instrument would fill a gap in the third category above where the text is silent on the applicability of the GATT general exceptions.[141] Alternatively, members could simply replace the existing exceptions and flexibilities with those in the new instrument.

6.6   Harmonization of the Trade and Environmental Regimes

In the Uruguay Round, the ministers agreed to establish the WTO Committee on Trade and Environment to address the intersectional issues, while desiring to coordinate trade and environmental policies "without exceeding the competence of the multilateral trading system."[142] Paragraph 31 of the Doha Ministerial Declaration (2001) set the goal of "enhancing the mutual supportiveness of trade and environment."

About 20 out of over 250 multilateral environmental agreements (MEAs) in force contain provisions that control trade in order to prevent environmental damage.[143] To name a few, the Basel Convention on the Control of Transboundary Movements of Hazardous Wastes and their Disposal, the UN Convention on International Trade in Endangered Species of Wild Fauna and Flora, and the Montreal Protocol on Substances that Deplete the Ozone Layer restrict trade in covered products among parties and generally apply a stricter policy vis-à-vis nonparties.[144] Such environmental rules imposing import/export quotas or

---

[141] *Ibid.*   [142] See the Uruguay Round Decision on Trade and Environment.

[143] WTO, "WTO Matrix on Trade-Related Measures Pursuant to Selected Multilateral Environmental Agreements (MEAs)," www.wto.org/english/tratop_e/envir_e/envir_matrix_e.htm.

[144] See WTO, Committee on Trade and Environment – Committee on Trade and Environment – Special Session – Matrix on Trade Measures Pursuant to Selected Multilateral

prohibitions and discriminating against nonparties may conflict with the WTO's ban on quantitative restrictions and discrimination.

Article 3.5 of the UN Framework Convention on Climate Change states that (unilateral) climate measures "should not constitute a means of arbitrary or unjustifiable discrimination or a disguised restriction on international trade." The preamble of the International Plant Protection Convention contains similar language in relation to phytosanitary measures. But not all environmental treaties include such a "trade-friendly" text.

6.6.1   Judicial Aspects of Harmonization

A formal "WTO vs. MEA" dispute could have potentially emerged in *Chile – Swordfish*. In April 2000, the EC filed a WTO complaint (DS193) claiming that Chile's legislation banning European fishing vessels from unloading their swordfish in Chilean ports for warehousing or transshipment was inconsistent with Articles V and XI of the GATT on transit and quantitative restrictions. But in the parallel proceedings in the International Tribunal for the Law of the Sea on the *Case Concerning the Conservation and Sustainable Exploitation of Swordfish Stocks in the South-Eastern Pacific Ocean*, Chile countered that the EC had failed to cooperate with the Chilean authorities to ensure the conservation of swordfish – a highly migratory species – contrary to the UN Convention on the Law of the Sea. Eventually, two proceedings were suspended, as the disputing parties had reached a mutually satisfactory solution. This case obviously shows that there is always a risk of mutually conflicting judgments under two distinct regimes.[145]

As part of public international law,[146] multilateral trade agreements cannot be read "in clinical isolation" therefrom.[147] Trade litigation involving non-WTO law raises the fundamental issues of (i) jurisdiction and (ii) applicable or relevant law, as follows.

With respect to the first issue, Article 7 of the DSU stipulates that panels "shall address the relevant provisions in any covered [WTO]

Enviro[. . .]e by the Secretariat – Revision, WT/CTE/W/160/Rev.7, TN/TE/S/5/Rev.5 (4 September 2015).

[145] WTO, "Trade and Environment at the WTO," 2004, pp. 37–8.

[146] See, e.g., Jackson, Ch. 1, *supra* note 63, p. 48; Joost Pauwelyn, *Conflict of Norms in Public International Law: How WTO Law Relates to Other Rules of International Law* (Cambridge: Cambridge University Press, 2003), pp. 25–88.

[147] Appellate Body Report, *US – Gasoline*, p. 17.

agreement or agreements cited by the parties to the dispute" in the standard terms of reference, but it allows parties to agree on nonstandard terms of reference. Therefore, the panel's jurisdiction can, in principle, be stretched to MEAs cited in nonstandard terms of reference, provided that: there is a close nexus between WTO law and the MEA at issue; the MEA is consistent with WTO objectives; and both parties agree on such widening of jurisdiction.[148]

As for the second issue, the DSU's silence on the scope of applicable law arguably supports rather than denies the applicability of MEAs to trade disputes,[149] with the caveat that a relevant MEA provision can be applied to the extent of its WTO-consistency.[150] The latter can be inferred from Articles 3.2 and 19.2 of the DSU barring panelists and the Appellate Body from "add[ing] to or diminish[ing] the rights and obligations provided in the covered agreements" of the WTO.[151] WTO adjudicators have developed quite a narrow definition of a "conflict," and have not lightly assumed the existence of normative discrepancies between WTO and other international systems, relying on a presumption against conflict in public international law.[152]

Finally, MEAs may be relevant to the interpretation of a particular WTO provision. They can be invoked as "any subsequent agreement between the parties" or "any relevant rules of international law applicable in the relations between the parties" that, pursuant to Article 31(3) of the VCLT, must be "taken into account, together with the context" of a given WTO provision. In *EC – Approval and Marketing of Biotech Products*, the panel recognized that the Convention on Biological Diversity and the associated Cartagena Protocol on Biosafety were "rules of international law" within the meaning of that VCLT clause, but it eventually did not

---

[148] These conditions are developed in the GATT/WTO judicial practice, as summarized in Vranes, *supra* note 47, n. 296 in p. 78.

[149] Indeed, WTO adjudicators did apply general international law and other non-WTO international rules independently of interpreting given WTO provisions. See Joost Pauwelyn, "The Role of Public International Law in the WTO: How Far Can We Go?," 95 *American Journal of International Law* 535 (2001), p. 563.

[150] For instance, it was found that only *WTO-consistent* customary international law is applicable within the WTO system. See Panel Report, *Korea – Procurement*, para. 7.96.

[151] See Lorand Bartels, "Applicable Law in WTO Dispute Settlement Proceedings," 35 *Journal of World Trade* 499 (2001), pp. 506–9.

[152] Graham Cook, *A Digest of WTO Jurisprudence on Public International Law Concepts and Principles* (Cambridge: Cambridge University Press, 2015), p. 61.

consider them in interpreting the SPS Agreement, as they did not apply to all disputing parties.[153]

6.6.2   *International and Domestic Harmonization*

Harmonization of the trade and environmental regimes is covered by the Doha negotiations on (i) clarifying the relationship between WTO rules and specific trade obligations under MEAs without prejudice to the WTO rights of non-MEA-party members and (ii) furthering cooperation between the relevant WTO committees and MEA secretariats.[154] These negotiated items represent normative and institutional ways of enhancing the mutual supportiveness of two systems. In April 2011, the Chairman of the WTO Committee on Trade and Environment issued a draft Ministerial Decision on Trade and Environment which, albeit not adopted, shows the areas of compromise and disagreement among members, as follows.[155]

With respect to the first item, some members (the United States, Australia, Argentina, etc.) consider the existing WTO rules to be sufficient and deny the need for legislative reforms, while others (the EU, Switzerland, etc.) insist on greater clarification of the WTO–MEA relationship. It is generally understood that specific trade obligations under MEAs are those that require an MEA party to take or refrain from a particular trade action. Most members wish the final document to underline the importance of national-level coordination in negotiating and implementing trade-related provisions of MEAs, with some suggesting similar language for international coordination as well. Proposed elements on dispute settlement over WTO–MEA matters include, inter alia, requests for the advice of experts on the MEA involved. There is also a wide support for provision of technical assistance in this sphere.[156]

---

[153] Panel Reports, *EC – Approval and Marketing of Biotech Products*, paras. 7.67, 7.74–7.75.

[154] See paragraph 31 of the Doha Ministerial Declaration (2001). Due to the spatial constraints, fisheries subsidies and trade liberalization for environmental goods and services are not considered here.

[155] WTO, Committee on Trade and Environment – Special Session – Report by the Chairman, Ambassador Manuel A. J. Teehankee, to the Trade Negotiations Committee, TN/TE/20 (21 April 2011).

[156] See *ibid.*; WTO, Committee on Trade and Environment – Special Session – Compilation of Submissions under Paragraph 31(i) of the Doha Declaration – Note by the Secretariat – Revision, TN/TE/S/3/Rev.1 (24 April 2003); WTO, Committee on Trade and Environment – Special Session – Multilateral Environmental Agreements (MEAs) and

For the second item, there is a substantial convergence of views on encouraging collaboration between the WTO and MEA institutions with regard to information exchanges, document sharing and preparation, technical assistance, and capacity building projects. The Committee on Trade and Environment is to grant observer status to MEA secretariats, taking into account mutual relevance of activities, an MEA secretariat's participation in the committee and previous contribution to the WTO work.[157]

As the Doha mandate prescribes, the outcome of the negotiations on both agenda items in question "shall be compatible with the open and non-discriminatory nature of the multilateral trading system, shall not add to or diminish the rights and obligations of members under existing WTO agreements ... nor alter the balance of these rights and obligations."[158] This arguably supports the idea about the WTO's primacy, as a general rule, over the conflicting MEA trade-related obligations as addressed within the WTO framework.

In addition to the harmonization on the international plane, there should be coherence in the domestic decision-making process as well. First, each government needs to have an operational mechanism of coordinating trade, environment, and industry agencies and considering all stakeholders' views. This will help countries pursue balanced internal and external policies on the issues concerned.

Second, governments should establish domestic procedures for environmental impact assessments of trade initiatives. These are *ex ante* and/or *ex post* environmental reviews of multilateral, plurilateral, and regional trade agreements that evaluate effects of market openings on the environment and identify any resulting constraints on the government's ability to protect the environment. Such a system necessitates an increased interaction of trade and environment officials and may involve the civil society. Environmental dimensions can be considered together with economic and social indices in carrying out comprehensive sustainability assessments. Depending on the outcomes, governments may make some environment-friendlier adjustments to the drafting or implementation of the trade agreements reviewed.[159]

WTO Rules; Proposals Made in the Committee on Trade [...] 2002 – Note by the Secretariat, TN/TE/S/1 (23 May 2002).

[157] See TN/TE/20, *supra* note 155.

[158] Paragraph 32 of the Doha Ministerial Declaration (2001).

[159] For details on trade-related environmental reviews, see WTO, Committee on Trade and Environment – Environmental (Sustainability) Assessments of Trade Liberalization Agreements at the National Level – Item 2 of the Work[...]ramme – Note by the

The significance of environmental reviews is already globally acknowledged.[160] But this is not enough. Indeed, unlike the case of commonly practiced economic impact evaluations of prospective or existing trade agreements, only a handful of WTO members (e.g., the EU, Canada, and the United States)[161] operate environmental assessment mechanisms for trade policies on a systematic basis. Therefore, the WTO and other relevant international organizations should intensively collaborate on developing appropriate assessment methodologies and spreading the know-how around the world.

6.7 Concluding Remarks

While the greening of industrial policies as such pursues good purposes, related governmental actions aimed at leveling the playing field and increasing competitiveness of local producers represent typical examples of WTO-challengeable measures. As a principle, the WTO accommodates environmental policies as far as they do not conflict with its regulations. But most of the WTO rules were created more than twenty years ago, and the key GATT provisions have remained virtually unchanged since the very inception of the multilateral trading system. However, meanwhile, environmental degradation in many parts of our planet has only worsened, and serious global-scale problems like climate change have become more acute.

In these circumstances, members should make real efforts to render the WTO rule book more responsive to today's environmental challenges. This concerns, inter alia, the Doha mandate on trade and environment, as well as the suggested revamping of WTO law of subsidies and general exceptions.[162] Until legislative amendments are enacted, the

---

Secretariat, WT/CTE/W/171 (20 October 2000); OECD, "Environment and Regional Trade Agreements," 2007, pp. 55–73.

[160] See Principle 17 of the Rio Declaration on Environment and Development (1992); the Plan of Implementation of the World Summit on Sustainable Development (2002); paragraphs 6 and 33 of the Doha Ministerial Declaration (2001).

[161] See WT/CTE/W/171, *supra* note 159.

[162] We also argue elsewhere that the WTO should adopt a separate agreement or sectoral provisions under the existing agreements that would regulate renewable energy trade more specifically. See Sherzod Shadikhodjaev, "Regulation of Renewable Energy Trade in the Megaregionals Era: Current Issues and Prospects for Rule-Making Reforms," in Shin-yi Peng, Han-Wei Liu, and Ching-Fu Lin (eds.), *Governing Science and Technology under the International Economic Order: Regulatory Divergence and Convergence in the Age of Megaregionals* (Cheltenham, the United Kingdom/Northampton, MA, the United States: Edward Elgar, 2018), pp. 160–82.

WTO judiciary may, of course, use its authority to interpret the existing rules in an environmentally friendly way to the permitted extent. But judicial interpretations have their own constraints, as they cannot create "rules" to be followed by all WTO members. At the domestic level, environmental impact assessments of trade arrangements should become a normal practice everywhere. We believe that such external and internal ways of greening industrial and trade policies will support timely transition to, and sustainability of, green economies all around the world.

7

Industrial Policy in the Age of Creative Economy

Following the first official use of the term "creative industries" in Australia and the United Kingdom in the 1990s, the concept of "creative economy" now frequently appears in national legislations, government programs, policy papers, and academic works. This is a relatively new industrial policy paradigm that combines culture/the arts, innovation, and a technological breakthrough into one regulatory framework. This topic was closely analyzed in reports of the UN Educational, Scientific, and Cultural Organization (UNESCO), the UNCTAD, the UN Development Program (UNDP), and the OECD, drawing policy-makers' interest on the international plane.[1] Creative industries are distinct in being culturally "sensitive," heavily dependent on innovative ideas, and quite often represented by small-scale businesses. Many governmental measures in this field affect the way creative industries engage in trade. This chapter discusses creative economy as a concept and part of national economic strategies and examines, in detail, associated trade issues.

7.1 Creative Economy as a New Paradigm of Industrial Policy

7.1.1 The Concept of "Creative Economy"

The term "creative economy" became especially popular with John Howkins' book entitled *The Creative Economy: How People Make Money from Ideas*, first published in 2001. According to Howkins, creativity is "a process of using ideas to produce a new idea." It is personal and subjective and leads to art and "innovation" – a new product or process that is, unlike creativity, public, objective, and repeatable by anyone. "Creative economy" represents "a system for the production, exchange and use of

---

[1] See UNESCO and UNDP, "Creative Economy Report," Special Edition, 2013; UNCTAD and UNDP, "Creative Economy: A Feasible Development Option," Joint Report, 2010; OECD, "Tourism and the Creative Economy," 2014.

creative products," namely, goods, services, or experiences resulting from, and having economic value based on, creativity.[2]

Creative industries embrace both cultural industries – typically, publishing, music, cinema, audiovisual production, multimedia, visual arts, performing arts, architecture, crafts, and design[3] – and innovation-intensive sectors, such as software, video games, digitalized creative content, R&D, and so on. One study argues that the term "creative industries" can only be understood in the context of information society policy, with ICT being part of it.[4]

In this chapter, we rely mainly on the UNCTAD classification of "creative industries." As in Table 7.1, they can be grouped into four categories: "heritage," "arts," "media," and "functional creations."

Creative industries operate in highly dynamic markets where changing preferences and tastes of consumers constantly necessitate innovations in both manufacturing and services sectors. In many countries, creative industries are dominated by SMEs and microfirms. They often require startup capital and investment, including governmental support for capacity building in utilizing domestic and overseas markets. Many entrepreneurs have insufficient business skills, as they are often more content-driven than commercially oriented, with most of their products being "cultural" by nature.[5]

Creative industries play a significant role in the development of each country. Reflecting local cultures, social values and traditions, creative industries participate in the evolution of national identity. Their economic impact cannot be underestimated either. Specifically, the contribution of creative industries to GDP and employment was, respectively, 10.4 percent and 4 percent in Austria (2010), 7.4 percent and 7.1 percent in Canada (2007), 7.2 percent and 8.2 percent in Indonesia (2012), 2.4 percent and 2.6 percent in Korea (2012), and 2.7 percent and 1.7 percent in Brazil (2011).[6] Virtually any country can benefit from creative

---

[2] John Howkins, *The Creative Economy: How People Make Money from Ideas*, 2nd edn (London: Penguin Books, 2013), pp. 4–6.

[3] See UNESCO, "Cultural Industries," www.unesco.org/bpi/pdf/memobpi25_culturalindustries_en.pdf.

[4] Nicholas Garnham, "From Cultural to Creative Industries," 11(1) *International Journal of Cultural Policy* 15 (2005), pp. 15–16, 20–1.

[5] HKU, "The Entrepreneurial Dimension of the Cultural and Creative Industries," Hogeschool vor de Kunsten Utrecht, Utrecht, 2010, p. 14.

[6] OECD, *supra* note 1, p. 40.

Table 7.1 *UNCTAD Classification of Creative Industries*

Groups	Subgroups	Description
Heritage	• *Traditional cultural expressions:* art crafts, festivals, and celebrations • *Cultural sites:* archaeological sites, museums, libraries, exhibitions, etc.	Cultural heritage is identified as the origin of all forms of arts and the soul of cultural and creative industries. It is heritage that brings together cultural aspects from the historical, anthropological, ethnic, esthetic, and societal viewpoints, influences creativity, and is the origin of a number of heritage goods and services, as well as cultural activities.
Arts	• *Visual arts:* painting, sculpture, photography, and antiques • *Performing arts:* live music, theater, dance, opera, circus, puppetry, etc.	This group includes creative industries based purely on art and culture. Artwork is inspired by heritage, identity values, and symbolic meaning.
Media	• *Publishing and printed media:* books, press, and other publications • *Audiovisuals:* film, television, radio, and other broadcasting	This group produces creative content with the purpose of communicating with large audiences.
Functional creations	• *Design:* interior, graphic, fashion, jewelry, toys • *New media:* software, video games, digitalized creative content • *Creative services:* architectural, advertising, cultural and recreational, creative R&D	This group comprises more demand-driven and services-oriented industries creating goods and services with functional purposes.

Source: Based on UNCTAD and UNDP, "Creative Economy: A Feasible Development Option," Joint Report, 2010, pp. 8–9.

industries, as there seems to be no clear relationship between the size of economy and the importance of creative industries.[7]

According to the UNCTAD's most recently presented data we could find, world trade in creative goods and services reached US$624 billion in 2011, up from US$559.5 billion in 2010. Developing country exports made up 50 percent of the global total. The top ten exporters of creative goods in 2011 were China, the United States, Germany, Hong Kong, Italy, India, the United Kingdom, France, Switzerland, and the Netherlands. Design had the largest share in global exports of creative goods, followed by new media, publishing, art crafts, and visual arts. Exports of creative services jumped to US$172 billion in 2011, up from US$163.8 billion in 2010. Demand for most creative goods and services – especially domestically consumed ones, such as interior design products, videos, video games, music, and new formats for TV/radio broadcasting – was strong in the first decade of this century.[8]

7.1.2 National Policies

It appears that the term "creative industries" was officially used, for the first time, in the Australian government report "Creative Nation" (1994) that formally announced the national cultural policy, linking the arts to new communications technologies. The term gained wider acceptance following its adoption by the UK Department of Culture, Media, and Sport.[9] In 1998, that agency released the "Creative Industries Mapping Document" highlighting major economic contributions of creative industries – "those industries which have their origin in individual creativity, skill and talent and which have a potential for wealth and job creation through the generation and exploitation of intellectual property." It featured thirteen sectors, including advertising, antiques, architecture, crafts, design, fashion, film, leisure software, music, performing arts, publishing, software, and TV/radio.[10]

Recently, many other countries have followed suit in pursuing tailor-made policies in this sphere, although the scope of creative industries

---

[7] *Ibid.*, p. 39.

[8] UNCTAD, "Trade in Creative Products Reached New Peak in 2011, UNCTAD Figures Show," http://unctad.org/en/pages/newsdetails.aspx?OriginalVersionID=498.

[9] David Throsby, *The Economics of Cultural Policy* (Cambridge: Cambridge University Press, 2010), p. 88.

[10] GOV.UK, "Creative Industries Mapping Documents 1998," www.gov.uk/government/publications/creative-industries-mapping-documents-1998.

varies, sometimes including science, technology, and ICT sectors. As one can see from the WTO sources, Hong Kong, Macao, Thailand, the UAE, Indonesia, and Seychelles have set their creative economy agenda,[11] but the actual geography of these policies is certainly wider than this. Moreover, many WTO members care about their creative industries' access to foreign markets. In this connection, LDCs have asked other members to provide preferential market access to their creative services and suppliers – performers, entertainers, dance and cultural troupes, sports professionals, and artists – under the LDC services waiver adopted at the WTO Eighth Ministerial Conference in 2011.[12]

A keen interest in creative economy can be explained with governments' attempt to find new engines of growth and job creation as a response to recent economic crises, declining manufacturing, and changing economic structures. The package of policy measures for creative economy is designed to improve education, support startups and SMEs, reinforce innovation capability, raise awareness of IPRs, globalize creative firms, develop creative cities and clusters, and explore new markets.[13]

Due to spatial limits, we wish to briefly outline the EU and Korean cases below to exemplify national practices of implementing creative economy policies. But, of course, the perception of creative economy and the related government-employed means differ from country to country.

---

[11] See WTO, TPRB – 1 and 3 December 2010 – TPR – Hong Kong, China – Record of the Meeting, WT/TPR/M/241/Add.1 (10 February 2011); WTO, TPRB – 13 and 15 May 2013 – TPR – Macao, China – Record of the Meeting – Addendum, WT/TPR/M/281/Add.1 (18 September 2013); WTO, TPRB – 28 and 30 November 2011 – TPR – Thailand – Record of the Meeting, WT/TPR/M/255 (30 January 2012); WTO, TPRB – 27 and 29 March 2012 – TPR – UAE – Record of the Meeting, WT/TPR/M/262 (9 May 2012); WTO, TPRB – TPR – Report by the Secretariat – Indonesia – Revision, WT/TPR/S/278/Rev.1 (16 July 2013); WTO, Working Party on the Accession of the Republic of Seychelles – Accession of Seychelles – Draft Report of the Working Party on the Accession of the Republic of Seychelles – Revision, WT/ACC/SPEC/SYC/6/Rev.2 (16 September 2014).

[12] WTO, Council for Trade in Services – Submission by the Delegation of Uganda on behalf of the LDC Group – Collective Request Pursuant to the Bali Decision on the o[. . .]rs of LDCs, S/C/W/356 (23 July 2014), p. 5; WTO, "LDCs Welcome Progress on Preferential Treatment for Services," 2 November 2015, www.wto.org/english/news_e/news15_e/serv_02nov15_e.htm.

[13] Jeong-gon Kim, Eun-ji Kim, and Yun-ok Kim, "Cases of Creative Economy Promotion and Their Implications," *World Economy Update*, vol. 3(36), Korea Institute for International Economic Policy, 2013, p. 3.

The EU places "cultural and creative industries" under the same policy framework. According to the European Commission, cultural industries embody or convey cultural expressions, irrespective of their commercial value, and comprise traditional arts (performing arts, visual arts, cultural heritage), as well as other sectors, such as film, digital video disc (DVD) and video, television and radio, video games, new media, music, books, and press. Creative industries – "which use culture as an input and have a cultural dimension, although their outputs are mainly functional" – include architecture and design and subsectors, such as graphic design, fashion design, or advertising.[14] The EU policy directions include funding these sectors, provision of a favorable business environment for SMEs, tax harmonization on cultural products, and full utilization of "digitisation, globalisation and access to international markets."[15] The European Commission promotes innovation in education to address changing skills needs, supports the mobility of artists, reforms regulatory environments, and promotes market access for and investment in these industries.[16] Through various schemes, such as Cohesion Policy Funds and Connecting Europe Facility, it provides financial, technical, or advisory assistance for the development of platforms and networks.[17] In addition, EU member States have their own strategies of supporting domestic cultural and creative firms.

In 2013, the Korean government announced its "Creative Economy Action Plan" with the purpose to create new jobs and markets through creativity and innovation, strengthen Korea's global leadership through a creative economy, and establish a society that respects creativity. The government launched six strategies and twenty-three implementation tasks aimed at, inter alia, establishing an ecosystem for nurturing startup firms, promoting venture businesses and creative SMEs, pioneering new markets and new industries, and improving the innovation capacity of

---

[14] European Commission Green Paper, "Unlocking the Potential of Cultural and Creative Industries," COM(2010) 183 final, 2010, pp. 5–6.
[15] European Parliament Resolution of 12 September 2013 on Promoting the European Cultural and Creative Sectors as Sources of Economic Growth and Jobs, 2012/2302 (INI).
[16] European Commission, "Supporting Cultural and Creative Industries," https://ec.europa .eu/culture/policy/cultural-creative-industries_en.
[17] European Commission, "European Union Funding," https://ec.europa.eu/culture/policy/ cultural-creative-industries/eu-funding_en.

science, technology, and ICT.[18] A number of newly opened creative economy innovation centers promote regional industries and SMEs in commercializing their creative products and expanding into the global market. The essence of the Korean model of creative economy consists in the idea of a convergence of different industries, of industries and culture through people's creativity, science, technology, and ICT.[19] In short, this model prioritizes intrasectoral industrial and technological targeting and makes creativity a tool for achieving transformation across the national economy.[20]

As the EU and Korean cases may suggest, creative industries are characterized by an increasing interaction of culture/the arts and technology. This, in turn, leads to the industrial convergence, with the borderline between traditional sectors getting blurred.[21]

7.2   The Status of Creative Products under the WTO Legal Framework

Except some specific restrictions like censorship, creative industries face, in principle, the same obstacles in entering foreign markets as other industries.[22] Such market barriers may stem from, inter alia, cultural policy considerations, inadequate protection of IPRs, and the way governments cope with technological developments. As the cases considered here show, WTO litigation on creative economy issues specifically concerned publishing, advertising, audiovisual, recreational, and R&D sectors.

Proper classification of creative items – hereinafter collectively referred to as "creative products" – as a good or service is a threshold issue

---

[18] Korea's Ministry of Strategy and Finance, "Creative Economy Action Plan and Measures to Establish a Creative Economic Ecosystem," Press Release, 5 June 2013, http://english .mosf.go.kr/pre/view.do?bcd=N0001&seq=3289.

[19] Korea's Ministry of Science, ICT, and Future Planning, "Creative Economy Opens up a New Era of Korea: Action Plan for the Creative Economy," 2013, p. 6.

[20] Kim, Kim, and Kim, *supra* note 13, p. 5.

[21] See Rostam J. Neuwirth, "Global Market Integration and the Creative Economy: The Paradox of Industry Convergence and Regulatory Divergence," 18 *Journal of International Economic Law* 21 (2015).

[22] For instance, State measures on audiovisual products – a subset of creative products – include subsidies, domestic content requirements, regulatory or licensing restrictions, tax measures, border restrictions, etc. See Michael Hahn, "A Clash of Cultures? The UNESCO *Diversity Convention* and International Trade Law," 9 *Journal of International Economic Law* 515 (2006), pp. 530–1.

defining applicable law. But this may not always be a straightforward exercise, given the emergence of new technologies and intangibility of some creative products. Because the WTO agreements do not provide a homogeneous definition of "goods" and "services," this issue is to be decided on a case-by-case basis. Moreover, some creative products constitute intellectual property.

7.2.1 Creative Products as Goods

The UNCTAD divides all creative goods in seven categories pursuant to HS 2002, as follows:[23]

- design, 102 codes (items related to architecture, fashion, interior, toys, jewelry, glassware);
- art crafts, 60 codes (carpet, yarn, wickerware, celebration articles, paperware, others);
- visual arts, 17 codes (photography, painting, sculpture, antiques);
- publishing, 15 codes (newspapers, books, other printing matter);
- performing arts, 7 codes (recorded laser discs, recorded magnetic tapes, printed or manuscript music);
- new media, 8 codes (recorded media for sound and image, video games);
- audiovisuals, 2 codes (exposed cinematographic film).

Some creative goods can be subjected to the government control because of their content. To give an example, Viet Nam bans domestic production, sales, exportation, and importation of "superstitious, depraved and reactionary cultural products," including audiovisual materials, due to their harmful content.[24] Cultural restrictions of this kind basically aim to protect public morals[25] and as such do not necessary conflict with WTO rules. Some members even secure the censorship right under their accession package.[26]

---

[23] UNCTAD and UNDP, *supra* note 1, p. 115; Statistical Annex thereto, http://unctadstat .unctad.org/UnctadStatMetadata/Documentation/CER2010_StatAnnex.pdf.

[24] WT/ACC/VNM/48, Ch. 2, *supra* note 33, paras. 211–15.

[25] Panel Report, *China – Publications and Audiovisual Products*, paras. 7.712, 7.766.

[26] See, e.g., WT/ACC/VNM/48, Ch. 2, *supra* note 33, paras. 211–15; WTO, Working Party on the Accession of China – Report of the Working Party on the Accession of China – Schedule CLII – The People's Republic of China – Part II –[. . .]le II MFN Exemptions – Addendum, WT/ACC/CHN/49/Add.2 (1 October 2001), p. 21 (inscribing commitments

But the way cultural restrictions are applied may cause trade frictions. The high-profile dispute in *China – Publications and Audiovisual Products* dealt with the policy of filtering cultural imports. In order to prevent negative influence of "undesirable" foreign culture on its people and political system,[27] China allowed only designated State-owned entities to import cultural goods and carry out their "content review" at the border. But this system was found to be contrary to the Accession Protocol that obligates China to "progressively liberalize the availability and scope of the right to trade" so that all enterprises in the country would eventually be able to freely import and export.[28]

The *Canada – Periodicals* case concerned a prohibitive excise tax on foreign split-run periodicals – special editions of foreign publications that contained country-of-origin material plus some "Canadian content" and advertisements primarily oriented for the Canadian market. The tax was set to prevent diversion of advertising opportunities from local publishers to US split-run companies that were able to offer price discounts on advertisement in Canada thanks to their sales of the main edition in the US market. Canada defended the discriminatory tax with unlikeness of foreign split-run and domestic non-split-run magazines, as the latter allegedly reflected a "Canadian perspective" on the covered topics and events. In Canada's view, magazines as a cultural good are different from ordinary articles of trade in being intended for intellectual consumption rather than physical use, which allegedly makes editorial content decisive in the likeness determination as opposed to the traditional approach of examining product's physical characteristics.[29] But the Appellate Body disagreed and said that the imported split-run and domestic non-split-run periodicals were, in fact, "directly competitive or substitutable" products within the meaning of the second sentence of Article III:2 of the GATT. The Appellate Body did underline the role of the content in defining a proper market for product comparisons, but doubted that the per se difference in the editorial content could make the periodicals on the same subject matter unlike:

on audiovisual services "without prejudice to China's right to examine the content of audio and video products").

[27] Julia Ya Qin, "Pushing the Limits of Global Governance: Trading Rights, Censorship and WTO Jurisprudence – A Commentary on the *China – Publications* Case," 10 *Chinese Journal of International Law* 271 (2011), p. 272.

[28] Panel Report, *China – Publications and Audiovisual Products*, para. 8.1.2.

[29] Panel Report, *Canada – Periodicals*, paras. 3.61–3.62, 3.67, 3.69.

Our conclusion that imported split-run periodicals and domestic non-split-run periodicals are "directly competitive or substitutable" does not mean that all periodicals belong to the same relevant market, whatever their editorial content. A periodical containing mainly current news is not directly competitive or substitutable with a periodical dedicated to gardening, chess, sports, music or cuisine. But newsmagazines, like TIME, TIME Canada and Maclean's, are directly competitive or substitutable *in spite of* the "Canadian" content of Maclean's. The competitive relationship is even closer in the case of more specialized magazines, like Pulp & Paper as compared with Pulp & Paper Canada, two trade magazines presented to the Panel by the United States.[30]

If the content is available to end users in a nonphysical medium, a very fundamental question is whether the related item is a good or service. Case law shows that a product's intangibility as such does not automatically render it a service. If the subject item is covered by tariff classification, this may be indicative of it being a good.

In *China – Publications and Audiovisual Products*, the Chinese authorities banned foreign entities from importing and distributing reading materials, audiovisual home entertainment products (e.g., videocassettes, video compact discs, DVDs), sound recordings (e.g., recorded audio tapes), and films for theatrical release. China argued that "motion pictures for theatrical release" – those intended to be shown in movie theaters – were not "goods" but part of the theatrical distribution service, even though they were carried by the tangible film reel which was merely "an accessory to the service" provided.[31] China also insisted that master copies with audiovisual content (e.g., videocassettes, DVDs, or physical sound recordings) used for making copies for domestic sales were not goods but merely part of copyright licensing.[32] But the panel disagreed, referring to the HS Code and its Explanatory Note, China's schedule of concessions, and the fact of collecting customs duties.[33] However, the caveat is that this particular case concerned audiovisual products as imported in *physical carrier materials* with embedded content. Thus, the panel's finding is not perfectly suitable for the audiovisual content delivered electronically,[34] which raises a controversial issue of a proper

---

[30] Appellate Body Report, *Canada – Periodicals*, p. 28 (emphasis added).
[31] Panel Report, *China – Publications and Audiovisual Products*, paras. 7.496–7.497, 7.500.
[32] *Ibid.*, paras. 7.615–7.618, 7.639.   [33] *Ibid.*, paras. 7.524–7.525, 7.640–7.642.
[34] Tania Voon, "China – Measures Affecting Trading Rights and Distribution Services for Certain Publications and Audiovisual Entertainment Products," 103 *American Journal of International Law* 710 (2009), p. 716.

classification under the goods/services rules as discussed in the WTO for many years without any clear-cut conclusion reached.[35]

The "good vs. service" issue can come into play where a service is related to or supplied in conjunction with a particular good. In *Canada – Periodicals*, Canada claimed that the GATT was not applicable, because the excise tax pertained to advertising services that were excluded from Canada's GATS schedule and thus exempt from WTO obligations. But the Appellate Body rightly concluded that the GATT was, in fact, applicable here, as the tax was imposed on the periodicals rather than advertising, and that, anyway, the GATT and the GATS could co-exist without overriding each other.[36]

7.2.2   Creative Products as Services

Pursuant to the UNCTAD, creative services comprise four groups: (i) advertising, market research, and public opinion services; (ii) architectural, engineering, and other technical services; (iii) research and development services; and (iv) personal, cultural, and recreational services, such as audiovisual and related services, as well as other personal, cultural, and recreational services associated with museums, libraries, archives, and recreational activities. Computer and information services and services associated with royalties and license fees – leasing or rental of video tapes/discs, licensing services for the use of computer software, entertainment, R&D products, and so on – constitute services related to creative industries.[37]

WTO members have great latitude in defining their commitments on creative services and making MFN exemptions. As of 1 September 2015, only forty-nine members included recreational, cultural, and sporting services in their respective GATS schedules; thirty-six members scheduled audiovisual services.[38] The exclusion of particular services from the scheduling scope would mean virtually unrestricted governmental control of market access and lawfulness of preferences given to domestic (but not foreign) operators. In practice, creative services are subject to, inter alia, government regulations regarding

---

[35] See Section 7.3.2.2.   [36] Appellate Body Report, *Canada – Periodicals*, pp. 17–20.
[37] UNCTAD and UNDP, *supra* note 1, p. 115; Statistical Annex thereto, http://unctadstat .unctad.org/UnctadStatMetadata/Documentation/CER2010_StatAnnex.pdf.
[38] Based on WTO, "I-TIP Services," http://i-tip.wto.org/services/default.aspx.

IPR protection, equity, competition, censorship, language and technical requirements, taxes, and subsidies.

According to the WTO Secretariat, the scheduled limitations for audiovisual services include, for example, content quotas on television and motion pictures, caps on foreign equity, restrictions on the type of legal entity, and discriminatory subsidies. The audiovisual sector accounts for most of the GATS MFN exemptions. Often justified by cultural policy reasons, such exemptions typically extend national treatment to works covered by coproduction agreements, support programs, or relevant treaties.[39]

In *US – Gambling*, Antigua challenged US measures that prevented its operators from supplying gambling and betting services – an essential part of its gaming industry – to the US market over the Internet. Sector 10 ("Recreational, Cultural, & Sporting Services") of the US schedule contained subsector D ("Other Recreational Services (except sporting)"), with no corresponding limitations ("None") being inscribed for market access in mode 1 (cross-border supply). Antigua argued that this would mean full market access for recreational services *including* gambling, but the United States countered that the words "except sporting" excluded gambling from its commitments. The Appellate Body emphasized the mutual exclusiveness of (sub)sectors in GATS schedules and eventually denied the US proposition. Specifically, the Appellate Body found some support for Antigua's claim in, inter alia, the document W/120 on "Services Sectoral Classification List" and the related WTO Scheduling Guidelines (1993).[40] But it considered these sources as merely supplementary means of interpretation,[41] which somewhat undermines their role in treaty interpretation.[42]

In the same case, the panel held that mode 1 under the GATS encompassed "all means of delivery, whether by mail, telephone, Internet etc., unless otherwise specified in a Member's Schedule." In the finding not reviewed by the Appellate Body, the panel opined that this was "in line" with the principle of technological neutrality that "seems to be largely shared among WTO Members" as shown in the WTO work

---

[39] WTO, Council for Trade in Services – Audiovisual Services – Background Note by the Secretariat, S/C/W/310 (12 January 2010), paras. 67, 69.

[40] Appellate Body Report, *US – Gambling*, paras. 196–213.   [41] *Ibid.*, para. 197.

[42] Federico Ortino, "Treaty Interpretation and the WTO Appellate Body Report in *US – Gambling*: A Critique," 9 *Journal of International Economic Law* 117(2006), pp. 128–30.

program on electronic commerce.[43] By contrast, the panel in *China – Publications and Audiovisual Products* refrained from invoking this "principle" and used general interpretation techniques to address China's argument that sound recording distribution services under its GATS schedule covered only distribution of sound recordings embedded in physical media, but not their electronic distribution. The latter, in China's view, was a new type of service – "network music services" – outside of the scheduling commitments.[44] The panel observed that neither the ordinary meaning of "sound recording distribution services" nor the language of China's schedule (as opposed to other members' schedules) excluded distribution through an electronic medium. The panel also noted that the electronic distribution of music was technically and commercially feasible even before China's accession to the WTO and hence known to the negotiators at the time of the service commitment at issue.[45]

Although technological neutrality does not seem to be fully accepted as an established *principle* yet, the *US – Gambling* panel's referral to this concept nevertheless makes sense. Indeed, technological neutrality allows much flexibility in sustaining national schedules even where they are not timely adjusted to rapid technological developments. It prevents members from invoking the emergence of so-called new (not-scheduled-yet) services as a pretext for circumventing scheduled commitments.

7.2.3   Creative Products as Intellectual Property

Intellectual property embodied in publications, music, movies, videos, and other relevant creative items is subject to the TRIPS Agreement. Protection and enforcement of IPRs are of particular importance to innovative activities. Given the close nexus between creativity/innovation and IPRs, it is not surprising that, for instance, several WTO members in a TPRB meeting called upon Thailand to strengthen the IPR system under its creative economy policy.[46]

Two IPR-related WTO disputes examined the extent to which governments may deviate from their TRIPS obligations on copyright and related

---

[43] Panel Report, *US – Gambling*, para. 6.285.
[44] Panel Report, *China – Publications and Audiovisual Products*, paras. 7.1144, 7.1167.
[45] *Ibid.*, paras. 7.1220, 7.1247, 7.1258.
[46] WT/TPR/M/255, *supra* note 11, paras. 97, 182, 256.

rights. In *US – Section 110(5) Copyright Act*, the EC challenged the US legislation that exempted certain public establishments playing radio or television music from paying royalties to songwriters and music publishers. In particular, a so-called "business exemption" permitted food, drink, and retail establishments under certain size and equipment restrictions to display audio or visual transmissions without an authorization of the right holders and payment of a royalty fee. In addition, a "homestyle exemption" gave the same exemption to small restaurants and retail outlets that used only broadcasting equipment commonly found in private homes. The homestyle exemption covered only "dramatic" musical works (e.g., operas, operettas, or musicals), while the business exemption was limited to "nondramatic" musical works. As many other countries have similar copyright exceptions, the panel decision has indirect repercussions for them as well.[47]

Article 9(1) of the TRIPS Agreement requires members to comply with, inter alia, the Berne Convention (1971) provisions that grant authors the exclusive right of authorizing the broadcasting of their works to the public. But the United States invoked Article 13 of the TRIPS Agreement, which allows limitations or exceptions to exclusive rights of copyright holders, provided that such limitations or exceptions (i) are confined to "certain special cases," (ii) "do not conflict with a normal exploitation of the work," and (iii) "do not unreasonably prejudice the legitimate interests of the right holder." The panel considered that, in order to meet the first condition, a limitation or exception in national legislation must be clearly defined and be narrow in its scope, with the public policy purposes being of "subsidiary relevance" only.[48] The "normal exploitation" in the second condition is something less than "full use" of an exclusive right.[49] The third condition means that the exception or limitation must not (threaten to) cause an unreasonable loss of income to the copyright holder.[50] The panel found that the business exemption was not covered by Article 13, because, inter alia, potential users of this exemption constituted the vast majority of eating and drinking establishments and almost half of retail establishments – the portion that was too broad in scope to qualify as a "special case[ ]" under the first condition. But the panel held that the homestyle exemption met

---

[47] See Helen A. Christakos, "WTO Panel Report on Section 110(5) of the U.S. Copyright Act," 17 *Berkeley Technology Law Journal* 595 (2002), pp. 604–6.

[48] Panel Report, *US – Section 110(5) Copyright Act*, paras. 6.111–6.113, 6.157.

[49] *Ibid.*, para. 6.167.   [50] *Ibid.*, para. 6.229.

the conditions of Article 13, given certain limits imposed on the beneficiaries of the exemption, permissible equipment, and categories of works, as well as the US judicial practice.[51]

In *China – Intellectual Property Rights*, the United States challenged China's denial of copyright protection and enforcement to creative works not authorized by Chinese censors for publication or distribution inside the country. Article 4(1) of China's Copyright Law provided that "[w]orks the publication and/or dissemination of which are prohibited by law shall not be protected by this Law." The panel found that the Copyright Law was inconsistent with Article 5(1) of the Berne Convention (1971) – as incorporated by Article 9.1 of the TRIPS Agreement – which says that, in signatory countries other than the country of origin, the authors "shall enjoy" the rights granted by this Convention in respect of protected works. The panel also faulted China, under Article 41.1 of the TRIPS Agreement, for not making its enforcement procedures available for the works whose copyright protection was denied.[52] But China countered that its law banned works with "completely unconstitutional or immoral content" and was justified by Article 17 of the Berne Convention which recognizes the right of the government to control or prohibit "the circulation, presentation, or exhibition of any work or production in regard to which the competent authority may find it necessary to exercise that right."[53] The panel held that, while Article 17 clearly covered censorship for public order reasons, it did not deny *all* rights granted by the Berne Convention, including the exclusive right of the owner to authorize specific acts with respect to its work. In the panel's assessment, China was unable to explain why censorship interfered with the copyright owners' right to prevent third parties from exploiting prohibited works. In fact, copyright and government censorship are not necessarily mutually exclusive, as they address private rights and public interests, respectively.[54]

Just like under many other WTO exceptions, the government seeking justification under the relevant TRIPS provisions must, first of all, be consistent in applying measures aimed at the protection of legitimate public interests. This reveals a weak point in China's defense. The United States stated that the denial of copyright protection under the challenged legislation unfairly profited copyright infringers, because legitimate

---

[51] See *ibid.*, paras. 6.114–6.272, 7.1.
[52] Panel Report, *China – Intellectual Property Rights*, paras. 7.139, 7.179–7.181.
[53] *Ibid.*, paras. 7.78, 7.120, 7.122.   [54] *Ibid.*, paras. 7.133–7.135.

right-holders were not able to take any action within China against pirated copies of publications, films, music, or other creative works that were well available in that market.[55] Obviously, the fundamental problem with China's policy was in that the government disallowed certain works due to their harmful content, while, at the same time, failing to effectively combat the in-country circulation of pirated copies with the *identical* content.

7.3   Creative Economy and Technological Progress under WTO Law

Creative industries are susceptible to any technological changes that affect the way they reach consumers and produce. We now discuss the WTO regime on R&D – an important constituent of creative economy. Then, we turn to the digitization of trade in creative products.

7.3.1   R&D Issues

The UNCTAD recommends that for fostering the creative economy governments should encourage technology acquisition and upgrading and have their science, technology, and innovation policies in place.[56] In this connection, R&D plays a crucial role in facilitating innovation. In the multilateral trading system, R&D issues are regulated mainly in the fields of services, government procurement, and subsidies.

The GATS applies to R&D services on natural sciences (CPC 851), R&D services on social sciences and humanities (CPC 852), and interdisciplinary R&D services (CPC 853).[57] Similarly, the UNCTAD's trade statistics on creative economy capture R&D services in the sciences, social sciences, and humanities.[58] To our knowledge, R&D services have not raised any serious issues in the GATS-related litigation. Thus, we focus on R&D-related government procurement and subsidy issues.

7.3.1.1   R&D and Government Procurement

The GPA of the 1994 and revised versions prefers open or selective tendering procedures to limited tendering – the least open way of procurement, whereby a procuring entity contacts suppliers of its choice.

---

[55] *Ibid.*, Annex A, p. A-11, para. 59.   [56] UNCTAD and UNDP, *supra* note 1, p. 9.
[57] MTN.GNS/W/120, Ch. 5, *supra* note 90.
[58] UNCTAD and UNDP, *supra* note 1, p. 115; Statistical Annex thereto, http://unctadstat .unctad.org/UnctadStatMetadata/Documentation/CER2010_StatAnnex.pdf.

Limited tendering is allowed in exceptional cases, including where the entity procures a prototype or a first product or service which is "developed at its request in the course of, and for, a particular contract for research, experiment, study or original development."[59]

Under the former GATT system, the *Norway – Trondheim Toll Ring* case centered on whether the Norwegian government's awarding of a contract on the purchase of an electronic toll collection system to a domestic company was a limited tendering – namely, a "single tendering" in the Tokyo Round text. The United States claimed that this was a contract for procurement of a product (i.e., toll collection equipment) rather than R&D, and that as such it could not constitute a legitimate single tendering for the production of a prototype or first product in order to execute an R&D contract.[60] The panel held that, in interpreting the GPA words "contract for research . . . or original development," one had to consider not the nature of the supplier's work but what the entity was procuring. Such a contract must lead to the public procurement of the results of research and/or original development, i.e. knowledge.[61] The panel determined further that, for a valid single tendering, the purchased products would qualify as prototypes if their main purpose was "the testing and furthering of the knowledge" procured by the government under the R&D contract.[62] Based on the evidence, the panel concluded that the transaction at issue did not meet the GPA requirements.[63]

7.3.1.2 R&D Subsidies

R&D activities generate knowledge – a public good – capable of spilling over to others not involved in those activities (i.e., "free riders"), which discourages many firms from investing in R&D. Thus, government subsidies are needed to address such a positive externality.

The forms of R&D subsidies vary. These could be direct payments as in, for example, Korea's "21st Century Frontier R&D progam," under which the government provided, in essence, long-term interest-free loans to cover a portion of R&D costs in science and technology projects.[64] Some R&D projects resemble a joint venture between the sponsor and

[59] Article XV:1(e) of the GPA; Article XIII:1(f) of the Revised GPA.
[60] GATT Panel Report, *Norway – Trondheim Toll Ring*, para. 4.1.   [61] *Ibid.*, para. 4.8.
[62] *Ibid.*, para. 4.9.   [63] *Ibid.*, para. 4.14.
[64] See US DOC, Issues and Decision Memorandum for the Final Determination in the Countervailing Duty Investigation of Dynamic Random Access Memory Semiconductors from the Republic of Korea [C-580–851], 68 FR 37122, 23 June 2003.

the beneficiary. In particular, the US National Aeronautics and Space Administration in *US – Large Civil Aircraft (2nd complaint)* not only paid Boeing to conduct R&D but also allowed access to its facilities, equipment, and employees, with the fruits of the research being shared between that agency and Boeing.[65] Furthermore, R&D projects can result in a transfer of associated IPRs from the subsidizing government to recipients. The panel in *US – Large Civil Aircraft (2nd complaint)* merely assumed *arguendo* that the allocation of patent rights was a "subsidy" and proceeded to see if it was "specific," but the Appellate Body warned against such an *arguendo* approach.[66] In our view, such transfer of IPRs could qualify as governmental provision of goods within the meaning of Article 1.1(a)(1)(iii) of the SCM Agreement, as the scope of "goods" under that provision is quite broad to comprise even some unconventional products.[67]

We now consider two particular issues WTO case law dealt with in relation to R&D subsidies, namely, specificity and adverse effects.

7.3.1.2.1 Specificity   Export-oriented or import-substitutive R&D subsidies are prohibited and deemed to be specific as such. With respect to de facto export conditionality, the panel in *Canada – Aircraft* held that the closer subsidies bring products to export markets, the greater the probability is that they are linked to export performance. In contrast, subsidies for "pure research" or "for general purposes such as improving efficiency or adopting new technology" would be less likely to give rise to de facto export contingency.[68] The Appellate Body cautioned that the mere presence of such a nearness-to-the-export-market factor would not create "a presumption" of de facto contingency. Thus, it did not rule out that, in the light of various factors taken together, a preproduction subsidy for R&D could, in fact, be contingent upon export performance.[69]

Specificity becomes a complicated issue if R&D subsidies are provided under a comprehensive support program that covers research activities in many sectors. But WTO adjudicators seem to have preferred a narrowing-down approach. In particular, the panel in *US – Large Civil*

---

[65] Appellate Body Report, *US – Large Civil Aircraft (2nd complaint)*, paras. 594–7.
[66] *Ibid.*, para. 739; Panel Report, *US – Large Civil Aircraft (2nd complaint)*, para. 7.1276.
[67] Appellate Body Report, *US – Softwood Lumber IV*, para. 67.
[68] Panel Report, *Canada – Aircraft*, paras. 9.337–9.339.
[69] Appellate Body Report, *Canada – Aircraft*, para. 174.

Aircraft (2nd complaint) said that the specificity analysis had to pertain to individual subprograms that have a narrow R&D scope.[70] In *EC and certain member States – Large Civil Aircraft*, EC framework programs sought to advance R&D activities in general, whereas related subprograms channelled dedicated funding to sector-specific research areas.[71] The EU argued that the specificity analysis concerned each framework program as a whole, which would make it nonspecific, as funds thereunder were allocated to a wide range of sectors and enterprises.[72] But the Appellate Body insisted on the fund-level assessment where the relevant fund was available to "certain enterprises" within the meaning of Article 2.1 of the SCM Agreement, regardless of whether other funds under the same framework program were accessible by different groupings of entities:

> [W]e do not consider that explicit limitations on access to a subsidy to entities active in one sector of the economy will produce a different result under Article 2.1(a) [of the SCM Agreement] by virtue of the fact that separate groupings of entities have access to other pools of funding under that programme. Certainly, if access to the same subsidy is limited to some grouping of enterprises or industries, an investigating authority or panel would be required to assess whether the eligible recipients can be collectively defined as "certain enterprises". Where access to certain funding under a subsidy programme is explicitly limited to a grouping of enterprises or industries that qualify as "certain enterprises", this in our view leads to a provisional indication of specificity within the meaning of Article 2.1(a), irrespective of how other funding under that programme is distributed.[73]

The following case-law lessons may help policy-makers design R&D programs in a nonspecific way. The UK Technology Program in *EC and certain member States – Large Civil Aircraft* was found to be nonspecific, because that program's overall budget was allocated across seven broad technology areas, subject to open competition among research themes, with no subbudgets set aside for research projects of particular industries.[74] Moreover, the panel in *US – Large Civil Aircraft (2nd complaint)* concluded that the US Advanced Technology Program was not specific, because it focused on R&D in "high risk, high pay-off, emerging and

---

[70] Panel Report, *US – Large Civil Aircraft (2nd complaint)*, paras. 7.1191–7.1196.
[71] Appellate Body Report, *EC and certain member States – Large Civil Aircraft*, para. 938.
[72] *Ibid.*, para. 946.   [73] *Ibid.*, para. 949.
[74] Panel Report, *EC and certain member States – Large Civil Aircraft*, paras. 7.1587, 7.1589, 7.1591.

enabling technologies," the factor that did not limit the subsidy to a sufficiently limited group of enterprises or industries.[75] The panel also observed that specificity could not be analyzed at the level of an individual project (payment) if it flowed from a broader, identifiable R&D program.[76]

As a final remark, it is worth noting that in this age of creative economy and the fourth industrial revolution when many new products tend to have technology-converging characteristics, the way of classifying technology by industrial sectors will likely change accordingly. Given this, the mere fact of technology convergence cutting across several sectors will probably not necessarily make associated R&D subsidies unspecific. This issue will need to be approached on a case-by-case basis.

7.3.1.2.2 Adverse Effects In *US – Large Civil Aircraft (2nd complaint)*, the panel considered "technology effects" – the impact of aeronautics R&D subsidies on the development of certain technologies – as part of a larger assessment of "serious prejudice" to EC commercial interests under Articles 5 and 6 of the SCM Agreement. The Appellate Body approved of the panel's counterfactual analysis of the technology effects on both Boeing (stage one) and its rival Airbus (stage two).

At stage one, the panel concluded that the R&D subsidies greatly contributed to Boeing's development of technologies, conferred a competitive advantage on Boeing, and enabled it to quickly launch and commercialize the aircraft incorporating all of the relevant technologies. For this, the panel considered the objectives, structure, design, and operation of the aeronautics R&D subsidies and the conditions of competition in the market.[77] Although the United States argued that the government's R&D funding was far smaller than Boeing's own R&D investments, the Appellate Body agreed with the panel's finding that the effects of subsidies could not be reduced to their cash value, and that even relatively small amounts of R&D subsidies may have "substantial" impacts in the market due to their "multiplier" effects. Indeed, it was found that the public R&D funding allowed Boeing to overcome significant disincentives in spending on highly risky aeronautics R&D.[78]

---

[75] Panel Report, *US – Large Civil Aircraft (2nd complaint)*, paras. 7.1241–7.1246.
[76] *Ibid.*, paras. 7.1252–7.1254.
[77] *Ibid.*, paras. 7.1773, 7.1775; Appellate Body Report, *US – Large Civil Aircraft (2nd complaint)*, para. 1030.
[78] Appellate Body Report, *US – Large Civil Aircraft (2nd complaint)*, paras. 1005–6, 1033–5.

At stage two, the panel found that, but for the R&D subsidies' effects, Airbus would have obtained additional orders for its aircraft, made additional sales of it, and would not have suffered significant price suppression. But the Appellate Body reversed the panel's finding that the R&D subsidies at issue threatened to cause displacement and impedance of EC exports in some third countries, because the panel failed to identify clear trends showing this effect.[79]

7.3.2   Creative Economy and Digitization

Digital technologies have changed the way many creative works are generated, distributed, and used.[80] ICTs affect the creative economy by facilitating the production of new creative products like software and videogames and the delivery of creative content to consumers via a greater range of media, such as video-on-demand, music podcasting, streaming, and cable/Internet TV.

The Internet has enabled electronic commerce involving creative goods and services. Under the WTO's working definition, "electronic commerce" (or "e-commerce") – the term used in many sources interchangeably with "digital trade" – means "the production, distribution, marketing, sale or delivery of goods and services by electronic means."[81]

Creative industries may face different obstacles to advancing their digital content in foreign markets. As listed here, a company survey by the US International Trade Commission distinguishes three sets of typical barriers that hinder digital trade in creative products. While the governmental measures among them are not necessarily WTO-inconsistent, they still may or do limit market access to creative industries.

First of all, an increasing number of countries apply localization policies to digital goods and services. Although the "shelf space" on the online marketplace is virtually unlimited, firms distributing digital content through the licensing of movies and television shows for streaming and downloading argue that the screen-quota-like restrictions of, for

---

[79] *Ibid.*, paras. 1040, 1126–7; Panel Report, *US – Large Civil Aircraft (2nd complaint)*, para. 7.1794.

[80] See Ruth Towse and Christian Handke (eds.), *Handbook on the Digital Creative Economy* (Cheltenham, the United Kingdom/Northampton, MA, the United States: Edward Elgar, 2013).

[81] WTO, Work Programme on Electronic Commerce – Adopted by the General Council on 25 September 1998, WT/L/274 (30 September 1998), para. 1.3.

example, Brazil, China, France, and Canada are impeding their online business.[82] The EU Audiovisual Media Services Directive (2007) is said to extend preferences for European content to on-demand or streaming video services.[83] Government subsidies in China for the online game sector reportedly increased the share of local companies from one-third of the domestic market in 2003 to about two-thirds in ten years.[84] In some countries, local creative industries and, in particular, software producers enjoy secured access to public procurement, with the government giving price preferences to indigenous innovative products.[85]

Furthermore, Internet piracy, which can be exacerbated by a government's weak or inefficient enforcement system, constitutes another barrier to digital trade. The International Intellectual Property Alliance illustrates how online wrongdoings may negatively affect creative industries:

> Unauthorized downloading or streaming of a motion picture, for example, often sourced to a single illegal camcording incident, can decimate box office sales and harm subsequent release windows. Online and mobile piracy threatens the viability of licensed platforms, and erodes the capacity of artists, musicians, filmmakers, performers and songwriters to earn a living from their craft. Online piracy of entertainment software continues at prolific rates, facilitated by sites that link to infringing copies stored on cyberlockers or through peer to peer-to-peer (P2P) networks. Book and journal publishers are harmed by sites that provide and deliver unauthorized digital copies of medical and scientific journal articles on an illegal subscription basis, as well as sites that traffic in illegally obtained subscription login credentials, and increasingly face online piracy of trade books (fiction and non-fiction) and academic textbooks. Infringing software of all types is also prevalent on online sites, which constitutes a major source for unlicensed software for both consumers and business enterprises.[86]

Finally, government censorship of Internet content and platforms may result in complete or partial denial of access to respective countries' markets. The censorship measures in the form of blocking or filtering websites make it difficult for digital content companies to reach their customers. Some countries like China and Viet Nam are said to carry out

---

[82] US International Trade Commission, Ch. 5, *supra* note 85, p. 84.
[83] US International Trade Commission, "Digital Trade in the U.S. and Global Economies, Part 1," 2013, p. 5–6.
[84] *Ibid.*, p. 5–7.   [85] *Ibid.*, pp. 5–7, 5–8.
[86] US International Trade Commission, Ch. 5, *supra* note 85, p. 94.

strict online censorship over foreign Internet intermediaries, music and entertainment software companies as opposed to a looser control of domestic counterparts.[87]

7.3.2.1   Availability of Electronic Infrastructure

The WTO plays an important role in facilitating access to the Internet and communication networks that enable trade in digital creative products. First, the IT Agreement removed tariffs on a number of IT products, including computers, telecommunication equipment, and software. Software here refers to the HS-classifiable carrier media – like diskettes, magnetic tapes, and compact discs – containing software. At the WTO's Tenth Ministerial Conference (2015) in Nairobi, a group of members participating in the negotiations on updating the IT Agreement agreed to eliminate customs duties on an extended list of 201 products.[88]

Second, WTO law regulates the supply of services. Digital trade comprises three different transactions involving services: (i) provision of Internet access services, (ii) electronic delivery of services (i.e., delivery of service products in the form of electronic information flows), and (iii) e-commerce as a form of distribution services (online shopping). It is the first type that provides access to the Internet network. According to the WTO Secretariat's note, the Internet was initially perceived to be a computer service, but it is currently widely viewed as a telecommunication service due to the convergence of telecommunications and computer technology. At least ten members made specific GATS commitments concerning Internet access in the context of basic telecommunications. On the other hand, the absence of specific commitments does not necessarily entail the outright ban on services by foreign Internet providers but may simply imply that there is no guarantee for their access to the respective member's market.[89]

In a monopolized telecommunications sector, the monopoly provider is typically the only supplier of Internet access. But even in that case, governments have the obligation under Article VIII of the GATS to ensure that the exclusive provider does not frustrate their commitments on other services supplied online. Members granting market access to

---

[87] US International Trade Commission, *supra* note 83, pp. 5–20, 5–21.

[88] WTO, "WTO Members Conclude Landmark $1.3 Trillion IT Trade Deal," 16 December 2015, www.wto.org/english/news_e/news15_e/ita_16dec15_e.htm.

[89] WTO, General Council – WTO Agreements and Electronic Commerce, WT/GC/W/90 (14 July 1998), p. 3, paras. 7, 12.

competitive Internet access providers are required by the GATS Annex on Telecommunications to give those providers reasonable and nondiscriminatory access to public telecommunications transport networks and services.

7.3.2.2   Creative Digital Content and Market Access

On 20 May 1998, the Ministerial Conference adopted a declaration urging the WTO General Council to establish a comprehensive work program on trade-related issues of electronic commerce and announcing that "Members will continue their current practice of not imposing customs duties on electronic transmission." The General Council launched the work program in the same year and has since then discussed numerous issues dealing with the classification of digital content, development, fiscal implications of e-commerce, relationship between e-commerce and traditional forms of commerce, imposition of customs duties on electronic transmissions, competition, jurisdiction, and applicable law.[90]

Under the work program, all members share the view that the existing WTO agreements apply to e-commerce – with many questioning the need for creating tailor-made rules – but they cannot agree to the extent of such applicability.[91] There is a common understanding that goods sold electronically but delivered physically across borders are subject to the WTO rules on goods, and that the electronic delivery of services falls within the ambit of the GATS.[92]

A host of issues remain controversial. With respect to the political commitment to suspend customs duties on electronic transmissions, it is not clear whether this moratorium is about nonimposition of duties on the digitally delivered content or on electronically delivered services. It is questionable whether the moratorium itself is meaningful, as it is technically difficult to collect such duties.[93]

---

[90] WTO, "Electronic Commerce: Work Continues on Issues Needing Clarification," www.wto.org/english/tratop_e/ecom_e/ecom_briefnote_e.htm.

[91] Sacha Wunsch-Vincent, *The WTO, the Internet and Trade in Digital Products: EC–US Perspectives* (Portland, OR: Hart Publishing, 2006), p. 19.

[92] WTO, Council for Trade in Goods – Work Programme on Electronic Commerce – Information Provided to the General Council, G/C/W/158 (26 July 1999), para. 4.2; WTO, Council for Trade in Services – Work Programme on Electronic Commerce – Interim Report to the General Council, S/C/8 (31 March 1999), para. 4.

[93] S/C/8, *supra* note 92, Annex, p. 10.

With respect to creative industries, the most fundamental question is, for example, whether music, videos, movies, entertainment games, or software programs available online should be classified as a good or service. The United States and other proponents of the pro-GATT classification are interested in furthering commercialization of digital content across the globe. They argue that trade in digital content would be more liberal in the GATT context as compared to the GATS regime with its positive listing of sectoral market openings. They add that nothing in the GATT indicates its applicability to physical goods only, and that the actual production of digital content, unlike services, does not coincide with its consumption. By contrast, a group of opponents led by the EU supports the idea of regulating digital content through the GATS, as it gives more policy space in protecting their cultural industries. A third group of members advocate a somewhat "hybrid" approach of applying the GATS regime to digital content while securing GATT-level market access through scheduling all respective sectors and removing MFN exemptions.[94]

We take the view that creative *content* – be it presented in a physical or digital format (e.g., music embedded in a CD or a downloadable file) – should be treated as a good, whereas the associated electronic transaction (e.g., downloading the file) should be considered as a service. The Appellate Body in *EC – Bananas III* admitted simultaneous applicability of the GATT and the GATS to the same measure that involves "a service relating to a particular good or a service supplied in conjunction with a particular good."[95] But a legal assessment of that measure under each of these agreements can lead to different outcomes. Thus, a member's trade restriction on digital creative content can be found GATT-inconsistent but still immune from the GATS disciplines if no specific commitments have been made for the service concerned.

In addition to the classification issue, there are unresolved questions in each respective context as well. In the goods sector, members differ on whether digital and comparable physical products are alike to be eligible for nondiscriminatory treatment.[96] Let us take the example of publications. Some countries levy lower VATs on print books than on e-books (i.e., digital formats of books displayable on a computer screen, tablets,

---

[94] For the discussion of this classification issue, see Wunsch-Vincent, *supra* note 91, pp. 48–79.

[95] Appellate Body Report, *EC – Bananas III*, para. 221.

[96] G/C/W/158, *supra* note 92, para. 2.6.

mobile phones, and e-readers),[97] which other countries may consider as discrimination against their e-books versus domestic or third-country print books. With the increasing rate of market penetration of e-books,[98] this issue may well be raised in the future.

As for services, the views differ on whether, for instance, an audio-visual content transmitted and consumed online is covered by mode 1 (cross-border supply) or mode 2 (consumption abroad).[99] In theory, mode 2 applies when a foreign service is consumed by a committing member's consumer outside the territory of that member. But because an electronic delivery of a foreign service, which is otherwise available within the respective foreign country, enables a consumer to enjoy that service without leaving his/her home country, the distinction between the two modes in question becomes blurred. As a practical matter, it is suggested that mode 1 or 2 should prevail if a particular restriction is placed on the supplier or the consumer, respectively.[100] However, this approach may not be helpful in reconciling differing opinions when there is a discrepancy of commitments between the two modes. In *US – Gambling*, Antigua invoked mode 1 commitments to challenge US restrictions on *providers* of online gambling services, although some restrictions were also directed at consumers.[101] The United States did not oppose the mode 1 consideration. The US schedule had the same entry "None" for both modes 1 and 2 in the same services sector under the market access and national treatment columns. But had the mode 2 commitment been "unbound," the United States could have insisted on mode 2 as a more appropriate basis for the assessment.

Since 2016, the WTO discussions on e-commerce have intensified. Members disagree on whether to stick to the initial WTO work program or move away from it to negotiate new rules in this field. The issues recently raised in these discussions include, inter alia, prohibition of customs duties on electronic transmissions, nondiscrimination, market

---

[97] See OECD, "E-books: Developments and Policy Considerations," OECD Digital Economy Paper No. 208, 2012, p. 51.

[98] For instance, e-book sales have recently shown dramatic rates of growth in many OECD countries. See *ibid.*, pp. 34–7.

[99] See S/C/8, *supra* note 92, para. 5.

[100] See WTO, Council for Trade in Services – The Work Programme on Electronic Commerce – Note by the Secretariat, S/C/W/68 (16 November 1998), pp. 2–3, para. 8.

[101] Panel Report, *US – Gambling*, para. 6.262; Appellate Body Report, *US – Gambling*, para. 253.

access liberalization in relevant services sectors, cross-border data flows, the Internet access, localization barriers, digital infrastructure problems, electronic signatures and authentication, paperless trade, e-payments, and policy transparency.[102]

Meanwhile, the lack of progress in the WTO work on e-commerce has accelerated rule-making at the regional level. At least thirty to forty RTAs include provisions on e-commerce[103] often contained in separate e-commerce chapters, chapters on cross-border supply of services, chapters on ICT cooperation, or IPR chapters. Those provisions define some core concepts, but generally avoid drawing a clear demarcation line between goods and services as tied to e-commerce or digital trade. For example, the Korea–US FTA defines "digital products" as "computer programs, text, video, images, sound recordings, and other products that are digitally encoded and produced for commercial sale or distribution, regardless of whether they are fixed on a carrier medium or transmitted electronically." But the agreement cautions that this definition is without prejudice to "a Party's view on whether trade in digital products through electronic transmission should be categorized as trade in services or trade in goods."[104]

Many RTAs confirm the WTO-applicability to e-commerce and recognize that the RTA provisions on cross-border trade in services cover electronically delivered services. RTAs typically incorporate the WTO duty-free moratorium on electronic transmissions, with some of them explicitly extending it to digital content. They ban discrimination against RTA-originating digital products and create carve-outs for subsidies and government procurement. Agreements like the US FTAs with Chile,

---

[102] See, e.g., WTO, Council for Trade in Services – Work Programme on Electronic Commerce – Report by the Chairman of the Council for Trade in Services to the General Council, S/C/52 (19 July 2017); WTO, Council for Trade in Goods – Work Programme on Electronic Commerce – Report by the Chairperson of the Council for Trade in Goods to the General Council, G/C/59 (21 July 2017); WTO, General Council – 7 December 2016 – Item – Work Programme on Electronic Commerce – Review of Progress – Report by the Chairman, WT/GC/W/728 (8 December 2016); South Center and ATPC, "The WTO's Discussions on Electronic Commerce," Analytical Note, SC/AN/TDP/2017/2, 2017.

[103] Lior Herman, "Multilateralising Regionalism: The Case of E-Commerce," OECD Trade Policy Paper No. 99, 2010, p. 10.

[104] Article 15.9 of the Korea–US FTA and accompanying n. 4.

Singapore, and Australia also make exceptions for local content measures on certain (digitized) audiovisual services.[105]

7.3.2.3 IPR Protection of Creative Works in the Digital Environment

The TRIPS Agreement is, in principle, applicable in the digital environment, given its "technologically neutral language."[106] The agreement provides for copyright protection of computer programs and databases, rental rights for computer programs, phonograms and cinematographic works, as well as protection of layout-designs of integrated circuits.[107]

The "borderless" nature of the Internet brings a number of legal problems. For instance, online piracy infringes the right of authors, performers, phonogram producers, or broadcasting organizations to authorize the reproduction of their works. The electronic transmission of protected materials entails storage and transient copies by Internet service providers between the points of uploading and downloading of the materials. The main controversy here is about the applicability of the reproduction right at this intermediate stage of the distribution chain and about liability of service providers for transmitting or storing potentially infringing content. On the enforcement front, it is not clear what country should have jurisdiction over illicit activities in cyberspace that is by nature global.[108]

While the TRIPS Agreement itself is silent on these and some other related issues, practical guidance on some of them can be found in the World Intellectual Property Organization (WIPO) Copyright Treaty and the WIPO Performances and Phonograms Treaty (collectively known as the "Internet treaties") adopted in 1996. These instruments intend to prevent unauthorized use of creative works on digital networks, while generally adhering to the preexisting international legal regimes concerned. An agreed statement on the WIPO Copyright Treaty recognizes that authors' right of reproduction fully applies in the digital environment, and that "the storage of a protected work in digital form in an

---

[105] This paragraph summarizes RTA practices on digital trade discussed in Wunsch-Vincent, *supra* note 91, pp. 206–19; Rolf H. Weber, "Digital Trade and E-Commerce: Challenges and Opportunities of the Asia-Pacific Regionalism," 10 *Asian Journal of WTO & International Health Law and Policy* 321 (2015), p. 334.

[106] WTO, Council for TRIPS – The Work Programme on Electronic Commerce – Background Note by the Secretariat, IP/C/W/128 (10 February 1999), para. 14.

[107] See Sections 1, 6 of Part II of the TRIPS Agreement.

[108] See IP/C/W/128, *supra* note 106, paras. 39–42, 68–73.

electronic medium constitutes a reproduction within the meaning of Article 9 of the Berne Convention." Such a statement itself is not a legal provision, but it reflects the common understanding of negotiators during the preparatory work.

Moreover, the Internet treaties make it clear that authors, performers, and phonogram producers enjoy "the exclusive right" of authorizing any communication (or the making available) to the public of their works, "by wire or wireless means," in such a way that members of the public can access these works from a place and at a time individually chosen by them. This clarifies the application of the communication right to on-demand delivery of works over the Internet. At the same time, a related agreed statement stipulates that "the mere provision of physical facilities for enabling or making a communication does not in itself amount to communication." As for the issue of liability of service providers, it is left to the discretion of national regulators.[109]

Since the WIPO instruments above are not incorporated into the WTO system, they are of limited applicability within this trade regime. In *China – Publications and Audiovisual Products*, China argued that, before the WIPO Copyright Treaty's entry into force in 2002, there was no international consensus on permissibility of worldwide exploitation of music over the Internet, but the panel found this alleged fact irrelevant to the GATS treatment of electronic distribution of sound recordings.[110]

Two more case-law findings on digital aspects of IPRs are noteworthy. As mentioned earlier, the panel in *US – Section 110(5) Copyright Act* agreed with the justification of the homestyle exemption for nonauthorized reproduction of broadcasted music in a public place under Article 13 of the TRIPS Agreement. Notwithstanding the lack of experience, at the time of litigation, with applying the homestyle exemption to online transmission of music, the panel did not rule out that the development of new technologies of music distribution could affect a future assessment of the homestyle exemption in the context of Article 13.[111]

In *China – Intellectual Property Rights*, the panel emphasized the technologically neutral language of the first sentence of Article 61 of

---

[109] Article 8 of the WIPO Copyright Treaty; Articles 10, 14 of the WIPO Performances and Phonograms Treaty. See also IP/C/W/128, *supra* note 106, paras. 43–5, 82; WTO, Council for TRIPS – The Work Programme on Electronic Commerce – Background Note by the Secretariat – Addendum, IP/C/W/128/Add.1 (15 May 2003), para. 25.

[110] Panel Report, *China – Publications and Audiovisual Products*, paras. 7.1164, 7.1243.

[111] Panel Report, *US – Section 110(5) Copyright Act*, para. 6.153.

the TRIPS Agreement which requires members to introduce criminal procedures and penalties for "wilful trademark counterfeiting or copyright piracy on a commercial scale." The panel admitted that the US concern regarding the volume of distribution via digital technology and the Internet was relevant to the assessment of a "commercial scale," but found related US evidence insufficient.[112]

7.4   Policy Space for Trade Restrictions on Creative Products

Apart from generic ways of contracting out of WTO rules (e.g., waivers and exclusions of certain services from scheduling), members may avail themselves of specific exceptions that are closely relevant to creative industries, especially cultural sectors. This part is dedicated to some representative flexibilities for trade-restrictive measures against foreign creative products.

7.4.1   Screen Quotas

In the late 1940s following World War II, when globalization was in its very infant stage, national cultures were not much exposed to foreign influences as they are today. Yet, local film industries did feel some cultural pressure from abroad, especially from Hollywood. This led to the insertion of Article IV (entitled "Special Provisions Relating to Cinematograph Films") into the GATT.[113]

Under Article IV, governments may impose screen quotas on "exposed cinematograph films" in the form of the specified proportion of the total screen time reserved for national films per theater per year, subject to quota-loosening negotiations. As a rule, they cannot allocate the remaining screen time among foreign sources. But Article IV(c) of the GATT allows minimum screen quotas for nonnational films – "films of a specified origin other than that of the [member] imposing such screen quotas" – that do not exceed "the level in effect on April 10, 1947." Thus, Article IV is an exception to both GATT principles of national treatment (as stated in Article III:10 of the GATT) and MFN.

---

[112] Panel Report, *China – Intellectual Property Rights*, paras. 7.654–7.657, n. 640 to para. 7.657.

[113] Chi Carmody, "When 'Cultural Identity Was Not at Issue': Thinking about *Canada – Certain Measures Concerning Periodicals*," 30 *Law and Policy in International Business* 231 (1999), pp. 254–5.

This clause has never been interpreted by GATT/WTO panels. In the early 1960s, a GATT working party considered the issue raised by the United States as to whether Article IV covered television programs recorded on video tapes or films. Beginning to export them in large quantities, the United States argued that overseas restrictions on the use of imported television material were contrary to Article III:4 of the GATT unless an Article IV-like specific provision would be introduced to extend the GATT to trade in television programs – a "new commodity." Such provision could reserve the exhibition time for national material, while assuring fair access for the imported product.[114] But the working party failed to reach any conclusion due to the divergence of opinion, with some sharing the US position and others insisting that television was a service outside of the GATT domain.[115]

The issue arose in 1989 again when the United States requested consultations under the GATT dispute settlement procedures over certain restrictions against showing non-European films on television, but the EC countered that broadcasting by television or any other means belonged to the area of services, which was the matter for the Uruguay Round negotiations.[116] In the Uruguay Round, the EC demanded insertion of a general cultural exception into trade rules or a specific exception for audiovisuals only, but failed to persuade all negotiating countries. This left the cultural exception issue to bilateral negotiations[117] and other forums, such as the UNESCO.

Even though it is clear from the text that Article IV of the GATT applies to cinematograph films screened in movie theaters, one commentator argues that evolutionary treaty interpretation still allows that clause

---

[114] GATT, Contracting Parties – Nineteenth Session – [13 November – 8 December 1961] – Application of GATT to International Trade in Television Programmes, L/1615 (16 November 1961); GATT, Contracting Parties – Nineteenth Session – [13 November – 8 December 1961] – Application of GATT to International Trade in Television Programmes – Statement Made by the US Representatives on 21 November 1961, L/1646 (24 November 1961).

[115] GATT, Application of GATT to International Trade in Television Programmes – Report of the Working Party, L/1741 (13 March 1962), paras. 4–11.

[116] GATT, Council – Minutes of Meeting – Held in the Center William Rappard on 11 October 1989, C/M/236 (6 November 1989), pp. 33–4

[117] Carmody, *supra* note 113, pp. 259–60.

to cover television broadcasting of movies, irrespective of whether the movies are exhibited from a videotape, DVD, or another medium.[118] Apart from Article IV, one will also need to additionally check the WTO-consistency of screen quotas under the GATS. If a member made full liberalization commitments in the audiovisual and related services, screen quotas can be found to violate the GATS even if they are justified under Article IV of the GATT.

7.4.2   Public Morals

Article XX(a) of the GATT is a general exception for measures "necessary to protect public morals." In services trade, Article XIV(a) of the GATS covers measures "necessary to protect public morals or to maintain public order." The term "public morals" in both contexts denotes "standards of right and wrong conduct" that can vary "depending upon a range of factors, including prevailing social, cultural, ethical and religious values." It is acknowledged that members have "some scope to define and apply for themselves the concepts of 'public morals' ... in their respective territories, according to their own systems and scales of values."[119] Thus, they have the right to determine the appropriate level of protection under the provisions in question.[120] Two cases discussed here are of relevance to creative industries.

The United States in *US – Gambling* argued that it imposed a ban on remote supply of gambling services to protect the society against the threat of money laundering, organized crime, fraud, and risks to children (underage gambling) and to health (pathological gambling). The Appellate Body found that the US restriction was indeed a "necessary" measure in the sense of Article XIV(a) of the GATS, as no other less-restrictive alternative was "reasonably available" to the US authorities. But in the *chapeau* context, it held that in the light of the Interstate Horseracing Act (which appeared to authorize domestic operators to engage in the remote supply of certain betting services), the United States had failed to

---

[118] See Lothar Ehring, "Article IV [of the GATT]," in Rüdiger Wolfrum, Peter-Tobias Stoll, and Holger P. Hestermeyer (eds.), *WTO – Trade in Goods* (Leiden: Martinus Nijhoff Publishers, 2011), pp. 171–3.

[119] Panel Report, *China – Publications and Audiovisual Products*, para 7.759 (intermediate footnotes omitted), referring to Panel Report, *US – Gambling*, paras. 6.461, 6.465; Appellate Body Report, *US – Gambling*, para. 299; See also Appellate Body Reports, *EC – Seal Products*, para. 5.199.

[120] Panel Report, *China – Publications and Audiovisual Products*, para. 7.819.

demonstrate that the restriction in question applied to both foreign and domestic service suppliers, that is, in a manner that did not constitute "arbitrary and unjustifiable discrimination."[121]

In *China – Publications and Audiovisual Products*, China invoked Article XX(a) of the GATT to defend its system of censorship by selected import entities over foreign publications and audiovisual products. China argued that cultural goods were unique in having "a potentially serious impact on societal and individual morals," and that imported cultural goods, being "vectors of different cultural values," might conflict with moral standards specific to China.[122] But neither the panel nor the Appellate Body were convinced that the requirement for authorized import entities to be wholly State-owned made a "material contribution" to the protection of public morals.[123] In particular, they observed that this requirement completely excluded non-wholly-State-owned (foreign) enterprises in China from the right to import cultural products in question.[124] As a possible alternative to the current system with selected importing entities, content reviews conducted solely by the Chinese government would, they said, have been less trade-restrictive and more capable of making an equivalent or better contribution to the protection of public morals.[125]

7.4.3   National Treasures

Article XX(f) of the GATT applies to measures "imposed for the protection of national treasures of artistic, historic or archaeological value." This exception does not have any equivalent in the GATS, which may probably imply that national treasures are deemed to be goods rather than services. It would typically accommodate export restrictions on qualifying cultural property. The latter may include the objects of "high culture" that can be found in museums, such as works of visual arts or

---

[121] Appellate Body Report, *US – Gambling*, paras. 315–18, 323–7, 361–9.

[122] Panel Report, *China – Publications and Audiovisual Products*, paras. 7.712, 7.754.

[123] *Ibid.*, para. 7.863; Appellate Body Report, *China – Publications and Audiovisual Products*, para. 269.

[124] Panel Report, *China – Publications and Audiovisual Products*, paras. 7.861–7.862; Appellate Body Report, *China – Publications and Audiovisual Products*, para. 311.

[125] Panel Report, *China – Publications and Audiovisual Products*, para. 7.908; Appellate Body Report, *China – Publications and Audiovisual Products*, para. 332.

archaeological artifacts of a certain age, with perhaps no room left for contemporary products of audiovisual industries.[126]

Like in the case of the other general exceptions, there must be some connection between an illegal trade measure and the covered public interest, although the words "imposed for the protection of" signify a degree of connection that may differ from that under the remaining paragraphs of Article XX. Article XX(f) has never come into play in GATT/WTO dispute settlement.

7.4.4   Security Exceptions

Certain unlawful trade measures concerning foreign creative products (e.g., software programs) can also fall under the security exceptions of, inter alia, Article XXI of the GATT, Article XIV *bis* of the GATS, Article 73 of the TRIPS Agreement, and Article XXIII of the GPA (or Article III:1 of the revised GPA). With the pervasive influence of ICTs, there is a growing potential for applying these exceptions to certain cybersecurity actions, such as, for instance, the US ban on certain public procurement of IT products from Chinese Huawei or China's "countermeasure" prohibiting governmental use of Microsoft's Windows 8 operating system. The US and Chinese restrictions in question have been introduced to allegedly prevent invisible software programs installed in computer hardware and telecommunications systems from stealing public secrets.[127] Today, cybersecurity is shifting from a merely computer security issue to the matter of national policy, as the illicit use of cyberspace endangers economic, public health, and national security activities.[128] Thus, cybersecurity can be said to be part of national security.

The GATT, the GATS, and the TRIPS Agreement do not preclude any member "from taking any action which it considers necessary for the protection of its essential security interests" in situations described by the respective provisions. The invoking party enjoys much discretion derivable from the words "which it considers" and the absence of any *chapeau* requirements. It can claim that, inter alia, it adopted cybersecurity

---

[126] Frederic Scott Galt, "The Life, Death, and Rebirth of the 'Cultural Exception' in the Multilateral Trading System: An Evolutionary Analysis of Cultural Protection and Intervention in the Face of American Pop Culture's Hegemony," 3 *Washington University Global Studies Law Review* 909 (2004), p. 913; Tania Voon, "A New Approach to Audiovisual Products in the WTO: Rebalancing GATT and GATS," 14 *UCLA Entertainment Law Review* 1, p. 13.

[127] See Peng, Ch. 1, *supra* note 98, pp. 450–4.   [128] *Ibid.*, p. 469.

measures to preserve its security interests "in time of war or *other emergency in international relations*" (emphasis added). The fact that all three agreements in question separate "other emergency" from "war" with the conjunction "or" suggests that the former is not necessarily associated with military operations. In the case of the (revised) GPA, this link to military affairs is even looser, as it allows protection of essential security interests "relating to the procurement of arms, ammunition or war materials, *or to procurement indispensable for national security* or for national defence purposes" (emphasis added). Whereas the invoking party has certain freedom to determine for itself the protectable security values within the defined parameters, the related measure is still subject to the necessity test.[129]

7.4.5   The UNESCO Regime on Cultural Diversity

The UNESCO was created in 1945 "for the purpose of advancing, through the educational and scientific and cultural relations of the peoples of the world, the objectives of international peace and of the common welfare of mankind."[130] Some UNESCO instruments acknowledge the importance of "the free exchange of ideas and knowledge" and provide for barrier-free international circulation of certain educational, scientific, and cultural materials like books, publications, and qualifying works of art.[131]

In *China – Publications and Audiovisual Products*, China cited the UNESCO Universal Declaration on Cultural Diversity (2001) that recognizes uniqueness of cultural goods as distinct from other articles of international trade.[132] In particular, Article 8 of the UNESCO declaration calls for a particular attention to "the diversity of the supply of creative work" and "the specificity of cultural goods and services which, as vectors of identity, values and meaning, must not be treated as mere commodities or consumer goods." China also referred to the UNESCO Convention on the Protection and Promotion of the Diversity of Cultural

---

[129] *Ibid.*, pp. 464, 472.   [130] Preamble of the Constitution of the UNESCO (1945).
[131] See the UNESCO Agreement on the Importation of Educational, Scientific and Cultural Materials (1950) and the related Protocol (1976).
[132] Panel Report, *China – Publications and Audiovisual Products*, para. 7.751.

Expressions (2005), which is closely related to the aforementioned declaration.[133] That convention was an outcome of the attempts of France, Canada, and other "culture-sensitive" countries to secure cultural exceptions outside the WTO after such attempts had failed in the multilateral trading system due to the strong opposition of the United States.[134] China invoked the UNESCO instruments in question to emphasize a potential negative impact of cultural goods on public morals, but did not make them part of legal defense under Article XX(a) of the GATT. Thus, the panel was able to avoid a substantive analysis of such non-WTO rules.[135]

But even if China had relied on those UNESCO instruments more "aggressively," it would not have succeeded. In particular, the UNESCO declaration apparently lacks a binding effect upon its parties. It is also unlikely that the related UNESCO convention would provide an effective defense for a WTO violation,[136] as an invoking WTO member would have to prove (i) that WTO adjudicators can or should apply the UNESCO convention in WTO dispute settlement, and (ii) that such a non-WTO treaty prevails over WTO rules in case of a conflict.[137] Even on the assumption that the first hurdle is cleared, there is no visible "conflict" between the UNESCO convention and WTO law under the second inquiry, as the invoking member may simultaneously comply with both regimes by refraining from applying a measure allowed by the UNESCO but banned by the WTO or otherwise applying a UNESCO-permitted measure in a WTO-consistent manner. For instance, Article 6 of the UNESCO convention entitles its parties to take measures of preserving cultural diversity within their territory that "may" include, inter alia, "regulatory measures aimed at protecting and promoting diversity of cultural expressions" or "measures aimed at providing

---

[133] Panel Report, *China – Publications and Audiovisual Products*, para. 4.207; Appellate Body Report, *China – Publications and Audiovisual Products*, para. 25.

[134] Hahn, *supra* note 22, p. 533.

[135] Panel Report, *China – Publications and Audiovisual Products*, n. 538 to para. 7.758. The UNESCO-based justification issue as such was not before the Appellate Body.

[136] See the US, Australian, and Korean statements in Panel Report, *China – Publications and Audiovisual Products*, paras. 4.207, 5.13, 5.61. See also Jingxia Shi and Weidong Chen, "The 'Specificity' of Cultural Products versus the 'Generality' of Trade Obligations: Reflecting on 'China – Publications and Audiovisual Products'," 45 *Journal of World Trade* 159 (2011), pp. 165–7; Hahn, *supra* note 22, pp. 539–47; Tania Voon, *Cultural Products and the World Trade Organization* (Cambridge: Cambridge University Press, 2007), pp. 202–16.

[137] Voon, *supra* note 136, pp. 202–3.

public financial assistance." To be in consistency with both regimes, a WTO member could simply opt not to adopt such regulatory and financial support measures altogether or to apply them in compliance with, for example, the GATT/TBT Agreement and the SCM Agreement, respectively. In any event, Article 20 of the UNESCO convention requires that its parties "foster mutual supportiveness" between this convention and other applicable treaties, with the former not being subordinated to and *not modifying* the latter.

7.5   Concluding Remarks

By implementing creative economy policies, countries demonstrate their support for content-driven and innovative sectors. This helps them secure a continuous economic growth through creativity, cultural products, and technological advancement of original ideas and knowledge. In a broad sense, such countries strive to raise their international competitiveness through promoting their creativity-based comparative advantages.

The concept of creative economy shows, among other things, how ICTs today make it possible to develop complex "products" representing some kind of a fusion of goods, services, and intellectual property. But as the case of digitization suggests, the multilateral trade rules need updating to address ICT-related aspects of the creative economy more adequately. In spite of the adoption of the work program on e-commerce two decades ago, the lack of progress in this important field undermines credibility of the WTO system. Since national (or indigenous) cultures and creative industries may be vulnerable to certain risks associated with technological changes, any new digital rule book in the WTO must leave enough room for governments to deal with those risks in cyberspace.

~

Conclusion

Industrial development in many countries is orchestrated by government strategies and policies that send certain encouraging, discouraging, or other behavior-correcting signals to market players. In theory, governments should intervene in narrowly defined scenarios of market failures, but in reality public interventions are more pervasive partly due to the pressure from interest groups. The practice shows that even policies with obviously good intentions may not succeed in the presence of government failures or when the market does not react in an anticipated way.

Industrial policies are subject to WTO rules as far as international trade is affected. Therefore, the less trade-restrictive an industrial policy is, the more tolerated it is under the WTO system. Typically, a hard industrial policy of direct market interventions is more likely to come under the WTO's scrutiny than a soft industrial policy consisting in the public–private collaboration.

For seventy years, the GATT/WTO system managed to create a complex rules-based environment for global trading. The general tendency in setting trade rules has been to squeeze a government's sovereignty over trade-related aspects of industrial policy, on the one hand, and to recognize its autonomy in addressing public interests, on the other. Overall, members have their hands tied by WTO strictures and may utilize the available policy space only under limited conditions. Such legal constraints and flexibilities discussed in this book may not necessarily constitute an ideal balance. But it is clear that without this system the virtually unrestrained freedom of countries in relation to their industrial policies would be outweighed by much more burdensome and unpredictable market barriers to their trading industries. This is what sustains the existence and expansion of the multilateral trade regime.

The East Asian miraculous growth in the past decades was possible with the reorientation from import substitution to export promotion. It is remarkable that this was a *shift* in the policy priority from one direction to the other. Arguably, *prioritizing both* import substitution and export promotion may turn out to be counterproductive, as they are mutually contradictory in principle. In particular, import substitution may cause the local currency to appreciate by restricting imports and consequently lowering demand for foreign exchange. But this makes exports more expensive, working against the very goals of export promotion. The SCM Agreement does not allow export subsidies, outlawing many export-boosting market interventions. Yet, monitoring and countering overseas trade restrictions through WTO-permitted ways, as well as providing exporters with administrative support is what many members can realistically do now in promoting their exports. Furthering trade liberalization at the multilateral and regional/bilateral levels is another legitimate way of increasing exports.

Part I of this book separately considered the role of the government in protecting and supporting domestic industries. But we admit, of course, that this is not a clear-cut delimitation of such governmental functions, as any protective measure could be considered as an indirect way of "subsidizing" local producers, and any price advantages given to domestic industries could "protect" them from competition with foreign rivals.

On the protection front, governments would be on a safer footing if they employ price-based instruments, such as tariffs and internal taxes, instead of quantitative restrictions that are banned in principle. Although trade remedies work against the philosophy of "free" trade, antidumping and countervailing duties are justified as contributors to "fair" trade, and safeguards are warranted as a means of facilitating trade concessions on a multilateral scale. Whereas it is clearly recognized that product standards are important in fulfilling legitimate societal objectives, any overly trade-restrictive way of their application may provide grounds for regarding them as unacceptable acts of protectionism. For services industries, national authorities have more space for self-defining their protective policies than for merchandise sectors.

As for the promotion of industries, government subsidies are not challengeable if they are provided across the board. Selective (or "specific") subsidies are tolerated as long as they are not given in an import-substitutive and export-stimulating manner or otherwise do not cause adverse effects to the interests of other members. In the services sector, governments may avail themselves of the lack of substantive WTO disciplines on subsidies, but they should take into account the applicability of the GATS antidiscrimination rules and the SCM Agreement where relevant.

In Part II of this book, we noted that free zones can be used for testing an industrial policy within a designated site to subsequently extend successful elements of the policy to the rest of the home country. Whereas the WCO rules recognize the "extraterritorial" nature of such zones, they do not prescribe the way of incentivizing resident enterprises, something that should conform to the WTO rules concerned.

LCRs have strong political appeal, which explains their wide use all over the world. But the economic literature has generally condemned them for their import-restrictiveness. In the same vein, the multilateral trade agreements significantly constrain localization measures, but provide more room for properly designed government procurement, services regulations, preferential rules of origin, and direct subsidization of input producers.

The intersection of trade and the environment has been a hot issue for a long time, but ironically some WTO provisions are rather outdated to appropriately handle the greening of industrial policies today. In particular, the environmental exceptions of GATT Article XX are hardly applicable beyond the GATT absent any textual basis, and the subsidy rules do not accommodate many environmental support measures. Moreover, the trade and environmental systems are in need of further harmonization on the international and domestic planes.

The policy of creative economy combining culture and technology exemplifies the area where WTO rules on goods, services, and IPRs are closely intertwined. The absence of any progress on e-commerce exacerbates the weakness of the WTO regime to promptly adapt to rapidly changing patterns of industrialization and international trade.

On the basis of the analysis throughout this book as summarized here, we wish to offer our concluding thoughts about what should be done to better tackle industrial policy issues at the WTO and national levels, as well as within academic circles.

Whereas the expanding global reach of the GATT/WTO legal order indicates its trustworthiness, this system risks losing its credibility if it continuously fails to deliver new substantive outcomes. More specifically, at the time when the world ecological situation is rapidly deteriorating, and many economies are entering the era of the fourth industrial revolution, the WTO rule book – mostly unchanged since the end of the Uruguay Round – is not fully capable of catching up with, or responding to, these important developments accordingly. The "ICTization" of industries and our daily life has been altering industrialization and the lifestyle of many people tremendously. The convergence of goods and services throughout the production and consumption chains enabled by technological transformations will likely necessitate the reshaping of traditional regulatory approaches in respective spheres.

At present, certain trade-related aspects of greening measures and pervasive digitization are among most pressing issues to be tackled by the WTO in the nearest future. Because artificial intelligence and other components of the fourth industrial revolution are rising in importance, it remains to be seen what implications they will have for WTO law.

It is true that treaty interpretation by the WTO judiciary helps "adapting" some old-fashioned rules to the current realities, but this approach is not without limitations. Given this factor and enormous difficulty in completing the multilateral trade negotiations, the decision-making process in the WTO should be reconsidered. With the increasing membership and issues on the table, the principle of consensus is no longer the right way of creating or amending rules. Where the "critical mass" technique is not practicable or effective, members should switch to voting as a second option, which is already provided for by the WTO Agreement. Any new trade initiative should foresee a maximum timeframe for the consensus-building attempts, beyond which voting should automatically take place.

Article X:9 of the WTO Agreement requires consensus on an inclusion of any new plurilateral agreement in Annex 4. This obviously preserves the integrity of the system. But in the current state of affairs, members should be more lenient toward plurilateralism so as to make rule-making in the WTO smoother and more operational. Indeed, the "multilateral vs. plurilateral" fragmentation *within the reach of the WTO* is better than a widening split between the WTO and non-WTO trade regimes fueled by the indefinite stalemate in multilateral talks. Otherwise, the WTO's position in the global trade governance may be damaged by an emergence of rival institutions like "mini-WTOs" – mega-regional groupings or even plurilateral WTOs. Unlike commonly perceived RTAs, such mini-WTOs – which could, for instance, result from a merger or expansion of existing trading blocs – may largely or completely replicate, and hence substitute for, the WTO within a smaller number of like-minded countries.

Furthermore, the deadlock in the Doha Round is, in our view, at least partly attributable to the concern by many developing countries that further trade openings could badly impact on their development. It is highly inconceivable that a real breakthrough on many substantive issues will be made without any visible deliverables for development issues, including S&D treatment. The lack of such deliverables will also increase skepticism of developing countries about any future negotiation proposals. In this book, we considered a number of S&D provisions that, in fact, merely constitute soft law. Given this, the S&D system should definitely be revamped in a way that would grant meaningful benefits to developing countries. But it appears that a WTO-wide agreement on stronger S&D would be politically feasible especially (or perhaps only) if clear-cut objective criteria for eligibility and graduation are introduced to confine exceptional flexibilities to most deserving countries. For this, a proper benchmark could be the current exemption for export subsidies of some developing countries, which is valid under the SCM Agreement as long as their subsidized exports remain internationally uncompetitive in accordance with a predetermined numerical threshold. Alternatively, some future S&D elements may follow the approach adopted in the Trade Facilitation Agreement where compliance with the self-selected obligations is conditional on availability of technical assistance and capacity building support.

As for actions to be taken at the national level, an industrial policy should be formulated and implemented through a trilateral cooperation of the government, industries, and academia. Whereas the concept of soft industrial policy calls for a government–industry dialogue, we believe that academics should also be part of this process. They should be involved as independent advisors or experts giving feedback on economic soundness and lawfulness of relevant government programs. In a sense, they could also act as "umpires" between the government and industrial circles in the course of allocating protective and supporting measures. This probably already works well in some countries but not in others. Therefore, to see whether and how such a collaborative triangle operates in different countries, the WTO should organize knowledge-sharing events among its members with the purpose to identify best practices or desirable "models" of the trade and industrial policy process.

Finally, we believe that there should be more communication across academic circles as well. National/international societies or associations dealing with, separately, the economics and law of industrial policy tend to work within their respective fields. As a result, lawyers and economists speaking different "languages" do not always follow each other on essentially the same subject matters. But they could definitely learn many things from each other. The multifaceted nature of the topic in question requires intensive interaction between them through joint activities in the form of research, conferences, seminars, and workshops with a view to stimulating mutual understanding and exploring interdisciplinary approaches to addressing common issues. Government officials should participate in such research sharing so that academic findings and recommendations would not just remain on paper but also would find a practical use in the real policy-making. The ultimate goal should be setting a worldwide trend toward making interdisciplinary academic research embedded in (inter)national policies.

BIBLIOGRAPHY

100 Pearls of Wisdom by Navoi (Tashkent: Yangi Asr Avlodi, 2016).

Address by Ujal Singh Bhatia (Chairman of the Appellate Body), "The Problems of Plenty: Challenging Times for the WTO's Dispute Settlement System," 8 June 2017, www.wto.org/english/news_e/news17_e/ab_08jun17_e.pdf.

Anderson, Kym, "Setting the Trade Policy Agenda: What Roles for Economists?," World Bank Policy Research Working Paper No. 3560, 2005.

Anderson, Robert D. and Kodjo Osei-Lah, "The Coverage Negotiations under the Agreement on Government Procurement: Context, Mandate, Process and Prospects," in Sue Arrowsmith and Robert D. Anderson (eds.), *The WTO Regime on Government Procurement: Challenge and Reform* (Cambridge: Cambridge University Press, 2011), pp. 149–74.

Anderson, Robert D. and Sue Arrowsmith, "The WTO Regime on Government Procurement: Past, Present and Future," in Sue Arrowsmith and Robert D. Anderson (eds.), *The WTO Regime on Government Procurement: Challenge and Reform* (Cambridge: Cambridge University Press, 2011), pp. 3–58.

APEC Leaders' Declaration (2011), www.apec.org/Meeting-Papers/Leaders-Declarations/2011/2011_aelm/2011_aelm_annexD.aspx.

APEC, "Progress Report on 2011 Baseline Study on Good Regulatory Practices," APEC#213-CT-01.13, 2014.

Asian Development Bank, "Asian Economic Integration Report 2015: How Can Special Economic Zones Catalyze Economic Development?," 2015.

Azmeh, Shamel and Christopher Foster, "The TPP and the Digital Trade Agenda: Digital Industrial Policy and Silicon Valley's Influence on New Trade Agreements," Working Paper No. 16–175, London School of Economics and Political Science, 2016.

Bacchetta, Marc and Michele Ruta (eds.), *The WTO, Subsidies and Countervailing Measures* (Cheltenham, the United Kingdom/Northampton, MA, the United States: Edward Elgar, 2011).

Bagwell, Kyle and Robert W. Staiger, "An Economic Theory of GATT," 89 *American Economic Review* 215 (1999).

"Will International Rules on Subsidies Disrupt the World Trading System?," 96 *American Economic Review* 877 (2006).

The Economics of the World Trading System (Cambridge, MA: MIT Press, 2002).

Bahar, Heymi, Jagoda Egeland, and Ronald Steenblik, "Domestic Incentive Measures for Renewable Energy with Possible Trade Implications," OECD Trade and Environment Working Paper No. 2013/01, 2013.

Baldwin, Robert E., "The Case against Infant-Industry Tariff Protection," 77 *Journal of Political Economy* 295 (1969).

Bartels, Lorand, "Applicable Law in WTO Dispute Settlement Proceedings," 35 *Journal of World Trade* 499 (2001).

"The Chapeau of the General Exceptions in the WTO GATT and GATS Agreements: A Reconstruction," 109 *American Journal of International Law* 95 (2015).

"The WTO Legality of the Application of the EU's Emission Trading System to Aviation," 23 *European Journal of International Law* 429 (2012).

Baschuk, Bryce, "U.S. Demands Exacerbate WTO Dispute Body Turmoil," Bloomberg BNA, *International Trade Daily*, 12 September 2017.

Berry, Renee and Matthew Reisman, "Policy Challenges of Cross-Border Cloud Computing," 4(2) *Journal of International Commerce and Economics* 1 (2012).

Bhagwati, Jagdish and V. K. Ramaswami, "Domestic Distortions, Tariffs and the Theory of Optimum Subsidy," 71 *Journal of Political Economy* 44 (1963).

Bhagwati, Jagdish, "More on the Equivalence of Tariffs and Quotas," 58 *American Economic Review* 142 (1968).

Blanchard, Emily J., Chad P. Bown, and Robert C. Johnson, "Global Supply Chains and Trade Policy," NBER Working Paper No. 21883, 2016.

Bonsi, Richard, A. L. Hammet, and Bob Smith, "Eco-Labels and International Trade: Problems and Solutions," 42 *Journal of World Trade* 407 (2008).

Bora, Bijit, Peter J. Lloyd, and Mary Pangestu, "Industrial Policy and the WTO," UNCTAD Policy Issues in International Trade and Commodities Study Series No. 6, 2000.

Bown, Chad P. *Self-Enforcing Trade: Developing Countries and WTO Dispute Settlement* (Washington, DC: Brookings Institution, 2009).

"Will the Proposed US Border Tax Provoke WTO Retaliation from Trading Partners?," Policy Brief No. PB17–11, Peterson Institute for International Economics, 2017.

Boyenge, Jean-Pierre Singa, "ILO Database on Export Processing Zones (Revised)," ILO Working Paper No. WP.251, 2007.

Brander, James A. and Barbara J. Spencer, "Export Subsidies and International Market Share Rivalry," 18 *Journal of International Economics* 83 (1985).

Brou, Daniel and Michele Ruta, "A Commitment Theory of Subsidy Agreements," WTO Staff Working Paper No. ERSD–2012–15, 2012.

Brou, Daniel, Edoardo Campanella, and Michele Ruta, "The Value of Domestic Subsidy Rules in Trade Agreements," WTO Staff Working Paper No. ERSD–2009–12, 2009.

Carmody, Chi, "When 'Cultural Identity Was Not at Issue': Thinking about Canada – Certain Measures Concerning Periodicals," 30 *Law and Policy in International Business* 231 (1999).

Chang, Ha-Joon, *Kicking Away the Ladder: Development Strategy in Historical Perspective* (London: Anthem Press, 2003).

Chang, Seung Wha, "GATTing a Green Trade Barrier: Eco-Labelling and the WTO Agreement on Technical Barriers to Trade," 31 *Journal of World Trade* 137 (1997).

Charnovitz, Steve, "The Law of Environmental 'PPMs' in the WTO: Debunking the Myth of Illegality," 27 *Yale Journal of International Law* 59 (2002).

Cheyne, Ilona, "Proportionality, Proximity and Environmental Labelling in WTO Law," 12 *Journal of International Economic Law* 927 (2009).

China's State Council, "Made in China 2025," http://english.gov.cn/2016special/madeinchina2025.

Choi, Won-mog, *"Like Products" in International Trade Law: Towards a Consistent GATT/WTO Jurisprudence* (New York: Oxford University Press, 2003).

Christakos, Helen A., "WTO Panel Report on Section 110(5) of the U.S. Copyright Act," 17 *Berkeley Technology Law Journal* 595 (2002).

Commission Regulation (EU) No. 473/2010 of 31 May 2010 Imposing a Provisional Countervailing Duty on Imports of Certain Polyethylene Terephthalate Originating in Iran, Pakistan and the United Arab Emirates, OJ L 134/25 (1 June 2010).

Conrad, Christiane R., *Processes and Production Methods (PPMs) in WTO Law: Interfacing Trade and Social Goals* (Cambridge: Cambridge University Press, 2011).

Cook, Graham, *A Digest of WTO Jurisprudence on Public International Law Concepts and Principles* (Cambridge: Cambridge University Press, 2015).

Coppens, Dominic, *WTO Disciplines on Subsidies and Countervailing Measures: Balancing Policy Space and Legal Constraints* (Cambridge: Cambridge University Press, 2014).

Cosbey, Aaron and Petros C. Mavroidis, "A Turquoise Mess: Green Subsidies, Blue Industrial Policy and Renewable Energy: The Case for Redrafting the Subsidies Agreement of the WTO," 17 *Journal of International Economic Law* 11 (2014).

Czapnik, Ben, "The Unique Features of the Trade Facilitation Agreement: A Revolutionary New Approach to Multilateral Negotiations or the Exception Which Proves the Rule?," 18 *Journal of International Economic Law* 773 (2015).

Davidson, Carl, Steven J. Matusz, and Mordechai E. Kreinin, "Analysis of Performance Standards for Direct Foreign Investments," 18 *Canadian Journal of Economics* 876 (1985).

Deardorff, Alan V., "The Economics of Government Market Intervention and Its International Dimension," in Marco Bronckers and Reinhard Quick (eds.), *New Directions in International Economic Law: Essays in Honour of John H. Jackson* (The Hague: Kluwer Law International, 2000), pp. 71–84.

Desai, Mihir A. and James R. Hines, "Market Reactions to Export Subsidies," 74 *Journal of International Economics* 459 (2008).

Directive 2008/101/EC of the European Parliament and of the Council of 19 November 2008 Amending Directive 2003/87/EC so as to Include Aviation Activities in the Scheme for Greenhouse Gas Emission Allowance Trading within the Community, OJ L 8 (13 January 2009).

Dixit, Avinash, "International Trade Policy for Oligopolistic Industries," 94 *Economic Journal* (supplement) 1–16 (1984).

Eaton, Jonathan and Gene M. Grossman, "Optimal Trade and Industrial Policy under Oligopoly," 101 *The Quarterly Journal of Economics* 383 (1986).

Ecolabel Index (the global directory of ecolabels), www.ecolabelindex.com.

Ehring, Lothar, "Article IV [of the GATT]," in Rüdiger Wolfrum, Peter-Tobias Stoll, and Holger P. Hestermeyer (eds.), *WTO – Trade in Goods* (Leiden: Martinus Nijhoff Publishers, 2011), pp. 166–82.

Eliason, Antonia, "The Trade Facilitation Agreement: A New Hope for the World Trade Organization," 14 *World Trade Review* 643 (2015).

Engman, Michael, Osamu Onodera, and Enrico Pinali, "Export Processing Zones: Past and Future Role in Trade and Development," OECD Trade Policy Working Paper No. 53, 2007.

Epps, Tracey and Andrew Green, *Reconciling Trade and Climate: How the WTO Can Help Address Climate Change* (Cheltenham, the United Kingdom/ Northampton, MA, the United States: Edward Elgar, 2010).

European Commission Green Paper, "Unlocking the Potential of Cultural and Creative Industries," COM(2010) 183 final, 2010.

European Commission, "European Union Funding," https://ec.europa.eu/culture/policy/cultural-creative-industries/eu-funding_en.

"Investing in a Smart, Innovative and Sustainable Industry: A Renewed EU Industrial Policy Strategy," Communication from the Commission, 13 September 2017.

"State of the Union 2017 – Industrial Policy Strategy: Investing in a Smart, Innovative and Sustainable Industry," Press Release, 18 September 2017, http://europa.eu/rapid/press-release_IP-17-3185_en.htm.

"Supporting Cultural and Creative Industries," https://ec.europa.eu/culture/policy/cultural-creative-industries_en.

"The EU Emissions Trading System (EU ETS)," 2016, https://ec.europa.eu/clima/sites/clima/files/factsheet_ets_en.pdf.

European Office of the UN, "Adoption and Signature of the Final Act," Second Session of the Preparatory Committee of the UN Conference on Trade and Employment, Press Release No. 469, 27 October 1947.

European Parliament Resolution of 12 September 2013 on Promoting the European Cultural and Creative Sectors as Sources of Economic Growth and Jobs, 2012/2302(INI).

Ezell, Stephen J., Robert D. Atkinson, and Michelle A. Wein, "Localization Barriers to Trade: Threat to the Global Innovation Economy," Information Technology and Innovation Foundation, 2013.

Feichtner, Isabel, *The Law and Politics of WTO Waivers: Stability and Flexibility in Public International Law* (New York: Cambridge University Press, 2011).

FIAS, "Special Economic Zones: Performance, Lessons Learned, and Implications for Zone Development," 2008.

Finger, J. M., "Effects of the Kennedy Round Tariff Concessions on the Exports of Developing Countries," 86 *The Economic Journal* 87 (1976).

Fliess, Barbara and Tarja Mård, "Taking Stock of Measures Restricting the Export of Raw Materials: Analysis of OECD Inventory Data," OECD Trade Policy Paper No. 140, 2012.

Fliess, Barbara, Christine Arriola, and Peter Liapis, "Recent Developments in the Use of Export Restrictions in Raw Materials Trade," in OECD, "Export Restrictions in Raw Materials Trade: Facts, Fallacies and Better Practices," 2014, pp. 17–61.

Friedman, Lisa and Brad Plumer, "E.P.A. Announces Repeal of Major Obama-Era Carbon Emissions Rule," New York Times, 9 October 2017, www.nytimes.com/2017/10/09/climate/clean-power-plan.html.

Fung, K.C. and Jane Korinek, "Economics of Export Restrictions as Applied to Industrial Raw Materials," OECD Trade Policy Paper No. 155, 2013.

Galt, Frederic Scott, "The Life, Death, and Rebirth of the 'Cultural Exception' in the Multilateral Trading System: An Evolutionary Analysis of Cultural Protection and Intervention in the Face of American Pop Culture's Hegemony," 3 *Washington University Global Studies Law Review* 909 (2004).

Garnham, Nicholas, "From Cultural to Creative Industries," 11(1) *International Journal of Cultural Policy* 15 (2005).

GATT Analytical Index, *Guide to GATT Law and Practice*, updated 6th edn., 2 vols. (Geneva: WTO, 1995).

GATT, Accession of Panama: Questions and Replies to the Memorandum on Foreign Trade Regime (L/7228), L/7426 (30 March 1994).

Application of GATT to International Trade in Television Programmes – Report of the Working Party, L/1741 (13 March 1962).

Contracting Parties – Nineteenth Session – [13 November – 8 December 1961] – Application of GATT to International Trade in Television Programmes, L/1615 (16 November 1961).

Contracting Parties – Nineteenth Session – [13 November – 8 December 1961] – Application of GATT to International Trade in Television Programmes – Statement Made by the US Representatives on 21 November 1961, L/1646 (24 November 1961).

Council – Minutes of Meeting – Held in the Center William Rappard on 11 October 1989, C/M/236 (6 November 1989).

Report of the Working Party on Border Tax Adjustments, L/3464, adopted 2 December 1970.

Uruguay Round – Group of Negotiations on Goods (GATT) – Negotiating Group on SCM – Draft Text on SCM, MTN.GNG/NG10/23 (7 November 1990).

Ghosh, Arunabha, "Information Gaps, Information Systems, and the WTO's Trade Policy Review Mechanism," GEG Working Paper No. 2008/40, University of Oxford, 2008.

GOV.UK, "Creative Industries Mapping Documents 1998," www.gov.uk/government/publications/creative-industries-mapping-documents-1998.

Granados, Jaime, "Export Processing Zones and Other Special Regimes in the Context of Multilateral and Regional Trade Negotiations," Occasional Paper No. 20, Inter-American Development Bank, 2003.

Grossman, Gene M., "The Theory of Domestic Content Protection and Content Preference," 96 Quarterly Journal of Economics 583 (1981).

Guan, Wenwei, "Consensus Yet Not Consented: A Critique of the WTO Decision-Making by Consensus," 17 Journal of International Economic Law 77 (2014).

Hahn, Michael, "A Clash of Cultures? The UNESCO Diversity Convention and International Trade Law," 9 Journal of International Economic Law 515 (2006).

Harrison, Ann and Andrés Rodríguez-Clare, "Trade, Foreign Investment, and Industrial Policy for Developing Countries," in Dani Rodrik and Mark Rosenzweig (eds.), Handbook of Development Economics (North-Holland: Elsevier, 2010), vol. 5, pp. 4039–214.

Herman, Lior, "Multilateralising Regionalism: The Case of E-Commerce," OECD Trade Policy Paper No. 99, 2010.

HKU, "The Entrepreneurial Dimension of the Cultural and Creative Industries," Hogeschool vor de Kunsten Utrecht, Utrecht, 2010.

Hoekman, Bernard, "Operationalizing the Concept of Policy Space in the WTO: Beyond Special and Differential Treatment," 8 Journal of International Economic Law 405 (2005).

Holcombe, Randall G., "South Korea's Economic Future: Industrial Policy, or Economic Democracy?," 88 Journal of Economic Behavior & Organization 3 (2013).

Horn, Henrik and Petros C. Mavroidis, "To B(TA) or Not to B(TA)? On the Legality and Desirability of Border Tax Adjustments from a Trade Perspective," 34 The World Economy 1911 (2011).

Howkins, John, *The Creative Economy: How People Make Money from Ideas*, 2nd edn. (London: Penguin Books, 2013).

Howse, Robert and Antonia L. Eliason, "Domestic and International Strategies to Address Climate Change: An Overview of the WTO Legal Issues," in Thomas Cottier, Olga Nartova, and Sadeq Z. Bigdeli (eds.), *International Trade Regulation and the Mitigation of Climate Change* (New York: Cambridge University Press, 2009), pp. 48–93.

Howse, Robert and Donald Regan, "The Product/Process Distinction – An Illusory Basis for Disciplining 'Unilateralism' in Trade Policy," 11 *European Journal of International Law* 249 (2000).

Hudec, Robert E., *The GATT Legal System and World Trade Diplomacy*, 2nd edn. (Salem, NH: Butterworth Legal Publishers, 1990).

Hufbauer, Gary Clyde et al., *Local Content Requirements: A Global Problem* (Washington, DC: Peterson Institute for International Economics, 2013).

Hufbauer, Gary Clyde, Steve Charnovitz, and Jisun Kim, *Global Warming and the World Trading System* (Washington, DC: Peterson Institute for International Economics, 2009).

ILO, "Good Practices in Labour Inspection in Export Processing Zones," 2012.

India's Ministry of Commerce and Industry, "Formulation of a New Industrial Policy," 29 August 2017, http://pib.nic.in/newsite/PrintRelease.aspx?relid=170319.

"Industrial Policy – 2017," Discussion Paper, 2017, http://dipp.nic.in/sites/default/files/Industrial_policy_2017_DP.pdf.

Intergovernmental Panel on Climate Change, "Climate Change 2014: Synthesis Report," 2015.

International Energy Agency, "Renewables," www.iea.org/topics/renewables.

International Institute for Sustainable Development, "The ISO 14020 Series," www.iisd.org/business/markets/eco_label_iso14020.aspx.

Irwin, Douglas A. and Nina Pavchik, "Airbus versus Boeing Revisited: International Competition in the Aircraft Market," 64 *Journal of International Economics* 223 (2004).

Irwin, Douglas A., "The Aftermath of Hamilton's 'Report on Manufactures'," 64 *The Journal of Economic History* 800 (2004).

Irwin, Douglas A., Petros C. Mavroidis, and Alan O. Sykes, *The Genesis of the GATT* (New York: Cambridge University Press, 2008).

Ismer, R. and K. Neuhoff, "Border Tax Adjustments: A Feasible Way to Address Nonparticipation in Emission Trading," CMI Working Paper No. 36, 2004.

Jackson, John H. "International Law Status of WTO Dispute Settlement Reports: Obligation to Comply or Option to 'Buy Out'?," 98 *American Journal of International Law* 109 (2004).

Sovereignty, the WTO and Changing Fundamentals of International Law (Cambridge: Cambridge University Press, 2006).

Johannesson, Louise and Petros C. Mavroidis, "Black Cat, White Cat: The Identity of the WTO Judges," 49 *Journal of World Trade* 685 (2015).

Johnson, Harry G., "Optimal Trade Intervention in the Presence of Domestic Distortions," in R.E. Caves, H.G. Johnson, and P.B. Kenen (eds.), *Trade, Growth, and the Balance of Payments: Essays in Honor of Gottfried Haberler* (Chicago: Rand McNally and Company, 1965), pp. 3–34.

Kaufmann, Christine and Rolf H. Weber, "Carbon-Related Border Tax Adjustment: Mitigating Climate Change or Restricting International Trade?," 10 *World Trade Review* 497 (2011).

KDI School of Public Policy and Management, "K-Developedia," www.kdevelopedia.org.

Keck, Alexander and Patrick Low, "Special and Differential Treatment in the WTO: Why, When and How?," WTO Staff Working Paper No. ERSD–2004–03, 2004.

Kennedy, Scott, "Made in China 2025," Center for Strategic and International Studies, 2015, www.csis.org/analysis/made-china-2025.

Kim, Jeong-gon, Eun-ji Kim, and Yun-ok Kim, "Cases of Creative Economy Promotion and Their Implications," *World Economy Update*, vol. 3(36), Korea Institute for International Economic Policy, 2013.

Kogan, Lawrence A., "Coherent International Trade Policies Hasten, Not Retard, Cloud Computing," 7 *Global Trade and Customs Journal* 379 (2012).

Korea's Ministry of Science, ICT, and Future Planning, "Creative Economy Opens up a New Era of Korea: Action Plan for the Creative Economy," 2013.

Korea's Ministry of Strategy and Finance, "Creative Economy Action Plan and Measures to Establish a Creative Economic Ecosystem," Press Release, 5 June 2013, http://english.mosf.go.kr/pre/view.do?bcd=N0001&seq=3289.

Korinek, Jane and Jessica Bartos, "Multilateralising Regionalism: Disciplines on Export Restrictions in Regional Trade Agreements," OECD Trade Policy Paper No. 139, 2012.

Krishna, Kala and Motoshige Itoh, "Content Protection and Oligopolistic Interactions," 55 *Review of Economic Studies* 107 (1988).

Krueger, Anne O., "The Political Economy of the Rent-Seeking Society," 64 *American Economic Review* 291 (1974).

Krugman, Paul R., "Targeted Industrial Policies: Theory and Evidence," Proceedings, Economic Policy Symposium, Jackson Hole, 1983, pp. 123–76.

Krugman, Paul R., Maurice Obstfeld, and Marc J. Melitz, *International Economics: Theory and Policy*, 10th edn. (Boston: Pearson, 2015).

Lall, Sanjaya, "Industrial Policy in Developing Countries: What Can We Learn from East Asia?," in Patrizio Bianchi and Sandrine Labory (eds.), *International Handbook on Industrial Policy* (Cheltenham, the United Kingdom/ Northampton, MA, the United States: Edward Elgar, 2006), pp. 79–97.

Lee, Juneyoung et al., "Energy-Related Rules in Accession Protocols: Where are They?," in Uri Dadush and Chiedu Osakwe (eds.), *WTO Accessions and*

Trade Multilateralism: Case Studies and Lessons from the WTO at Twenty (Cambridge: Cambridge University Press, 2015), pp. 701–28.

Leitner, Kara and Simon Lester, "WTO Dispute Settlement 1995–2015 – A Statistical Analysis," 19 *Journal of International Economic Law* 289 (2016).

Lim, Wonhyuk, "The Chaebol and Industrial Policy in Korea," in Joseph E. Stiglitz and Justin Yifu Lin (eds.), *The Industrial Policy Revolution I: The Role of Government Beyond Ideology* (Basingstoke, UK: Palgrave Macmillan, 2013), pp. 348–70.

List, Friedrich, *The National System of Political Economy* (originally published in 1841), translated by Sampson S. Lloyd (London: Longmans, Green and Co., 1909).

Lui, Francis T. and Larry D. Qiu, "Taiwan: Thriving High-Technology Industries and SMEs," in Kwong Kai-Sun et al. (eds.), *Industrial Development in Singapore, Taiwan, and South Korea* (Singapore: World Scientific, 2001), pp. 56–117.

Maggi, Giovanni and Andres Rodriguez-Clare, "The Value of Trade Agreements in the Presence of Political Pressures," 106 *Journal of Political Economy* 574 (1998).

Mah, Jai S., "Industrial Policy and Economic Development: Korea's Experience," 41 *Journal of Economic Issues* 77 (2007).

Marceau, Gabrielle Z. and Jennifer K. Hawkins, "Experts in WTO Dispute Settlement," 3 *Journal of International Dispute Settlement* 493 (2012).

Meier, Gerald M., "The Tokyo Round of Multilateral Trade Negotiations and the Developing Countries," 13 *Cornell International Law Journal* 239 (1980).

Melitz, Marc J., "When and How Should Infant Industries be Protected?," 66 *Journal of International Economics* 177 (2005).

Meltzer, Joshua, "Climate Change and Trade – The EU Aviation Directive and the WTO," 15 *Journal of International Economic Law* 111 (2012).

Moran, Theodore H., "The Impact of TRIMs on Trade and Development," 1 *Transnational Corporations* 55 (1992).

Mussa, Michael, "The Economics of Content Protection," NBER Working Paper No. 1457, 1984.

Nathan, Max and Henry Overman, "Agglomeration, Clusters, and Industrial Policy," 29 *Oxford Review of Economic Policy* 383 (2013).

National Board of Trade (Sweden), "How Borderless is the Cloud? An Introduction to Cloud Computing and International Trade," 2012.

Naudé, Wim, "Industrial Policy: Old and New Issues," UNU–WIDER Working Paper No. 2010/106, 2010.

"New Challenges for Industrial Policy," UNU–WIDER Working Paper No. 2010/107, 2010.

Neuwirth, Rostam J., "Global Market Integration and the Creative Economy: The Paradox of Industry Convergence and Regulatory Divergence," 18 *Journal of International Economic Law* 21 (2015).

Noland, Marcus and Howard Pack, *Industrial Policy in an Era of Globalization: Lessons from Asia* (Washington, DC: Institute for International Economics, 2003).

OECD, "E-books: Developments and Policy Considerations," OECD Digital Economy Paper No. 208, 2012.

"Effects of Eco-Labelling Schemes: Compilation of Recent Studies," Joint Working Party on Trade and Environment, COM/ENV/TD(2004)34/FINAL, 2005.

"Environment and Regional Trade Agreements," 2007.

"Export Restrictions in Raw Materials Trade: Facts, Fallacies and Better Practices," 2014.

"Objectives and Instruments of Industrial Policy: A Comparative Study," 1975.

"Tax: Tax Revenue," https://data.oecd.org/tax/tax-revenue.htm.

"Tourism and the Creative Economy," 2014.

OECD–WTO, "Aid for Trade at a Glance 2015: Reducing Trade Costs for Inclusive, Sustainable Growth," 2015.

Oh, Wonsun, "Export Processing Zones in the Republic of Korea: Economic Impact and Social Issues," ILO Working Paper No. 75, 1993.

Ohashi, Hiroshi, "Learning by Doing, Export Subsidies, and Industry Growth: Japanese Steel in the 1950s and 1960s," 66 *Journal of International Economics* 297 (2005).

Ortino, Federico, "Treaty Interpretation and the WTO Appellate Body Report in *US – Gambling*: A Critique," 9 *Journal of International Economic Law* 117 (2006).

Osakwe, Chiedu "Contributions and Lessons from WTO Accessions: The Present and Future of the Rules-based Multilateral Trading System," in Uri Dadush and Chiedu Osakwe (eds.), *WTO Accessions and Trade Multilateralism: Case Studies and Lessons from the WTO at Twenty* (Cambridge: Cambridge University Press, 2015), pp. 219–308.

Osakwe, Chiedu and Juneyoung Lee, "The Future of Multilateral Investment Rules in the WTO: Contributions from WTO Accession Outcomes," in Uri Dadush and Chiedu Osakwe (eds.), *WTO Accessions and Trade Multilateralism: Case Studies and Lessons from the WTO at Twenty* (Cambridge: Cambridge University Press, 2015), pp. 818–49.

Pack, Howard and Kamal Saggi, "Is There a Case for Industrial Policy? A Critical Survey," 21 *The World Bank Research Observer* 267 (2006).

Pal, Rajib, "Has the Appellate Body's Decision in Canada – *Renewable Energy* / Canada – *Feed-in Tariff Program* Opened the Door for Production Subsidies?," 17 *Journal of International Economic Law* 125 (2014).

Park, Nohyoung and Myung-Hyun Chung, "Analysis of a New Mediation Procedure under the WTO SPS Agreement," 50 *Journal of World Trade* 93 (2016).

Pauwelyn, Joost, "The Role of Public International Law in the WTO: How Far Can We Go?," 95 *American Journal of International Law* 535 (2001).

"The Use of Experts in WTO Dispute Settlement," 51 *International and Comparative Law Quarterly* 325 (2002).

"U.S. Federal Climate Policy and Competitiveness Concerns: The Limits and Options of International Trade Law," Working Paper No. NI WP 07–02, Nicholas Institute for Environmental Policy Solutions at Duke University, 2007.

Conflict of Norms in Public International Law: How WTO Law Relates to Other Rules of International Law (Cambridge: Cambridge University Press, 2003).

Peng, Shin-yi and Han-wei Liu, "The Legality of Data Residency Requirements: How Can the Trans-Pacific Partnership Help?," 51 *Journal of World Trade* 183 (2017).

Peng, Shin-yi, "Cybersecurity Threats and the WTO National Security Exceptions," 18 *Journal of International Economic Law* 449 (2015).

Peres, Wilson and Annalisa Primi, "Theory and Practice of Industrial Policy: Evidence from the Latin American Experience," CEPAL Desarrollo Productivo Serie No. 187, 2009.

Perkins, Dwight H., *East Asian Development: Foundations and Strategies* (Cambridge, MA: Harvard University Press, 2013).

Pogoretskyy, Vitaliy, "Energy Dual Pricing in International Trade: Subsidies and Anti-Dumping Perspectives," in Yulia Selivanova (ed.), *Regulation of Energy in International Trade Law: WTO, NAFTA and Energy Charter* (Alphen aan den Rijn: Kluwer Law International, 2011), pp. 181–228.

Qin, Julia Ya, "Pushing the Limits of Global Governance: Trading Rights, Censorship and WTO Jurisprudence – A Commentary on the *China – Publications* Case," 10 *Chinese Journal of International Law* 271 (2011).

"Reforming WTO Discipline on Export Duties: Sovereignty over Natural Resources, Economic Development and Environmental Protection," 46 *Journal of World Trade* 1147 (2012).

Raff, Horst and Young-Han Kim, "Optimal Export Policy in the Presence of Informational Barriers to Entry and Imperfect Competition," 49 *Journal of International Economics* 99 (1999).

REN21, "Renewables 2016: Global Status Report," 2016.

Richardson, Martin, "The Effects of a Content Requirement on a Foreign Duopsonist," 31 *Journal of International Economics* 143 (1991).

Ripinsky, Sergey, "The System of Gas Dual Pricing in Russia: Compatibility with WTO Rules," 3 *World Trade Review* 463 (2004).

Rodrik, Dani "Industrial Policy for the Twenty-First Century," Harvard University Faculty Research Working Paper No. RWP04–047, 2004.

"Normalizing Industrial Policy," Working Paper No. 3, Commission on Growth and Development, 2008.

"Taking Trade Policy Seriously: Export Subsidization as a Case Study in Policy Effectiveness," in Jim Levinsohn, Alan V. Deardorff, and Robert M. Stern (eds.), *New Directions in Trade Theory* (Ann Arbor: University of Michigan Press, 1995), pp. 347–84.

Rolland, Sonia E., *Development at the World Trade Organization* (Oxford: Oxford University Press, 2012).

Rubini, Luca, "'The Good, the Bad, and the Ugly.' Lessons on Methodology in Legal Analysis from the Recent WTO Litigation on Renewable Energy Subsidies," 48 *Journal of World Trade* 895 (2014).

Schwab, Klaus, "The Fourth Industrial Revolution: What It Means and How to Respond," *Foreign Affairs*, 12 December 2015.

"The Fourth Industrial Revolution," World Economic Forum, 2016.

Schwartz, Gerd and Benedict Clements, "Government Subsidies," 13 *Journal of Economic Surveys* 119 (1999).

Selivanova, Julia, "World Trade Organization Rules and Energy Pricing: Russia's Case," 38 *Journal of World Trade* 559 (2004).

Shadikhodjaev, Sherzod, "Checking RTA Compatibility with Global Trade Rules: WTO Litigation Practice and Implications from the Transparency Mechanism for RTAs," 45 *Journal of World Trade* 529 (2011).

"Customs Duty or Internal Charge? Revisiting the Delineation Issue within Treaty Interpretation in the *China – Auto Parts* Case," 7 *Asian Journal of WTO & International Health Law and Policy* 195 (2012).

"Duty Drawback and Regional Trade Agreements: Foes or Friends?," 16 *Journal of International Economic Law* 587 (2013).

"First WTO Judicial Review of Climate Change Subsidy Issues," 107 *American Journal of International Law* 864 (2013).

"How to Pass a Pass-Through Test: The Case of Input Subsidies," 15 *Journal of International Economic Law* 621 (2012).

"India – Certain Measures Relating to Solar Cells and Solar Modules," 111 *American Journal of International Law* 139 (2017).

"Input Cost Adjustments and WTO Anti-Dumping Law: A Closer Look at the EU Practice," *World Trade Review, forthcoming*. Published online 21 January 2018, DOI: 10.1017/S1474745617000568.

"International Regulation of Free Zones: An Analysis of Multilateral Customs and Trade Rules," 10 *World Trade Review* 189 (2011).

"Promotion of 'Green' Electricity and International Dispute Settlement: Trade and Investment Issues," 49 *International Lawyer* 343 (2016).

"Regulation of Renewable Energy Trade in the Megaregionals Era: Current Issues and Prospects for Rule-Making Reforms," in Shin-yi Peng, Han-Wei Liu, and Ching-Fu Lin (eds.), *Governing Science and Technology under the International Economic Order: Regulatory Divergence and Convergence in the Age of Megaregionals* (Cheltenham, the United Kingdom/Northampton, MA, the United States: Edward Elgar, 2018), pp. 160–82.

"Renewable Energy and Government Support: Time to 'Green' the SCM Agreement?," 14 *World Trade Review* 479 (2015).

"The 'Regionalism vs Multilateralism' Issue in International Trade Law: Revisiting the *Peru–Agricultural Products* Case," 16 *Chinese Journal of International Law* 109 (2017).

Retaliation in the WTO Dispute Settlement System (Alphen aan den Rijn: Kluwer Law International, 2009).

Shafaeddin, Mehdi, "How Did Developed Countries Industrialize? The History of Trade and Industrial Policy: The Cases of Great Britain and the USA," UNCTAD Discussion Paper No. 139, 1998.

Shaffer, Gregory, Robert Wolfe, and Vinhcent Le, "Can Informal Law Discipline Subsidies?," 18 *Journal of International Economic Law* 711 (2015).

Shi, Jingxia and Weidong Chen, "The 'Specificity' of Cultural Products versus the 'Generality' of Trade Obligations: Reflecting on 'China – Publications and Audiovisual Products'," 45 *Journal of World Trade* 159 (2011).

South Center and ATPC, "The WTO's Discussions on Electronic Commerce," Analytical Note, SC/AN/TDP/2017/2, 2017.

Staiger, Robert W. and Guido Tabellini, "Discretionary Trade Policy and Excessive Protection," 77 *American Economic Review* 823 (1987).

Stern, David I., "The Rise and Fall of the Environmental Kuznets Curve," 32 *World Development* 1419 (2004).

Stiglitz, Joseph E., "Some Lessons from the East Asian Miracle," 11 *The World Bank Research Observer* 151 (1996).

Stiglitz, Joseph E., Justin Yifu Lin, and Célestin Monga, "The Rejuvenation of Industrial Policy," Policy Research Working Paper No. WPS6628, World Bank, 2013.

Stone, Susan, James Messent, and Dorothee Flaig, "Emerging Policy Issues: Localisation Barriers to Trade," OECD Trade Policy Paper No. 180, 2015.

Sykes, Alan O., "Countervailing Duty Law: An Economic Perspective," 89 *Columbia Law Review* 199 (1989).

"The Economics of WTO Rules on Subsidies and Countervailing Measures," John M. Olin Law & Economics Working Paper No. 186, University of Chicago Law School, 2003.

"The Questionable Case for Subsidies Regulation: A Comparative Perspective," 2 *Journal of Legal Analysis* 473 (2010).

The WTO Agreement on Safeguards: A Commentary (New York: Oxford University Press, 2006).

Takechi, Kazutaka and Kazuharu Kiyono, "Local Content Protection: Specific-Factor Model for Intermediate Goods Production and Market Segmentation," 15 *Japan and the World Economy* 69 (2003).

Throsby, David, *The Economics of Cultural Policy* (Cambridge: Cambridge University Press, 2010).

Torres, Raúl A., "Free Zones and the World Trade Organization Agreement on Subsidies and Countervailing Measures," 5 *Global Trade and Customs Journal* 217 (2007).

Towse, Ruth and Christian Handke (eds.), *Handbook on the Digital Creative Economy* (Cheltenham, the United Kingdom/Northampton, MA, the United States: Edward Elgar, 2013).

UN Conference on Environment and Development, "Agenda 21," 1992.

UN Division for Sustainable Development, "A Guidebook to the Green Economy – Issue 3: Exploring Green Economy Policies and International Experience with National Strategies," 2012.

UN General Assembly Resolution 1803 (XVII) on Permanent Sovereignty over Natural Resources, 14 December 1962.

"The Future We Want," A/RES/66/288 (27 July 2012).

UN Economic and Social Council – Preparatory Committee of the International Conference on Trade and Employment – Verbatim Report of the Second Plenary Meeting Held at Church House, Westminster, S.W.1, on 17 October 1946, E/PC/T/PV/2 (17 October 1946).

UNCTAD and UNDP, "Creative Economy: A Feasible Development Option," Joint Report, 2010.

UNCTAD, "About GSP," http://unctad.org/en/Pages/DITC/GSP/About-GSP.aspx.

"Trade in Creative Products Reached New Peak in 2011, UNCTAD Figures Show," http://unctad.org/en/pages/newsdetails.aspx?OriginalVersionID=498.

UNEP, "Criterial in Environmental Labelling: A Comparative Analysis of Environmental Criteria in Selected Labelling Schemes," Environment and Trade, No. 13, cited in WTO, Committee on Trade and Environment – Market Access Impact of Eco-Labelling Requirements – Note by the Secretariat, WT/CTE/W/79 (9 March 1998).

UNESCO and UNDP, "Creative Economy Report," Special Edition, 2013.

UNESCO, "Cultural Industries," www.unesco.org/bpi/pdf/memobpi25_culturalindustries_en.pdf.

US DOC, Decision Memorandum (17 October 2007), Final Determination in the Countervailing Duty Investigation of Coated Free Sheet from the People's Republic of China [C-570–907], 72 FR 60645, 25 October 2007.

Issues and Decision Memorandum for the Final Determination in the Countervailing Duty Investigation of Dynamic Random Access Memory Semiconductors from the Republic of Korea [C-580–851], 68 FR 37122, 23 June 2003.

US International Trade Commission, "Digital Trade in the U.S. and Global Economics, Part 2," 2014.

"Digital Trade in the U.S. and Global Economies, Part 1," 2013.

US White House, "America First Foreign Policy," www.whitehouse.gov/america-first-foreign-policy.

"An America First Energy Plan," www.whitehouse.gov/america-first-energy.

VanGrasstek, Craig, *The History and Future of the World Trade Organization* (Geneva: WTO, 2013).

Veel, Paul-Erik, "Carbon Tariffs and the WTO: An Evaluation of Feasible Policies," 12 *Journal of International Economic Law* 749 (2009).

Vermulst, Edwin, *The WTO Anti-Dumping Agreement: A Commentary* (Oxford: Oxford University Press, 2005).

Voon, Tania, "A New Approach to Audiovisual Products in the WTO: Rebalancing GATT and GATS," 14 *UCLA Entertainment Law Review* 1.

"China – Measures Affecting Trading Rights and Distribution Services for Certain Publications and Audiovisual Entertainment Products," 103 *American Journal of International Law* 710 (2009).

Cultural Products and the World Trade Organization (Cambridge: Cambridge University Press, 2007).

Vranes, Erich, *Trade and the Environment: Fundamental Issues in International Law, WTO Law, and Legal Theory* (New York: Oxford University Press, 2009).

Wang, Zhongmei, "Negative List in the SHPFTZ and Its Implications for China's Future FDI Legal System," 50 *Journal of World Trade* 117 (2016).

Warwick, Ken, "Beyond Industrial Policy: Emerging Issues and New Trends," OECD Science, Technology and Industry Policy Paper No. 2, 2013.

WCO, "The Revised Kyoto Convention," www.wcoomd.org/en/topics/facilitation/instrument-and-tools/conventions/pf_revised_kyoto_conv.aspx.

Weber, Rolf H. and Rika Koch, "International Trade Law Challenges by Subsidies for Renewable Energy," 49 *Journal of World Trade* 757 (2015).

Weber, Rolf H., "Digital Trade and E-Commerce: Challenges and Opportunities of the Asia-Pacific Regionalism," 10 *Asian Journal of WTO & International Health Law and Policy* 321 (2015).

"Regulatory Autonomy and Privacy Standards under the GATS," 7 *Asian Journal of WTO & International Health Law and Policy* 25 (2012).

Wikipedia, "Colón Free Trade Zone," http://en.wikipedia.org/wiki/Col%C3%B3n_Free_Trade_Zone.

Williams, Peter John, *A Handbook on Accession to the WTO* (Cambridge: Cambridge University Press, 2008).

Williamson, John, "What Washington Means by Policy Reform," in John Williamson (ed.), *Latin American Adjustment: How Much Has Happened?* (Washington, DC: Peterson Institute for International Economics, 1990), available at https://piie.com/commentary/speeches-papers/what-washington-means-policy-reform.

World Bank and Ecofys, "State and Trends of Carbon Pricing," Joint Report, 2015.

World Bank, *The East Asian Miracle: Economic Growth and Public Policy* (New York: Oxford University Press, 1993).

WTO Analytical Index, *Guide to WTO Law and Practice*, www.wto.org/english/res_e/booksp_e/analytic_index_e/analytic_index_e.htm.

WTO and UNEP, "Trade and Climate Change," Joint Report, 2009.

WTO, "Appellate Body Members," www.wto.org/english/tratop_e/dispu_e/ab_members_descrp_e.htm.

"Azevêdo: Global Trading System Has Constructive Role to Play to Help Drive Inclusivity," Speech, 30 October 2017, www.wto.org/english/news_e/spra_e/spra195_e.htm.

"Business Leaders Call for WTO to Address Pressing Business Issues," 30 May 2016, www.wto.org/english/news_e/news16_e/bus_30may16_e.htm.

"Businesses Share Ideas on Rules for Inclusive Trade," 28 September 2016, www.wto.org/english/news_e/news16_e/bus_28sep16_e.htm.

"Chronological List of Disputes Cases," www.wto.org/english/tratop_e/dispu_e/dispu_status_e.htm.

"Detailed Presentation of Environmental Requirements and Market Access, including Labelling for Environmental Purposes," WTO E-Learning, 2013, https://ecampus.wto.org/admin/files/Course_385/Module_2423/ModuleDocuments/TE_Req-L2-R2-E.pdf.

"Disputes by Agreement: Subsidies and Countervailing Measures," www.wto.org/english/tratop_e/dispu_e/dispu_agreements_index_e.htm?id=A20#.

"Electronic Commerce: Work Continues on Issues Needing Clarification," www.wto.org/english/tratop_e/ecom_e/ecom_briefnote_e.htm.

"Exploring the Links between Subsidies, Trade and the WTO," World Trade Report, 2006.

"Exploring the Links between Trade, Standards and the WTO," World Trade Report, 2005.

"I-TIP Services," http://i-tip.wto.org/services/default.aspx.

"LDCs Welcome Progress on Preferential Treatment for Services," 2 November 2015, www.wto.org/english/news_e/news15_e/serv_02nov15_e.htm.

"Recent Developments in Regional Trade Agreements (July–December 2016)," INT/SUB/RTA/153, www.wto.org/english/tratop_e/region_e/rtajuly-dec16_e.pdf.

"Six Decades of Multilateral Trade Cooperation: What Have We Learnt?," World Trade Report, 2007.

"Special and Differential Treatment: Grappling with 88 Proposals," www.wto.org/english/thewto_e/minist_e/min03_e/brief_e/brief21_e.htm.

"Statistics on Subsidies and Countervailing Measures," www.wto.org/english/tratop_e/scm_e/scm_e.htm.

"Technical Barriers to Trade Information Management System," http://tbtims.wto.org.

"The WTO and Trade Economics: Theory and Policy," WTO E-Learning, 2012, https://ecampus.wto.org/admin/files/Course_492/CourseContents/TEC-E-Print.pdf.

"Trade and Environment at the WTO," 2004.

"Trade and Public Policies: A Closer Look at Non-Tariff Measures in the 21st Century," World Trade Report, 2012.

"Trade in Natural Resources," World Trade Report, 2010.

"Trade in Services: The Most Dynamic Segment of International Trade," www.wto.org/english/thewto_e/20y_e/services_brochure2015_e.pdf.

"Trade Monitoring Database," http://tmdb.wto.org.

"Trade Policy Commitments and Contingency Measures," World Trade Report, 2009.

"Understanding the WTO," 5th edn., 2015.

"World Tariff Profiles," 2016.

"WTO Business Survey," www.wto.org/english/res_e/booksp_e/survey13_e.pdf.

"WTO Matrix on Trade-Related Measures Pursuant to Selected Multilateral Environmental Agreements (MEAs)," www.wto.org/english/tratop_e/ envir_e/envir_matrix_e.htm.

"WTO Members Conclude Landmark $1.3 Trillion IT Trade Deal," 16 December 2015, www.wto.org/english/news_e/news15_e/ita_16dec15_e.htm.

Accession of Ecuador – Decision of 16 August 1995, WT/ACC/ECU/5 (22 August 1995).

Accession of the People's Republic of China – Decision of 10 November 2001, WT/L/432 (23 November 2001).

China – Measures Concerning Wind Power Equipment – Request for Consultations by the US, WT/DS419/1, G/L/950, G/SCM/D86/1 (6 January 2011).

Committee on Antidumping Practices – Recommendation Regarding Annual Reviews of the Anti-Dumping Agreement – Adopted by the Committee on 27 November 2002, G/ADP/9 (29 November 2002).

Committee on Government Procurement – Minutes of the Formal Meeting of 11 February 2015, GPA/M/59 (4 May 2015).

Committee on Government Procurement – Minutes of the Formal Meeting of 29 October 2014, GPA/M/57 (22 December 2014).

Committee on Government Procurement – Minutes of the Formal Meeting of 25 June 2014, GPA/M/56 (4 September 2014).

Committee on Market Access – Canadian Government Actions to Unilaterally Eliminate Certain Most-Favoured-Nation Applied Tariffs – Communication from Canada, G/MA/W/101 (19 April 2010).

Committee on Market Access – Minutes of the Meeting Held on 29 April 2009, G/MA/M/51 (26 May 2010).

Committee on Market Access – Minutes of the Meeting Held on 16 October 2012, G/MA/M/56 (8 January 2013).

Committee on Market Access – Situation of Schedules of WTO Members – Note by the Secretariat – Revision, G/MA/W/23/Rev.12 (11 April 2016).

Committee on Safeguards – Formats for Certain Notifications under the Agreement on Safeguards – Note from the Secretariat, G/SG/1/Rev.1, G/SG/N/6/Rev.1, G/SG/89 (5 November 2009).

Committee on SCM – Minutes of the Regular Meeting Held on 25 October 2016, G/SCM/M/99 (16 January 2017).

Committee on SCM – Minutes of the Regular Meeting Held on 26 and 27 October 2011, G/SCM/M/79 (2 February 2012).

Committee on SCM – Minutes of the Special Meeting Held on 4 May 1999, G/SCM/M/21 (21 September 1999).

Committee on SCM – Notification Requirements under the SCM Agreement – Background Note by the Secretariat – Revision, G/SCM/W/546/Rev.7 (31 March 2016).

Committee on SCM – Questionnaire Format for Subsidy Notifications under Article 25 of the Agreement on Subsidies and Counte[...]cle XVI of GATT 1994 – Revision, G/SCM/6/Rev.1 (11 November 2003).

Committee on SCM – Subsidies – New and Full Notification Pursuant to Article XVI:1 of the GATT 1994 and Article 25 of the A[...]Countervailing Measures – Korea, G/SCM/N/220/KOR (23 September 2011).

Committee on SCM – Subsidies – Replies to Questions Posed by the EC Regarding the New and Full Notification of Panama – Revision, G/SCM/Q2/PAN/6/Rev.1 (13 April 1999).

Committee on SCM – Subsidies – Requests Pursuant to Article 27.4 of the SCM Agreement – Requests Pursuant to the Procedure in Document G/SCM/39 – Costa Rica, G/SCM/N/74/CRI (20 December 2001).

Committee on Specific Commitments – Report of the Meeting Held on 14 October 2015 – Note by the Secretariat, S/CSC/M/74 (27 November 2015).

Committee on SPS Measures – SPS Agreement and Developing Countries – Statement by Egypt at the Meeting of 7–8 July 1999, G/SPS/GEN/128 (16 July 1999).

Committee on SPS Measures – STCs – Note by the Secretariat – Revision, G/SPS/GEN/204/Rev.16 (23 February 2016).

Committee on SPS Measures – Summary of the Meeting Held on 21–22 June 2000 – Note by the Secretariat, G/SPS/R/19 (1 August 2000).

Committee on TBT – Decisions and Recommendations adopted by the WTO Committee on TBT since 1 January 1995 – Note by the Secretariat – Revision, G/TBT/1/Rev.12 (21 January 2015).

Committee on TBT – Fifth Triennial Review of the Operation and Implementation of the Agreement on TBT under Article 15.4, G/TBT/26 (13 November 2009).

Committee on TBT – Seventh Triennial Review of the Operation and Implementation of the Agreement on TBT under Article 15.4, G/TBT/37 (3 December 2015).

Committee on TBT – Twenty-first Annual Review of the Implementation and Operation of the TBT Agreement – Note by the Secretariat – Revision, G/TBT/38/Rev.1 (24 March 2016).

Committee on Trade and Development – S&D Treatment Provisions in WTO Agreements and Decisions – Note by the Secretariat, WT/COMTD/W/219 (22 September 2016).

Committee on Trade and Environment – Committee on TBT – Negotiating History of the Coverage of the Agreement on TBT [. . .]stics – Note by the Secretariat, WT/CTE/W/10, G/TBT/W/11 (29 August 1995).

Committee on Trade and Environment – Committee on Trade and Environment – Special Session – Matrix on Trade Measures Pursuant to Selected Multilateral Enviro[. . .]e by the Secretariat – Revision, WT/CTE/W/160/Rev.7, TN/TE/S/5/Rev.5 (4 September 2015).

Committee on Trade and Environment – Environmental (Sustainability) Assessments of Trade Liberalization Agreements at the National Level – Item 2 of the Work[. . .]ramme – Note by the Secretariat, WT/CTE/W/171 (20 October 2000).

Committee on Trade and Environment – Internationally Agreed Definitions of Environmental Labelling within the International Organization for Standardization[. . .]rk – Communication from the ISO, WT/CTE/W/114 (31 May 1999).

Committee on Trade and Environment – Report of the Meeting Held on 2 May 2007 – Note by the Secretariat, WT/CTE/M/44 (13 June 2007).

Committee on Trade and Environment – Report of the Meeting Held on 3 November 2008 – Note by the Secretariat, WT/CTE/M/46 (12 January 2009).

Committee on Trade and Environment – Report of the Meeting Held on 16 October 2013 – Note by the Secretariat, WT/CTE/M/56 (31 January 2014).

Committee on Trade and Environment – Report of the Meeting Held on 6 July 2011 – Note by the Secretariat, WT/CTE/M/52 (6 September 2011).

Committee on Trade and Environment – Report of the Meeting Held on 22 June 2015 – Note by the Secretariat, WT/CTE/M/59 (3 September 2015).

Committee on Trade and Environment – Report of the Meeting Held on 29 September 2010 – Note by the Secretariat, WT/CTE/M/50 (2 November 2010).

Committee on Trade and Environment – Report of the Meeting Held on 27–28 June 2001 – Note by the Secretariat, WT/CTE/M/27 (8 August 2001).

Committee on Trade and Environment – Report of the Meeting Held on 20 April 2004 – Note by the Secretariat, WT/CTE/M/36 (19 May 2004).

Committee on Trade and Environment – Report of the Meeting Held on 20 April 2004 – Note by the Secretariat, WT/CTE/M/34 (29 July 2003).

Committee on Trade and Environment – Report of the Meeting Held on 14 November 2011 – Note by the Secretariat, WT/CTE/M/53 (27 January 2012).

Committee on Trade and Environment – Report of the Meeting Held on 9 November 2010 – Note by the Secretariat, WT/CTE/M/51 (31 May 2011).

Committee on Trade and Environment – Report of the Meeting Held on 30 June 2014 – Note by the Secretariat, WT/CTE/M/57 (30 September 2014).

Committee on Trade and Environment – Report to the 5th Session of the Ministerial Conference in Cancún – Paragraphs 32 and 33 of the Doha Ministerial Declaration, WT/CTE/8 (11 July 2013).

Committee on Trade and Environment – Special Session – Compilation of Submissions under Paragraph 31(i) of the Doha Declaration – Note by the Secretariat – Revision, TN/TE/S/3/Rev.1 (24 April 2003).

Committee on Trade and Environment – Special Session – Multilateral Environmental Agreements (MEAs) and WTO Rules; Proposals Made in the Committee on Trade [. . .] 2002 – Note by the Secretariat, TN/TE/S/1 (23 May 2002).

Committee on Trade and Environment – Special Session – Report by the Chairman, Ambassador Manuel A. J. Teehankee, to the Trade Negotiations Committee, TN/TE/20 (21 April 2011).

Committee on Trade and Environment – Summary Report of the Information Session on Product Carbon Footprint and Labelling Schemes – 17 February 2010 – Note by the Secretariat – Addendum, WT/CTE/M/49/Add.1 (28 May 2010).

Committee on Trade and Environment – Taxes and Charges for Environmental Purposes – Border Tax Adjustment – Note by the Secretariat, WT/CTE/W/47 (2 May 1997).

Committee on TRIMs – Minutes of the Meeting Held on 16 April 2015, G/TRIMS/M/38 (27 July 2015).

Committee on TRIMs – Minutes of the Meeting Held on 30 September and 1 November 1996, G/TRIMS/M/5 (27 November 1996).

Committee on TRIMs – Minutes of the Meeting Held on 4 October 2013, G/TRIMS/M/35 (20 December 2013).

Committee on TRIMs – Minutes of the Meeting Held on 4 October 2013, G/TRIMS/M/35 (20 December 2013).

Committee on TRIMs – Minutes of the Meeting Held on 8 October 2014, G/TRIMS/M/37 (21 November 2014).

Committee on TRIMs – Minutes of the Special Meeting Held on 1 October 2012 – Note by the Secretariat, G/TRIMS/M/33 (22 November 2012).

Committee on TRIMs – Notification under Article 5.1 of the Agreement on TRIMs – Dominican Republic, G/TRIMS/N/1/DOM/1 (10 May 1995).

Committee on TRIMs – Notification under Article 5.1 of the Agreement on TRIMs – Thailand, G/TRIMS/N/1/THA/1 (28 April 1995).

Côte d'Ivoire – Schedule of Specific Commitments, GATS/SC/23 (15 April 1994).

Council for Trade in Goods – TRIMs and Other Performance Requirements – Joint Study by the WTO and UNCTAD Secretariats – Part II – Addendum, G/C/W/307/Add.1 (8 February 2002).

Council for Trade in Goods – Work Programme on Electronic Commerce – Information Provided to the General Council, G/C/W/158 (26 July 1999).

Council for Trade in Goods – Work Programme on Electronic Commerce – Report by the Chairperson of the Council for Trade in Goods to the General Council, G/C/59 (21 July 2017).

Council for Trade in Services – Audiovisual Services – Background Note by the Secretariat, S/C/W/310 (12 January 2010).

Council for Trade in Services – Communication by the US – Work Programme on Electronic Commerce, S/C/W/359 (17 December 2014).

Council for Trade in Services – Report of the Meeting Held on 18 March 2015 – Note by the Secretariat, S/C/M/122 (1 May 2015).

Council for Trade in Services – Submission by the Delegation of Uganda on behalf of the LDC Group – Collective Request Pursuant to the Bali Decision on the o[. . .]rs of LDCs, S/C/W/356 (23 July 2014).

Council for Trade in Services – The Work Programme on Electronic Commerce – Note by the Secretariat, S/C/W/68 (16 November 1998).

Council for Trade in Services – Work Programme on Electronic Commerce – Interim Report to the General Council, S/C/8 (31 March 1999).

Council for Trade in Services – Work Programme on Electronic Commerce – Report by the Chairman of the Council for Trade in Services to the General Council, S/C/52 (19 July 2017).

Council for TRIPS – Paragraph 6 of the Doha Declaration on the TRIPS Agreement and Public Health [. . .] – Note by the Secretariat, IP/C/W/387 (24 October 2002).

Council for TRIPS – The Work Programme on Electronic Commerce – Background Note by the Secretariat, IP/C/W/128 (10 February 1999).

Council for TRIPS – The Work Programme on Electronic Commerce – Background Note by the Secretariat – Addendum, IP/C/W/128/Add.1 (15 May 2003).

Decision-Making Procedures under Articles IX and XII of the WTO Agreement – Statement by the Chairman – As Agreed by the General Council on 15 November 1995, WT/L/93 (24 November 1995).

General Council – 7 December 2016 – Item – Work Programme on Electronic Commerce – Review of Progress – Report by the Chairman, WT/GC/W/728 (8 December 2016).

General Council – Article 27.4 of the SCM Agreement – Decision of 27 July 2007, WT/L/691 (31 July 2007).

General Council – Minutes of the Meeting – Held in the Center William Rappard on 21 October 2014, WT/GC/M/153 (2 December 2014).

General Council – Transparency Mechanism for Regional Trade Agreements – Decision of 14 December 2006, WT/L/671 (18 December 2006).

General Council – WTO Agreements and Electronic Commerce, WT/GC/W/90 (14 July 1998).

Israel – Schedule of Specific Commitments, GATS/SC/44 (15 April 1994).

Mexico – Schedule of Specific Commitments, GATS/SC/56 (15 April 1994).

Ministerial Conference – Fourth Session – Doha, 9–13 November 2001 – Report of the Working Party on the Accession of the Separate Customs Territory of Taiwan, Penghu, Kinmen and Matsu, WT/MIN(01)/4 (11 November 2001).

Ministerial Conference – Fourth Session – Doha, 9–13 November 2001 – Report of the Working Party on the Accession of China, WT/MIN(01)/3 (10 November 2001).

Ministerial Conference – Fourth Session – Doha, 9–14 November 2001 – Ministerial Declaration – Adopted on 14 November 2001, WT/MIN(01)/DEC/1 (20 November 2001).

Ministerial Conference – Ninth Session – Bali, 3–6 December 2013 – Monitoring Mechanism on S&D Treatment – Ministerial Decision of 7 December 2013, WT/MIN(13)/45, WT/L/920 (11 December 2013).

Ministerial Conference – Sixth Session – Hong Kong, 13–18 December 2005 – Doha Work Programme – Ministerial Declaration – Adopted on 18 December 2005, WT/MIN(05)/DEC (22 December 2005).

Ministerial Conference – Tenth Session – Nairobi, 15–18 December 2015 – Implementation of Preferential Treatment in Favour of Services and Service Supplier[. . .]al Decision of 19 December 2015, WT/MIN(15)/48, WT/L/982 (21 December 2015).

Ministerial Conference – Tenth Session – Nairobi, 15–18 December 2015 – Export Competition – Ministerial Decision of 19 December 2015, WT/MIN (15)/45, WT/L/980 (21 December 2015).

Preferential Treatment to Services and Service Suppliers of LDCs – Decision of 17 December 2011, WT/L/847 (19 December 2011).

Report (2008) of the Committee on TRIMs, G/L/860 (29 October 2008).

Technical Note on the Accession Process – Note by the Secretariat – Revision, WT/ACC/7/Rev.2 (1 November 2000).

TPRB – 1 and 3 December 2010 – TPR – Hong Kong, China – Record of the Meeting, WT/TPR/M/241/Add.1 (10 February 2011).

TPRB – 13 and 15 May 2013 – TPR – Macao, China – Record of the Meeting – Addendum, WT/TPR/M/281/Add.1 (18 September 2013).

TPRB – 27 and 29 March 2012 – TPR – UAE – Record of the Meeting, WT/TPR/M/262 (9 May 2012).

TPRB – 28 and 30 November 2011 – TPR – Thailand – Record of the Meeting, WT/TPR/M/255 (30 January 2012).

TPRB – TPR – Report by the Secretariat – Brazil, WT/TPR/S/358 (12 June 2017).

TPRB – TPR – Report by the Secretariat – Indonesia – Revision, WT/TPR/S/278/Rev.1 (16 July 2013).

TPRB – TPR – Report by the Secretariat – Kyrgyz Republic – Revision, WT/TPR/S/170/Rev.1 (12 January 2007).

TPRB – TPR – Report by the Secretariat – Panama – Revision, WT/TPR/S/186/Rev.1 (3 December 2007).

TPRB – TPR – Report by the Secretariat – Republic of Korea – Revision, WT/TPR/S/204/Rev.1 (4 December 2008).

Trade in Services – Guidelines for the Scheduling of Specific Commitments under the GATS – Adopted by the Council for Trade in Services on 23 March 2001, S/L/92 (28 March 2001).

Trade in Services – Russian Federation – Schedule of Specific Commitments, GATS/SC/149 (5 November 2012).

Trade in Services – The Republic of Kazakhstan – Schedule of Specific Commitments, GATS/SC/154 (15 February 2016).

Work Programme on Electronic Commerce – Adopted by the General Council on 25 September 1998, WT/L/274 (30 September 1998).

Working Party on GATS Rules – Subsidies for Services Sectors – Information Contained in WTO TPRs – Background Note by the Secretariat – Revision, S/WPGR/W/25/Add.7/Rev.1 (13 January 2015).

Working Party on the Accession of Armenia – Report of the Working Party on the Accession of the Republic of Armenia, WT/ACC/ARM/23 (26 November 2002).

Working Party on the Accession of China – Report of the Working Party on the Accession of China, WT/ACC/CHN/49 (1 October 2001).

Working Party on the Accession of China – Report of the Working Party on the Accession of China – Schedule CLII – The People's Republic of China – Part II –[. . .]le II MFN Exemptions – Addendum, WT/ACC/CHN/49/Add.2 (1 October 2001).

Working Party on the Accession of Saudi Arabia – Report of the Working Party on the Accession of the Kingdom of Saudi Arabia to the WTO, WT/ACC/SAU/61 (1 November 2005).

Working Party on the Accession of the Former Yugoslav Republic of Macedonia – Report of the Working Party on the Accession of the Former Yugoslav Republic of Macedonia, WT/ACC/807/27 (26 September 2002).

Working Party on the Accession of the Republic of Kazakhstan – Report of the Working Party on the Accession of the Republic of Kazakhstan, WT/ACC/KAZ/93 (23 June 2015).

Working Party on the Accession of the Republic of Seychelles – Accession of Seychelles – Draft Report of the Working Party on the Accession of the Republic of Seychelles – Revision, WT/ACC/SPEC/SYC/6/Rev.2 (16 September 2014).

Working Party on the Accession of the Republic of Tajikistan – Report of the Working Party on the Accession of the Republic of Tajikistan, WT/ACC/TJK/30 (6 November 2012).

Working Party on the Accession of the Russian Federation – Report of the Working Party on the Accession of the Russian Federation to the WTO, WT/ACC/RUS/70, WT/MIN(11)/2 (17 November 2011).

Working Party on the Accession of Ukraine – Report of the Working Party on the Accession of Ukraine to the WTO, WT/ACC/UKR/152 (25 January 2008).

Working Party on the Accession of Viet Nam – Accession of Viet Nam – Report of the Working Party on the Accession of Viet Nam, WT/ACC/VNM/48 (27 October 2006).

Wunsch-Vincent, Sacha, *The WTO, the Internet and Trade in Digital Products: EC–US Perspectives* (Portland, OR: Hart Publishing, 2006).

Yao, Daqing and John Whalley, "The China (Shanghai) Pilot Free Trade Zone: Background, Developments and Preliminary Assessment of Initial Impacts," 39 *The World Economy* 2 (2016).

Yoo, Ji Yeong and Dukgeun Ahn, "Security Exceptions in the WTO System: Bridge or Bottle-Neck for Trade and Security?," 19 *Journal of International Economic Law* 417 (2016).

INDEX